ABRIDGMENT

OF

MENTAL PHILOSOPHY,

INCLUDING THE THREE DEPARTMENTS

OF THE

INTELLECT, SENSIBILITIES, AND WILL.

DESIGNED AS A TEXT-BOOK

FOR

ACADEMIES AND HIGH SCHOOLS.

BY THOMAS C. UPHAM,

PROFESSOR OF MENTAL AND MORAL PHILOSOPHY IN BOWDOIN COLLEGE.

NEW YORK:

HARPER & BROTHERS, PUBLISHERS,

FRANKLIN SQUARE.

PREFACE

The Philosophy of the Mind has grown up, like other sciences, from small beginnings. Many propositions, coming too, in many instances, from able writers, have been thrown aside; truth has been sifted out from the mass of error, until at last a great number of important principles is ascertained. But while it is exceedingly necessary that our youth should be made acquainted with these principles, it is impossible that they should go through with all the complicated discussions which have been held in respect to them. Many of the books in which these discussions are contained have become exceedingly rare; and, if they were not so, no small number of students, who are now in the course of as thorough an education as our country affords, would not be able to purchase them. And besides, by placing before the student a mass of crude and conflicting statements, his mind becomes perplexed. To be able to resolve such a mass into its elements, and to separate truth from error, implies an acquaintance with the laws of the intellect, and a degree of mental discipline, which he is not yet supposed to have acquired; and hence, instead of obtaining much important knowledge, he becomes distrustful of everything

Now these evils, saying nothing of the loss of time attendant on such a course, are to be remedied in the same way as in other sciences. In other departments of learning, ingenious men discuss points of difficulty; conflicting arguments are accumulated, until the preponderance on one side is such that the question in debate is considered settled Others employ themselves in collecting facts, in classifying them, and in deducing general principles; and when all this is done, the important truths of the science, collected from such a variety of sources, and suitably arranged and expressed, are laid before the student, in order that he may become acquainted with them. And this is what is attempted, to some extent, to be done in the present work, which is an abridgment of a larger work on the same subject. In the larger work, the principles of Eclecticism and Induction, which have just been referred to, are applied on a more extensive scale than in the present. I have been obliged necessarily to exclude from the abridgment many interesting and striking illustrations and facts, and some general philosophical views, which would have had a place if our limits had permitted. I indulge the hope, nevertheless, as the abridgment has been made with no small degree of care, that it will answer the purpose for which it is particularly designed; viz., the assistance of those youth who need some knowledge of Mental Philosophy, but are not in a situation to prosecute the subject to any great extent.

THOMAS C UPHAM

Bowdoin College, May, 1840

CONTENTS.

DIVISION I.

THE INTELLECT OR UNDERSTANDING.

[illegible]NTELLECTIVE OR INTELLECTUAL STATES OF THE MIND.

PART I.

INTELLECTUAL STATES OF EXTERNAL ORIGIN.

CHAPTER I.

ORIGIN OF KNOWLEDGE IN GENERAL.

Section		Page
1.	The mind susceptible of a threefold division	17
2.	The Intellect susceptible of a subordinate division	ib.
3.	Of the connexion of the mind with the material world	18
4.	Our first knowledge in general of a material or external origin	19
5.	Shown further from what we notice in children	20
6.	Further proof of the beginnings of knowledge from external causes	21
7.	The same subject further illustrated	22
8.	Illustration from the case of James Mitchell	23

CHAPTER II.

SENSATION AND PERCEPTION.

9.	Sensation a simple mental state originating in the senses	24
10.	All sensation is properly and truly in the mind	25
11.	Sensations are not images or resemblances of objects	ib.
12.	The connexion between the mental and physical change not capable of explanation	26
13.	Of the meaning and nature of perception	27
14.	Perception makes us acquainted with a material world	27
15.	Of the primary and secondary qualities of matter	28
16.	Of the secondary qualities of matter	29

CHAPTER III.

THE SENSES OF SMELL AND TASTE.

17.	Nature and importance of the senses as a source of knowledge	30
18.	Connexion of the brain with sensation and perception	31
19.	Order in which the senses are to be considered	32
20.	Of the sense and sensations of smell	ib.
21.	Of perceptions of smell in distinction from sensations	33
22.	Of the sense and the sensations of taste	34

CHAPTER IV.

THE SENSE OF HEARING.

23.	Organ of the sense of hearing	35
24.	Varieties of the sensation of sound	36
25.	Manner in which we learn the place of sounds	[illegible]

CHAPTER V.

THE SENSE OF TOUCH.

Section		Page
26.	Of the sense of touch in general and its sensations	38
27.	Idea of externality suggested in connexion with the touch	ib.
28.	Origin of the notion of extension, and of form or figure	40
29.	On the sensations of heat and cold	41
30.	Of the sensations of hardness and softness	42
31.	Of certain indefinite feelings sometimes ascribed to the touch	44
32.	Relation between the sensation and what is outwardly signified	45

CHAPTER VI.

THE SENSE OF SIGHT.

33.	Of the organ of sight, and the uses or benefits of that sense	46
34.	Statement of the mode or process in visual perception	47
35.	Of the original and acquired perceptions of sight	48
36.	The idea of extension not originally from sight	49
37.	Of the knowledge of the figure of bodies by the sight	50
38.	Illustration of the subject from the blind	51
39.	Measurements of magnitude by the eye	52
40.	Of objects seen in a mist	53
41.	Of the sun and moon when seen in the horizon	ib.
42.	Of the estimation of distances by sight	54
43.	Signs by means of which we estimate distance by sight	55
44.	Estimation of distance when unaided by intermediate objects	56
45.	Of objects seen on the ocean, &c.	57

CHAPTER VII.

HABITS OF SENSATION AND PERCEPTION.

46.	General view of the law of habit and of its applications	58
47.	The law of habit applicable to the mind as well as the body	ib.
48.	Of habit in relation to the smell	59
49.	Of habit in relation to the taste	60
50.	Of habit in relation to the hearing	62
51.	Application of habit to the touch	64
52.	Other striking instances of habits of touch	65
53	Habits considered in relation to the sight	66
54.	Sensations may possess a relative, as well as positive increase of power	68
55.	Of habits as modified by particular callings and arts	69
56.	The law of habit considered in reference to the perception of the outlines and forms of objects	70
57.	Notice of some facts which favour the above doctrine	71
58.	Additional illustrations of Mr. Stewart's doctrine	72

CHAPTER VIII.

CONCEPTIONS.

59	Meaning and characteristics of conceptions	73
60.	Of conceptions of objects of sight	74
61.	Of the influence of habit on our conceptions	76
62.	Influence of habit on conceptions of sight	77
63.	Of the subserviency of our conceptions to description	ib.
64	Of conceptions attended with a momentary belief	78
65.	Conceptions which are joined with perceptions	81
66.	Conceptions as connected with fictitious representations	82

CHAPTER IX.

SIMPLICITY AND COMPLEXNESS OF MENTAL STATES.

Section Page
67. Origin of the distinction of simple and complex 83
68. Nature and characteristics of simple mental states . . . ib.
69. Simple mental states not susceptible of definition . . . 84
70. Simple mental states representative of a reality 85
71. Origin of complex notions, and their relation to simple . . 86
72. Supposed complexness without the antecedence of simple feelings 87
73. The precise sense in which complexness is to be understood 88
74. Illustrations of analysis as applied to the mind . . . 89
75. Complex notions of external origin 90
76. Of objects contemplated as wholes 91

CHAPTER X.

ABSTRACTION.

77. Abstraction implied in the analysis of complex ideas . . 92
78. Instances of particular abstract ideas 93
79. Mental process in separating and abstracting them . . 94
80. General abstract notions the same with genera and species 95
81. Process in classification, or the forming of genera and species 96
82. Early classifications sometimes incorrect 97
83. Illustrations of our earliest classifications . . . . ib.
84. Of the nature of general abstract ideas 98
85. The power of general abstraction in connexion with numbers, &c. 99
86. Of general abstract truths or principles . . . . . ib.
87. Of the speculations of philosophers and others 100

CHAPTER XI.

OF ATTENTION.

88. Of the general nature of attention 101
89. Of different degrees of attention 102
90. Dependence of memory on attention 103
91. Of exercising attention in reading 104
92. Alleged inability to command the attention 105

CHAPTER XII.

DREAMING.

93. Definition of dreams and the prevalence of them 107
94. Connexion of dreams with our waking thoughts . . . . . ib.
95. Dreams are often caused by our sensations 108
96. Explanation of the incoherency of dreams. (1st cause) . 110
97. Second cause of the incoherency of dreams . . . . . ib.
98. Apparent reality of dreams. (1st cause) 111
99. Apparent reality of dreams. (2d cause) 112
100. Of our estimate of time in dreaming 113
101. Explanation of the preceding statements 114

PART II.

INTELLECTUAL STATES OF INTERNAL ORIGIN.

CHAPTER I.

INTERNAL ORIGIN OF KNOWLEDGE.

102. The soul has fountains of knowledge within 119
103. Declaration of Locke, that the soul has knowledge in itself 120

Section		Page
104.	The beginning of knowledge is in the senses	120
105.	There may also be internal accessions to knowledge	121
106.	Instances of notions which have an internal origin	122
107.	Other instances of ideas which have an internal origin	ib

CHAPTER II.

ORIGINAL SUGGESTION.

108.	Import of suggestion, and its application in Reid and Stewart	123
109.	Ideas of existence, mind, self-existence, and personal identity	124
110	Of the nature of unity, and the origin of that notion	126
111.	Nature of succession, and origin of the idea of succession	127
112.	Origin of the notion of duration	128
113.	Illustrations of the nature of duration	ib.
114.	Of time and its measurements, and of eternity	129
115.	The idea of space not of external origin	130
116.	The idea of space has its origin in suggestion	131
117.	Of the origin of the idea of power	132
118.	Occasions of the origin of the idea of power	ib.
119.	Of the ideas of right and wrong	133
120.	Origin of the ideas of moral merit and demerit	134
121.	Of other elements of knowledge developed in suggestion	135
122.	Suggestion a source of principles as well as of ideas	ib

CHAPTER III.

CONSCIOUSNESS.

123.	Consciousness the 2d source of internal knowledge; its nature	136
124.	Further remarks on the proper objects of consciousness	137
125.	Consciousnes a ground or law of belief	138
126.	Instances of knowledge developed in consciousness	ib.

CHAPTER IV.

RELATIVE SUGGESTION OR JUDGMENT.

127.	Of the susceptibility of perceiving or feeling relations	140
128	Occasions on which feelings of relation may arise	141
129.	Of the use of correlative terms	142
130.	Of relations of identity and diversity	ib.
131.	(II.) Relations of degree, and names expressive of them	143
132.	(III.) Of relations of proportion	144
133.	(IV.) Of relations of place or position	145
134.	(V.) Of relations of time	146
135.	(VI.) Of ideas of possession	147
136.	(VII.) Of relations of cause and effect	148
137.	Of complex terms involving the relation of cause and effect	149
138.	Connexion of relative suggestion with reasoning	150

CHAPTER V.

ASSOCIATION. (I.) PRIMARY LAWS.

139	Reasons for considering this subject here	151
140.	Meaning of association and illustrations	ib.
141.	Of the general laws of association	152
142.	Resemblance the first general law of association	153
143.	Of resemblance in the effects produced	154
144.	Contrast the second general or primary law	155
145.	Contiguity the third general or primary law	157
146.	Cause and effect the fourth primary law	158

CHAPTER VI.

ASSOCIATION. (II.) SECONDARY LAWS.

Section — Page

147. Secondary laws, and their connexion with the primary . 159
148. Of the influence of lapse of time 160
149. Secondary law of repetition or habit 161
150. Of the secondary law of co-existent emotion . . . 162
151. Original difference in the mental constitution . . . 163
152. The foregoing as applicable to the sensibilities . . . 164

CHAPTER VII.

MEMORY.

153. Remarks on the general nature of memory 166
154. Of memory as a ground or law of belief 167
155. Of differences in the strength of memory 168
156. Of circumstantial memory, or that species of memory which is based on the relations of contiguity in time and place . . 169
157. Illustrations of specific or circumstantial memory . . . 170
158. Of philosophic memory, or that species of memory which is based on other relations than those of contiguity 171
159. Illustrations of philosophic memory 172
160. Of that species of memory called intentional recollection . . 173
161. Nature of intentional recollection 174
162. Instance illustrative of the preceding statements . . . . ib.
163. Marks of a good memory 175
164. Directions or rules for the improvement of the memory . . 177
165. Further directions for the improvement of the memory . . 179
166. Of observance of the truth in connexion with memory . . 180

CHAPTER VIII.

DURATION OF MEMORY.

167. Restoration of thoughts and feelings supposed to be forgotten . 181
168. Mental action quickened by influence on the physical system . 183
169. Other instances of quickened mental action, and of a restoration of thoughts 184
170 Effect on the memory of a severe attack of fever . . . . ib.
171. Approval and illustrations of these views from Coleridge . . 185
172. Application of the principles of this chapter to education . . 187
173. Connexion of this doctrine with the final judgment and a future life 189

CHAPTER IX.

REASONING.

174. Reasoning a source of ideas and knowledge 190
175. Definition of reasoning, and of propositions 191
176. Process of the mind in all cases of reasoning . . . 192
177. Illustration of the preceding statement 193
178. Grounds of the selection of propositions 194
179. Reasoning implies the existence of antecedent or assumed propositions 195
180 Further considerations on this subject 196
181. Of differences in the power of reasoning 197
182. Of habits of reasoning 198
183 Of reasoning in connexion with language or expression . 199
184 Illustration of the foregoing section 200

CHAPTER X.

DEMONSTRATIVE REASONING

Section / Page
185 Of the subjects of demonstrative reasoning . . . 201
186. Use of definitions and axioms in demonstrative reasoning 202
187. The opposites of demonstrative reasonings absurd . 203
188 Demonstrations do not admit of different degrees of belief . 204
189. Of the use of diagrams in demonstrations . . . 205

CHAPTER XI.

MORAL REASONING.

190. Of the subjects and importance of moral reasoning . . . 206
191. Of the nature of moral certainty 207
192. Of reasoning from analogy 208
193. Of reasoning by induction 209
194. Of combined or accumulated arguments 210

CHAPTER XII.

PRACTICAL DIRECTIONS IN REASONING.

195. Rules relating to the practice of reasoning . . . . . 21.
196. Of being influenced in reasoning by a love of the truth . ib
197. Care to be used in correctly stating the subject of discussion . 212
198. Consider the kind of evidence applicable to the subject . . 213
199. Reject the aid of false arguments or sophisms il
200. Fallacia equivocationis, or the use of equivocal terms and phrases 215
201. Of the sophism of estimating actions and character from the circumstances of success merely 216
202. Of adherence to our opinions 217
203. Effects on the mind of debating for victory instead of truth . 218

CHAPTER XIII.

IMAGINATION.

204. Imagination an intellectual rather than a sensitive process . . 219
205. The imagination closely related to the reasoning power . 220
206. Definition of the power of imagination 221
207. Process of the mind in the creations of the imagination . . 222
208. Further remarks on the same subject 223
209. Illustration from the writings of Dr. Reid . . . . . ib.
210. Grounds of the preference of one conception to another . 224
211. Illustration of the subject from Milton 22
212. The creations of imagination not entirely voluntary . . . ib.
213. Illustration of the statements of the preceding section . . 227
214. On the utility of the faculty of the imagination 228
215. Importance of the imagination in connexion with reasoning . 229

CHAPTER XIV.

DISORDERED INTELLECTUAL ACTION.

(I.) EXCITED CONCEPTIONS OR APPARITIONS.

216. Disordered intellectual action as connected with the body . . 231
217. Of excited conceptions and of apparitions in general . . . 232
218. Of the less permanent excited conceptions of sight . . . ib.
219. Of the less permament excited conceptions of sound . . . 234
220. First cause of permanently vivid conceptions or apparitions.— Morbid sensibility of the retina of the eye 235

Section Page
221. Second cause of permanently excited conceptions or apparitions. Neglect of periodical blood-letting 237
222. Methods of relief adopted in this case 239
223. Third cause of excited conceptions. Attacks of fever . . 240
224. Fourth cause of apparitions and other excited conceptions. Inflammation of the brain 241
225. Facts having relation to the fourth cause of excited conceptions . 242
226. Fifth cause of apparitions. Hysteria 243

CHAPTER XV.

DISORDERED INTELLECTUAL ACTION.

(II.) INSANITY.

227. Meaning of the term insanity 244
228. Of disordered or alienated sensations 245
229. Of disordered or alienated external perception 246
230. Disordered state or insanity of original suggestion . . . 247
231. Unsoundness or insanity of consciousness 248
232. Insanity of the judgment or relative suggestion 249
233. Disordered or alienated association. Light-headedness . . 250
234. Illustrations of this mental disorder 251
235. Of partial insanity or alienation of the memory . . . . ib.
236. Of the power of reasoning in the partially insane 25-
237. Instance of the above form of insanity of reasoning . . 25-
238. Partial mental alienation by means of the imagination . . 255
239. Insanity or alienation of the power of belief . . . 256

DIVISION II.

THE SENSIBILITIES.

SENTIENT OR SENSITIVE STATES OF THE MIND.—SENTIMENTS

INTRODUCTION.

CLASSIFICATION OF THE SENSIBILITIES.

240. Reference to the general division of the whole mind . . . 261
241. The action of the sensibilities implies that of the intellect . . ib.
242. Division of the sensibilities into natural or pathematic, and moral 262
243. The moral and natural sensibilities have different objects . . 263
244. The moral sensibilities higher in rank than the natural . . 264
245. The moral sensibilities wanting in brutes . . . . . . ib.
246. Classification of the natural sensibilities 265
247 Classification of the moral sensibilities . . . 266

PART I.

NATURAL OR PATHEMATIC SENSIBILITIES.

NATURAL OR PATHEMATIC SENTIMENTS.

CLASS I.

EMOTIONS OR EMOTIVE STATES OF THE MIND.

CHAPTER I.

NATURE OF THE EMOTIONS.

248. We have a knowledge of emotions by consciousness . . . 269
249. The place of emotions, considered in reference to other mental acts 270
250. The character of emotions changes so as to comform to that of perceptions 271
251. Emotions characterized by rapidity and variety . . . 272

CHAPTER II.

EMOTIONS OF BEAUTY.

Section — Page
252. Characteristics of emotions of beauty . . 273
253. Of what is meant by beautiful objects . . . 274
254. Of the distinction between beautiful and other objects . . 275
255. Grounds or occasions of emotions of beauty various . . 276
256. All objects not equally fitted to cause these emotions . . . 277
257. A susceptibility of emotions of beauty an ultimate principle of our mental constitution 278
258. Remarks on the beauty of forms.—The circle 279
259. Original or intrinsic beauty.—The circle 280
260. Of the beauty of straight and angular forms . . . . ib.
261. Of square, pyramidal, and triangular forms 281
262. Of the original or intrinsic beauty of colours . . 283
263. Further illustrations of the original beauty of colours . . 284
264. Of sounds considered as a source of beauty 286
265. Illustrations of the original beauty of sounds 287
266. Further instances of the original beauty of sounds . . . 290
267. The permanency of musical power dependent on its being intrinsic ib.
268. Of motion as an element of beauty 291
269. Explanation of the beauty of motion from Kaimes . . . 292

CHAPTER III.

ASSOCIATED BEAUTY.

270. Associated beauty implies an antecedent or intrinsic beauty . 293
271. Objects may become beautiful by association merely . . . 294
272. Further illustrations of associated feelings 295
273. Instances of national associations 297
274. The sources of associated beauty coincident with those of human happiness 298
275. Summary of views in regard to the beautiful 299

CHAPTER IV

EMOTIONS OF SUBLIMITY.

276. Connexion between beauty and sublimity 300
277. The occasions of the emotions of sublimity various . . . 301
278. Great extent or expansion an occasion of sublimity . . . 302
279. Great height an element or occasion of sublimity . . . ib.
280. Of depth in connexion with the sublime 303
281. Of colours in connexion with the sublime 304
282. Of sounds as furnishing an occasion of sublime emotions . . ib.
283. Of motion in connexion with the sublime 305
284. Indications of power accompanied by emotions of the sublime 306
285. Of the original or primary sublimity of objects . . . 307
286. Considerations in proof of the original sublimity of objects . ib.
287. Influence of association on emotions of sublimity . . . 308

CHAPTER V.

EMOTIONS OF THE LUDICROUS

288. General nature of emotions of the ludicrous . . 309
289. Occasions of emotions of the ludicrous 310
290. Of what is understood by wit 311
291. Of wit as it consists in burlesque or in debasing objects . . ib.
292. Of wit when employed in aggrandizing objects 312
293. Of the character and occasions of humour 313
294. Of the practical utility of feelings of the ludicrous . . 314

CHAPTER VI.

INSTANCES OF OTHER SIMPLE EMOTIONS.

Section Page
295. Emotions of cheerfulness, joy, and gladness . . 314
296. Emotions of melancholy, sorrow, and grief . . . 315
297. Emotions of surprise, astonishment, and wonder . . . 316
298. Emotions of dissatisfaction, displeasure, and disgust . . ib.
299 Emotions of diffidence, modesty, and shame . . 317
300. Emotions of regard, reverence, and adoration . . . ib

CLASS II.

THE DESIRES.

CHAPTER I.

NATURE OF DESIRES.

301. Of the prevalence of desire in this department of the mind . 321
302. The nature of desires known from consciousness . . . ib.
303. Of the place of desires in relation to other mental states . . 322
304. The desires characterized by comparative fixedness and permanency 323
305. Desires always imply an object desired 324
306. The fulfilment of desires attended with enjoyment . . . ib.
307. Of variations or degrees in the strength of the desires . . . 325
308. Tendency to excite movement an attribute of desire . . . ib
309. Classification of this part of the sensibilities 326
310. The principles, based upon desire, susceptible of a twofold operation 327

CHAPTER II.

INSTINCTS.

311. Of instincts in man as compared with those of inferior animals 328
312. Illustrations of the instincts of brute animals . . . . . ib.
313. Instances of instincts in the human mind 330
314. Further instances of instincts in men 331
315. Of the final cause or use of instincts 332

CHAPTER III.

APPETITES.

316 Of the general nature and characteristics of the appetites . . 333
317 The appetites necessary to our preservation, and not originally of a selfish character . . . . ib
318. Of the prevalence and origin of appetites for intoxicating drugs . 334
319. Of the twofold operation and the morality of the appetites . . 335

CHAPTER IV.

PROPENSITIES.

320. General remarks on the nature of the propensities . . . 336
321. Principle of self-preservation, or the desire of continued existence 337
322. Of the twofold action of the principle of self-preservation . . 338
323 Of curiosity, or the desire of knowledge . . . . . . ib.
324 Further illustrations of the principle of curiosity 339
325 Of the twofold operation and the morality of the principle of curiosity 340
326. Imitativeness, or the propensity to imitation 341
327 Practical results of the principle of imitation . . . 342

Section | Page

328. Of the natural desire of esteem 344
329. Of the desire of esteem as a rule of conduct 345
330. Of the desire of possession 346
331. Of the moral character of the possessory principle . . 347
332. Of perversions of the possessory desire 348
333. Of the desire of power 349
334. Of the moral character of the desire of power 350
335. Propensity of self-love, or the desire of happiness . . . 351
336. Of selfishness as distinguished from self-love 352
337. Reference to the opinions of philosophical writers . . . 353
338. The principle of sociality original in the human mind . . . 354
339 Evidence of the existence of this principle of sociality . . 355
340. Other illustrations of the existence of this principle . . . 356
341. Relation of the social principle to civil society 357

CHAPTER V.

THE MALEVOLENT AFFECTIONS

342. Of the comparative rank of the affections 358
343. Of the complex nature of the affections 359
344. Of resentment or anger 360
345. Illustrations of instinctive resentment 361
346. Uses and moral character of instinctive resentment . . . ib.
347. Of voluntary in distinction from instinctive resentment . . 362
348. Tendency of anger to excess, and the natural checks to it . . 363
349. Other reasons for checking and subduing the angry passions . 365
350. Modifications of resentment. Peevishness 366
351. Modifications of resentment. Envy 367
352. Modifications of resentment. Jealousy 368
353. Modifications of resentment. Revenge 369
354 Nature of the passion of fear . . . . ib

CHAPTER VI.

THE BENEVOLENT AFFECTIONS.

355. Of the nature of love or benevolence in general . . . 371
356. Love, in its various forms, characterized by a twofold action . 372
357. Of the parental affection . . . . ib.
358. Illustrations of the strength of the parental affection . . . 374
359. Of the filial affection 375
360. The filial affection original or implanted 376
361. Illustrations of the filial affection 377
362. Of the nature of the fraternal affection 379
363. On the utility of the domestic affections 380
364. Of the moral character of the domestic affections, and of the benevolent affections generally 381
365. Of the moral character of the voluntary exercises of the benevolent affections 382
366. Of the connexion between benevolence and rectitude . 383
367 Of humanity, or the love of the human race . 384
368. Further proofs in support of the doctrine of an innate humanity, or love for the human race 386
369. Proofs of a humane or philanthropic principle from the existence of benevolent institutions 387
370 Other remarks in proof of the same doctrine . . . 388
371. Of patriotism or love of country 389
372. Of the affection of friendship 390
373. Of the affection of pity or sympathy 391
374 Of the moral character of pity 392
375 Of the affection of gratitude 394

CHAPTER VII.

THE BENEVOLENT AFFECTIONS.

LOVE TO THE SUPREME BEING.

Section | Page
376. Man created originally with the principle of love to God . 395
377. That man was originally created with a principle of love to God, further shown from the Scriptures 396
378. Further proof that man was thus created 398
379. Relation of the principle of supreme love to God to the other principles of the pathematic sensibilities . . . . . . ib
380. The absence of this principle attended with an excessive and sinful action of other principles 400
381. Further illustrations of the results of the absence of this principle 401

CHAPTER VIII.

HABITS OF THE SENSIBILITIES.

382. Meaning of the term habit 404
383. Of habits in connexion with the appetites . . . . . . ib.
384. Of habits in connexion with the propensities . . . 405
385. Of habits in connexion with the affections 406
386. Of the origin of secondary active principles 408

PART II.

THE MORAL SENSIBILITIES OR CONSCIENCE.

MORAL OR CONSCIENTIOUS STATES OF THE MIND.—MORAL SENTIMENTS

CHAPTER I.

EMOTIONS OF MORAL APPROVAL AND DISAPPROVAL.

387. Reference to the general division 413
388. Classification of the moral sensibilities 414
389. Nature of the moral emotions of approval and disapproval . . ib.
390. Of the place or position, mentally considered, of the emotions of approval or disapproval 416
391. Changes in the moral emotions take place in accordance with changes in the antecedent perceptions . . . . . ib.
392. Of objects of moral approval and disapproval 418

CHAPTER II.

RELATION OF REASONING TO THE MORAL NATURE

393. Of the doctrine which confounds reasoning and conscience . 419
394. Of the close connexion between conscience and reasoning . . 420
395. Illustration of the preceding section 421
396. Of the training or education of the conscience 422
397. Of guilt, when a person acts conscientiously 423

CHAPTER III.

FEELINGS OF MORAL OBLIGATION.

398. Feelings of moral obligation distinct from feelings of moral approval and disapproval 424
399. Proof of the existence of obligatory feelings from consciousness . ib.
400. Further proof from the conduct of men 425
401. Further proof from language and literature 426
402. Further proof from the necessity of these feelings . . . 427

Section Page
403. Feelings of obligation simple and not susceptible of definition . 427
404. They are susceptible of different degrees 428
405. Of their authoritative and enforcing nature . . . . . . ib.
406. Feelings of obligation differ from those of mere approval and disapproval 429
407. Feelings of obligation have particular reference to the future . 430
408. Feelings of obligation subsequent in time to the moral emotions of approval and disapproval 431
409. Feelings of obligation differ from desires 432
410. Further considerations on this subject . . . . ib.

CHAPTER IV

UNIFORMITY OF ACTION IN THE MORAL SENSIBILITIES.

41 . Of uniformity in the decisions of the moral nature and the principle on which it is regulated 433
412. The nature of conscience, considered as a uniform principle of action, requires that it should vary in its decisions with circumstances 434
413. Diversities in moral decisions dependent on differences in the amount of knowledge 436
414. Of diversities in moral judgment in connexion with differences in civil and political institutions 437
415 Of diversities and obliquities of moral judgment in connexion with speculative opinions . . . . ib.
416. Further illustrations of the influence of wrong speculative opinions 439
417. Influence of early associations on moral judgments . . . 440
418. Of diversities in the moral judgment in connexion with an excited state of the passions 441

CHAPTER V.

MORAL EDUCATION.

419. Suggestions on the importance of moral education . . . 442
420. The mind early occupied either with good or bad principles . 443
421. Of the time when moral instruction ought to commence . . 444
422. Of the discouragements attending a process of moral instruction 445
423. Of the importance, in a moral point of view, of adopting correct speculative opinions 446
424. Of the knowledge of the Supreme Being, and of the study of religious truth generally 447

THE SENSIBILITIES, OR SENSITIVE NATURE.

SENSITIVE STATES OF THE MIND OR SENTIMENTS.

PART III.

IMPERFECT OR DISORDERED SENSITIVE ACTION.

CHAPTER I.

DISORDERED AND ALIENATED ACTION OF THE APPETITES AND PROPENSITIES.

425. Introductory remarks on disordered sensitive action . . . 451
426. Of what is meant by a disordered and alienated state of the sensibilities . . . . ib.
427. Of the disordered and alienated action of the appetites . 452

Section | Page
428. Disordered action of the principle of self-preservation . . 454
429. Disordered and alienated action of the possessory principle . . 455
430. Instances of the second kind or form of disordered action of the possessory principle . . . . ib.
431. Disordered action of imitativeness, or the principle of imitation . 456
432. Disordered action of the principle of sociality 457
433. Further remarks on the disordered action of the social propensity 458
434. Of the disordered action of the desire of esteem 459
435 Disordered action of the desire of power 460

CHAPTER II.

SYMPATHETIC IMITATION.

436. Of sympathetic imitation, and what is involved in it . . . 461
437. Familiar instances of sympathetic imitation 462
438. Instances of sympathetic imitation at the poor-house of Harlem . 463
439. Other instances of this species of imitation 464

CHAPTER III.

DISORDERED ACTION OF THE AFFECTIONS.

440. Of the states of mind denominated presentiments . . 465
441. Of sudden and strong impulses of the mind 467
442. Insanity of the affections or passions 468
443. Of the mental disease termed hypochondriasis 469
444. Of intermissions of hypochondriasis, and of its remedies . . 471
445. Disordered action of the passion of fear 473
446. Perversions of the benevolent affections . . . . . ib.

CHAPTER IV.

DISORDERED ACTION OF THE MORAL SENSIBILITIES.

447. Nature of voluntary moral derangement 475
448. Of accountability in connexion with this form of disordered conscience 476
449. Of natural or congenital moral derangement 477
450. Moral accountability in cases of natural moral derangement . 479

DIVISION III.

THE WILL.

VOLITIONS, OR VOLITIONAL STATES OF MIND.

CHAPTER I.

GENERAL NATURE OF THE WILL.

451. The will the third and last department of the mind . . 483
452. On the nature of the will . . . . ib.
453. Of the nature of the acts of the will or volitions . . . 484
454. Volition never exists without some object . . . . . ib.
455. It exists in reference to what we believe to be in our power . 485
456. Volition relates to our own action and to whatever else may be dependent upon us 486
457. Volitions involve a prospective element 488
458. Volitions may exist with various degrees of strength . . ib.

CHAPTER II.

ON THE LAWS OF THE WILL.

459. On the universality of law 490
460. Remarks of Hooker on the universality of law 491
461. A presumption thus furnished for subjection of the will to law 492

CHAPTER III.

LAWS OF THE WILL IMPLIED IN THE PRESCIENCE OR FORESIGHT OF THE DEITY.

Section | Page
462. The notion which men naturally form of the Deity implies foreknowledge 493
463. The prescience of God directly taught in the Scriptures . . ib.
464. The foreknowledge of events implies the foreknowledge of volitions 494
465. Application of these views to the will 495
466. The views of this chapter in harmony with the doctrine of the influences of the Holy Spirit . . . . ib.

CHAPTER IV.

LAWS OF THE WILL IMPLIED IN THE PRESCIENCE OF MEN.

467. Man as well as Deity susceptible of foresight 497
468. Prescience of men in respect to their own situation, &c. . . 498
469. Foresight of men in respect to the conduct of others . . 499
470. Other familiar instances of this foresight. 500
471. Argument from the regularity of voluntary contributions . 501
472. Of sagacity in the estimate of individual character. . . 502
473. Foresight of the conduct of masses of men and nations . . 503

CHAPTER V.

ON THE FREEDOM OF THE WILL.

474. Of the freedom of the will, and of the relation of its freedom to its subjection to law 505
475. Circumstances under which freedom of the will exists . . 506
476. Evidence of the freedom of tbe will from consciousness . . 507
477. Objection to the argument from consciousness . . . 508

CHAPTER VI.

FREEDOM OF THE WILL IMPLIED IN MAN'S MORAL NATURE.

478. Of the elements of man's moral nature 509
479. Evidence of freedom of the will from feelings of approval and disapproval 510
480. Proof of freedom from feelings of remorse 511
481. Without the possession of liberty of will man could never have framed the abstract notions of right and wrong . . . 512
482. Proof from feelings of moral obligation 513
483. Evidence from men's views of crimes and punishments . . 514
484. Prevalent opinions of mankind on this subject 516
485. Both views are to be fully received 517
486. The doctrine of the will's freedom equally important with that of its subjection to law 518

CHAPTER VII.

ON THE POWER OF THE WILL.

487. Proof of power in the will from the analogy of the mind . 519
488. Proof of power in the will from internal experience . . 520
489. Proved from the ability which we have to direct our attention to particular subjects 521
490. Proof of power in the will from observation . . . . ib.
491. Illustration of the subject from the command of temper . 523
492. Further illustrations of this subject . . . . ib.
493. Illustrated from the prosecution of some general plan . . 524
494. The subject illustrated from the first settlers of New England . 526
495. Illustrated by the fortitude exhibited by Savages . . . ib.

MENTAL PHILOSOPHY.

DIVISION FIRST.

THE INTELLECT OR UNDERSTANDING.

INTELLECTIVE OR INTELLECTUAL STATES OF THE MIND.

PART FIRST.

INTELLECTUAL STATES OF EXTERNAL ORIGIN

MENTAL PHILOSOPHY.

CHAPTER I.

ORIGIN OF KNOWLEDGE IN GENERAL.

§ 1. The mind susceptible of a threefold division.

THE Human Mind, regarded as a whole, is undoubtedly to be considered as constituting a nature or existence which is truly, and in the strictest sense, one and indivisible. At the same time, if we would have a correct and thorough knowledge of it, it is necessary to contemplate it in three distinct points of view. Accordingly, the leading Divisions in which the Mind presents itself to our notice, are the Understanding or Intellect, the Sensibilities, and the Will. The states of mind which are the results of the action of these leading mental departments, are appropriately expressed by the phrases INTELLECTUAL, SENSITIVE OR SENTIENT, and VOLUNTARY states of the mind. —It is the object of this Abridgment to examine, in as brief a manner as possible, the Divisions which naturally come first in order, viz., the Intellect and the Sensibilities The limits which we find it necessary to assign to the present undertaking, do not allow us to enter into an examination of the distinct and important department of the Will.

§ 2. The Intellect susceptible of a subordinate division.

We begin with the Intellect or Understanding; that department of the mind by means of which we perceive, compare, and reason; and which, in its various modes of action, is the source of all our knowledge. The Intellectual part of man may be considered under two points of view, viz., the External Intellect and the Internal Intellect; in other words, intellectual states of External, and intellectual states of Internal origin.—Intellectual states of External origin depend for their existence upon the existence and presence of external objects. If the mind were insulated and cut off from the outward and material world, or if there were no such outward world, we could not touch, nor hear, nor see. All those mental states which we express when we speak of the diversities of touch, and smell, and taste, of sound and sight, are immediately dependent on the existence and presence of something which is exterior to the intellect itself.

But there are other states of the Intellect, such, for instance, as are expressed by the words TRUTH, FALSEHOOD, POWER, INTELLIGENCE, MERIT, DEMERIT, CAUSE, OBLIGATION, &c., which are not thus closely connected with external things. And these, in distinction from those of External origin, are denominated intellectual states of Internal origin.

§ 3. Of the connexion of the mind with the material world.

As a general statement, the knowledge which is External in its origin is acquired first; the knowledge which is Internal is subsequent. The mind, whatever may ultimately be found to be the extent of its powers of perception, appears, in the first instance, to be wholly destitute of any actual knowledge; and is first brought into action and is put in the way of acquiring knowledge, by means of its connexion with the material or outward world.

This leads us to remark, that there is a correspondence, a mutual adaptation, between the mind and outward material things. They appear to be made for each other. The Creator has obviously established a close relation between them; and it is a striking and important fact, that, in this connexion of the mental and material world, as we have just had occasion to intimate, we are probably to look for the commencement of the mind's activity, and for the beginnings of knowledge.

The soul, considered in its relationship to external nature, may be compared to a stringed instrument. Regarded in itself, it is an invisible existence, having the capacity and elements of harmony The nerves, the eye, and the senses generally, are the chords and artificial framework which God has woven round its unseen and unsearchable essence. This living and curious instrument, made up of the invisible soul and the bodily framework which surrounds it, is at first voiceless and silent. Nor does it appear that it will ever send forth its sounds of harmony, until it is touched and operated upon by those outward influences which exist in the various forms and adaptations of the material world. Under these influences it is first awakened into activity.

§ 4. Our first knowledge in general of a material or external origin.

In accordance with what has been said, we lay down the general principles, FIRST, that during the early period of life there is an intimate connexion between the mind and the material world; and, SECOND, that far the greater portion of the mind's acts during that period can be traced to a material source. In proof of both positions, particularly the latter, we may properly attend to the following considerations.

(I.) What has been said will, in the first place, be found agreeable to each one's individual experience. If we look back to the early periods of life, we discover not merely that our ideas are then comparatively few in number, but that far the greater proportion of them are suggested by external objects. They are forced upon us by our immediate wants; they have relation to what we ourselves see, or hear, or touch; and only a small proportion are internal and abstract. As we advance in years, susceptibilities of the mind are brought into exercise, which have a less intimate connexion with things external; and thoughts from within are more rapidly multiplied than from without. We have in some measure exhausted that which is external; and as the mind, awakened to a love of knowledge and a consciousness of its powers, has at last been brought fully into action by means of repeated affections of the senses, a new world (as yet in some degree a TERRA INCOGNITA) projects itself upon our attention, where we are called upon to push our researches and gratify our curiosity.—This is the general experience, the testimony which each one can give for himself.

§ 5. Shown further from what we notice in children.

In the second place, what has been said finds confirmation in what we observe of the progress of the mind in infants and children generally. The course of things which we observe in them, agrees with what our personal consciousness and remembrance, as far back as it goes, enables us to testify with no little confidence in our own case. No one can observe the operations of the mind in infants and children, without being led to believe, that the Creator has instituted a connexion between the mind and the material world, and that the greater portion of our early knowledge is from an outward source.

To the infant its nursery is the world. The first ideas of the human race are its particular conceptions of its nurse and mother; and the origin and history of all its notions may be traced to its animal wants, to the light that breaks in from its window, and to the few objects in the immediate neighbourhood of the cradle and hearth. When it has become a few years of age, there are other sources of information, other fountains of thought, but they are still external and material. The child then learns the topography of his native village; he explores the margin of its river, ascends its flowering hills, and penetrates the seclusion of its valleys. His mind is full of activity; new and exalting views crowd upon his perceptions; he beholds, and hears, and handles; he wonders, and is delighted. And it is not till after he has grasped the elements of knowledge which the outward world gives, that he retires within himself, compares, reasons, and seeks for causes and effects.

It is in accordance with what has now been stated of the tendencies of mind in children, that we generally find them instructed by means of sensible objects, or by pictures of such objects. When their teachers make an abstract statement to them of an action or event, they do not understand it; they listen to it with an appearance of confusion and vacancy, for the process is undoubtedly against nature. But show them the objects themselves, or a faithful picture of them, and interpret your abstract expressions by a reference to the object or picture, and they are observed to learn with rapidity and pleasure. The time has not yet arrived for the springing up and growth of thoughts of an internal and abstract origin.

§ 6. Further proof of the beginnings of knowledge from external causes.

In the third place, the history of language is a strong proof of the correctness of the position, that the mind is first brought into action by means of the senses, and acquires its earliest knowledge from that source. At first words are few in number, corresponding to the limited extent of ideas. The vocabulary of savage tribes (those, for example, which inhabit the American continent) is in general exceedingly limited. The growth of a language corresponds to the growth of mind; it extends itself by the increased number and power of its words, nearly in exact correspondence with the multiplication and the increased complexity of thought. Now the history of all languages teaches us, that words, which were invented and brought into use one after another in the gradual way just mentioned, were first employed to express external objects, and afterward were used to express thoughts of internal origin.

Almost all the words in every language, expressive of the susceptibilities and operations of the mind, may be clearly shown to have had an external origin and application before they were applied to the mind. To IMAGINE, in its literal signification, implies the forming of a picture; to IMPRESS conveys the idea of leaving a stamp or mark, as the seal leaves its exact likeness or stamp on wax; to REFLECT literally means to turn back, to go over the ground again, &c. These words cannot be applied to the mind in the literal sense; the nature of the mind will not admit of such an application; the inference therefore is, that they first had an external application. Now if it be an established truth, as the history of languages seems to show that it is, that all language has a primary reference to external objects, and that there is no term expressive of mental acts which was not originally expressive of something material, the conclusion would seem to be a fair one, that the part of our knowledge which has its rise by means of the senses, is, as a general statement, first in origin. And the more so, when we combine with these views the considerations which have been previously advanced.

§ 7. The same subject further illustrated.

And, in the fourth place, it is not too much to say, that all the observations which have been made on persons who, from their birth or at any subsequent period, have been deprived of any of the senses, and all the extraordinary facts which have come to knowledge, having a bearing on this inquiry, go strongly in favour of the views which have been given.—It appears, for instance, from the observations which have been made in regard to persons who have been deaf until a particular period, and then have been restored to the power of hearing, that they have never previously had those ideas which naturally come in by that sense. If a person has been born blind, the result is the same; or if, having the sense of sight, it has so happened that he has never seen any colours of a particular description. In the one case, he has no ideas of colours at all; and in the other, only of those colours which he has seen.—It may be said, perhaps, that this is what might be expected, and merely proves the senses to be a source of knowledge, without necessarily involving the priority of that knowledge to what has an internal origin. But then observe the persons referred to a little further, and it will be found, as a general statement, that the internal powers of their minds have not been unfolded; they lay wrapped up in a great measure in their original darkness; no inward light springs up to compensate for the absence of that which, in other cases, bursts in from the outward world. This circumstance evidently tends to confirm the principles which we are endeavouring to illustrate.

Of those extraordinary instances to which we alluded, as having thrown some light on the history of our intellectual acquisitions, is the account which is given in the Memoirs of the French Academy of Sciences for the year 1703, of a deaf and dumb young man in the city of Chartres At the age of three-and-twenty, it so happened, to the great surprise of the whole town, that he was suddenly restored to the sense of hearing, and in a short time he acquired the use of language. Deprived for so long a period of a sense which, in importance, ranks with the sight and the touch, unable to hold communion with his fellow-beings by means of oral or written language, and not particularly compelled, as he had every care taken of him by his friends and relations, to bring his faculties into exercise, the powers of his mind remained without having opportunity to unfold themselves. Being examined by some men of discernment, it was found that he had no idea of a God, of a soul, of the moral merit or demerit of human actions, and, what might seem to be yet more remarkable, he knew not what it was to die; the agonies of dissolution, the grief of friends, and the ceremonies of interment being to him inexplicable mysteries.

Here we see how much knowledge a person was deprived of, merely by his wanting the single sense of hearing; a proof that the senses were designed by our Creator to be the first source of knowledge, and that without them the faculties of the soul would never become operative.

§ 8. Illustration from the case of James Mitchell.

But this is not the only instance of this sort which ingenious men have noticed and recorded. In the Transactions of the Royal Society at Edinburgh, (vol. vii., part i.,) is a Memoir communicated by Dugald Stewart, which gives an account of James Mitchell, a boy born deaf and blind. The history of this lad, who laboured under the uncommon affliction of this double deprivation, illustrates and confirms all that has been above stated. He made what use he could of the only senses which he possessed, those of touch, taste, and smell, and gained from them a number of ideas. It was a proof of the diligence with which he employed the limited means which were given him, that he had by the sense of touch thoroughly explored the ground in the neighbourhood of the house where he lived for hundreds of yards. But deprived of sight, of hearing, and of intercourse by speech, it was very evident to those who observed him, as might be expected, that his knowledge was in amount exceedingly small. He was destitute of those perceptions which are appropriate to the particular senses of which he was deprived; and also of many other notions of an internal origin, which would undoubtedly have arisen, if the powers of the mind had previously been rendered fully operative by means of those assistances which it usually receives from the bodily organs.—Such instances as these, however they may at first appear, are extremely important. They furnish us with an appeal, not to mere speculations, but to fact. And it is only by checking undue speculation, and by continually recurring to facts, that our progress in this science will become sure, rapid, and delightful.

CHAPTER II.

SENSATION AND PERCEPTION.

§ 9. Sensation a simple mental state originating in the senses.

In tracing the history of that portion of human thought which is of external origin, we have frequent occasion to make use of the words Sensation and Perception. The term SENSATION is not of so general a nature as to include every variety of mental state, but is limited to such as answer to a particular description. It does not appear that the usage of language would forbid our speaking of the feelings of warmth, and coldness, and hardness, as well as of the *feelings* of love, and benevolence, and anger, but it would clearly forbid our using the term SENSATION with an application equally extensive. Its application is not only limited, but is fixed with a considerable degree of precision.

Sensation, being a simple act or state of the mind, is unsusceptible of definition; and this is one of its characteristics. As this alone, however, would not separate it from many other mental states, it has this peculiarity to distinguish it, that *it is immediately successive to a change in some organ of sense, or, at least, to a bodily change of some kind.* But it is evident, that, in respect to numerous other feelings, this statement does not hold good. They are immediately subsequent, not to bodily impressions, but to other states of the soul itself. Hence it is, that while we speak of the sensations of heat and cold, of hardness, of smoothness, roughness, and the like, we do not commonly apply this term to joy and sorrow, hatred and love, and other emotions and passions.

§ 10. All sensation is properly and truly in the mind.

Sensation is often regarded as something having a position, and as taking place in the body, and particularly in the organ of sense. The sensation of touch, as we seem to imagine, is in the hand, which is the organ of touch, and is not truly internal; the hearing is in the ear, and the vision in the eye, and not in the soul. But all we can say with truth and on good grounds is, that the organs of sense are accessory to sensation and necessary to it; but the sensation or feeling itself is wholly in the mind. How often it is said the eye sees; but the proper language, if we look at the subject philosophically, is, that the soul sees; for the eye is only the organ, instrument, or minister of the soul in visual perceptions.

"A man," says Dr Reid, "cannot see the satellites of Jupiter but by a telescope. Does he conclude from this that it is the telescope that sees those stars? By no means; such a conclusion would be absurd. It is no less absurd to conclude that it is the eye that sees, or the ear that hears. The telescope is an artificial organ of sight, but it sees not. The eye is a natural organ of sight, by which we see; but the natural organ sees as little as the artificial."

§ 11. Sensations are not images or resemblances of objects.

But while we are careful to assign sensations their true place in the mind, and to look upon what is outward in the body as merely the antecedents or cause of them, it is a matter of some consequence to guard against a danger directly the reverse of that which has been remarked on. We are apt to transfer to the sensation, considered as existing in the mind, some of those qualities which belong to the external object. But in point of fact, our sensations are by no means copies, pictures, or images of outward objects; nor are they representations of them in any material sense whatever; nor do they possess any of their qualities

It is true, we often think it otherwise; constantly occupied with external objects, when in the act of contemplation we retire within the mind, we unwarily carry with us the form and qualities of matter, and stamp its likeness on the thought itself. But the thought, whatever it may by the constitution of our nature be the sign of, has no form, and presents no image analogous to what are outwardly objects of touch and sight; nor has it form or image in any sense which we can conceive of. When, therefore, we have an idea of some object as round, we are not to infer, from the existence of the quality in the outward object, that the mental state is possessed of the same quality. When we think of anything as extended, it is not to be supposed that the thought itself has extension. When we behold and admire the varieties of colour, we are not at liberty to indulge the presumption that the inward feelings are painted over, and radiant with corresponding hues. There is nothing of the kind; and the admission of such a principle would lead to a multitude of errors.

§ 12. The connexion between the mental and physical change not capable of explanation.

(I.) External bodies operate on the senses, before there is any affection of the mind, but it is not easy to say what the precise character and extent of this operation is. We know that some object capable of affecting the organ must be applied to it in some way either directly or indirectly, and it is a matter of knowledge also, that some change in the organ actually takes place; but further than this we are involved in uncertainty. All we can undertake to do at present is merely to make a statement of the facts, viz., the application of an external body, and some change in consequence of it in the organ of sense.

(II.) Subsequently to the change in the organ, either at its extremity and outward developement or in the brain, with which it is connected, and of which it may be considered as making a part, a change in the mind or a new state of the mind immediately takes place. Here also we are limited to the mere statement of the fact

We here touch upon one of those boundaries of the intellect which men are probably not destined to pass in the present life. We find ourselves unable to resolve and explain the connexion between mind and matter in this case, as we do in all others. All we know, and all we can state with confidence is, that a mental affection is immediately subsequent to an affection or change which is physical. Such is our nature, and such the appointment of Him who ordered it.

§ 13. Of the meaning and nature of perception.

We next come to the subject of PERCEPTION, which is intimately connected with that of sensation. This term, like many others, admits of a considerable latitude in its application. In common language we are not only said to have the power of perceiving outward objects, but also of perceiving the agreement or disagreement in the acts of the mind itself. Accordingly, we perceive a tree in the forest or a ship at sea, and we also perceive that the whole is greater than a part, and that the three angles of a triangle are equal to two right angles. But what we have to say here does not concern internal perception, but merely that which relates to objects exterior to the mind

Perception, using the term in its application to outward objects, differs from sensation as a whole does from a part; it embraces more. It may be defined, therefore, an affection or state of the mind *which is immediately successive to certain affections of the organs of sense, and which is referred by us to something external as its cause.*

§ 14. Perception makes us acquainted with a material world.

It will be recollected, that the term SENSATION, when applied to the mind, expresses merely the state of the mind, without reference to anything external, which might be the cause of it, and that it is the name of a truly simple feeling. Perception, on the contrary, is the name of a complex mental state, including not merely the internal affection of the mind, but also a reference to the exterior cause. Sensation is wholly within; but Perception carries us, as it were, out of ourselves, and makes us acquainted with the world around us. It is especially by means of this last power, that material nature, in all its varieties of form and beauty, is brought within the range of our inspection. If we had but sensation alone, there would still be form, and fragrance, and colour, and harmony of sound, but it would seem to be wholly inward The mind would seem to constitute everything; we could know no other world, no other form of being. Perception prevents the possibility of such a mistake; it undeceives and dissipates the flattering notion, that all things are in the soul; it leads us to other existences, and, in particular, to the knowledge of the vast and complicated fabric of the material creation.

§ 15. Of the primary and secondary qualities of matter

From what has been said, it will be noticed that SENSATION implies the existence of an external material world as its cause, and that PERCEPTION implies the same existence both as cause and object. It is hardly necessary to say, that we are altogether ignorant of the subjective or real essence of matter. Our knowledge embraces merely its qualities or properties, and nothing more. Without proposing to enter into a minute examination of them, it will be proper to state here, that the qualities of material bodies have been ranked by writers under the two heads of Primary and Secondary.

The PRIMARY QUALITIES are known by being essential to the existence of all bodies. They are extension, figure, divisibility, and solidity; and some writers have included motion. They are called PRIMARY for the reason already distinctly referred to, that all men embrace them in the notions which they form of matter, and that they are essential to its existence. All bodies have extension, all bodies have figure, all are capable of division, all possess the attribute of solidity.

By SOLIDITY in bodies (perhaps some would prefer the term RESISTANCE) is to be understood that quality by which a body hinders the approach of others between which it is interposed. In this sense even water, and all other fluids are solid. If particles of water could be prevented from separating, they would oppose so great resistance, that it would be impossible for any two bodies between which they might be to come in contact. This was shown in an experiment which was once made at Florence. A quantity of water was enclosed in a gold ball, which, on the most violent pressure, could not be made to fill the internal cavity until the water inside was forced through the pores.

There is reason also for that part of the arrangement which includes DIVISIBILITY. We cannot conceive of a particle so small as not to be susceptible of division. And to that small particle must belong, not only divisibility, but the qualities of solidity, extension, and figure.

§ 16. *Of the secondary qualities of matter.*

The SECONDARY qualities of bodies are of two kinds. (1.) Those which have relation to the perceiving and sentient mind; (2.) Those which have relation to other bodies.

Under the first class are to be included sound, colour, taste, smell, hardness and softness, heat and cold, roughness and smoothness, &c. When we say of a body it has sound, we imply in this remark that it possesses qualities which will cause certain effects in the mind; the term sound being applicable, by the use of language, both to the qualities of the external object and to the effect produced within. When we say it has colour, we always make a like reference to the mind, which beholds and contemplates it; and it is the same of the other secondary qualities of this description.

The other class of secondary qualities, (or properties, as they are not unfrequently termed,) those which have relation to other material bodies, are exceedingly various and numerous. The material substance which, in relation to the mind, possesses the qualities of sound and colour, may possess also, in relation to other bodies, the qualities or properties of malleability, fusibility, solubility, permeability, and the like.

CHAPTER III.

THE SENSES OF SMELL AND TASTE.

§ 17. Nature and importance of the senses as a source of knowledge.

It is desirable to keep clearly in mind the precise relation of the senses to the origin, progress, and amount of our knowledge, and to possess, if possible, a correct understanding of their true value. In a certain sense, the possession of the bodily organs with which we are furnished, is not essential and prerequisite to the possession of that knowledge which we are accustomed to ascribe to them. There is nothing unwarrantable and unreasonable in the supposition, that the knowledge which we now have by their means might have been possessed without their aid, either immediately, or in some way altogether different. Their use and indispensableness in the acquisition of a certain portion of what men are permitted to know, is a matter of arrangement and appointment on the part of our Maker. It is undoubtedly an evidence of the correctness of this remark, that the Supreme Being has a full acquaintance with all those outward objects which present themselves to our notice, without being indebted to any material instrumentality and mediation. He perceives in another way, or, rather, all knowledge is inherent in, and originally and unalterably essential to himself.

It is not so, as we have reason to believe, with any other beings, and certainly not with man. Although a great part of his knowledge relates to material things, he is so formed, and his constitution is so ordered, that he is wholly dependent for it on the senses.—Deprive him of the ear, and all nature becomes silent; deprive him of the eye, and the sun and moon withdraw their light, and the universe becomes darkened; deprive him of the sense of touch, and he is then entirely insulated, and as much cut off from all communication with others as if he were the only being in existence.

§ 18. Connexion of the brain with sensation and perception

(I.) It may perhaps be asked, Whether these views are intended to exclude the brain, as having a connexion with the senses in the results which are here ascribed to them? And this inquiry leads us to observe, (what has been before alluded to,) that the brain is a prominent organ in the material part of the process of sensation and of external perception. The senses evidently cannot be separated from the nervous system. But the substance which is found in the nerves, excepting the coat in which it is enveloped, is the same as in the brain, being of the same soft and fibrous texture, and in continuity with it. As a general statement, when the brain has been in any way injured, the inward sensation, which would otherwise be distinct on the presence of an external body, is imperfect. Also, if the nerve be injured, or if its continuity be disturbed by the pressure of a tight ligature, the effect is the same; a circumstance which goes to confirm the alleged identity of substance in the two.

(II.) The brain, therefore, and whatever of the same substance is in continuity with it, particularly the nerves, constitutes the *sensorial organ*, which, in the subordinate organs of taste, smell, sight, touch, and hearing, presents itself under different modifications to external objects. On this organ, the *sensorial*, as thus explained, an impression must be made before there can be sensation and perception.

An impression, for instance, is made on that part of the sensorial organ called the auditory nerve, and a state of mind immediately succeeds which is variously termed, according to the view in which it is contemplated, either the sensation or the perception of sound.

An impression is made by the rays of light on that expansion of the optic nerve which forms what is called the RETINA of the eye, and the intellectual principle is immediately brought into that new position, which is termed visual perception or a perception of sight.

The hand is impressed on a body of an uneven and rough surface, and immediately consequent on this application and pressure is that state of mind which is termed a sensation or perception of roughness.

§ 19. Order in which the senses are to be considered.

In considering those ideas which we become possessed of by means of the senses, it is natural to begin with that sense which will cause us the least difficulty in the analysis of its results; and to proceed to others successively, as we find them increasing in importance. It may not be altogether easy to apply this principle with strictness, but it will answer all the purpose for which it is here introduced, if we consider the senses in the following order, the smell, taste, hearing, touch, and sight.

The mind holds a communication with the material world by means of the sense of smelling. All animal and vegetable bodies (and the same will probably hold good of other bodies, though generally in a less degree) are continually sending out effluvia of great subtilty. These small particles are rapidly and widely scattered abroad in the neighbourhood of the body from which they proceed. No sentient being can come within the circumference occupied by these continually moving and volatile atoms, without experiencing effects from it.

§ 20. Of the sense and sensations of smell.

The medium through which we have the sensations and perceptions of smell, is the organ which is termed the olfactory nerve, situated principally in the nostrils, but partly in some continuous cavities. When some odoriferous particles, sent from external objects, affect this organ, there is a certain state of mind produced which varies with the nature of the odoriferous bodies. But we can no more infer from the sensation itself merely, that there exists any necessary connexion between the smell and the external objects, than that there exists a connexion between the emotions of joy and sorrow and the same objects. It might indeed be suggested to us by the change in our mental states, that there must be some cause or antecedent to the change, but this suggestion would be far from implying the necessity of a *corporeal* cause.

(II.) How then does it happen, that we are not merely sensible of the particular sensation, but refer it at once to some external object, to the rose, or the honeysuckle? In answer it may be remarked, if we had always been destitute of the senses of sight and touch, this reference never could have been made; but, having been furnished with them by the beneficent Author of our being, we make this reference by experience. When we have seen the rose, when we have been near to it and handled it, we have uniformly been conscious of that state of mind which we term a sensation of smell. When we have come into the neighbourhood of the honeysuckle, or when it has been gathered and presented to us, we have been reminded of its fragrance. And thus, having learned by experience that the presence of the odoriferous body is always attended with the sensations of smell, we form the habit of attributing the sensations to that body as their cause

§ 21. Of perceptions of smell in distinction from sensations.

The mental reference spoken of in the last section is made with almost as much promptness as if it were necessarily involved in the sensation itself. It is at least so rapid, that we find ourselves utterly unable to mark the mind's progress from the inward feeling to the conception of the outward cause. Nor is this inability surprising, when we consider that we have repeated this process, both in this and in analogous cases, from our earliest childhood. No object has ever been present to us capable of operating on the senses, where this process has not been gone through. The result of this long-continued and frequent repetition has been an astonishing quickness in the mental action; so much so that the mind leaps outward with the rapidity of lightning, to be present with, and to comprehend the causes of the feeling within.

This view, it will be seen, helps in illustrating the nature of PERCEPTION as distinguished from sensation. The outlines of that distinction have already been given; and every one of the senses, as well as that now under consideration, will furnish proofs and illustrations of it. Accordingly, when we are said to perceive the smell, or to have perceptions of the smell of a body, the rapid process which has been described is gone through, and the three things which were involved in the definition of Perception, already given, are supposed to exist; (1.) The presence of the odoriferous body and the affection of its appropriate organ; (2.) The change or sensation in the mind; and, (3.) The reference of the sensation to the external body as its cause.

§ 22. Of the sense and the sensations of taste

The tongue, which is covered with numerous nervous papillæ, forms essentially the organ of taste, although the papillæ are found scattered in other parts of the cavity of the mouth. The application of any sapid body to this organ immediately causes in it a change or affection; and that is at once followed by a mental affection or a new state of the mind. In this way we have the sensations and perceptions, to which we give the names sweet, bitter, sour, acrid, &c.

Having experienced the inward sensation, the affections of the mind are then referred by us to something external as their *cause*. We do not, however, always, nor even generally, distinguish the qualities which constitute this cause by separate and appropriate designations; but express them by the names that are employed for the internal feeling, viz., sweetness, bitterness, sourness, &c. This reference of what is internally experienced to its external cause is very rapidly made; so that we at once say of one apple it is sweet, and of another it is sour. Still it is to be kept in mind, that, in point of fact, it is subsequent, both in the order of nature and of time, to the mere sensation; although we may not be able, in consequence of its rapidity, to mark distinctly the progress of the mental action from the one to the other. As in the case of smells, which have already been remarked upon, the reference is the result of our former experience. We say of one body it is sweet, and of another it is sour, because we have ever observed that the mental states indicated by those terms have always existed in connexion with the presence of those bodies.

Whenever, therefore, we say of any bodies that they are sweet, bitter, sour, or apply any other epithets expressive of sapid qualities, we mean to be understood to say that such bodies are fitted, in the constitution of things, to cause in the mind the sensations of sweetness, bitterness, and sourness, or other sensations expressed by denominations of taste. Or, in other words, that they are the established antecedents of such mental states, as there is, further than this, no necessary connexion between them.

CHAPTER IV.

THE SENSE OF HEARING.

§ 23. Organ of the sense of hearing.

FOLLOWING the order which has been proposed, we are next to consider the sense of HEARING. And, in proceeding to the consideration of this subject, the remark is a very obvious one, that we should be unable to hear if we had not a sense designed for, and appropriate to, that result. The air, when put strongly in motion, is distinctly perceived by the touch; but no impression which it could make on that sense would cause that internal feeling which is termed a sensation of sound. Our Creator, therefore, has taken care that these sensations shall have their own organ; and it is obviously one of precise and elaborate workmanship.

The ear is designedly planted in a position where, with the greatest ease, it takes cognizance of whatever is going on in the contiguous atmosphere. When we examine it externally, we not only find it thus favourably situated, but presenting a hollowed and capacious surface, so formed as to grasp and gather in the undulations of air, continually floating and in motion around it. Without, however, delaying to give a minute description of the internal construction of the ear, which belongs rather to the physiologist, it will answer our present purpose merely to add, that these undulations are conducted by it through various windings, till they are brought in a state of concentration, as it were, against the membrane called the TYMPANUM.—It is worthy of notice, that on the internal surface of this membrane (the drum, as it is popularly called) there is a nerve spread out in a manner analogous to the expansion of the optic nerve at the bottom of the eye. Whether this nervous expansion be indispensably necessary to the result or not, it is certain that a pressure upon or affection of the tympanum by the external air, is followed by a new state of the mind, known as the sensation or perception of sound.

§ 24. Varieties of the sensation of sound.

The sensations which we thus become possessed of by the hearing are far more numerous than the words and the forms of speech, having relation to them in different languages, would lead us to suppose. It will help to illustrate this subject if we recur a moment to the sense of TASTE. The remark has somewhere been made to this effect, and probably with much truth, that if a person were to examine five hundred different wines, he would hardly find two of them of precisely the same flavour. The diversity is almost endless, although there is no language which distinguishes each variety of taste by a separate name. It is the same in respect to the sensations of sound. These sensations exhibit the greatest variety, although their differences are too minute to be separately and distinctly represented by language.

These views will appear the less objectionable when it is remembered that sounds differ from each other both in the tone and in the strength of the tone. It is remarked by Dr. Reid, that five hundred variations of tone may be perceived by the ear, also an equal number of variations in the strength of the tone; making, as he expressly informs us, by a combination of the tones and of the degrees of strength, more than twenty thousand simple sounds, differing either in tone or strength.

In a perfect tone, a great many undulations of elastic air are required, which must be of equal duration and extent, and follow each other with perfect regularity. Each undulation is made up of the advance and retreat of innumerable particles, whose motions are all uniform in direction, force, and time. Accordingly, there will be varieties also and shades of difference in the same tone, arising from the position and manner of striking the sonorous body, from the constitution of the elastic medium, and from the state of the organ of hearing.

Different instruments, such as a flute, a violin, and a bass-viol, may all sound the same tone, and yet be easily distinguishable. A considerable number of human voices may sound the same note, and with equal strength, and yet there will be some difference. The same voice, while it maintains the proper distinctions of sound, may yet be varied many ways by sickness or health, youth or age, and other alterations in our bodily condition to which we are incident.

§ 25. Manner in which we learn the place of sounds.

It is a fact particularly worthy of notice in respect to sounds, that we should not know, previous to all experience on the subject, whether a sound came from the right or left, from above or below, from a smaller or greater distance. And this will appear the less surprising when we remember that the undulations of air are always changed from their original direction by the channels and the windings of the ear before they strike the tympanum. Abundant facts confirm this statement.

Dr. Reid mentions, that once, as he was lying in bed, having been put into a fright, he heard his own heart beat. He took it to be some one knocking at the door, and arose and opened the door oftener than once before he discovered that the sound was in his own breast. Some traveller has related that, when he first heard the roaring of a lion in a desert wilderness, not seeing the animal, he did not know on what side to apprehend danger, as the sound seemed to him to proceed from the ground, and to enclose a circle, of which he and his companions stood in the centre.

It is by custom or experience that we learn to distinguish the place of things, and, in some measure also, their nature, by means of their sound. It is thus that we learn that one noise is in a contiguous room, that another is above our heads, and another is in the street. And what seems to be an evidence of this is, that when we are in a strange place, after all our experience, we very frequently find ourselves mistaken in these respects

If a man born deaf were suddenly made to hear, he would probably consider his first sensations of sound as originating wholly within himself. But in process of time we learn not only to refer the origin of sounds to a position above or below, to the right or left; but to connect each particular sound with a particular external cause, referring one to a bell as its appropriate external cause, another to a flute, another to a trumpet.

CHAPTER V.

THE SENSE OF TOUCH.

§ 26. Of the sense of touch in general and its sensations.

We are next to consider the sense of TOUCH. The principal organ of this sense is the hand, although it is not limited to that part of our frame, but is diffused over the whole body. The hand principally arrests our attention as the organ of this sense, because, being furnished with various articulations, it is easily moveable by the muscles, and can readily adapt itself to the various changes of form in the objects to which it is applied.

The senses, which have hitherto been examined, are more simple and uniform in their results than that of the touch. By the ear we merely possess that sensation which we denominate hearing; we have the knowledge of sounds, and that is all. By the palate we acquire a knowledge of tastes, and by the sense of smelling we become acquainted with the odours of bodies. The knowledge which is directly acquired by all these senses is limited to the qualities which have been mentioned. By the sense of touch, on the contrary, we become acquainted not with one merely, but with a variety of qualities, such as the following, heat and cold, hardness and softness, roughness and smoothness, solidity or resistance, extension, and figure; and, in particular, it gives occasion for the origin of the antecedent and more general notion of externality.

§ 27. Idea of externality suggested in connexion with the touch.

If man were possessed of the sense of smell alone, it would be found that the earliest elements of his knowl edge consisted exclusively in sensations of odours. According, however, as these sensations were agreeable or disagreeable, he would acquire the additional ideas of pleasure and pain. And having experienced pleasure and pain, we may suppose that this would subsequently give rise both to the feelings and the abstract conceptions of desire and aversion. But if he had no other sense, all these feelings would seem to him to be internal, not only in their experience, but their origin; in other words, to be mere emanations from the soul itself; and he would be incapable of referring them to an external cause.—If he were possessed of the sense of hearing alone, the result would be similar; his existence would then seem to consist essentially of sounds, as in the other case it would be made up of odours; nor, indeed, by the aid of merely both these senses combined would he be able to form an idea of externality or outwardness.

But this idea is a most important one; it is the connecting thought which introduces us to an acquaintance with a new form of existence, different from that interior existence which we variously call by the names spirit, mind, or soul. This idea first arises in the mind, although it is not directly addressed to that sense, by means of the touch.

There is no question that the other senses might of themselves furnish a basis of considerable extent for the mental action. By means of their aid alone, such a developement of the mind might take place, that we could perceive, think, compare, abstract, reason, and will. And although, under such circumstances, everything would seem to us to be internal, yet we should probably find the mental action unembarrassed and easy, and a source of pleasure. But after a time we decide to move the limbs in a particular direction, and to press the hand or some other part of the body through some hard and resisting substance. It is when we attempt to do anything of this kind, which calls the sense of touch into action, that we find the wonted series of thoughts disturbed, the desire checked, and the volition counteracted. It is probably at this precise position of the mind, with scarcely the interval of a momentary pause of wonder, that there arises vividly in the soul a new perception, a new thought, which we call the idea of externality or outness. It is the sense of touch which impinges upon the obstacle that stands in our way; and no other sense admits of this peculiar application. It is thus the means of partially disturbing the previous connexion and tendency of thought, and of giving occasion for the rise of the new idea which is under consideration. And this idea, called into existence under these circumstances, becomes associated with all those notions which we subsequently form of matter.—It may be of some importance to add here, that we shall have occasion to refer to this idea again under the head of Original Suggestion. It is to be remembered, that externality is not a direct object of the touch, as extension and hardness are, but that the tactual sense simply furnishes the *occasion* on which it is formed.

§ 28. Origin of the notion of extension, and of form or figure.

The idea of EXTENSION has its origin by means of the sense of touch. When the touch is applied to bodies, where in the intermediate parts there is a continuity of the same substance, we necessarily form that notion. It is not, however, to be imagined that Extension, as it exists outwardly, and the corresponding notion in the mind, actually resemble each other. So far from any imitation and copying from one to the other, or resemblance in any way, there is a radical and utter diversity. As to outward, material extension, it is not necessary to attend to it here; our business at present is with the corresponding inward feeling Nor will it be necessary to delay even upon that; the more we multiply words upon it, the more obscure it becomes. As it is a simple idea, we cannot resolve it into others, and in that way make it clearer by defining it. We must refer in this case, as in others like it, to each one's personal experience. It will be better understood in that way than by any form of words.

The notion of extension is intimately connected with, and may be considered in some sort the foundation of, that of the FORM or figure of bodies.—Dr. Brown somewhere calls the Form of bodies their relation to each other in space. This is thought to afford matter for reflection;

but when we consider that SPACE, whatever it may be objectively or outwardly, exists in the mind as a simple notion, and that the particular relation here spoken of is not pointed out, the remark may not be found to throw much light on the subject. Still we do not suppose that any one is ignorant of what FORM is; men must be supposed to know that, if they are thought to know anything. All that is meant to be asserted here is, that the idea of extension is antecedent, in the order of nature, to that of form; and that the latter could not exist without the other; but that both, nevertheless, are simple, and both are to be ascribed to the sense of touch.

§ 29. On the sensations of heat and cold.

Among the states of mind which are usually classed with the intimations of the sense under consideration, are those which are connected with changes in the temperature of our bodies. Some writers, it is true, have been inclined to dissent from this arrangement, and have hazarded an opinion that they ought not to be ascribed to the sense of TOUCH; but Dr. Reid, on the contrary, who gave to our sensations the most careful and patient attention, has decidedly assigned to them this origin. Among other remarks, he has expressed himself on this subject to this effect.

"The words HEAT and COLD," he remarks, (Inquiry into the Human Mind, ch. v.,) "have each of them two significations; they sometimes signify certain sensations of the mind, which can have no existence when they are not felt, nor can exist anywhere but in the mind or sentient being; but more frequently they signify a quality in bodies, which, by the laws of nature, occasions the sensations of heat and cold in us; a quality which, though connected by custom so closely with the sensation that we cannot without difficulty separate them, yet hath not the least resemblance to it, and may continue to exist when there is no sensation at all.

"The sensations of heat and cold are perfectly known, for they neither are, nor can be, anything else than what we feel them to be; but the qualities in bodies, which we call *heat* and *cold*, are unknown. They are only conceiv ed by us as unknown causes or occasions of the sensations, to which we give the same names. But though common sense says nothing of the nature of the qualities, it plainly indicates the existence of them; and to deny that there can be heat and cold when they are not felt, is an absurdity too gross to merit confutation. For what could be more absurd than to say that the thermometer cannot rise or fall unless some person be present, or that the coast of Guinea would be as cold as Nova Zembla if it had no inhabitants.

"It is the business of philosophers to investigate, by proper experiments and induction, what heat and cold are in bodies. And whether they make heat a particular element diffused through nature, and accumulated in the heated body, or whether they make it a certain vibration of the parts of the heated body; whether they determine that heat and cold are contrary qualities, as the sensations undoubtedly are contrary, or that heat only is a quality, and cold its privation; these questions are within the province of philosophy; for common sense says nothing on the one side or the other.

"But, whatever be the nature of that quality in bodies which we call *heat*, we certainly know this, that it cannot in the least resemble the sensation of heat. It is no less absurd to suppose a likeness between the sensation and the quality, than it would be to suppose that the pain of the gout resembles a square or a triangle. The simplest man that hath common sense does not imagine the sensation of heat, or anything that resembles that sensation, to be in the fire. He only imagines that there is something in the fire which makes him and other sentient beings feel heat. Yet as the name of *heat*, in common language, more frequently and more properly signifies this unknown something in the fire than the sensation occasioned by it, he justly laughs at the philosopher who denies that there is any heat in the fire, and thinks that he speaks contrary to common sense."

§ 30. Of the sensations of hardness and softness.

"Let us next consider," continues the same writer, "HARDNESS and SOFTNESS; by which words we always understand real properties or qualities of bodies, of which we have a distinct conception.

"When the parts of a body adhere so firmly that it cannot easily be made to change its figure, we call it *hard;* when its parts are easily displaced, we call it *soft.* This is the notion which all mankind have of hardness and softness: they are neither sensations nor like any sensation; they were real qualities before they were perceived by touch, and continue to be so when they are not perceived: for if any man will affirm that diamonds were not hard till they were handled, who would reason with him?

"There is, no doubt, a sensation by which we perceive a body to be hard or soft. This sensation of hardness may easily be had by pressing one's hand against a table, and attending to the feeling that ensues, setting aside as much as possible all thought of the table and its qualities, or of any external thing. But it is one thing to have the sensation, and another to attend to it and make it a distinct object of reflection. The first is very easy; the last, in most cases, extremely difficult.

"We are so accustomed to use the sensation as a sign, and to pass immediately to the hardness signified, that, as far as appears, it was never made an object of thought, either by the vulgar or by philosophers; nor has it a name in any language. There is no sensation more distinct or more frequent; yet it is never attended to, but passes through the mind instantaneously, and serves only to introduce that quality in bodies which, by a law of our constitution, it suggests.

"There are, indeed, some cases wherein it is no difficult matter to attend to the sensation occasioned by the hardness of a body; for instance, when it is so violent as to occasion considerable pain: then nature calls upon us to attend to it; and then we acknowledge that it is a mere sensation, and can only be in a sentient being. If a man runs his head with violence against a pillar, I appeal to him whether the pain he feels resembles the hardness of the stone; or if he can conceive anything like what he feels to be in an inanimate piece of matter.

"The attention of the mind is here entirely turned towards the painful feeling; and, to speak in the common language of mankind, he feels nothing in the stone, but feels a violent pain in his head. It is quite otherwise when he leans his head gently against the pillar; for then he will tell you that he feels nothing in his head, but feels hardness in the stone. Hath he not a sensation in this case as well as in the other? Undoubtedly he hath; but it is a sensation which nature intended only as a sign of something in the stone; and, accordingly, he instantly fixes his attention upon the thing signified; and cannot, without great difficulty, attend so much to the sensation as to be persuaded that there is any such thing distinct from the hardness it signifies.

"But however difficult it may be to attend to this fugitive sensation, to stop its rapid progress, and to disjoin it from the external quality of hardness, in whose shadow it is apt immediately to hide itself: this is what a philosopher by pains and practice must attain, otherwise it will be impossible for him to reason justly upon this subject, or even to understand what is here advanced. For the last appeal, in subjects of this nature, must be to what a man feels and perceives in his own mind."

§ 31. *Of certain indefinite feelings sometimes ascribed to the touch*

In connexion with these views on the sensations of touch, it is proper to remark, that certain feelings have been ascribed to that sense, which are probably of a character too indefinite to admit of a positive and undoubted classification. Although they clearly have their place in the general arrangement which has been laid down, with the states of mind which we are now considering; that is to say, are rather of an external and material, than of an internal origin; still they do not so evidently admit of an assignment to a particular sense. Those sensations to which we now refer, (if it be proper to use that term in application to them,) appear to have their origin in the human system considered as a whole, made up of bones, flesh, muscles, the senses, &c., rather than to be susceptible of being traced to any particular part. Of this description are the feelings expressed by the terms uneasiness, weariness, weakness, sickness, and those of an opposite character, as ease, hilarity, health, vigour, &c

Similar views will be found to apply, in part at least, to the sensations which we express by the terms HUNGER and THIRST. These appear to be complex in their nature, including a feeling of uneasiness, combined with a desire to relieve that uneasiness. When we say that these views will apply in part to hunger and thirst, the design is to limit the application of them to the element of *uneasiness*. This elementary feeling undoubtedly has its origin in the bodily system, and therefore comes in this case under the general class of notions of an EXTERNAL origin; but still it is not easy to say that it should be arranged with our tactual feelings, which has sometimes been done. Every one must be conscious, it is thought, that the feeling of hunger does not greatly resemble the sensations of hardness and softness, roughness or smoothness, or other sensations which are usually ascribed to the touch.—The cause of that peculiar state of the nerves of the stomach, which is antecedent to the uneasy feeling involved in what is termed hunger, has been a subject of difference of opinion, and does not appear to be well understood. If we were fully acquainted with this we might perhaps be less at a loss where to arrange the feeling in question.

§ 32. Relation between the sensation and what is outwardly signified.

We here return a moment to the subject of the relation between the internal sensation and the outward object; and again repeat, that the mental state and the corresponding outward object are altogether diverse. This view holds good in the case of the secondary, as well as of the primary qualities of matter. Whether we speak of extension, or resistance, or heat, or colour, or roughness, there are, in all cases alike, two things, the internal affection and the outward quality; but they are utterly distinct, totally without likeness to each other. But how it happens that one thing which is totally different from another can nevertheless give us a knowledge of that from which it differs, it would be a waste of time to attempt to explain. Our knowledge is undoubtedly limited to the mere fact.

This is one those of difficult but decisive points in MENTAL PHILOSOPHY, of which it is essential to possess a precise and correct understanding. The letters which cover over the page of a book are a very different thing from the thought and the combinations of thought which they stand for. The accountant's columns of numerals are not identical with the quantities and their relations which they represent. And so in regard to the mind; all its acts are of one kind, and what they stand for is of another. The mind, in all its feelings and operations, is governed by its own laws, and characterizes its efforts by the essential elements of its own nature. Nothing which is seen or heard, nothing which is the subject of taste, or touch or any other sense, nothing material, which can be imagined to exist in any place or in any form, can furnish the least positive disclosure either of its intrinsic nature or of the mode of its action.

What, then, is the relation between the sensation and the outward object, between the perception and the thing perceived? Evidently that of the sign and the thing signified. And as, in a multitude of cases, the sign may give a knowledge of its objects without any other grounds of such knowledge than mere institution or appointment, so it is in this. The mind, maintaining its appropriate action, and utterly rejecting the intervention of all images and visible representations, except what are outward and material, and totally distinct from itself both in place and nature, is, notwithstanding, susceptible of the knowledge of things exterior, and can form an acquaintance with the universe of matter.

CHAPTER VI.

THE SENSE OF SIGHT.

§ 33. Of the organ of sight, and the uses or benefits of that sense.

Of those instruments of external perception with which a benevolent Providence has favoured us, a high rank must be given to the sense of seeing. If we were restricted in the process of acquiring knowledge to the informations of the touch merely, how many embarrassments would attend our progress, and how slow it would prove! Having never possessed sight, it would be many years before the most acute and active person could form an idea of a mountain or even of a large edifice. But by the additional help of the sense of seeing, he not only observes the figure of large buildings, but is in a moment possessed of all the beauties of a wide and variegated landscape.

The organ of this sense is the eye. On a slight examination, the eye is found to be a sort of telescope, having its distinct parts, and discovering throughout the most exquisite construction. The medium on which this organ acts are rays of light, everywhere diffused, and always advancing, if they meet with no opposition, in direct lines. The eye, like all the other senses, not only receives externally the medium on which it acts, but carries the rays of light into itself; and on principles purely scientific, refracts and combines them anew.

It does not, however, fall within our plan to give a minute description of the eye, which belongs rather to the physiologist; but such a description, with the statement of the uses of the different parts of the organ, must be, to a candid and reflecting mind, a most powerful argument in proof of the existence and goodness of the Supreme Being. How wonderful, among other things, is the adaptation of the rays of light to the eye! If these rays were not of a texture extremely small, they would cause much pain to the organ of vision, into which they so rapidly pass. If they were not capable of exciting within us the sensations of colour, we should be deprived of much of that high satisfaction which we now take in beholding surrounding objects; showing forth, wherever they are to be found, the greatest variety and the utmost richness of tints.

§ 34. Statement of the mode or process in visual perception.

In the process of vision, the rays of light, coming from various objects and in various directions, strike in the first place on the pellucid or transparent part of the ball of the eye.

If they were to continue passing on precisely in the

same direction, they would produce merely one mingled and indistinct expanse of colour. In their progress, however, through the crystalline humour, they are refracted or bent from their former direction, and are distributed to certain focal points on the retina, which is a white, fibrous expansion of the optic nerve.

The rays of light, coming from objects in the field of vision, whether it be more or less extensive, as soon as they have been distributed on their distinct portions of the retina, and have formed an image there, are immediately followed by the sensation or perception which is termed sight. The image which is thus pictured on the retina is the last step which we are able to designate in the material part of the process in visual perception; the mental state follows; but it is not in our power to trace, even in the smallest degree, any physical connexion between the optical image and the corresponding state of the mind.—All that we can say in this case is, that we suppose them to hold to each other the relation of antecedent and consequent by an ultimate law of our constitution.

§ 35. Of the original and acquired perceptions of sight.

In speaking of those sensations and perceptions, the origin of which is generally attributed to the sense of sight, it is necessary to make a distinction between those which are ORIGINAL and those which are ACQUIRED. Nothing is properly original with the sense of sight but the sensations of colour, such as red, blue, yellow. These sensations (or perceptions, as they are otherwise called, when the internal feeling is combined with a reference to the external cause) are exceedingly numerous. In this respect, the intimations of the sense of sight stand on the same footing with those of taste and hearing; although distinctive names, in consequence of the difficulty of accurately separating and drawing the line between each, are given only in a few cases. All the sensations of colour are original with the sight, and are not to be ascribed to any other sense.

A part, however, of that knowledge, which we attribute to the sight, and which has the appearance of being immediate and original in that sense, is not so. Some of its alleged perceptions are properly the results of sensations, combined not only with the usual reference to an external cause, but with various other acts of the judgment. In some cases the combination of the acts of the judgment with the visual sensation is carried so far, that there is a sort of transfer to the sight of the knowledge which has been obtained from some other source. And not unfrequently, in consequence of a long and tenacious association, we are apt to look upon the knowledge thus acquired as truly original in the seeing power. This will suffice, perhaps, as a statement of the general fact, while the brief examination of a few instances will help to the more thorough understanding of those acquired perceptions of the sight which are here referred to.

§ 36. The idea of extension not originally from sight.

It is well known that there is nothing more common than for a person to say, that he sees the length or breadth of any external object; that he sees its extent, &c. These expressions appear to imply (and undoubtedly are so understood) that extension is a direct object of sight. There is no question that such is the common sentiment, viz., that the outlines and surface which bodies permanently expand and present to the view, are truly seen. An opinion different from this might even incur the charge of great absurdity.

But, properly, the notion of extension, as we have already seen, has its origin in the sense of touch. Being a simple and elementary thought, it is not susceptible of definition; nor, when we consider extension as existing outwardly and materially, can we make it a matter of description without running into the confusion of using synonymous words. But, whatever it is, (and certainly there can be neither ignorance nor disagreement on that point, however much language may fail of conveying our ideas,) the knowledge of it is not to be ascribed originally to the sight.

The notion of extension is closely connected with externality. It is not possible to form the idea of extension from mere consciousness, or a reflection on what takes place within us. But making a muscular effort, and thus applying the touch to some resisting body, we first have the notion of outness; and either from the same application of that sense, or when we have repeated it continuously on the same surface, we have the additional notion of its being extended or spread out. If a man were fixed immoveably in one place, capable of smelling, tasting, hearing, and seeing, but without tactual impressions originating from a resisting body, he would never possess a knowledge of either. Having first gained that knowledge from the touch in the way just mentioned, he learns in time what appearance extended bodies (which are, of course, coloured bodies) make to the eye. At a very early period, having ascertained that all coloured bodies are spread out or extended, he invariably associates the idea of extension with that coloured appearance. Hence he virtually and practically transfers the knowledge obtained by one sense to another; and even after a time imagines extension to be a direct object of sight, when, in fact, what is seen is only a sign of it, and merely suggests it. An affection of the sense of touch is the true and original occasion of the origin of this notion; and it becomes an idea of sight only by acquisition or transference.

§ 37. Of the knowledge of the figure of bodies by the sight.

Views similar to those which have been already advanced will evidently apply to the figure of bodies. We acquire a knowledge of the figure or form of bodies originally by the sense of touch. But it cannot be doubted that this knowledge is often confidently attributed to the sense of sight as well as the touch. Although there is reason to believe that men labour under a mistake in this, it is not strange, when we trace back our mental history to its earlier periods, that such a misapprehension should exist.

A solid body presents to the eye nothing but a certain disposition of colours and light. We may imagine ourselves to see the prominences or cavities in such bodies, when in truth we only see the light or the shade occasioned by them. This light and shade, however, we learn by experience to consider as the sign of a certain solid figure.—A proof of the truth of this statement is, that a painter, by carefully imitating the distribution of light and shade which he sees in objects, will make his work very naturally and exactly represent, not only the general outline of a body, but its prominences, depressions, and other irregularities. And yet his delineation, which, by the distribution of light and shade, gives such various representations, is on a smooth and plain surface

§ 38. Illustration of the subject from the blind.

It was a problem submitted by Mr. Molyneux to Mr. Locke, whether a blind man, who has learned the difference between a cube and a sphere by the touch, can, on being suddenly restored to sight, distinguish between them, and tell which is the sphere and which is the cube, by the aid of what may be called his *new* sense merely? And the answer of Mr. Locke was, in agreement with the opinion of Molyneux himself, that he cannot. The blind man knows what impressions the cube and sphere make on the organ of *touch*, and by that sense is able to distinguish between them; but, as he is ignorant what impression they will make on the organ of sight, he is not able, by the latter sense alone, to tell which is the round body and which is the cubic.

It was remarked that solid bodies present to the eye nothing but a certain disposition of light and colours.—It seems to follow from this, that the first idea which will be conveyed to the mind on seeing a globe, will be that of a circle variously shadowed with different degrees of light. This imperfect idea is corrected in this way. Combining the suggestions of the sense of touch with those of sight, we learn by greater experience what kind of appearance solid, convex bodies will make to us. That appearance becomes to the mind the sign of the presence of a globe; so that we have an idea of a round body by a very rapid mental correction, whereas the notion first conveyed to the mind is truly that of a plane, circular surface, on which there is a variety in the dispositions of light and shade. It is an evidence of the correctness of this statement, that in paintings, plane surfaces, variously shaded, represent convex bodies, and with great truth and exactness.

It appears, then, that extension and figure are originally perceived, not by sight, but by touch. We do not judge of them by sight until we have learned by our experience that certain visible appearances always accompany and signify the existence of extension and of figure. This knowledge we acquire at a very early period in life; so much so, that we lose, in a great measure, the memory both of its commencement and progress.

§ 39. Measurements of magnitude by the eye.

What has been said naturally leads us to the consideration of MAGNITUDE. This is a general term for Extension, when we conceive of it not only as limited or bounded, but as related to, and compared with, other objects. Although we make use of the eye in judging of it, it is to be kept in mind that the knowledge of magnitude is not an original intimation of the sight, but is at first acquired by the aid of touch. So well known is this, that it has been common to consider Magnitude under the two heads of tangible or real, and visible or apparent; the tangible magnitude being always the same, but the visible varying with the distance of the object. A man of six feet stature is always that height, whether he be a mile distant, or half a mile, or near at hand; the change of place making no change in his real or tangible magnitude. But the visible or apparent magnitude of this man may be six feet or two feet, as we view him present with us and immediately in our neighbourhood, or at two miles' distance; for his magnitude appears to our eye greater or less, according as he is more or less removed.

In support of the doctrine that the knowledge of magnitude is not an original intimation of the sight, but is at first acquired by the aid of touch, we may remark, that, in judging of magnitude by the sight, we are much influenced, not merely by the visual perception, but particularly by comparison with other objects, the size of which is known or supposed to be known. "I remember once," says Dr. Abercrombie (Intellectual Powers, pt. ii., sect. i.), "having occasion to pass along Ludgate Hill when the great door of St. Paul's was open, and several persons were standing in it. They appeared to be very little children; but, on coming up to them, were found to be full-grown persons. In the mental process which here took place, the door had been assumed as a known magnitude, and the other objects judged of by it. Had I attended to the door being much larger than any door that one is in the habit of seeing, the mind would have made allowance for the apparent size of the persons; and, on the other hand, had these been known to be full-grown persons, a judgment would have been formed of the size of the door."

§ 40. Of objects seen in a mist.

In accordance with the above-mentioned principle, it happens that objects seen by a person in a mist seem larger than life. Their faint appearance rapidly conveys to the mind the idea of being considerably removed, although they are actually near to us. And the mind immediately draws the conclusion, (so rapidly as to seem a simple and original perception,) that the object having the same visible or apparent magnitude, and yet supposed to be at a considerable distance, is greater than other objects of the same class. So that it is chiefly the view of the mind, a law or habit of the intellect, which, in this particular case, gives a fictitious expansion to bodies; although it is possible that the result may in part be attributed to a difference in the refraction of the rays of light, caused by their passing through a denser and less uniform medium than usual.

§ 41. Of the sun and moon when seen in the horizon.

These remarks naturally remind us of the well-known fact, that the sun and moon seem larger in the horizon than in the meridian. Three reasons may be given for this appearance; and perhaps ordinarily they are combined together.—(1.) The horizon may seem more distant than the zenith, in consequence of intervening objects. We measure the distance of objects in part by means of those that are scattered along between, and any expanse of surface, where there are no such intervening objects, appears to us of less extent than it actually is. Now if the rays of light form precisely the same image in the eye, but the source of them is supposed to be further off in the horizon than in the zenith, such have been our mental habits, that the object in the horizon will probably appear the largest.—(2.) Another reason of the enlarged appearance of the sun and moon in the horizon is, that the rays from them fall on the body of the atmosphere obliquely, and, of course, are reflected downward towards the beholder, and subtend a larger angle at his eye. Hence, as we always see objects in the direction of the ray just before it enters the eye, if we follow the rays back in the precise direction of their approach, they will present to the eye the outlines of a larger object as their source than they would if they had not been refracted.—Also, when the atmosphere is not clear, but masses of vapour exist in it, the refraction is increased and the object proportionally enlarged.—(3.) The sun and moon appear enlarged when other objects of considerable dimensions, but so distant as to subtend a very small angle at the eye, are seen in the same direction or in the moment of passing their disk, such as distant trees in the horizon, or ships far off at sea. These objects, though small in the eye or in their *visual* appearance, are yet, in consequence of our previous knowledge, enlarged in our *conceptions* of them. And this conceptive enlargement communicates itself, by a sort of mental illusion, to other objects with which they seem to come in contact.

§ 42. Of the estimation of distances by sight.

We are next led to the consideration of distances as made known and ascertained by the sight. By the distance of objects, when we use the term in reference to ourselves, we mean the space which is interposed between those objects and our own position. It might be objected, that space interposed is only a synonymous expression for the thing to be defined. Nevertheless, no one can be supposed to be ignorant of what is meant. Even blind men have a notion of distance, and can measure it by the touch, or by walking forward until they meet the distant object.

The perception of distance by the sight is an acquired and not an original perception; although the latter was universally supposed to be the fact until comparatively a recent period.

All objects in the first instance appear to touch the eye; but our experience has corrected so many of the representations of the senses, before the period which we are yet able to retrace by the memory, that we cannot prove this by a reference to our own childhood and infancy. It appears, however, from the statement of the cases of persons born blind on the sudden restoration of their sight.—"When he first saw," says Cheselden, the anatomist, when giving an account of a young man whom he had restored to sight by couching for the cataract, "he was so far from making any judgment about distance, that he thought all objects touched his eye, as he expressed it, as what he felt did his skin; and thought no objects so agreeable as those which were smooth and regular, although he could form no judgment of their shape, or guess what it was in any object that was pleasing to him."

This anatomist has further informed us, that he has brought to sight several others who had no remembrance of ever having seen; and that they all gave the same account of their learning to see, as they called it, as the young man already mentioned, although not in so many particulars; and that they all had this in common, that, having never had occasion to move their eyes, they knew not how to do it, and, at first, could not at all direct them to a particular object; but in time they acquired that faculty, though by slow degrees.

§ 43. Signs by means of which we estimate distance by sight.

Blind persons, when at first restored to sight, are unable to estimate the distance of objects by that sense, but soon observing that certain changes in the visible appearance of bodies always accompany a change of distance, they fall upon a method of estimating distance by the visible appearance. And it would no doubt be found, if it could be particularly examined into, that all mankind come to possess the power of estimating the distances of objects by sight in the same way. When a body is removed from us and placed at a considerable distance, it becomes smaller in its visible appearance, its colours are less lively, and its outlines less distinct; and we may expect to find various intermediate objects, more or fewer in number, corresponding with the increase of the distance, showing themselves between the receding object and the spectator. And hence it is, that a certain visible appearance comes to be the sign of a certain distance.

Historical and landscape painters are enabled to turn these facts to great account in their delineations. By means of dimness of colour, indistinctness of outline, and the partial interposition of other objects, they are enabled apparently to throw back to a very considerable distance from the eye those objects which they wish to appear remote. While other objects, that are intended to appear near, are painted vivid in colour, large in size, distinct in outline, and are separated from the eye of the spectator by few or no intermediate objects.

§ 44. Estimation of distance when unaided by intermediate objects.

(1.) As we depend, in no small degree, upon intermediate objects in forming our notions of distance, it results, that we are often much perplexed by the absence of such objects. Accordingly, we find that people frequently mistake, when they attempt to estimate by the eye the length or width of unoccupied plains and marshes, generally making the extent less than it really is. For the same reason they misjudge of the width of a river, estimating its width at half or three quarters of a mile at the most, when it is perhaps not less than double that distance. The same holds true of other bodies of water; and of all other things which are seen by us in a horizontal position and under similar circumstances.

(2.) We mistake in the same way also in estimating the height of steeples, and of other bodies that are perpendicular, and not on a level with the eye, provided the height be considerable. As the upper parts of the steeple out-top the surrounding buildings, and there are no contiguous objects with which to compare it, any measurement taken by the eye must be inaccurate, but is generally less than the truth.

(3) The fixed stars, when viewed by the eye, all appear to be alike indefinitely and equally distant. Being scattered over the whole sky, they make every part of it

seem, like themselves, at an indefinite and equal distance, and therefore contribute to give the whole sky the appearance of the inside of a sphere. Moreover, the horizon seems to the eye to be further off than the zenith; because between us and the former there lie many things, as fields, hills, and waters, which we know to occupy a great space; whereas between us and the zenith there are no considerable things of known dimensions. And, therefore, the heavens appear like the segment of a sphere, and less than a hemisphere, in the centre of which we seem to stand.—And the wider our prospect is, the greater will the sphere appear to be, and the less the segment.

§ 45. Of objects seen on the ocean, &c.

A vessel seen at sea by a person who is not accustomed to the ocean, appears much nearer than it actually is; and on the same principles as already illustrated. In his previous observations of the objects at a distance, he has commonly noticed a number of intermediate objects, interposed between the distant body and himself. It is probably the absence of such objects that chiefly causes the deception under which he labours in the present instance.

In connexion with what has been said, we are led to make this further remark, that a change in the purity of the air will perplex in some measure those ideas of distance which we receive from sight. Bishop Berkeley remarks, while travelling in Italy and Sicily, he noticed that cities and palaces seen at a great distance appeared nearer to him by several miles than they actually were. The cause of this he very correctly supposed to be the purity of the Italian and Sicilian air, which gave to objects at a distance a degree of brightness and distinctness which, in the less clear and pure atmosphere of his native country, could be observed only in those towns and separate edifices which were near. At home he had learned to estimate the distances of objects by their appearance; but his conclusions failed him when they came to be applied to objects in countries where the air was so much clearer.—And the same thing has been noticed by other travellers, who have been placed in the like circumstances.

CHAPTER VII.

HABITS OF SENSATION AND PERCEPTION.

§ 46. General view of the law of habit and of its applications.

THERE is an important law of the mental constitution known as the law of Habit, which may be described in general terms as follows: *That the mental action acquires facility and strength from repetition or practice.* The fact that the facility and the increase of strength, implied in HABIT, is owing to mere repetition, or what is more frequently termed practice, we learn, as we do other facts and principles in relation to the mind, from the observation of men around us, and from our own personal experience. And as it has hitherto been found impracticable to resolve it into any general fact or principle more elementary, it may justly be regarded as something ultimate and essential in our nature.

The term Habit, by the use of language, indicates the facility and strength acquired in the way which has been mentioned, including both the result and the manner of it. As the law of habit has reference to the whole mind of man, the application of the term which expresses it is, of course, very extensive. We apply it to the dexterity of workmen in the different manual arts, to the rapidity of the accountant, to the coup d'œil or eye-glance of the military engineer, to the tact and fluency of the extemporaneous speaker, and in other like instances.—We apply it also in cases where the mere exercise of emotion and desire is concerned; to the avaricious man's love of wealth, the ambitious man's passion for distinction, the wakeful suspicions of the jealous, and the confirmed and substantial benevolence of the philanthropist.

§ 47. The law of habit applicable to the mind as well as the body.

It is remarkable, that the law under consideration holds good in respect to the body as well as the mind. In the mechanical arts, and in all cases where there is a corporeal as well as mental effort, the effect of practice will be found to extend to both. Not only the acts of the mind are quickened and strengthened, but all those muscles which are at such times employed, become stronger and more obedient to the will. Indeed, the submission of the muscular effort to the volition is oftentimes rendered so prompt by habit, that we are unable distinctly to recollect any exercise of volition previous to the active or muscular exertion. It is habit which is the basis of those characteristic peculiarities that distinguish one man's handwriting from another's; it is habit which causes that peculiarity of attitude and motion so easily discoverable in most persons, termed their gait; it is habit also which has impressed on the muscles, immediately connected with the organs of speech, that fixed and precise form of action, which, in different individuals, gives rise, in part at least, to characteristics of voice. The habit, in the cases just mentioned, is both bodily and mental, and has become so strong, that it is hardly possible to counteract it for any length of time.—The great law of Habit is applicable to all the leading divisions of our mental nature, the Intellect, the Sensibilities, and the Will; and as we advance from one view of the mind to another, we shall have repeated occasion to notice its influence. In the remainder of this chapter we shall limit our remarks to Habit, considered in connexion with the Sensations and Perceptions.

§ 48. Of habit in relation to the smell.

We shall consider the application of the principle of Habit to the senses in the same order which has already been observed. In the first place, there are habits of Smell.—This sense, like the others, is susceptible of cultivation. As there are some persons whose power of distinguishing the difference of two or more colours is feeble; so there are some who are doubtful and perplexed in like manner in the discrimination of odours. And as the inability may be overcome in some measure in the former case, so it may be in the latter. The fact that the powers of which the smell is capable are not more frequently brought out and quickened, is owing to the circumstance that it is not ordinarily needed. It sometimes happens, however, that men are compelled to make an uncommon use of it, when, by a defect in the other senses, they are left without the ordinary helps to knowledge. It is then we see the effects of the law of Habit. It is stated in Mr. Stewart's account of James Mitchell, who was deaf, sightless, and speechless, and, of course, strongly induced by his unfortunate situation to make much use of the sense we are considering, that his smell would immediately and invariably inform him of the presence of a stranger, and direct to the place where he might be; and it is repeatedly asserted, that this sense had become in him extremely acute.—"It is related," says Dr. Abercrombie, "of the late Dr. Moyse, the well-known blind philosopher, that he could distinguish a black dress on his friends by its smell."

In an interesting account of a deaf, dumb, and blind girl in the Hartford Asylum, recently published, statements are made on this subject of a similar purport.—"It has been observed," says the writer, "of persons who are deprived of a particular sense, that additional quickness or vigour seems to be bestowed on those which remain. Thus blind persons are often distinguished by peculiar exquisiteness of touch; and the deaf and dumb, who gain all their knowledge through the eye, concentrate, as it were, their whole souls in that channel of observation. With her whose eye, ear, and tongue are alike dead, the capabilities both of touch and smell are exceedingly heightened. Especially the *latter* seems almost to have acquired the properties of a new sense, and to transcend the sagacity even of a spaniel."—Such is the influence of habit on the intimations of the sense under consideration.

§ 49. Of habit in relation to the taste.

The same law is applicable to the Taste. We see the results of the frequent exercise of this sense in the quickness which the dealer in wines discovers in distinguishing the flavour of one wine from that of another. So marked are the results in cases of this kind, that one is almost disposed to credit the story which Cervantes relates of two persons, who were requested to pass their judgment upon a hogshead which was supposed to be very old and excellent. One of them tasted the wine, and pronounced it to be very good, with the exception of a slight taste of leather which he perceived in it. The other, after mature reflection and examination, pronounced the same favourable verdict, with the exception of a taste of iron, which he could easily distinguish. On emptying the hogshead, there was found at the bottom an old key with a leathern thong tied to it.

Another practical view of this subject, however, presents itself here. The sensations which we experience in this and other like cases, not only acquire by repetition greater niceness and discrimination, but increased strength; (and perhaps the increased strength is in all instances the foundation of the greater power of discrimination.) On this topic we have a wide and melancholy source of illustration. The bibber of wine and the drinker of ardent spirits readily acknowledge, that the sensation was at first only moderately pleasing, and perhaps in the very slightest degree. Every time they carried the intoxicating potion to their lips, the sensation grew more pleasing, and the desire for it waxed stronger. Perhaps they were not aware that this process was going on in virtue of a great law of humanity; but they do not pretend to deny the fact. They might, indeed, have suspected at an early period that chains were gathering around them, whatever might be the cause; but what objection had they to be bound with links of flowers; delightful while they lasted, and easily broken when necessary! But here was the mistake. Link was added to link; chain was woven with chain, till he who boasted of his strength was at last made sensible of his weakness, and found himself a prisoner, a captive, a deformed, altered, and degraded slave.

There is a threefold operation. The sensation of taste acquires an enhanced degree of pleasantness; the feeling of uneasiness is increased in a corresponding measure when the sensation is not indulged by drinking; and the desire, which is necessarily attendant on the uneasy feeling, becomes in like manner more and more imperative

To alleviate the uneasy feeling and this importunate desire, the unhappy man goes again to his cups, and with a shaking hand pours down the delicious poison. What then? He has added a new link to his chain; at every repetition it grows heavier and heavier, till that, which at first he bore lightly and cheerfully, now presses him like a coat of iron, and galls like fetters of steel. There is a great and fearful law of his nature bearing him down to destruction. Every indulgence is the addition of a new weight to what was before placed upon him, thus lessening the probability of escape, and accelerating his gloomy, fearful, and interminable sinking. We do not mean to say that he is the subject of an implacable destiny, and cannot help himself. But it would seem that he can help himself only in this way; by a prompt, absolute, and entire suspension of the practice in all its forms, which has led him into this extremity. But few, however, have the resolution to do this; the multitude make a few unwilling and feeble efforts, and resign themselves to the horrors of their fate.

§ 50. Of habit in relation to the hearing.

There is undoubtedly a natural difference in the quickness and discrimination of hearing. This sense is more acute in some than in others; but in those who possess it in much natural excellence, it is susceptible of a high degree of cultivation. Musicians are a proof of this, whose sensibility to the melody and concord of sweet sounds continually increases with the practice of their art.

The increase of sensibility in the perceptions of hearing is especially marked and evident, when uncommon causes have operated to secure such practice. And this is the state of things with the Blind. The readers of Sir Walter Scott may not have forgotten the blind fiddler, who figures so conspicuously with verse and harp in Red Gauntlet; a character sufficiently extraordinary, but by no means an improbable exaggeration. The blind necessarily rely much more than others on the sense of hearing. By constant practice they increase the accuracy and power of its perceptions. Shut out from the beauties that are seen, they please themselves with what is heard, and greedily drink in the melodies of song. Accordingly, music is made by them not only a solace, but a business and a means of support; and in the Institutions for the Blind this is considered an important department of instruction.

Many particular instances on record, and well authenticated, confirm the general statement, that the ear may be trained to habits, and that thus the sensations of sound may come to us with new power and meaning. It is related of a celebrated blind man of Puiseaux in France, that he could determine the quantity of fluid in vessels by the sound it produced while running from one vessel into another. "Dr. Rush," as the statement is given in Abercrombie's Intellectual Powers, "relates of two blind young men, brothers, of the city of Philadelphia, that they knew when they approached a post in walking across a street by a peculiar sound which the ground under their feet emitted in the neighbourhood of the post; and that they could tell the names of a number of tame pigeons, with which they amused themselves in a little garden, by only hearing them fly over their heads." Dr. Saunderson, who became blind so early as not to remember having seen, when happening in any new place, as a room, piazza, pavement, court, and the like, gave it a character by means of the sound and echo from his feet; and in that way was able to identify pretty exactly the place, and assure himself of his position afterward. A writer in the First Volume of the Manchester Philosophical Memoirs, who is our authority also for the statement just made, speaks of a certain blind man in that city as follows: "I had an opportunity of repeatedly observing the peculiar manner in which he arranged his ideas and acquired his information. Whenever he was introduced into company, I remarked that he continued some time silent. The sound directed him to judge of the dimensions of the room, and the different voices of the number of persons that were present. His distinction in these respects was very accurate, and his memory so retentive that he was seldom mistaken. I have known him instantly recognise a person on first hearing him, though more than two years had elapsed since the time of their last meeting. He determined pretty nearly the stature of those he was conversing with by the direction of their voices; and he made tolerable conjectures respecting their tempers and dispositions by the manner in which they conducted their conversation."

§ 51. Application of habit to the touch.

The sense of touch, like the others, may be exceedingly improved by habit. The more we are obliged to call it into use, the more attention we pay to its intimations. By the frequent repetition, therefore, under such circumstances, these sensations not only acquire increased intenseness in themselves, but particularly so in reference to our notice and remembrance of them. But it is desirable to confirm this, as it is all other principles from time to time laid down, by an appeal to facts, and by careful inductions from them.

Diderot relates of the blind man of Puiseaux, mentioned in a former section, that he was capable of judging of his distance from the fireplace by the degree of heat, and of his approach to any solid bodies by the action or pulse of the air upon his face. The same thing is recorded of many other persons in a similar situation; and it may be regarded as a point well established, that blind people who are unable to see the large and heavy bodies presenting themselves in their way as they walk about, generally estimate their approach to them by the increased resistance of the atmosphere. A blind person, owing to the increased accuracy of his remaining senses, especially of the touch, would be better trusted to go through the various apartments of a house in the darkness of midnight, than one possessed of the sense of seeing without any artificial light to guide him.

In the celebrated Dr. Saunderson, who lost his sight in very early youth, and remained blind through life, although he occupied the professorship of mathematics in the English University of Cambridge, the touch acquired such acuteness that he could distinguish, by merely letting them pass through his fingers, spurious coins, which were so well executed as to deceive even skilful judges who could see.*

* Memoirs of the Manchester Philosophical Society, vol. i., p. 164.

The case of a Mr. John Metcalf, otherwise called Blind Jack, which is particularly dwelt upon by the author of the Article in the Memoirs just referred to, is a striking one. The writer states that he became blind at an early period; but, notwithstanding, followed the profession of a wagoner, and occasionally of a guide in intricate roads during the night, or when the tracks were covered with snow. At length he became a projector and surveyor of highways in difficult and mountainous districts; an employment for which one would naturally suppose a blind man to be but indifferently qualified. But he was found to answer all the expectations of his employers, and most of the roads over the Peak in Derbyshire, in England, were altered by his directions. Says the person who gives this account of Blind Jack, "I have several times met this man, with the assistance of a long staff, traversing the roads, ascending precipices, exploring valleys, and investigating their several extents, forms, and situations, so as to answer his designs in the best manner."

In the interesting Schools for the Blind which have recently been established in various parts of the world, the pupils read by means of the fingers. They very soon learn by the touch to distinguish one letter from another, which are made separately for that purpose of wood, metals, or other hard materials. The printed sheets which they use are conformed to their method of studying them. The types are much larger than those ordinarily used in printing; the paper is very thick, and being put upon the types while wet, and powerfully pressed, the letters on it are consequently *raised*, and appear in relief. The pupils having before learned to distinguish one letter from another, and also to combine them into syllables and words, are able after a time to pass their fingers along the words and sentences of these printed sheets, and ascertain their meaning, with a good degree of rapidity.

§ 52. Other striking instances of habits of touch.

The power of the touch will increase in proportion to the necessity of a reliance on it. The more frequent the resort to it, the stronger will be the habit; but the necessity of this frequent reference to it will be found to be peculiarly great where a person is deprived of two of his other senses. It is noticed of James Mitchell, whose case has been already referred to, that he distinguished such articles as belonged to himself from the property of others by this sense. Although the articles were of the same form and materials with those of others, it would seem that he was not at a loss in identifying what was his own. It will be recollected that he could neither see nor hear, and was, of course, speechless. He was obliged, therefore, to depend chiefly on the touch. This sense was the principal instrument he made use of in forming an acquaintance with the strangers who frequently visited him. And what is particularly remarkable, he actually explored by it, at an early period, a space round his father's residence of about two hundred yards in extent, to any part of which he was in the practice of walking fearlessly and without a guide, whenever he pleased.

It is related of the deaf and blind girl in the Hartford Asylum, that it is impossible to displace a single article in her drawers without her perceiving and knowing it; and that, when the baskets of linen are weekly brought from the laundress, she selects her own garments without hesitation, however widely they may be dispersed among the mass. This is probably owing, at least in great part, to habits of touch, by means of which the sense is rendered exceedingly acute.—Diderot has even gone so far as to conjecture that persons deprived of both sight and hearing would so increase the sensibility of touch as to locate the seat of the soul in the tips of the fingers.

§ 53. Habits considered in relation to the sight.

The law of habit affects the sight also. By a course of training this sense seems to acquire new power. The length and acuteness of vision in the mariner who has long traversed the ocean has been frequently referred to. —A writer in the North American Review (July, 1833) says, he once "knew a man, in the Greek island of Hydra, who was accustomed to take his post every day for thirty years on the summit of the island, and look out for the approach of vessels; and although there were over three hundred sail belonging to the island, he would tell the name of each one as she approached with unerring certainty, while she was still at such a distance as to present to a common eye only a confused white blur upon the clear horizon." There are numerous instances to the same effect, occasioned by the situations in which men are placed, and the calls for the frequent exercise of the sight. The almost intuitive vision of the skilful engineer is, beyond doubt, in most cases merely a habit. He has so often fixed his eye upon those features in a country which have a relation to his peculiar calling, that he instantly detects the bearing of a military position, its susceptibility of defence, its facilities of approach and retreat, &c.

No man is born without the sense of touch, but many are born without the sense of hearing; and, wherever this is the case, we are entitled to look for habits of sight Persons under such circumstances naturally and necessarily rely much on the visual sense, whatever aids may be had by them from the touch. Hence habits; and these imply increased quickness and power, wherever they exist. It is a matter of common remark, that the keenness of visual observation in the DEAF and DUMB is strikingly increased by their peculiar circumstances. Shut out from the intercourse of speech, they read the minds of men in their movements, gestures, and countenances. They notice with astonishing quickness, and apparently without any effort, a thousand things which escape the regards of others. This fact is undoubtedly the foundation of the chief encouragement which men have to attempt the instruction of that numerous and unfortunate class of their fellow-beings. They can form an opinion of what another says to them by the motion of the lips; and sometimes even with a great degree of accuracy. That this last, however, is common, it is not necessary to assert; that it is possible, we have the testimony of well-authenticated facts. In one of his letters, Bishop Burnet mentions to this effect the case of a young lady at Geneva.—"At two years old," he says, "it was perceived that she had lost her hearing, and ever since, though she hears great noises, yet hears nothing of what is said to her; but, by observing the motion of the lips and mouths of others, she acquired so many words, that out of these she has formed a sort of jargon in which she can hold conversation whole days with those who can speak her language. She knows nothing of what is said to her, unless she sees the motion of their lips that speak to her; one thing will appear the strangest part of the whole narrative. She has a sister with whom she has practised her language more than with anybody else, and in the night, by laying her hand on her sister's mouth, she can perceive by that what she says, and so can discourse with her in the dark." (London Quarterly Review, vol. xxiv, p. 399.)

Such are the views which have been opened to us in considering the law of HABIT in connexion with the senses; and we may venture to say with confidence, that they are exceedingly worthy of notice. There are two suggestions which they are especially fitted to call up. They evince the striking powers of the human mind, its irrepressible energies, which no obstacles can bear down. They evince also the benevolence of our Creator, who opens in the hour of misery new sources of comfort, and compensates for what we have not, by increasing the power and value of what we have.

§ 54. Sensations may possess a relative, as well as positive increase of power.

There remains a remark of some importance to be made in connexion with the general principle which has been brought forward, and as in some measure auxiliary to it; for it will help to explain the more striking instances of habits, if any should imagine that the fact of mere repetition is not sufficient to account for them. Our sensations and perceptions may acquire not only a direct and positive, but a relative and virtual increase of power.

This remark is thus explained. We shall hereafter see the truth of an important principle to this effect, that there will be a weakness of remembrance in any particular case in proportion to the want of interest in it. Now hundreds and thousands of our sensations and perceptions are not remembered, because we take no interest in them. Of course they are the same, relatively to our amount of knowledge and our practice, as if they had never existed at all. But when we are placed in some novel situation, or when, in particular, we are deprived of any one of the senses, the pressure of our necessities creates that interest which was wanting before. Then we delay upon, and mark, and remember, and interpret a multitude of evanescent intimations which were formerly neglected. The senses thus acquire a very considerable relative power and value. And in order to make out a satisfactory explanation of some instances of habits, it is perhaps necessary that this relative increase should be added to the direct and positive augmentation of vigour and quickness resulting from mere repetition or exercise.

§ 55. Of habits as modified by particular callings and arts.

Hitherto it has been our chief object to examine habits in their relation to the senses separately; it is proper also to take a general view of them, as formed and modified by the particular callings and employments of men. Habits of perception are frequently formed under such circumstances, where all the senses are not only possessed, but where they exist with their ordinary aptitudes and powers.—In consequence of the habits which he has been called upon to form by his particular situation, a farmer of a tolerable degree of experience and discernment requires but a slight inspection, in order to give an opinion on the qualities of a piece of land, and its suitableness for a settlement. A skilful printer will at once notice everything of excellence or of deficiency in the mechanical execution of a printed work.—The same results are found in all who practise the fine arts. An experienced painter at once detects a mannerism in colouring, combinations and contrasts of light and shade, and peculiarities of form, proportion, or position, which infallibly escape a person of more limited experience.

Dr. Reid speaks on this subject in the following characteristic manner.—"Not only men, but children, idiots, and brutes, acquire by habit many perceptions which they had not originally. Almost every employment in life hath perceptions of this kind that are peculiar to it. The shepherd knows every sheep of his flock, as we do our acquaintance, and can pick them out of another flock one by one. The butcher knows by sight the weight and quality of his beeves and sheep before they are killed The farmer perceives by his eye very nearly the quantity of hay in a .ick, or of corn in a heap. The sailor sees the burden, the built, and the distance of a ship at sea, while she is a great way off. Every man accustomed to writing, distinguishes acquaintances by their handwriting, as he does by their faces. And the painter distinguishes, in the works of his art, the style of all the great masters. In a word, acquired perception is very different in different persons, according to the diversity of objects about which they are employed, and the application they bestow in observing them."*

§ 56. The law of habit considered in reference to the perception of the outlines and forms of objects.

Before leaving the subject of Habit, considered as influencing Sensation and Perception, there is one other topic which seems to be entitled to a brief notice; we refer to the manner in which we perceive the outlines and forms of bodies. In discussing the subject of Attention, Mr. Stewart, in connexion with his views on that subject, introduces some remarks in respect to vision. He makes this supposition, That the eye is fixed in a particular position, and the picture of an object is painted on the retina. He then starts this inquiry: Does the mind perceive the complete figure of the object at once, or is this perception the result of the various perceptions we have of the different points in the outline?—He holds the opinion, that the perception is the result of our perceptions of the different points in the outline, which he adopts as naturally consequent on such views, as the following The outline of every body is made up of points or smallest visible portions; no two of these points can be in precisely the same direction; therefore every point by itself constitutes just as distinct an object of attention to the mind, as if it were separated by some interval of empty space from all the other points. The conclusion therefore is, as every body is made up of parts, and as the per-

* Reid's Inquiry into the Human Mind, chap. vi., § 20.

ception of the figure of the whole object implies a knowledge of the relative situation of the different parts with respect to each other, that such perception is the result of a number of different acts of attention.

But if we adopt this view of Mr. Stewart, it is incumbent upon us to show how it happens that we appear to see the object at once. The various facts which have been brought forward in this chapter appear to furnish us with a solution of this question. The answer is, that the acts of perception are performed with such rapidity, that the effect with respect to us is the same as if it were instantaneous. A habit has been formed; the glance of the mind, in the highest exercise of that habit, is indescribably quick; time is virtually annihilated; and separate moments are to our apprehension of them crowded into one.

§ 57. Notice of some facts which favour the above doctrine.

Some persons will probably entertain doubts of Mr. Stewart's explanation of the manner in which we perceive the outlines of objects; but there are various circumstances which tend to confirm it.—When we look for the first time on any object which is diversified with gaudy colours, the mind is evidently perplexed with the variety of perceptions which arise; the view is indistinct, which would not be the case if there were only one, and that an immediate perception. And even in paintings, which are of a more laudable execution, the effects at the first perception will be similar.

But there is another fact which comes still more directly to the present point. We find that we do not have as distinct an idea, at the first glance, of a figure of a hundred sides, as we do of a triangle or square. But we evidently should, if the perception of visible figure were the immediate consequence of the picture on the retina, and not the combined result of the separate perceptions of the points in the outline. Whenever the figure is very simple, the process of the mind is so very rapid that the perception seems to be instantaneous. But when the sides are multiplied beyond a certain number, the interval of time necessary for these different acts of attention becomes perceptible. We are then distinctly conscious that the mind labours from one part of the object to another, and that some time elapses before we grasp it as a whole.

§ 58. Additional illustrations of Mr. Stewart's doctrine.

These views and illustrations are still further confirmed by some interesting, and perhaps more decisive facts. In 1807, Sir Everard Home, well known for his various philosophical publications, read before the Royal Society an account of two blind children whom he had couched for the cataract. One of these was John Salter. Upon this boy various experiments were made, for the purpose, among other things, of ascertaining whether the sense of sight does originally, and of itself alone, give us a knowledge of the true figure of bodies. Some of the facts elicited under these circumstances have a bearing upon the subject now before us. In repeated instances, on the day of his restoration to sight, the boy called square and triangular bodies, which were presented to the visual sense merely, *round*. On a square body being presented to him, he expressed a desire to touch it. "This being refused, he examined it for some time, and said at last that he had found a corner, and then readily counted the four corners of the square; and afterward, when a triangle was shown him, he counted the corners in the same way; but, in doing so, his eye went along the edge from corner to corner, naming them as he went along." On the thirteenth day after the cataract was removed, the visual power he had acquired was so small, that he could not by sight tell a square from a circle, without previously directing his sight to the corners of the square figure as he did at first, and thus passing from corner to corner, and counting them one by one. It was noticed that the sight seemed to labour slowly onward from one point and angle to another, as if it were incapable of embracing the outline by a simultaneous and undivided movement. The process, however, became more and more easy and rapid, until the perception, which at first was obviously made up of distinct and successive acts, came to be in appearance (and we may suppose it was only in appearance) a concentrated and single one.

It was the same with Caspar Hauser. It is remarked by his biographer, that whenever a person was introduced to him, (this was probably soon after his release from his prison,) he went up very close to him, regarded him with a sharp, staring look, and noticed particularly each distinct part of his face, such as the forehead, eyes, nose, mouth, and chin. He then collected and consolidated all the different parts of the countenance, which he had noticed separately and piece by piece, into one whole. And it was not till after this process that he seemed to have a knowledge of the countenance or face, in distinction from the parts of the face.

CHAPTER VIII.

CONCEPTIONS.

§ 59. Meaning and characteristics of conceptions.

We are now led, as we advance in the general subject of intellectual states of EXTERNAL ORIGIN, to contemplate the mind in another view, viz., as employed in giving rise to what are usually termed CONCEPTIONS. Without professing to propose a definition in all respects unexceptionable, we are entitled to say, in general terms, that this name is given to any re-existing sensations whatever which the mind has felt at some former period, and to the ideas which we frame of absent objects of perception. Whenever we have conceptions, our sensations and perceptions are replaced, as Shakspeare expresses it, in the "mind's eye," without our at all considering at what time or in what place they first originated. In other words, they are revived or recalled, and nothing more.— Using, therefore, the term CONCEPTIONS to express a class of mental states, and, in accordance with the general plan, having particular reference in our remarks here to such as are of external origin, it may aid in the better understanding of their distinctive character if we mention more particularly how they differ both from sensations and perceptions, and also from remembrances, with which last some may imagine them to be essentially the same.

(I.) Conceptions differ from the ordinary sensations and perceptions in this respect, that both their causes and their objects are absent. When the rose, the honeysuckle, or other odoriferous body is presented to us, the effect which follows in the mind is termed a sensation. When we afterward think of that sensation, (as we sometimes express it,) when the sensation is recalled, even though very imperfectly, without the object which originally caused it being present, it then becomes, by the use of language, a CONCEPTION. And it is the same in any instance of perception. When, in strictness of speech, we are said to perceive anything, as a tree, a building, or a mountain, the objects of our perceptions are in all cases before us. But we may form conceptions of them; they may be recalled and exist in the *mind's eye*, however remote they may be in fact, both in time and place.

(II.) They differ also from remembrances or ideas of memory. We take no account of the period when those objects which laid the foundation of them were present; whereas, in every act of the memory, there is combined with the conception a notion of the past. Hence, as those states of mind, which we call conceptions, possess these distinctive marks, they are well entitled to a separate name.

CONCEPTIONS are regulated in their appearance and disappearance by the principles of Association, which will be explained hereafter.—Whenever at any time we may use the phrase "power of conception" or "faculty of conception," nothing more is to be understood by such expressions than this, that there is in the mind a susceptibility of feelings or ideas possessing the marks which we have ascribed to this class.

§ 60. Of conceptions of objects of sight.

One of the striking facts in regard to our conceptions is, that we can far more easily conceive of the objects of some senses than of others. He who has visited the Pyramids of Egypt and the imposing remains of Grecian temples, or has beheld, among nature's still greater works, the towering heights of the Alps and the mighty cataract of Niagara, will never afterward be at a loss in forming a vivid conception of those interesting objects. The visual perceptions are so easily and so distinctly recalled, that it is hardly too much to say of them, that they seem to exist as permanent pictures in the mind. It is related of Carsten Niebuhr, a well-known traveller in the East, that, in extreme old age, after he had become blind, he entertained his visiters with interesting details of what he had seen many years before at Persepolis; describing the walls on which the inscriptions and bas-reliefs of which he spoke were found, just as one would describe a building which he had recently visited. His son, who has given an account of his life, remarks, in connexion with this fact: "We could not conceal our astonishment. He said to us, that, as he lay blind upon his bed, the images of all that he had seen in the East were ever present to his soul; and it was therefore no wonder that he should speak of them as of yesterday. In like manner, there was vividly reflected to him, in the hours of stillness, the nocturnal view of the deep Asiatic heavens, with their brilliant host of stars, which he had so often contemplated; or else their blue and lofty vault by day; and this was his greatest enjoyment."

There seems to be less vividness in the conceptions of sound, touch, taste, and smell; particularly the last three. Every one knows that it is difficult in ordinary cases to recall with much distinctness a particular pain which we have formerly experienced, or a particular taste, or smell. The fact that the perceptions of sight are more easily and distinctly recalled than others, may be thus partially explained.—Visible objects, or, rather, the outlines of them, are complex; that is, they are made up of a great number of points or very small portions. Hence the conception which we form of such an object as a whole, is aided by the principles of association. The reason is obvious. As every original perception of a visible object is a compound made up of many parts, whenever we subsequently have a conception of it, the process is the same; we have a conception of a part of the object, and the principles of association help us in conceiving of the other parts. Association connects the parts together; it presents them to the mind in their proper arrangement, and helps to sustain them there.

We are not equally aided by the laws of association in forming our conceptions of the objects of the other senses. When we think of some sound, taste, touch, or smell, the object of our conception is either a single detached sensation or a series of sensations. In every such detached sensation of sound, taste, touch, or smell, whether we consider it at its first origin, or when it is subsequently recalled, there is not necessarily that fixed and intimate association of the parts which we suppose to exist in every visual perception, and which must exist also in every conception of objects of sight which subsequently takes place. Accordingly, our conceptions of the latter objects arise more readily, and are more distinct, than of the others.—There is a greater readiness and distinctness also, when there is a *series* of sensations and perceptions of sight, for the subsequent visual conceptions are aided by associations both in time and place; but the recurrence of other sensations and perceptions is aided only by associations in time.

§ 61. Of the influence of habit on our conceptions.

It is another circumstance worthy of notice in regard to conceptions, that the power of forming them depends in some measure on HABIT.—A few instances will help to illustrate the statement, that what is termed Habit may extend to the susceptibility of conceptions; and the first to be given will be of conceptions of sound. Our conceptions of sound are not, in general, remarkably distinct, as was intimated in the last section. It is nevertheless true, that a person may by practice acquire the power of amusing himself with merely reading written music. Having frequently associated the sounds with the notes, he has at last such a strong conception of the sounds, that he experiences, by merely reading the notes, a very sensible pleasure. It is for the same reason, viz., because our conceptions are strengthened by repetition or practice, that readers may enjoy the harmony of poetical numbers without at all articulating the words. In both cases they truly hear nothing; there is no actual sensation of sound; and yet there is a virtual enunciation and melody in the mind. It seems to be on this principle we are enabled to explain the fact, that Beethoven composed some of his most valued musical pieces after he had become entirely deaf; originating harmonic combinations so profound and exquisite as to require the nicest ear as a test, at the very time he was unable to hear anything himself.

§ 62. Influence of habit on conceptions of sight.

That our power of forming conceptions is strengthened by habit, is capable of being further illustrated from the sight. A person who has been accustomed to drawing, retains a much more perfect notion of a building landscape, or other visible object, than one who has not A portrait painter, or any person who has been in the practice of drawing such sketches, can trace the outlines of the human form with very great ease; it requires hardly more effort from them than to write their names. —This point may also be illustrated by the difference which we sometimes notice in people in their conceptions of colours. Some are fully sensible of the difference between two colours when they are presented to them, but cannot with confidence give names to these colours when they see them apart, and may even confound the one with the other. Their original sensations and perceptions are supposed to be equally distinct with those of other persons; but their subsequent conception of the colours is far from being so. This defect arises partly, at least, from want of practice; that is to say, from the not having formed a habit. The persons who exhibit this weakness of conception have not been compelled, by their situation nor by mere inclination, to distinguish and to name colours so much as is common.

§ 63. Of the subserviency of our conceptions to description.

It is highly favourable to the talent for lively description, when a person's conceptions are readily suggested and are distinct. Even such a one's common conversation differs from that of those whose conceptions arise more slowly and are more faint. One man, whether in conversation or in written description, seems to place the object which he wishes to describe directly before us; it is represented distinctly and to the life. Another, although not wanting in a command of language, is confused and embarrassed amid a multitude of particulars, which, in consequence of the feebleness of his conceptions, he finds himself but half acquainted with; and he therefore gives us but a very imperfect and confused notion of the thing which he desires to make known.

It has been by some supposed, that a person might give a happier description of an edifice, of a landscape, or other object, from the conception than from the actual perception of it. The perfection of a description does not always consist in a minute specification of circumstances; in general, the description is better when there is a judicious selection of them. The best rule for making the selection is to attend to the particulars that make the deepest impression on our own minds, or, what is the same thing, that most readily and distinctly take a place in our conceptions.—When the object is actually before us, it is extremely difficult to compare the impressions which different circumstances produce. When we afterward conceive of the object, we possess merely the outline of it; but it is an outline made up of the most striking circumstances. The circumstances, it is true, will not impress all persons alike, but will somewhat vary with the degree of their taste. But when, with a correct and delicate taste, any one combines lively conceptions, and gives a description from those conceptions, he can hardly fail to succeed in it. And, accordingly, we find here one great element of poetic power. It is the ability of forming vivid conceptions which bodies forth

"The forms of things unknown; the poet's pen
Turns them to shape, and gives to airy nothing
A local habitation and a name."

§ 64. Of conceptions attended with a momentary belief.

Our conceptions are sometimes attended with belief; when they are very lively, we are apt to ascribe to them a real outward existence, or believe in them. We do not undertake to assert that the belief is permanent; but a number of facts strongly lead to the conclusion that it has a momentary existence.

(1.) A painter, in drawing the features and bodily form of an absent friend, may have so strong a conception, so vivid a mental picture, as to believe for a moment that his friend is before him. After carefully recalling his thoughts at such times, and reflecting upon them, almost every painter is ready to say that he has experienced some illusions of this kind. "We read," says Dr. Conolly, "that, when Sir Joshua Reynolds, after being many hours occupied in painting, walked out into the street, the lamp-posts seemed to him to be trees, and the men and women moving shrubs." It is true, the illusion is in these cases very short, because the intensity of conception, which is the foundation of it, can never be kept up long when the mind is in a sound state. Such intense conceptions are unnatural. And, further, all the surrounding objects of perception, which no one can altogether disregard for any length of time, tend to check the illusion and terminate it.

(2.) When a blow is aimed at any one, although in sport, and he fully knows it to be so, he forms so vivid a conception of what might possibly be the effect, that his belief is for a moment controlled, and he unavoidably shrinks back from it. This is particularly the case if the blow approaches the eye. Who can help winking at such times? It is a proof of our belief being controlled under such circumstances, that we can move our own hands rapidly in the neighbourhood of the eye, either perpendicularly or horizontally; and, at the same time, easily keep our eyelids from motion. But when the motion is made by another, the conception becomes more vivid, and a belief of danger inevitably arises.—Again, place a person on the battlements of a high tower; his reason tells him he is in no danger; he knows he is in none. But, after all, he is unable to look down from the battlements without fear; his conceptions are so exceedingly vivid as to induce a momentary belief of danger in opposition to all his reasonings.

(3.) When we are in pain from having struck our foot against a stone, or when pain is suddenly caused in us by any other inanimate object, we are apt to vent a momentary rage upon it That is to say, our belief is so affected for an instant, that we ascribe to it an accountable existence, and would punish it accordingly. This is observed particularly in children and in Savages. It is on the principle of our vivid conceptions being attended with belief, that poets so often ascribe life, and agency, and intention to the rain and winds, to storms, and thunder and lightning. How natural are the expressions of King Lear, overwhelmed with the ingratitude of his daughters, and standing with his old head bared to the pelting tempest!

> "Nor rain, wind, thunder, fire are my daughters;
> I tax not you, ye elements, with unkindness;
> I never gave you kingdoms, called you children."

(4.) There are persons who are entirely convinced of the folly of the popular belief of ghosts and other nightly apparitions, but who cannot be persuaded to sleep in a room alone, nor go alone into a room in the dark. Whenever they happen out at night, they are constantly looking on every side; their quickened perceptions behold images, which never had any existence except in their own minds, and they are the subjects of continual disquiet and even terror.—"It was my misfortune," says Dr. Priestly, "to have the idea of darkness, and the ideas of invisible malignant spirits and apparitions very closely connected in my infancy; and to this day, notwithstanding I believe nothing of those invisible powers, and, consequently, of their connexion with darkness, or anything else, I cannot be perfectly easy in every kind of situation in the dark, though I am sensible I gain ground upon this prejudice continually."

In all such cases we see the influence of the prejudices of the nursery. Persons who are thus afflicted were taught in early childhood to form conceptions of ghosts, visible hobgoblins, and unearthly spirits; and the habit still continues. It is true, when they listen to their reasonings and philosophy, they may well say they do not believe in such things. But the effect of their philosophy is merely to check their belief; not in ten cases in a thousand is the belief entirely overcome. Every little hile, in all solitary places, and especially in the dark, it returns, and, when banished, returns again; otherwise we cannot give an explanation of the conduct of these persons.

§ 65. Conceptions which are joined with perceptions.

The belief in our mere conceptions is the more evident and striking whenever at any time they are joined with our perceptions.—A person, for instance, is walking in a field in a foggy morning, and perceives something, no matter what it is; but he believes it to be a man, and does not doubt it. In other words, he truly perceives some object, and, in addition to that perception, has a mental conception of a man, attended with belief. When he has advanced a few feet further, all at once he perceives that what he conceived to be a man is merely a stump with a few stones piled on its top. He perceived at first, as plainly or but little short of it, that it was a stump, as in a moment afterward; there were the whole time very nearly the same visible form and the same dimensions in his eye. But he had the conception of a man in his mind at the same moment, which overruled and annulled the natural effects of the visual perception; the conception, being associated with the present visible object, acquired peculiar strength and permanency; so much so, that he truly and firmly believed that a human being was before him. But the conception has departed; the present object of perception has taken its place, and it is now impossible for him to conjure up the phantom, the reality of which he but just now had no doubt of.

One of the numerous characters whom Sir Walter Scott has sketched with so much truth to nature, speaks of himself as being banished, on a certain occasion, to one of the sandy Keys of the West Indies, which was reputed to be inhabited by malignant demons. This person, after acknowledging he had his secret apprehensions upon their account, remarks, "In open daylight or in absolute darkness I did not greatly apprehend their approach; but in the misty dawn of the morning, or when evening was about to fall, I saw, for the first week of my abode on the Key, many a dim and undefined spectre; now resembling a Spaniard, with his capa wrapped around him, and his huge sombrera, as large as an umbrella, upon his head; now a Dutch sailor, with his rough cap and trunk hose; and now an Indian Cacique, with his feathery crown and long lance of cane. I always approached them, but, whenever I drew near, the phantom changed into a bush, or a piece of driftwood, or a wreath of mist, or some such cause of deception."

But it is unnecessary to resort to books for illustrations of this topic. Multitudes of persons have a conceptive facility of creations, which is often troublesome and perplexing; especially in uncommon situations, and in the night. And in all cases this tendency is greatly strengthened, whenever it can lay hold of objects, the outlines of which it can pervert to its own purposes.—In instances of this kind, where the conceptions are upheld, as it were, by present objects of perception, and receive a sort of permanency from them, nothing is better known than that we often exercise a strong and unhesitating belief. These instances, therefore, can properly be considered as illustrating and confirming the views in the preceding section.

§ 66. Conceptions as connected with fictitious representations.

These observations suggest an explanation, at least in part, of the effects which are produced on the mind by exhibitions of fictitious distress. In the representation of tragedies, for instance, it must be admitted, that there is a general conviction of the whole being but a fiction. But, although persons enter the theatre with this general conviction, it does not always remain with them the whole time. At certain peculiarly interesting passages in the poet, and at certain exhibitions of powerful and well-timed effort in the actor, this general impression, that all is a fiction, fails. The feelings of the spectator may be said to rush into the scenes; he mingles in the events; carried away and lost, he for a moment believes all to be real, and the tears gush at the catastrophe which he witnesses. The explanation, therefore, of the emotions felt at the exhibition of a tragedy, such as indignation, pity, and abhorrence, is, that at certain parts of the exhibition we have a momentary belief in the reality of the events which are represented. And after the illustrations which have been given, such a belief cannot be considered impossible.—The same explanation will apply to the emotions which follow our reading of tragedies when alone, or any other natural and affecting descriptions. In the world of conceptions which the genius of the writer conjures up, we are transported out of the world of real existence, and for a while fully believe in the reality of what is only an incantation.

CHAPTER IX.

SIMPLICITY AND COMPLEXNESS OF MENTAL STATES

§ 67. Origin of the distinction of simple and complex.

In looking at our thoughts and feelings, as they continually pass under the review of our internal observation, we readily perceive that they are not of equal worth; we do not assign to them the same estimate; one state of mind is found to be expressive of one thing only, and that thing, whatever it is, is precise, and definite, and inseparable; while another state of mind is found to be expressive of, and virtually equal to, many others. And hence we are led, not only with the utmost propriety, but even by a sort of necessity, to make a division of the whole body of our mental affections into the two classes of SIMPLE and COMPLEX. Nature herself makes the division; it is one of those characteristics which gives to the mind, in part at least, its greatness; one of those elements of power, without which the soul could not be what it is, and without a knowledge of which it is difficult to possess a full and correct understanding of it in other respects.

§ 68. Nature and characteristics of simple mental states.

We shall first offer some remarks on those mental states which are simple, and shall aim to give an understanding of their nature, so far as can be expected on a subject, the clearness of which depends more on a reference to our own personal consciousness than on the teachings of others.

Let it be noticed then, in the first place, that a simple idea CANNOT BE SEPARATED INTO PARTS.—It is clearly implied in the very distinction between simplicity and complexity, considered in relation to the states of the mind, that there can be no such separation, no such division. It is emphatically true of our simple ideas and emotions, and of all other simple states of the mind, that they are one and indivisible. Whenever you can detect in them more than one element, they at once lose their character of simplicity, and are to be regarded as complex, however they may have previously appeared. Inseparableness consequently is their striking characteristic; and it may be added, that they are not only inseparable in themselves, but are separate from everything else. There is nothing which can stand as a substitute for them where they are, or represent them where they are not; they are independent unities, constituted exclusively by the mind itself, having a specific and positive character, but never theless known only in themselves.

§ 69. Simple mental states not susceptible of definition.

Let it be observed, in the second place, that our simple notions CANNOT BE DEFINED.—This view of them follows necessarily from what has been said of their oneness and inseparableness, compared with what is universally understood by defining. In respect to definitions, it is undoubtedly true, that we sometimes use synonymous words, and call such use a definition; but it is not properly such. In every legitimate definition, the idea which is to be defined is to be separated, as far as may be thought necessary, into its subordinate parts; and these parts are to be presented to the mind for its examination, instead of the original notion into which they entered. This process must be gone through in every instance of accurate defining; this is the general and authorized view of definition; and it is not easy to see in what else it can well consist.

But this process will not apply to our simple thoughts and feelings, because, if there be any such thing as sim ple mental states, they are characterized by inseparableness and oneness. And furthermore, if we define ideas by employing other ideas, we must count upon meeting at last with such as shall be ultimate, and will reject all verbal explanation; otherwise we can never come to an end in the process.—So that the simple mental affections are not only undefinable in themselves; but if there were no such elementary states of mind, there could be no defining in any other case; it would be merely analysis upon analysis, a process without completion, and a labour without end; leaving the subject in as much darkness as when the process was begun.

When we speak of simple ideas and feelings, and a person, in consequence of our inability to define them, professes to be ignorant of the terms we use, we can frequently aid him in understanding them by a statement of the circumstances, as far as possible, under which the simple mental state exists. But having done this, we can merely refer him to his own senses and consciousness, as the only teachers from which he can expect to receive satisfaction.

§ 70. Simple mental states representative of a reality.

A third mark or characteristic of simple mental states is, that they always stand for or REPRESENT A REALITY. In other words, no simple idea is, in its own nature, delusive or fictitious, but always has something precisely corresponding to it.—It is not always so with complex ideas; these, as Mr. Locke justly gives us to understand, are sometimes CHIMERICAL. That is to say; the elements of which they are composed are so brought together and combined as to form something, of which nature presents no corresponding reality. If, for instance, a person had an idea of a body, yellow, or of some other colour, malleable, fixed; possessing, in a word, all the qualities of iron or of gold, with this difference only, of its being lighter than water, it would be what Mr. Locke terms a CHIMERICAL idea; because the combination of the elements here exists only in the human mind, and not in nature; the thing has no outward or objective reality. The words CENTAUR, DRAGON, and HYPOGRIFF, which are the well known names for imaginary beings possessing no actual existence, are expressive of chimerial complex ideas These ideas have nothing corresponding to them. But it is not so with the simple states of the mind. If it were otherwise, since in our inquiries after truth we naturally proceed from what is complex to what is simple, there would be no sure foundation of knowledge. Whenever, in our analysis of a subject, we arrive at truly simple ideas, we have firm footing; there is no mistake, no delusion. Nature, always faithful to her own character, gives utterance to the truth alone. But man, in combining together the elements which nature furnishes, does not always avoid mistakes.

§ 71. Origin of complex notions, and their relation to simple.

Our simple states of mind, which we have thus endeavoured to explain, were probably first in origin. There are reasons for considering them as antecedent in point of time to our complex mental states, although in many cases it may not be easy to trace the progress of the mind from the one to the other. The complex notions of external material objects embrace the separate and simple notions of resistance, extension, hardness, colour, taste, and others. As these elementary perceptions evidently have their origin in distinct and separate senses, it is but reasonable to suppose that they possess a simple, before they are combined together in a complex existence. Simple ideas, therefore, may justly be regarded as antecedent, in point of time, to those which are complex, and as laying the foundation of them.

Hence we see that it is sufficiently near the truth, and that it is not improper, to speak of our complex ideas as derived from, or made up of, simple ideas. This is the well-known language of Mr. Locke on this subject; and when we consider how much foundation there is for it in the constitution and operations of the human mind, there is good reason for retaining it.—Although purely simple states of the mind are few in number, vast multitudes of a complex nature are formed from them. The ability which the mind possesses of originating complex thoughts and feelings from elementary ones, may be compared to our power of uniting together the letters of the alphabet in the formation of syllables and words.

§ 72. Supposed complexness without the antecedence of simple feelings.

It is possible that some persons may object to the doctrine proposed in the last section, that complex mental states are subsequent in point of time to those which are simple; and may be inclined to adopt the opinion, that some, at least, of our complex notions are framed at once and immediately, whenever an occasion presents itself, and are not necessarily dependent on the prior existence of any other feelings. When the eye, for instance, opens on a wide and diversified landscape, they suppose the whole to be embraced in one complex mental state, the formation of which is not gradual and susceptible of measurement by time, but is truly instantaneous. When we direct our attention to objects of less extent, as a portrait, a landscape, or historical painting, they imagine it to be still more evident, that the complexity of mind, corresponding to the complexity of the object, is a result without any antecedent process. Without doubt, what has now been said is, in some instances, apparently the case; but this appearance (for we cannot speak of it as anything more than such) is susceptible of an obvious explanation, without an abandonment of the general principle which has been laid down. No one is ignorant that the mind often passes with exceeding rapidity along the successive objects of its contemplation. This rapidity may, in some cases, be so great, that no foundation will be laid for remembrance; and of course, in such cases, the complex feeling has the appearance of being formed without the antecedence of other simple feelings. Often the eye glances so rapidly over the distinct parts of the portrait, the historical painting, or even the wide landscape, that we are utterly unable in our recollection to detect the successive steps of its progress. There naturally seems, therefore, to be but one view, instead of distinct and successive glances of the mind from hill to hill, from forest to forest, and from one verdant spot to another, prior to the supposed one and instantaneous comprehension of the whole. But there is much reason for saying that this oneness of comprehension is in seeming and appearance only, and not in fact. (See § 57, 58.)

§ 73. The precise sense in which complexness is to be understood.

But while we distinctly assert the frequent complexness of the mental affections, it should be particularly kept in mind, that they are not to be regarded in the light of a material compound, where the parts, although it may sometimes appear to be otherwise, necessarily possess no higher unity than that of juxtaposition, and, of course, can be literally separated from each other, and then put together again. There is nothing of this kind; neither putting together nor taking asunder, in this literal and material sense.—But if our thoughts and feelings are not made up of others, and are not complex in the material sense of the expressions, what then constitutes their complexness? This inquiry gives occasion for the important remark, that complexness in relation to the mind is not literal, but virtual only. What we term a complex feeling is in itself truly simple, but at the same time it is equal to many others, and is complex only in that sense. Thought after thought, and emotion following emotion, passes through the mind; and as they are called forth by the operation of the laws of association, many of them necessarily have relation to the same object. Then there follows a new state of mind, which is the result of those previous feelings, and is complex in the sense already explained. That is to say, it is felt by us to possess a virtual equality to those separate antecedent thoughts and emotions. Our simple feelings are like streams coming from different mountains, but meeting and mingling together at last in the common centre of some intermediate lake; the tributary fountains are no longer separable; but have disappeared, and become merged and confounded in the bosom of their common resting-place. Or they may be likened to the cents and dimes of the American coinage, tens and hundreds of which are represented by a single EAGLE; and yet the eagle is not divided into a hundred or thousand parts, but has as much unity as the numerous pieces for which it stands.

The language which expresses the composition and

complexity of thought is, therefore, to be regarded as wholly metaphorical when applied to the mind, and is not to be taken in its literal meaning. We are under the necessity of employing in this case, as in others, language which has a material origin, but we shall not be led astray by it if we carefully attend to what has been said, and endeavour to aid our conception of it by a reference to our internal experience.

§ 74. Illustrations of analysis as applied to the mind.

The subject of the preceding section will be the better understood by the consideration of Analysis as applicable to the mind. As we do not combine literally, so we do not untie or separate literally; as there is no literal complexness, so there is no literal resolution or analysis of it. Nevertheless, we have a meaning when we speak of analyzing our thoughts and feelings. And what is it? What are we to understand by the term analysis?

Although this subject is not without difficulty, both in the conception and in the expression of it, it is susceptible of some degree of illustration.—It will be remembered that there may be an analysis of material bodies. The chemist analyzes when he takes a piece of glass, which appears to be one substance, and finds that it is not one, but is separable into silicious and alkaline matter. He takes other bodies, and separates them in like manner; and whenever he does this, the process is rightly called analysis.

Now we apply the same term to the mind; but the thing expressed by it, the process gone through, is not the same. All we can say is, there is something like this. We do not resolve and separate a complex thought, as we do a piece of glass or other material body, into its parts; we are utterly unable to do it, if we should seriously make the attempt; every mental state is, in itself and in fact, simple and indivisible, and is complex only virtually. Complex notions are the results rather than the compounds of former feelings; and though not literally made up of parts, have the relation to them which any material whole has to the elements composing it; and in that particular sense may be said to comprehend or embrace the subordinate notions. Mental analysis accordingly concerns merely this relation. We perform such an analysis when, by the aid of our reflection and consciousness, we are able to indicate those separate and subordinate feelings to which, in our conception of it, the complex mental state is virtually equal.

The term GOVERNMENT, for instance, when used in reference to the mental perception of the thing thus named, expresses a complex state of the mind; we may make this mental state, which is in fact only one, although it is virtually more than one, a subject of contemplation; and we are said to analyze it when we are able to indicate those separate and more elementary notions, without the existence and antecedence of which it could not have been formed by the mind. We do not literally take the complex state in pieces, but we designate other states of mind which, every one's knowledge of the origin of thought convinces him, must have preceded it, such as the ideas of power, right, obligation, command, and the relative notions of superior and inferior.

§ 75. Complex notions of external origin.

The doctrine of simplicity and complexness of mental states is applicable, in both its forms, to the Intellective and Sensitive parts of our nature; in other words, there may be a complex affection or passion, as well as a complex perception. The acts of the Will, the other great Division of the mental nature, are always simple. When we consider the subject in reference to the intellect alone, we may add further, that there is complexity of the Intellect both in its internal and external action; and it seems proper, in this connexion, to say something in particular of COMPLEX NOTIONS OF EXTERNAL ORIGIN.

What we term our simple ideas are representative of the parts of objects only. The sensations of colour, such as red, white, yellow; the original intimations from the touch, such as resistance, extension, hardness, and softness, do not, in themselves considered, give us a knowledge of substances, but only of the parts, attributes, or elements of substances. Accordingly, the ideas which we have of the various objects of the external world are, for the most part, complex. We speak of a house, a tree, a flower, a plant, a mineral, an animal; and in none of these cases are the ideas which we have simple; but, on the contrary, embrace a considerable number of elements

§ 76. Of objects contemplated as wholes.

In point of fact, the various external objects which come under our notice are presented to us as *wholes;* and, as such, (whatever may have been the original process leading to that result,) we very early contemplate them.—Take, for instance, a LOADSTONE In their ordinary and common thoughts upon it, (the result probably of some antecedent and very early training), men undoubtedly contemplate it as a whole; the state of mind which has reference to it embraces it as such. This complex notion, like all others which are complex, is virtually equal to a number of others of a more elementary character.—Hence, when we are called upon to give an account of the loadstone, we can return no other answer than by an enumeration of its elements. It is something which has weight, colour, hardness, power to draw iron, and whatever else we discover in it.

We use the term GOLD. This is a complex term, and implies a complexity in the corresponding mental state. But if we use the word gold, or any other synonymous word, in the hearing of a man who has neither seen that substance nor had it explained to him, he will not understand what is meant to be conveyed. We must enter into an analysis; and show that it is a combination of the qualities of yellowness, great weight, fusibility, ductility, &c. We look upward to the sun in the heavens. But what should we know of that great aggregate, if we could not contemplate it in the elements of form and extension, of brightness and heat, of roundness and regularity of motion?—All the ideas, therefore, which we form of external objects considered as wholes, are complex; and all such complex notions are composed of those which are simple.

CHAPTER X.

ABSTRACTION

§ 77. Abstraction implied in the analysis of complex ideas

THE remarks which have been made in the course of the foregoing chapter, on the analysis and examination of our Complex Intellectual states, naturally lead to the consideration of another subject, in some respects intimately connected with that topic. When we have once formed a complex notion (no matter at what period, in what way, or of what kind,) it not unfrequently happens that we desire, for various reasons, to examine more particularly some of its parts. Very frequently this is absolutely necessary to the full understanding of it. Although undoubtedly its elementary parts once came under review, that time is now long past; it has become important to institute a new inspection, to take each simple notion involved in it, and examine it by itself. And this is done by means of the process of ABSTRACTION, and in no other way.

By the aid of that process, our complex notions, however comprehensive they may be, are susceptible, if one may be allowed so to speak, of being taken to pieces, and the elementary parts may be abstracted or separated from each other; that is, they are made subjects of consideration apart from other ideas, with which they are ordinarily found to be associated. And hence, whenever this is the case in respect to the states of the mind, they are sometimes called ABSTRACTIONS, and still more frequently are known by the name of ABSTRACT IDEAS.—For the purpose of distinctness in what we have to say, they may be divided into the two classes of Particular and General; that is to say, in some cases the abstraction relates only to a single idea or element, in others it includes more

§ 93. Instances of particular abstract ideas.

We shall proceed, therefore, to remark first on Particular abstractions. Of this class, the notions which we form of the different kinds of colours may be regarded as instances. For example, we hold in our hand a rose; it has extension, colour, form, fragrance. The mind is so deeply occupied with the colour as almost wholly to neglect the other qualities. This is a species of abstraction, although perhaps an imperfect one, because, when an object is before us, it is difficult, in our most attentive consideration of any particular quality or property, to withdraw the mind wholly from the others. When, on the contrary, any *absent* object of perception occurs to us, when we think of or form a conception of it, our thoughts will readily fix upon the colour of such object, and make that the subject of consideration, without particularly regarding its other qualities, such as weight, hardness, taste, form, &c. We may also distinguish in any body (either when present, or still more perfectly when absent) its solidity from its extension, or we may direct our attention to its weight, or its length, or breadth, or thickness, and make any one of these a distinct object in our thoughts.

And hence, as it is a well-known fact that the properties of any body may be separated in the view and examination of the mind, however closely they may be connected in their appropriate subjects, we may lay down this statement in respect to the states of the mind before us, viz.: When any quality or attribute of an object, which does not exist by itself, but in a state of combination, is detached by our minds from its customary associates, and is considered separately, the notion we form of it becomes a particular abstract idea.—The distinctive mark of this class is, that the abstraction is limited to one quality. It should perhaps be particularly added, that the abstraction or separation may exist mentally, when it cannot take place in the object itself. For instance, the size, the figure, length, breadth, colour, &c., of a building, may each of them be made subjects of separate mental consideration, although there can be no real or actual separation of these things in the building itself. If there be any one of these properties, there must necessarily be all

§ 79. Mental process in separating and abstracting them.

The manner of expressing ourselves on the subject of our abstract notions, to which we have been accustomed, is apt to create and cherish a belief in the existence of a separate mental faculty, adapted solely to this particular purpose. But the doctrine of a power or faculty of abstraction, which is exclusive of other mental susceptibilities, and is employed solely for this purpose, does not appear to be well founded. It will convey an impression nearer the truth to speak of the PROCESS rather than the power of abstraction.—The following statement will be sufficient to show how those of the first class, or particular abstract ideas, are formed.

Although our earliest notions, whether they arise from the senses or are of an internal origin, are simple, existing in an independent and separate state, yet those simple thoughts are very soon found to unite together with a considerable degree of permanency, and out of them are formed complex states of mind. Many are in this way combined together in one, and the question is, how this combination is to be loosened, and the elementary parts are to be extracted from their present complexity?

In answer, it may be said that, in every case of separating a particular abstract idea, there must necessarily be a determination, a choice, an act of the will. This voluntary state of mind must concern the previous complex mental state, when viewed in one respect, rather than another; or, what is the same thing, it will concern one part of the complex idea rather than another. So that we may truly and justly be said to have not only a desire, but a determination to consider or examine some part of the complex idea more particularly than the others. When the mind is in this manner directed to any particular part of a complex notion, we find it to be the fact, that the principle of association, or whatever principle it is which keeps the other parts in their state of union with it, ceases, in a greater or less degree, to operate and to maintain that union; the other parts rapidly fall off and disappear, and the particular quality, towards which the mind is especially directed, remains the sole subject of consideration. That is to say, it is abstracted, or becomes an abstract idea.—If, for example, we have in mind the complex notion of any object, a house, tree, plant, flower, and the like, but have a desire and determination to make the colour, which forms a part of this complex notion, a particular subject of attention, the consequence is, that, while the quality of colour occupies our chief regard, the other qualities will disappear and no more be thought of. If we determine to examine the weight or extension of an object, the result will be the same; in other words, the extension, weight, colour, &c., becoming distinct and exclusive objects of attention, will be abstracted.

This, in the formation of particular abstract ideas, seems to be the process of the mind, and nothing more; viz., The direction of an act of the will to a particular part of a complex notion, and the consequent detention of the part towards which the mental choice is directed, and the natural and necessary disappearance, under such circumstances, of the other parts.

§ 80. General abstract notions the same with genera and species.

We proceed now to consider the other class of abstract ideas.—General Abstract ideas are not only different, in consequence of embracing a greater number of elementary parts, from those which are Particular, but are also susceptible of being distinguished from the great body of our other complex notions.—The idea, for example, which we form of any individual, of John, Peter, or James, is evidently a complex one, but it is not necessarily a general one. The notion which we frame of a particular horse or of a particular tree, is likewise a complex idea, but not a general one. There will be found to be a clear distinction between them, although it may not be perfectly obvious at first. GENERAL ABSTRACT IDEAS are our notions of the classes of objects, that is, of Genera and Species They are expressed by general names, without, in most cases, any defining or limitation, as when we use the words ANIMAL, MAN, HORSE, BIRD, SHEEP, FISH, TREE, not to express any one in particular of these various classes, but animals, men, horses, &c., in general.

§ 81. Process in classification, or the forming of genera and species.

Now if our general abstract ideas, so far as they relate to external objects, are truly notions of SPECIES and GENERA, it will aid us in the better understanding of them if we briefly consider how species and genera are formed. Men certainly find no great practical difficulty in forming these classifications, since we find that they do in fact make them in numberless instances, and at a very early period of life. They seem to be governed in the process by definite and uniform mental tendencies.—What, then, in point of fact, is the process in classification? It is obvious, in the first place, that no classification can be made without considering two or more objects together. A number of objects, therefore, are first presented to us for our observation and inquiry, which are to be examined first in themselves, and then in comparison with each other. We will take a familiar scene to illustrate what takes place.

We suppose ourselves to stand on the bank of a navigable river; we behold the flowing of its waters, the cliffs that overhang it, the trees that line its shore, the boats and boatmen on its bosom, the flocks and herds that press down to drink from its waves. With such a scene before us, it is to be expected that the mind will rapidly make each and all of these the subjects of its contemplation; nor does it pursue this contemplation and inquiry far, without perceiving certain relations of agreement or difference. Certain objects before it are felt to be essentially alike, and others to be essentially different; and hence they are not all arranged in one class, but a discrimination is made, and different classes are formed The flocks and herds are formed into their respective classes. The tall and leafy bodies on the river's bank, although they differ from each other in some respects, are yet found to agree in so many others, that they are arranged together in another class, and called by the general name of TREE. The living, moving, and reasoning beings that propel the boats on its waters, form another class, and are called MAN.—And there is the same process and the same result in respect to all other bodies coming within the range of our observation.

§ 82. Early classifications sometimes incorrect.

It has been intimated, that, in making these classifications, men are governed by definite and uniform mental tendencies; still it must be acknowledged that mistakes are sometimes committed, especially in the early periods of society, and in all cases where the opportunities of examination and comparison are imperfect. When man first opens his eyes on nature, (and in the infancy of our race he finds himself a novice wherever he goes,) objects so numerous, so various in kind, so novel and interesting, crowd upon his attention, that, attempting to direct himself to all at the same time, he loses sight of their specifical differences, and blends them together more than a calm and accurate examination would justify. And hence it is not to be wondered at that our earliest classifications, the primitive genera and species, are sometimes incorrectly made.

Subsequently, when knowledge has been in some measure amassed, and reasoning and observation have been brought to a greater maturity, these errors are attended to; individuals are rejected from species where they do not properly belong, and species from genera. The most savage and ignorant tribes will in due season correct their mistakes and be led into the truth.

§ 83. Illustrations of our earliest classifications.

We are naturally led to introduce one or two incidents here which throw light on this part of our subject. What we wish to illustrate is the simple fact that men readily perceive the resemblances of objects, and exhibit a disposition to classify them in reference to such resemblance. The first case which we shall mention in illustration of this, is that of Caspar Hauser. The principal objects which Caspar had to amuse himself with in his prison were two little wooden horses, which, in his entire ignorance, he believed to be possessed of life and sensibility. After the termination of his imprisonment, his biographer informs us, that to "every animal he met with, whether quadruped or biped, dog, cat, goose, or fowl, he gave the name of horse."

In the year 1814, Pitcairn's Island, a solitary spot in

the Pacific Ocean, was visited by two English cruisers. Two of the young men that belonged on the island, and whose knowledge was, of course, extremely limited, came on board one of the vessels. "The youths," says the Narrative, "were greatly surprised at the sight of so many novel objects; the size of the ship, the guns, and everything around them. Observing a cow, they were at first somewhat alarmed, and expressed a doubt whether it was a huge goat or a horned hog, these being the only two species of quadrupeds they had ever seen."—Travellers mention other instances where there is the same tendency to classify, which we have not room to repeat

§ 84. Of the nature of general abstract ideas.

The notions which are thus formed in all cases of classification, are commonly known, in the Treatises having relation to these subjects, as General Abstract ideas. And they are no less numerous than the multiplied varieties of objects which are found to exist everywhere around us. It is thus that we form the general notions of animal and of all the subordinate species of animals; of tree and its numerous varieties; of earths, and minerals, and whatever else is capable of being arranged into classes.

But it is to be noticed that the general idea, whatever objects it may be founded upon, does not embrace every particular which makes a part of such objects. When we look at a number of men, we find them all differing in some respects, in height, size, colour, tone of the voice, and in other particulars. The mind fixes only upon those traits or properties with which it can combine the notion of resemblance; that is to say, those traits, qualities, or properties in which the individuals are perceived to be like, or to resemble each other.—The complex mental state, which embraces these qualities and properties, and nothing more, (with the exception of the superadded notion of other bodies having resembling qualities,) is a General Abstract idea.

And hence the name. Such notions are called ABSTRACT, because, while embracing many individuals in certain respects, they detach and leave out altogether a variety of particulars in which those individuals disagree

If there were not this discrimination and leaving out of certain parts, we never could consider these notions, regarded as wholes, as otherwise than individual or particular.—They are called GENERAL, because, in consequence of the discrimination and selection which has just been mentioned, they embrace such qualities and properties as exist not in one merely, but in many.

§ 85. The power of general abstraction in connexion with numbers, &c.

The ability which the mind possesses of forming general abstract ideas, is of much practical importance. It is not easy to estimate the increase of power which is thus given to the action of the human mind, particularly in reasoning. By means of general abstract propositions, we are able to state volumes in a few sentences; that is to say, the truths, stated and illustrated in a few general propositions, would fill volumes in their particular applications.

Without the ability of forming general notions, we should not be able to *number*, even in the smallest degree. Before we can consider objects as forming a multitude, or are able to number them, it seems necessary to be able to apply to them a common name. This we cannot do until we have reduced them to a genus; and the formation of a genus implies the power (or process, rather) of abstraction. Consequently, we should be unable, without such power, to number.—How great, then, is the practical importance of that intellectual process by which general abstractions are formed!—Without the ability to number, we should be at a loss in our investigations where this ability is required; without the power to classify, all our speculations must be limited to particulars, and we should be capable of no general reasoning.

§ 86. Of general abstract truths or principles.

There are not only general abstract ideas, but abstract truths or principles also of a general nature, which are deserving of some attention, especially in a practical point of view. Although enough has already been said to show the importance of abstraction, it may yet be desirable to have a more full view of its applications

The process, in forming general truths or principles of an abstract nature, seems to be this. We must begin undoubtedly with the examination and study of particulars; with individual objects and characters, and with insulated events. We subsequently confirm the truth of whatever has been ascertained in such inquiry, by an observation of other like objects and events. We proceed from one individual to another, till no doubt remains.—Having in this way arrived at some general fact or principle, we thenceforward throw aside the consideration of the particular objects on which it is founded, and make it alone, exclusively and abstractly, the subject of our mental contemplations. We repeat this process again and again, till the mind, instead of being wholly taken up with a multitude of particulars, is stored with truths of a general kind. These truths it subsequently combines in trains of reasoning, compares together, and deduces from them others of still wider application.

§ 87. Of the speculations of philosophers and others.

What has been said leads us to observe, that there is a characteristical difference between the speculations of men of philosophic minds and those of the common mass of people, which is worthy of some notice. The difference between the two is not so much, that philosophers are accustomed to carry on processes of reasoning to a greater extent, as this, that they are more in the habit of employing general abstract ideas and general terms, and that, consequently, the conclusions which they form are more comprehensive. Nor are their general reasonings, although the conclusions at which they arrive seem, in their particular applications, to indicate wonderful fertility of invention, so difficult in the performance as is apt to be supposed. They have so often and so long looked at general ideas and general propositions; have been so accustomed, as one may say, to contemplate the general nature of things, divested of all superfluous and all specific circumstances, that they have formed a *habit;* and the operation is performed without difficulty. It requires in such persons no greater intellectual effort than would be necessary in skilfully managing the details of ordinary business.

The speculations of the great bulk of mankind differ from those of philosophers in being, both in the subjects of them and in their results, particular. They discover an inability to enlarge their view to universal propositions, which embrace a great number of individuals. They may possess the power of mere argument, of comparing propositions together which concern particulars, and deducing inferences from them to a great degree; but when they attempt to contemplate general propositions, their minds are perplexed, and the conclusions which are drawn from them appear obscure, however clearly the previous process of reasoning may have been expressed.

CHAPTER XI.

OF ATTENTION.

§ 88. Of the general nature of attention.

WITHOUT considering it necessary to speak of attention as a separate intellectual power or faculty, as some may be inclined to do, it seems to be sufficient to say, that ATTENTION expresses the state of the mind, when it is steadily directed, for a length of time, to some object of sense or intellect, exclusive of other objects. When we say that any external object, or any subject of thought which is purely internal, receives attention, it seems to be the fact, as far as we are able to determine, that the intellect is occupied with the subject of its attention, whatever it is, for a certain period, and that all other things are, for the time being, shut out. In other words, the grasp which the perceptive power fixes upon the object of its contemplations is an undivided, an unbroken one.—But this does not appear to be all. There is not only a distinct and exclusive mental perception; but also an act of the will, directing, condensing, and confining the perception. So that, in all cases of attention, the act of the mind may be regarded as a complex one, involving not only the mere perception or series of perceptions, but also an act of the will, founded on some feeling of desire or sentiment of duty. It is the act of the will, prompted in general by the feeling of desire or interest, which keeps the mind intense and fixed in its position.

§ 89. Of different degrees of attention.

In agreement with this view of the subject, we often speak of attention as great or small, as existing in a very high or a very slight degree. When the view of the mind is only momentary, and is unaccompanied, as it generally is at such times, with any force of emotion or energy of volitive action, then the attention is said to be slight. When, on the contrary, the mind directs itself to an object, or series of objects, with earnestness, and for a considerable length of time, and refuses to attend to anything else, then the attention is said to be intense.

We commonly judge at first of the degree of attention to a subject from the length of time during which the mind is occupied with it. But when we look a little further, it will be found that the time will generally depend upon the strength and permanency of the attendant emotion of interest. And hence, both the time and the degree of feeling are to be regarded in our estimate of the power of attention in any particular case; the former being the result, and, in some sense, a measure of the latter.

Of instances of people who are able to give but slight attention to any subject of thought, who cannot bring their minds to it with steadiness and power, we everywhere find multitudes, and there are some instances where this ability has been possessed in such a high degree as to be worthy of notice. There have been mathematicians who could investigate the most complicated problems amid every variety and character of disturbance. It was said of Julius Cæsar, that, while writing a despatch, he could at the same time dictate four others to his secretaries; and if he did not write himself, could dictate seven letters at once. The same thing is asserted also of the Emperor Napoleon, who had a wonderful capability of directing his whole mental energy to whatever came before him.*

* Segur's History of the Expedition to Russia, bk. vii., ch. xiii.

§ 90 Dependence of memory on atten.ion.

There seems to be no doctrine in mental philosophy more clearly established than this, that memory depends on attention; that is, where attention is very slight, remembrance is weak, and where attention is intense, remembrance continues longer.—There are many facts which confirm this statement.

(1.) In the course of a single day, persons who are in the habit of winking will close their eyelids perhaps thousands of times, and, as often as they close them, will place themselves in utter darkness. Probably they are conscious at the time both of closing their eyelids and of being in the dark; but, as their attention is chiefly taken up with other things, they have entirely forgotten it.—(2.) Let a person be much engaged in conversation, or occupied with any very interesting speculation, and the clock will strike in the room where he is, apparently without his having any knowledge of it. He hears the clock strike as much as at any other time, but, not attending to the perception of sound, and having his thoughts directed another way, he immediately forgets.—(3.) In the occupations of the day, when a multitude of cares are pressing us on every side, a thousand things escape our notice; they appear to be neither seen nor heard, nor to affect us in any way whatever. But at the stillness of evening, when anxieties and toils are quieted, and there is a general pause in nature, we seem to be endued with a new sense, and the slightest sound attracts our attention. Shakspeare has marked even this

> "The crow doth sing as sweetly as the lark
> When neither is attended; and, I think,
> The nightingale, if she should sing by day,
> When every goose is cackling, would be thought
> No better a musician than the wren."

It is on the same principle that people dwelling in the vicinity of waterfalls do not appear to notice the sound. The residents in the neighbourhood even of the great Cataract of Niagara are not seriously disturbed by it, although it is an unbroken, interminable thunder to all others.—The reason in all these cases is the same, as has already been given. There is no attention and no remembrance, and, of course, virtually no perception.

(4.) Whenever we read a book, we do not observe

the words merely as a whole, but every letter of which they are made up, and even the minute parts of these letters. But it is merely a glance; it does not for any length of time occupy our attention; we immediately forget, and with great difficulty persuade ourselves that we have truly perceived the letters of the word. The fact that every letter is in ordinary cases observed by us, may be proved by leaving out a letter of the word, or by substituting others of a similar form. We readily, in reading, detect such omissions or substitutions.

(5.) An expert accountant can sum up, almost with a single glance of the eye, a long column of figures. The operation is performed almost instantaneously, and yet he ascertains the sum of the whole with unerring certainty. It is impossible that he should learn the sum without noticing every figure in the whole column, and without allowing each its proper worth; but the attention to them was so very slight, that he is unable to remember this distinct notice.

Many facts of this kind evidently show, as we think, that memory depends upon attention, or rather upon a continuance of attention, and varies with that continuance.

§ 91. Of exercising attention in reading.

If attention, as we have seen, be requisite to memory, then we are furnished with a practical rule of considerable importance. The rule is, *Not to give a hasty and careless reading of authors, but read them with a suitable degree of deliberation and thought.*—If we are asked the reason of this direction, we find a good and satisfactory one in the fact referred to at the head of this section, that there cannot be memory without attention, or, rather, that the power of memory will vary with the degree of attention. By yielding to the desire of becoming acquainted with a greater variety of departments of knowledge than the understanding is able to master, and, as a necessary consequence, by bestowing upon each of them only a very slight attention, we remain essentially ignorant of the whole.

(1.) The person who pursues such a course finds himself unable to recall what he has been over; he has a great many half-formed notions floating in his mind, but these are so ill shaped and so little under his control as to be but little better than actual ignorance. This is one evil result of reading authors and of going over sciences in the careless way which has been specified, that the knowledge thus acquired, if it can be called knowledge, is of very little practical benefit, in consequence of being so poorly digested and so little under control.—(2.) But there is another, and perhaps more serious evil. This practice greatly disqualifies one for all intellectual pursuits. To store the mind with new ideas is only a part of education. It is, at least, a matter of equal importance, to impart to all the mental powers a suitable discipline, to exercise those that are strong, to strengthen those that are weak, and to maintain among all of them a suitable balance. An attentive and thorough examination of subjects is a training up of the mind in both these respects. It furnishes it with that species of knowledge which is most valuable, because it is not mixed up with errors; and, moreover, gives a strength and consistency to the whole structure of the intellect. Whereas, when the mind is long left at liberty to wander from object to object, without being called to account and subjected to the rules of salutary discipline, it entirely loses, at last, the ability to dwell upon the subjects of its thoughts, and examine them. And, when this power is once lost, there is but little ground to expect any solid attainments.

§ 92. Alleged inability to command the attention.

We are aware that those who, in accordance with these directions, are required to make a close and thorough examination of subjects, will sometimes complain that they find a great obstacle in their inability to fix their attention. They are not wanting in ability to comprehend; but find it difficult to retain the mind in one position so long as to enable them to connect together all the parts of a subject, and duly estimate their various bearings. When this intellectual defect exists, it becomes a new reason for that thorough examination of subjects, which has been above recommended. It has probably been caused by a neglect of such strictness of examination, and by a too rapid and careless transition from one subject to another

ATTENTION, it will be recollected, expresses the state of the mind when it is steadily directed for some time, whether longer or shorter, to some object of sense or intellect, exclusive of other objects. All other objects are shut out; and when this exclusion of everything else continues for some time, the attention is said to be intense.—Now it is well known that such an exclusive direction of the mind cannot exist for any long period without being accompanied with a feeling of desire or of duty. In the greatest intellectual exertions, not the mere powers of judging, of abstracting, and of reasoning are concerned; there will also be a greater or less movement of the feelings. And it will be found that no feeling will effectually confine the minds of men in scientific pursuits, but a love of the truth.

Mr. Locke thought that the person who should discover a remedy for wandering thoughts would do a great service to the studious and contemplative part of mankind. We know of no other effective remedy than the one just mentioned, A LOVE OF THE TRUTH, a desire to know the nature and relations of things, merely for the sake of knowledge. It is true, that a conviction of duty will do much; ambition and interest may possibly do more; but when the mind is led to deep investigations by these views merely, without finding something beautiful and attractive in the aspect of knowledge itself, it is likely to prove a tiresome process. The excellence of knowledge, therefore, considered merely in the light of its being suited to the intellectual nature of man, and as the appropriate incentive and reward of intellectual activity, ought to be frequently impressed.—"I saw D'Alembert," says a recent writer, "congratulate a young man very coldly who brought him a solution of a problem. The young man said, 'I have done this in order to have a seat in the Academy.' 'Sir,' answered D'Alembert, 'with such dispositions you never will earn one. Science must be loved for its own sake, and not for the advantage to be derived. No other principle will enable a man to make progress in the sciences!'"*

* Memoirs of Montlosier, vol. i., page 58, as quoted in Mackintosh's Ethical Philosophy, sect. vii.

CHAPTER XII

DREAMING.

§ 93. Definition of dreams and the prevalence of them.

Among numerous other subjects in mental philosophy which claim their share of attention, that of Dreaming is entitled to its place; nor can we be certain that any other will be found more appropriate to it than the present, especially when we consider how closely it is connected in all its forms with our sensations and conceptions. And what are Dreams? It approaches, perhaps, sufficiently near to a correct general description to say, that they are our mental states and operations while we are asleep. But the particular views which are to be taken in the examination of this subject will not fail to throw light on this general statement.

The mental states and exercises which go under this name have ever excited much interest. It is undoubtedly one reason of the attention, which the subject of our dreams has ever elicited among all classes of people, that they are so prevalent; it being very difficult, if not impossible, to find a person who has not had more or less of this experience. Mr. Locke, however, tells us of an individual who never dreamed till the twenty-sixth year of his age, when he happened to have a fever, and then dreamed for the first time. Plutarch also mentions one Cleon, a friend of his, who lived to an advanced age, and yet had never dreamed once in his life; and remarks that he had heard the same thing reported of Thrasymedes.

Undoubtedly these persons dreamed very seldom, as we find that some dream much more than others; but it is possible that they may have dreamed at some time and entirely forgotten it. So that it cannot with certainty be inferred from such instances as these, that there are any who are entirely exempt from dreaming.

§ 94. Connexion of dreams with our waking thoughts.

In giving an explanation of dreams, our attention is

first arrested by the circumstance that they have an intimate relationship with our waking thoughts. The great body of our waking experiences appear in the form of trains of associations; and these trains of associated ideas, in greater or less continuity, and with greater or less variation, continue when we are asleep.—Condorcet (a name famous in the history of France) told some one, that, while he was engaged in abstruse and profound calculations, he was frequently obliged to leave them in an unfinished state, in order to retire to rest, and that the remaining steps and the conclusion of his calculations have more than once presented themselves in his dreams.—Franklin also has made the remark, that the bearings and results of political events, which had caused him much trouble while awake, were not unfrequently unfolded to him in dreaming.—Mr. Coleridge says, that, as he was once reading in the Pilgrimage of Purchas an account of the palace and garden of the Khan Kubla, he fell into a sleep, and in that situation composed an entire poem of not less than two hundred lines, some of which he afterward committed to writing. The poem is entitled Kubla Khan, and begins as follows:

"In Xanadu did Kubla Khan
A stately pleasure-dome decree;
Where Alph, the sacred river, ran
Through caverns measureless to man
Down to a sunless sea."

It is evident from such statements as these, which are confirmed by the experience of almost every person, that our dreams are fashioned from the materials of the thoughts and feelings which we have while awake; in other words, they will, in a great degree, be merely the repetition of our customary and prevailing associations. So well understood is this, that President Edwards, who was no less distinguished as a mental philosopher than as a theologian, thought it a good practice to take particular notice of his dreams, in order to ascertain from them what his predominant inclinations were.

§ 95. Dreams are often caused by our sensations.

But while we are to look for the materials of our dreams in thoughts which had previously existed, we further find that they are not beyond the influence of those slight bodily sensations of which we are susceptible even in hours of sleep. These sensations, slight as they are, are the means of introducing one set of associations rather than another.—Dugald Stewart relates an incident which may be considered an evidence of this, that a person with whom he was acquainted had occasion, in consequence of an indisposition, to apply a bottle of hot water to his feet when he went to bed, and the consequence was, that he dreamed he was making a journey to the top of Mount Ætna, and that he found the heat of the ground almost insupportable. There was once a gentleman in the English army who was so susceptible of audible impressions while he was asleep, that his companions could make him dream of what they pleased. Once, in particular, they made him go through the whole process of a duel, from the preliminary arrangements to the firing of the pistol, which they put into his hand for that purpose, and which, when it exploded, waked him.

A cause of dreams, closely allied to the above, is the variety of sensations which we experience from the stomach, viscera, &c.—Persons, for instance, who have been for a long time deprived of food, or have received it only in small quantities, hardly enough to preserve life, will be likely to have dreams in some way or other directly relating to their condition. Baron Trenck relates, that, being almost dead with hunger when confined in his dungeon, his dreams every night presented to him the well-filled and luxurious tables of Berlin, from which, as they were presented before him, he imagined he was about to relieve his hunger. "The night had far advanced," says Irving, speaking of the voyage of Mendez to Hispaniola, "but those whose turn it was to take repose were unable to sleep, from the intensity of their thirst; or if they slept, it was to be tantalized with dreams of cool fountains and running brooks."

The state of health also has considerable influence, not only in producing dreams, but in giving them a particular character. The remark has been made by medical men, that acute diseases, particularly fevers, are often preceded and indicated by disagreeable and oppressive dreams

§ 96. Explanation of the incoherency of dreams. (1st cause.)

There is frequently much of wildness, inconsistency, and contradiction in our dreams. The mind passes very rapidly from one object to another; strange and singular incidents occur. If our dreams be truly the repetition of our waking thoughts, it may well be inquired, How this wildness and inconsistency happen?

The explanation of this peculiarity resolves itself into two parts.—The FIRST ground or cause of it is, that our dreams are not subjected, like our waking thoughts, to the control and regulation of surrounding objects. While we are awake, our trains of thought are kept uniform and coherent by the influence of such objects, which continually remind us of our situation, character, and duties; and which keep in check any tendency to revery. But in sleep the senses are closed; the soul is accordingly, in a great measure, excluded from the material world, and is thus deprived of the salutary regulating influence from that source.

§ 97. Second cause of the incoherency of dreams.

In the second place, when we are asleep, our associated trains of thought are no longer under the control of the WILL. We do not mean to say that the operations of the will are suspended at such times, and that volitions have no existence. On the contrary, there is sufficient evidence of the continuance of these mental acts, in some degree at least; since volitions must have made a part of the original trains of thought which are repeated in dreaming; and furthermore, we are often as conscious of exercising or putting forth volitions when dreaming as of any other mental acts; for instance, imagining, remembering, assenting, or reasoning. When we dream that we are attacked by an enemy sword in hand, but happen, as we suppose in our dreaming experiences, to be furnished in self-defence with an instrument of the same kind, we dream that we *will* to exert it for our own safety and against our antagonist; and we as truly in this case put forth the mental exercise which we term *volition*, as, in any other, we exercise remembrance, or imagine, or reason in our sleep.

Admitting, however, that the will continues to act in sleep, it is quite evident that the volitions which are put forth by it have ceased to exercise their customary influence in respect to our mental operations. Ordinarily we are able, by means of an act of the will, to fix our attention upon some particular part of any general subject which has been suggested, or to transfer it to some other part of such subject, and thus to direct and to regulate the whole train of mental action. But the moment we are soundly asleep, this influence ceases, and hence, in connexion with the other cause already mentioned, arise the wildness, incoherency, and contradictions which exist.

A person, while he is awake, has his thoughts under such government, and is able, by the direct and indirect influence of volitions, so to regulate them as generally to bring them in the end to some conclusion, which he foresees and wishes to arrive at. But in dreaming, as all directing and governing influence, both internal and external, is at an end, our thoughts and feelings seem to be driven forward, much like a ship at sea without a rudder, wherever it may happen.

§ 98. Apparent reality of dreams. (1st cause.)

When objects are presented to us in dreams, we look upon them as real; and events, and combinations and series of events appear the same. We feel the same interest and resort to the same expedients as in the perplexities and enjoyments of real life. When persons are introduced as forming a part in the transactions of our dreams, we see them clearly in their living attitudes and stature; we converse with them, and hear them speak, and behold them move, as if actually present.

One reason of this greater vividness of our dreaming conceptions and of our firm belief in their reality seems to be this. The subjects upon which our thoughts are then employed, occupy the mind *exclusively*. We can form a clearer conception of an object with our eyes shut than we can with them open, as any one will be convinced on making the experiment; and the liveliness of the conception will increase in proportion as we can suspend the exercise of the other senses. In sound sleep, not only the sight, but the other senses also, may be said to be closed; and the attention is not continually diverted by the multitude of objects, which arrest the hearing and touch when we are awake.—It is, therefore, a most natural supposition, that our conceptions must at such times be extremely vivid and distinct. At § 64 we particularly remarked upon conceptions, or those ideas which we have of absent objects of perception, which possess this vividness of character. And it there appeared that they might be attended with a momentary belief even when we are awake But as conceptions exist in the mind when we are asleep in a much higher degree distinct and vivid, what was in the former case a momentary, becomes in the latter a permanent belief. Hence everything has the appearance of reality; and the mere thoughts of the mind are virtually transformed into persons, and varieties of situation, and events, which are regarded by us in precisely the same light as the persons, and situations, and events of our every day's experience.

§ 99. Apparent reality of dreams. (2d cause.)

A second circumstance which goes to account for the fact that our dreaming conceptions have the appearance of reality is, that they are not susceptible of being controlled, either directly or indirectly, by mere volition.—We are so formed as almost invariably to associate reality with whatever objects of perception continue to produce in us the same effects. A hard or soft body, or any substance of a particular colour, or taste, or smell, are always, when presented to our senses, followed by certain states of mind essentially the same; and we yield the most ready and firm belief in the existence of such objects. In a word, we are disposed, from our very constitution, to believe in the existence of objects of perception, the perceptions of which do not depend on the WILL, but which we find to be followed by certain states of the mind, whether we choose it or not.—But it is to be recollected that our dreaming thoughts are mere conceptions; our senses being closed and shut up, and external objects not being presented to them. This is true. But if we conclude in favour of the real existence of objects of perception, because they produce in us sensations independently of our volitions, it is but natural to suppose that we shall believe in the reality of our conceptions also whenever they are in like manner beyond our voluntary control They are both merely states of the mind; and if belief always attends our perceptions, wherever we find them to be independent of our choice, there is no reason why conceptions, which are ideas of absent objects of perception, should not be attended with a like belief under the same circumstances.—And essentially the same circumstances exist in dreaming; that is, a train of conceptions arise in the mind, and we are not conscious at such times of being able to exercise any direction or control whatever over them. They exist, whether we will or not; and we regard them as real.

§ 100. Of our estimate of time in dreaming.

Our estimate of time in dreaming differs from that when awake. Events which would take whole days or a longer time in the performance, are dreamed in a few moments. So wonderful is this compression of a multitude of transactions into the very shortest period, that, when we are accidentally awakened by the jarring of a door which is opened into the room where we are sleeping, we sometimes dream of depredations by thieves or destruction by fire in the very instant of our awaking.—"A friend of mine," says Dr. Abercrombie, "dreamed that he crossed the Atlantic, and spent a fortnight in America. In embarking on his return, he fell into the sea; and, having awoke with the fright, discovered that he had not been asleep above ten minutes." Count Lavallette, who some years since was condemned to death in France, relates a dream which occurred during his imprisonment as follows. "One night while I was asleep, the clock of the Palais de Justice struck twelve and awoke me. I heard the gate open to relieve the sentry; but I fell asleep again immediately. In this sleep I dreamed that I was standing in the Rue St. Honoré, at the corner of the Rue de l'Echelle. A melancholy darkness spread around me; all was still; nevertheless, a low and uncertain sound soon arose. All of a sudden, I perceived at the bottom of the street, and advancing towards me, a troop of cavalry, the men and horses, however, all flayed. This horrible troop continued passing in a rapid gallop, and casting frightful looks on me. Their march, I thought, continued for five hours; and they were followed by an immense number of artillery-wagons full of bleeding corpses, whose limbs still quivered; a disgusting smell of blood and bitumen almost choked me. At length, the iron gate of the prison shutting with great force, awoke me again. I made my repeater strike; it was no more than midnight, so that the horrible phantasmagoria had lasted no more than two or three minutes; that is to say, the time necessary for relieving the sentry and shutting the gate. The cold was severe and the watchword short. The next day the turnkey confirmed my calculations."

Our dreams will not unfrequently go through all the particulars of some long journey, or of some military expedition, or of a circumnavigation of the globe, or of other long and perilous undertakings, in a less number of hours than it took weeks, or months, or even years in the actual performance of them. We go from land to land, and from city to city, and into desert places; we experience transitions from joy to sorrow and from poverty to wealth; we are occupied in the scenes and transactions of many long months; and then our slumbers are scattered, and behold, they are the doings of a fleeting watch of the night!

§ 101. Explanation of the preceding statements.

This striking circumstance in the history of our dreams is generally explained by supposing that our thoughts, as they successively occupy the mind, are more rapid than while we are awake. But their rapidity is at all times very great; so much so, that, in a few moments, crowds of ideas pass through the mind which it would take a long time to utter, and a far longer time would it take to perform all the transactions which they concern. This explanation, therefore, is not satisfactory, for our thoughts are oftentimes equally rapid in our waking moments.

The true reason, we apprehend, is to be found in those preceding sections which took under examination the apparent reality of dreams. Our conceptions in dreaming are considered by us real; every thought is an action; every idea is an event; and successive states of mind are successive actions and successive events. He who in his sleep has the conception of all the particulars of a long military expedition or of a circumnavigation of the globe, seems to himself to have actually experienced all the various and multiplied fortunes of the one and the other. Hence what appears to be the real time in dreams, but is only the apparent time, will not be that which is sufficient for the mere thought, but that which is necessary for the successive actions.

"Something perfectly analogous to this may be remarked," says Mr. Stewart, "in the perceptions we obtain by the sense of sight.* When I look into a show-box where the deception is imperfect, I see only a set of paltry daubings of a few inches in diameter; but if the representation be executed with so much skill as to convey to me the idea of a distant prospect, every object before me swells in its dimensions in proportion to the extent of space which I conceive it to occupy; and what seemed before to be shut within the limits of a small wooden frame, is magnified in my apprehension to an immense landscape of woods, rivers, and mountains."

Stewart's Elements, chapter on Dreaming.

MENTAL PHILOSOPHY

DIVISION FIRST.

THE INTELLECT OR UNDERSTANDING.

INTELLECTIVE OR INTELLECTUAL STATES OF THE MIND.

PART SECOND.

INTELLECTUAL STATES OF INTERNAL ORIGIN.

CHAPTER I.

INTERNAL ORIGIN OF KNOWLEDGE.

§ 102. The soul has fountains of knowledge within.

WE have traced the history of the mind thus far with continued and increased satisfaction, because we have been guided solely by well-known facts, without any desire of exciting wonder by exaggeration, and with no other feeling than that of knowing the truth. With cautious endeavours not to trespass upon those limits which the Creator himself has set to our inquiries, we have seen the mind placed in the position of a necessary connexion with the material world through the medium of the senses, and in this way awakened into life, activity, and power. Inanimate matter seems to have been designed and appointed by Providence as the handmaid and nurse of the mind in the days of its infancy; and for that purpose to have been endued with form, fragrance, and colour. Material eyes were given to the soul, (not made a part of its nature, but assigned to it as an instrumental and auxiliary agent,) that it might see; and material hands, that it might handle; and hearing, that it might hear. By means of these and other senses we become acquainted with whatever is visible and tangible, and has outline and form; but there are also inward powers of perception, hidden fountains of knowledge, which open themselves and flow up in the remote and secret places of the soul. In other words, the soul finds knowledge in itself which neither sight, nor touch, nor hearing, nor any other sense, nor any outward forms of matter, could give.

"The natural progress of all true learning," says the author of Hermes, "is from sense to intellect." Having begun with the senses, and first considered the sensations and ideas which we there receive, we are next to enter more exclusively into the mind itself, and to explore the fruitful sources of knowledge which are internal. And in thus doing, it is a satisfaction to know that we are treading essentially in the steps of Mr. Locke, whose general doctrine undoubtedly is, that a part of our ideas only may be traced to the senses, and that the origin of others is to be sought wholly in the intellect itself.

§ 103. Declaration of Locke, that the soul has knowledge in itself.

After alluding to the senses as one great source of knowledge, "the other fountain," says Locke, "from which experience furnisheth the understanding with ideas, is the perception of the operations of our own minds within us, as it is employed about the ideas it has got; which operations, when the soul comes to reflect on and consider, do furnish the understanding with another set of ideas, which could not be had from things without, and such are perception, thinking, doubting, believing, reasoning, knowing, willing, and all the different actings of our own minds, which, we being conscious of, and observing in ourselves, do from these receive into our understandings ideas as distinct as we do from bodies affecting our senses. This source of ideas every man has wholly within himself. And though it be not sense, as having nothing to do with EXTERNAL objects, yet it is very like it, and might properly enough be called INTERNAL SENSE. But as I call the other Sensation, so I call this Reflection; the ideas it affords being such only as the mind gets by reflecting on its own operations within itself."

§ 104. The beginning of knowledge is in the senses.

In order to have a clear understanding of the particular topic before us, let us briefly advert to certain general views, already more or less attended to, having a connexion with it. In making the human soul a subject of inquiry, it is an obvious consideration that a distinction may be drawn between the soul contemplated in itself, and its acts or states, or the knowledge which it possesses. The inquiry, therefore, naturally arises, Under what circumstances the acquisition of knowledge begins?

Now this is the very question which has already been considered; nor can it be deemed necessary to repeat here the considerations which have been brought up in reference to it. It is enough to express our continued reliance on the general experience and testimony of man kind, so far as it is possible to ascertain them on a subject of so much difficulty, that the beginnings of thought and knowledge are immediately subsequent to certain affections of those bodily organs which we call the SENSES. In other words, were it not for impressions on the senses, which may be traced to objects external to them, our mental capabilities, whatever they may be, would in all probability have remained folded up, and have never been redeemed from a state of fruitless inaction.—Hence the process which is implied in the perception of external things, or what is commonly termed by Mr. Locke *sensation*, may justly be considered the OCCASION or the introductory step to all our knowledge.

§ 105. There may also be internal accessions to knowledge.

But it does not follow from this, nor is it by any means true, that the whole amount of knowledge in its ultimate progress is to be ascribed directly to an external source. All that can be said with truth is, that the mind receives the earliest part of its ideas by means of the senses, and that, in consequence of having received these elementary thoughts, all its powers become rapidly and fully operative.—And here we come to the SECOND great source of knowledge. The powers of the mind being thus fairly brought into exercise, its various operations then furnish us with another set of notions, which, by way of distinguishing them from those received through the direct mediation of the senses, may be called, in the language of Mr. Locke, ideas of reflection, or, to use a phraseology embracing all possible cases, ideas of INTERNAL ORIGIN.

These two sources of human thought, the Internal and External, however they may have been confounded by some writers, are entirely distinct. The ideas which arise in the mind, solely from the fact of the previous existence of certain mental operations, could not have been suggested by anything which takes place in the external world independently of those operations. Of this last class, some instances, with illustrations of the same, may properly be mentioned here.

§ 106. Instances of notions which have an internal origin.

Among other notions which are to be ascribed to the second great source, are those expressed by the terms THINKING, DOUBTING, BELIEVING, and CERTAINTY.—It is a matter of internal observation, (that is, of consciousness or of reflection, which are synonymous with internal observation,) that the mind does not, and cannot, for any length of time, remain inactive. Hence there is occasion given for the origin of that idea which we denominate THINKING. The notion which we thus denominate is framed by the mind under these circumstances; the name is given, and nobody is ignorant as to what is meant. But then it is to be remarked that its origin is wholly internal; it is not an object of touch, or taste, or sight; it is to be ascribed to the mind itself alone, and to its inherent activity, unaided by the senses, or by anything operating upon them.

Again, in the examination of some topic which is proposed for discussion, a proposition is stated with little or no evidence attending it, and the mind, in reference to that proposition, is brought into a position to which we give the name of *doubting*. It is by no means easy, or rather it is impossible, to trace this idea directly to the senses. All we can say of it is, that it has its origin within, and necessarily exists immediately subsequent to certain other mental states of which we are conscious.

But then, in this very instance, if the evidence be considerably increased, the mental estimation which we form is altered in regard to it, and to this new state of the mind we give the name of *belief* or *believing*. And in case the evidence of the proposition is of a higher and more decided character, there then arises another state of the mind which we denominate *certainty*.

§ 107. Other instances of ideas which have an internal origin.

The ideas of right and wrong, of unity and number, of time and space, order, proportion, similitude, truth, wisdom, power, obligation, succession, cause, effect, and many others, have a like origin; at least there are none of them to be ascribed directly and exclusively to the senses.—It is cheerfully granted that, in determining this point, it is proper to refer to the common experience of mankind, and to rely upon it. But it is believed in all these instances, (certainly in the most of them,) such a reference will be amply decisive.

Let it then be left to the candid internal examination of each individual to determine, Whether a distinction be not rightly drawn between the origin of these ideas and that of those which we attribute to the senses, such as red, blue, sweet, fragrant, bitter, hard, smooth, loud, soft, extended, &c.? On this question it is thought that, in general, there can be but one answer, although some writers, through the love of excessive simplification, have been betrayed into error in regard to it.

Hence it is distinctly to be kept in mind, that there are two sources of thought and knowledge. An affection of the senses by means of external objects is the immediate occasion of one portion; the constitution of the mind and its operations are the occasions or source of the other. Those notions which can be ascribed directly to any one of the senses as their specific source, and not merely as an indirect and general occasion of their origin, are External, while all others seem to be entitled to be called Internal.

CHAPTER II

ORIGINAL SUGGESTION, OR THE INTUITIONAL POWER.

§ 108. Import of suggestion, and its application in Reid and Stewart.

Some of the cases of thought and knowledge which the mind becomes possessed of in itself, without the direct aid of the senses, are to be ascribed to Suggestion. This word, in its application here, is used merely to express a simple but important fact, viz., that the mind, by its own activity and vigour, gives rise to certain thoughts. Without any mixture of hypothesis, or any qualifying intimation whatever, it gives the fact, and that is all. The use of this word, as applicable to the origin of a portion of human knowledge, is distinctly proposed by Dr. Reid

In his Inquiry into the Human Mind, (ch. ii., § vii.,) he speaks of certain notions (for instance, those of existence, mind, person, &c.) as the "judgments of nature, judgments not got by comparing ideas, and perceiving agreements and disagreements, but immediately inspired by our constitution." Pursuing this train of thought, he ascribes those notions which cannot be attributed directly to the senses on the one hand, nor to the reasoning power on the other, to an internal or mental Suggestion, as follows.—"I beg leave to make use of the word SUGGESTION, because I know not one more proper, to express a power of the mind which seems entirely to have escaped the notice of philosophers, and to which we owe many of our simple notions."

Mr. Stewart also, in his Philosophical Essays, speaks of certain mental phenomena as attendant upon the objects of our consciousness, and as SUGGESTED by them. The notions of time, number, motion, memory, sameness, personal identity, present existence, &c., he ascribes neither to the external world on the one hand, nor the internal mental operations, of which we are conscious, on the other; except so far as they are the *occasions* on which the mind brings them out, or SUGGESTS them from its own inherent energy. Of the notion of DURATION, for instance, he would say, I do not see it, nor hear it, nor feel it, nor become acquainted with it by means of any other of the senses; nor am I conscious of it, as I am of believing, reasoning, imagining, &c., but it is SUGGESTED by the mind itself; it is an intimation absolutely essential to the mind's nature and action.

§ 109. Ideas of existence, mind, self-existence, and personal identity.

We shall now mention a few ideas which have this origin, without undertaking to give a complete enumeration of them. (I.) EXISTENCE. Among the various notions, the origin of which naturally requires to be considered under the head of Suggestion, is that of Existence. What existence is in itself, (that is to say, independently of any existent being,) it would be useless to inquire. Using the word as expressive of a mental state, it is the name of a purely simple idea, and cannot be defined. The history of its rise is briefly this. Such is our nature that we cannot exist, without having the notion of existence. So that the origin of the idea of existence is inseparable from the mere fact, that we have a percipient and sentient nature. An insentient being may exist without having any such idea. But man, being constituted with powers of perception, cannot help perceiving that he is what he is. If we think, then there is something which has this capability of thought; if we feel, then there is not only the mere act of feeling, but something also which puts forth the act.

(II.) MIND. The origin of the notion of Mind is similar to that of existence. Neither of them can be strictly and properly referred to the senses. We do not see the mind, nor is it an object of touch, or of taste, or of any other sense. Nor, on the other hand, is the notion of mind a direct object of the memory, or of reasoning, or of imagination. The notion arises naturally, or is SUGGESTED from the mere fact that the mind actually exists, and is susceptible of various feelings and operations. —The same may be said of all the distinct powers of the mind, such as the power of perception, of memory, of association, of imagination, of the will; not of the *acts* or *exercises* of these powers, it will be noticed, but of the powers themselves. That is to say, they are made known to us, considered abstractly and as distinct subjects of thought, not by *direct* perception, either inward or outward, but by spontaneity or suggestion. We say, not by *direct* perception, because there is something intermediate between the power and the knowledge of it, viz., the act or exercise of the power, which is the *occasion* of the knowledge of the power itself. The principle of Original Suggestion, availing itself of this occasion, gives us a knowledge of the distinct susceptibilities of the mind, just as it does of the mind as a whole.

(III.) Similar remarks, as far as spontaneity is concerned, will apply to the notions (whether we consider them as simple or complex) of SELF-EXISTENCE and PERSONAL IDENTITY. At the very earliest period they flow out, as it were, from the mind itself; not resulting from any prolonged and laborious process, but freely and spontaneously suggested by it. This is so true, that no one is able to designate either the precise time or the precise circumstances under which they originate; for they spring into being under all circumstances. We cannot look, or touch, or breathe, or move, or think without them. These are products of our mental nature too essential and important to be withheld, or to be given only on rare and doubtful occasions; but are brought into existence in all times and places, and under all the varieties of action and feeling.

§ 110. Of the nature of unity, and the origin of that notion.

Another important notion, properly entitled to a consideration here, is that of UNITY. We shall decline attempting to explain the nature of unity, for the simple reason that nothing is more easy to be understood; every child knows what is meant by *One*. And how can we explain it, if we would? We can explain a hundred by resolving it into parts; we can explain fifty or a score by making a like separation of the whole number into the subordinate portions of which it is made up; but when we arrive at unity, we must stop, and can go no further.

It is true, attempts have been made to define it; but, like many other such attempts, they have proved futile. Unity has been called *a thing indivisible in itself, and divided from everything else.* But this makes us no wiser. Is it anything more than to say that the unity of an object is its indivisibility? Or, in other words, that its unity is its unity?

As the idea of unity is one of the simplest, so it is one of the earliest notions which men have. It originates in the same way, and very nearly at the same time, with the notions of existence, self-existence, personal identity, and the like. When a man has a notion of himself, he evidently does not think of himself as two, three, or a dozen men, but as *one*. As soon as he is able to think of himself as distinct from his neighbour, as soon as he is in no danger of mingling and confounding his own identity with that of the multitude around him, so soon does he form the notion of unity. It exists as distinct in his mind as the idea of his own existence does; and arises there immediately successive to that idea, because it is impossible, in the nature of things, that he should have a notion of himself as a twofold or divided person.

Unity is the fundamental element of all enumeration. By the repetition or adding of this element, we are able to form numbers to any extent. These numbers may be combined among themselves, and employed merely as expressive of mutual relations, or we may apply them, if we choose, to all external objects whatever, to which we are able to give a common name.

§ 111. Nature of succession, and origin of the idea of succession.

Another of those conceptions which naturally offer themselves to our notice here, is that of SUCCESSION. This term (when we inquire what succession is in itself) is one of general application, expressive of a mode of existence rather than of existence itself; and in its application to mind in particular, expressive of a condition of the mind's action, but not of the action itself, which that condition regulates. It is certainly a fact too well known to require comment, that our minds exist at different periods in successive states; that our thoughts and feelings, in obedience to a permanent law, follow each other in a train. This is the simple fact. And the fact of such succession, whenever it takes place, forms the occasion on which the notion or idea of succession is SUGGESTED to the mind. Being a simple mental state, it is not susceptible of definition; yet every man possesses it, and every one is rightly supposed to understand its nature.

Accordingly, it is not necessary to refer the origin of this idea to anything external. It is certain, that the sense of smell cannot directly give us the idea of succession, nor the sense of taste, nor of touch. And we well know that the deaf and dumb possess it not less than others. The blind also, who have never seen the face of heaven, nor beheld that sun and moon which measure out for us days, and months, and years, have the notion of succession. They feel, they think, they reason, at least in some small degree, like other men; and it is impossible that they should be without it. The origin, therefore, of this notion is within; it is the unfailing result of the inward operation to call it forth, however true it may be, that it is subsequently applied to outward objects and events.

§ 112. Origin of the notion of duration.

There is usually understood to be a distinction between the idea of succession and that of duration, though neither can be defined. The idea of succession is supposed to be antecedent in point of time to that of duration (we speak now of succession and duration relatively to our conception of them, and not in themselves considered.) Duration must be supposed to exist antecedently to succession in the order of nature; but succession is the form in which it is made to apply to men; and is, therefore, naturally the occasion on which the idea of it arises in men's minds. Having the notion of succession, and that of personal or self-existence, a foundation is laid for the additional conception of permanency or duration; in other words, it naturally arises in the mind, or is suggested under these circumstances.

As we cannot, according to this view of its origin, have the notion of duration without succession, hence it happens that we know nothing of duration when we are perfectly asleep, because we are not then conscious of those intellectual changes which are involved in succession. If a person could sleep with a perfect suspension of all his mental operations from this time until the resurrection, the whole of that period would appear to him as nothing. Ten thousand years passed under such circumstances would be less than a few days, or even hours.

§ 113. Illustrations of the nature of duration.

That the notion of succession (we do not say succession itself, but only our *notion* or *idea* of it) is antecedent to, and is essential to that of duration, is in some measure proved by various facts. There are on record a number of cases of remarkable somnolency, in which persons have slept for weeks and even months. One of the most striking is that of Samuel Chilton, a labourer of Tinsbury, near Bath in England. On one occasion, in the year 1696, he slept from the ninth of April to the seventh of August, about seventeen weeks, being kept alive by small quantities of wine poured down his throat. He then awoke, dressed himself, and walked about the room, "being perfectly unconscious that he had slept more than one night. Nothing, indeed, could make him believe that he had slept so long, till, upon going to the fields, he saw crops of barley and oats ready for the sickle, which he remembered were only sown when he last visited them."—In the proceedings of the French Royal Academy of Sciences in 1719, there is also a statement, illustrative of the subject under consideration, to the following effect. There was in Lausanne a nobleman, who, as he was giving orders to a servant, suddenly lost his speech and all his senses.—Different remedies were tried, but, for a very considerable time, without effect. For six months he appeared to be in a deep sleep, unconscious of everything. At the end of that period, however, resort having been had to certain surgical operations, he was suddenly restored to his speech and the exercise of his understanding. When he recovered, the servant to whom he had been giving orders happening to be in the room, he asked him if he had done what he had ordered him to do, not being sensible that any interval, except perhaps a very short one, had elapsed during his illness.

§ 114. *Of time and its measurements, and of eternity.*

When duration is estimated or measured, then we call it Time. Such measurements, as every one is aware, are made by means of certain natural or artificial motions. The annual revolution of the sun (using language in accordance with the common apprehensions on the subject) marks off the portion of duration which we call a YEAR; the revolution of the moon marks off another portion, which we call a MONTH; the diurnal revolution of the sun gives us the period of a DAY; the movements of the hands over the face of a clock or watch give the diminished durations of hours and minutes. This is TIME, which differs from duration only in the circumstance of its being measured.

What we call Eternity is only a modified or imperfect time, or, rather, time not completed. We look back over the months, and days, and years of our former existence; we look forward and onward, and behold ages crowding on ages, and time springing from time. And in this way we are forcibly led to think of time unfinished, of time progressive but never completed; and to this complex notion we give the name of Eternity

§ 115. The idea of space not of external origin.

Another of those notions, the origin of which we propose to consider under the head of Suggestion, is the idea of SPACE.—If this idea were of external origin, if it could properly be said to come into the mind by the way of sensation, we should be able to make such a reference of it. But let us inquire. It will evidently not be pretended that the notion of space is to be ascribed to the senses of taste, of smell, or of hearing. And can it be ascribed to the sense of touch? Is it a matter of feeling? A single consideration will suggest a satisfactory answer. It will certainly be acknowledged, that we can have no knowledge, by the sense of touch, (with the single exception, perhaps, of the sensations of heat and cold which are commonly ascribed to it,) of anything which does not present some resistance. The degree of resistance may greatly vary, but there will always be some. But no one will undertake to say that resistance is a quality of space, or enters in any way into his notion of it.

Nor are there less obvious objections to regarding it as a direct object of sight. The sense of sight gives us no direct knowledge of anything but colours; all other visual perceptions are original in the sense of touch, and are made the property of the sight by transference. No one certainly ever speaks of space as red or white, or of any other colour, or conceives of it as such.

There is another consideration, adverse to ascribing the idea of space to the senses, applicable equally to the sight and the touch. Everything coming within the cognizance of those two senses, (with the exception already alluded to,) has form, limits, bounds, place, &c. But the idea to which we are now attending is utterly exclusive of everything of this nature; it is not susceptible of circumscription and figure. So far from it, when we escape beyond the succession of circumscribed and insulated objects, we have but just entered within its empire. If we let the mind range forth beyond the forms immediately surrounding us, beyond the world itself, beyond all the systems of worlds in the universe; if we stand in our conception on the verge of the remotest star, and look downward and upward, it is then the idea of space rushes upon the mind with a power before unknown.—These considerations clearly lead to the conclusion, that the notion of space is not susceptible of being ascribed directly to sensation in any of its forms, and is not, in the proper sense of the terms, of external origin.

§ 116. The idea of space has its origin in suggestion.

What, then, shall we say of the origin of the notion of space? When pressed on this point we have but one answer to give; it is the natural offspring of the mind; it is a creation of the soul, wholly inseparable from its elementary constitution and action; an intimation coming from an interior and original impulse.—It remains to be added, that, while we cannot directly refer the notion in question to the senses, but must ascribe its origin to the suggestive principle, we cannot even state with certainty any particular occasion on which it arises, for we have the notion at a period further back than we can remember. On this point, however, it is undoubtedly true, that we may advance opinions more or less probable. It is, for instance, a supposition not altogether worthless, that motion may have been the original occasion of the rise of this idea. At an early period we moved the hand, either to grasp something removed at a little distance, or in the mere playful exercise of the muscles, or perhaps we transferred the whole body from one position to another; and it is at least no impossibility, that on such an occasion the idea of space may have been called forth in the soul.

But there is another supposition still more entitled to notice. Our acquaintance with external bodies, by means of the senses, may have been the *occasion* of its rise, although the senses themselves are not its direct source. It is certain that we cannot contemplate any body whatever, an apple, a rose, a tree, a house, without always finding the idea of space a ready and necessary concomitant. We cannot conceive of a body which is *nowhere*. So that we may at least date the origin of the idea of space as early as our acquaintance with any external body whatever. In other words, it is a gift of the mind, made simultaneously with its earliest external perceptions.

§ 117. Of the origin of the idea of power.

Under the head of Suggestion the idea of POWER properly belongs. Every man has this notion; every one feels, too, that there is a corresponding reality; in other words, power is not only a mere subject of thought, but has, in some important sense, a real existence. And we may add, that every one knows, although there is somewhere a great original fountain of power, independent of all created beings, that he has a portion (small indeed it may be, but yet a portion) of the element of power in his own mind and in his own person. There is indeed a Power, unexplored and invisible, which has reared the mountains, which rolls the ocean, and which propels the sun in his course; but it is nevertheless true, that man, humble as he is in the scale of rational and accountable beings, possesses, as an attribute of his own nature, an amount of real efficiency, suited to the limited sphere which Providence has allotted him. This is a simple statement of the fact. Power goes hand in hand with existence, intelligence, and accountability. There is no existence, either intelligent or unintelligent, without power, either in the thing itself, or in something else which sustains it. There is no *accountable* existence without power, existing in and participating in such existence, and constituting the basis of its accountability.

§ 118. Occasions of the origin of the idea of power.

But the principal question here is, not what power is in itself, nor whether man possesses power in fact, but under what circumstances the notion or idea of power arises in the human mind. The occasions of the origin of this idea, so far as we are able to judge, appear to be threefold —(1.) All cases of antecedence and sequence in the natural world. We are so constituted, that, in connexion with such cases of antecedence and sequence, we are led at a very early period of life to frame the proposition and to receive it as an undeniable truth, that there can be no beginning or change of existence without a cause. This proposition involves the idea of efficiency or power.—(2.) The control of the will over the muscular action. We are so constituted, that, whenever we will to put a part of the body in motion, and the motion follows the volition, we have the idea of power.—(3.) The control of the will over the other mental powers. Within certain limits and to a certain extent, there seems to be ground for supposing that the will is capable of exercising a directing control over the mental as well as over the bodily powers. And whenever we are conscious of such control being exercised, whether it be greater or less, occasion is furnished for the origin of this idea. It is then called forth or SUGGESTED. It is not seen by the material eye, nor reached by the sense of touch; but, emerging of itself from the mind, like a star from the depths of the firmament, it reveals itself distinctly and brightly to the intellectual vision.

§ 119. Of the ideas of right and wrong.

Right and Wrong also are conceptions of the pure Understanding; that is, of the Understanding operating in virtue of its own interior nature, and not as dependent on the senses. We are constituted intellectually in such a manner, that, whenever occasions of actual right or wrong occur, whenever objects fitted to excite a moral approval or disapproval are presented to our notice, the ideas of RIGHT and WRONG naturally and necessarily arise within us. In respect to these ideas or *intellections*, (if we choose to employ an expressive term partially fallen into disuse,) Cudworth, Stewart, Cousin, and other writers of acknowledged discernment and weight, appear to agree in placing the origin of them here. And this arrangement of them is understood to be important in connexion with the theory of Morals. If these ideas originate in the pure intellect, and are simple, as they obviously are, then each of them necessarily has its distinctive nature, each of them is an entity by itself; and it is impossible to conceive of them as identical or interchangeable with each other. They are as truly unlike as our conceptions of *unity* and *time*, or of *space* and *power*. And if this is true of our *ideas* of right and wrong, it is not less so of right and wrong themselves. In other words, right can never become wrong, nor wrong right; they are placed for ever apart, each occupying its own sphere; and thus we have a foundation laid for the important doctrine of the immutability of moral distinctions.—"The distinction between right and wrong," says Cousin, (Psychology, ch. v.,) "may be incorrectly applied, may vary in regard to particular objects, and may become clearer and more correct in time, without ceasing to be with all men the same thing at the bottom. It is a universal conception of Reason, and hence it is found in all languages, those products and faithful images of the mind.—Not only is this distinction universal, but it is a necessary conception. In vain does the reason, after having once received, attempt to deny it, or call in question its truth. It cannot. One cannot at will regard the same action as just and unjust. These two ideas baffle every attempt to commute them, the one for the other. Their objects may change, but never their nature."

§ 120. Origin of the ideas of moral merit and demerit.

Closely connected with the ideas of right and wrong are the ideas of moral MERIT and DEMERIT. In the order of nature, (what is sometimes called the *logical* order,) the ideas of right and wrong come first. Without possessing the antecedent notions of right and wrong, it would be impossible for us to frame the ideas of moral merit and demerit. For what merit can we possibly attach to him in whom we discover no rectitude? or what demerit in him in whom we discover no want of it? Merit always implies virtue as its antecedent and necessary condition, while demerit as certainly implies the want of it, or vice. Although the ideas of merit and demerit, in consequence of being simple, are undefinable, there can be no doubt of their existence, and of their being entirely clear to our mental perception; and that they furnish a well-founded and satisfactory basis for many of our judgments in respect to the moral character and conduct of mankind.

§ 121. Of other elements of knowledge developed in suggestion.

In giving an account of the ideas from this source, we have preferred as designative of their origin the term SUGGESTION, proposed and employed by Reid and Stewart, to the word REASON, proposed by Kant, and adopted by Cousin and some other writers, as, on the whole, more conformable to the prevalent usage of the English language. In common parlance, and by the established usage of the language, the word REASON is expressive of the deductive rather than of the suggestive faculty; and if we annul or perplex the present use of that word by a novel application of it, we must introduce a new word to express the process of deduction. Whether we are correct in this or not, we shall probably find no disagreement or opposition in asserting, not only the existence, but the great importance of the intellectual capability which we have been considering. The thing, and the nature of the thing, is undoubtedly of more consequence than the mere name.

In leaving this interesting topic, we would not be understood to intimate that the notions of existence, mind, personal identity, unity, succession, duration, power, and the others which have been mentioned, are all which Suggestion furnishes. It might not be easy to make a complete enumeration; but, in giving an account of the genesis of human knowledge, we may probably ascribe the ideas of truth, freedom, design or intelligence, necessity, fitness or congruity, reality, order, plurality, totality, immensity, possibility, infinity, happiness, reward, punishment, and perhaps many others, to this source.

§ 122. Suggestion a source of principles as well as of ideas.

One more remark remains to be made. Original Suggestion is not only the source of ideas, (and particularly of ideas fundamental and unalterable,) but also of *principles*. The reasoning faculty, which in its nature is essentially comparative and deductive, must have something to rest upon back of itself, and of still higher authority than itself, with which, as a first link in the chain, the process of deduction begins. It is the suggestive intellect which is the basis of the action of the comparative and deductive intellect. Of those elementary or transcendental propositions which are generally acknowledged to be prerequisites and conditions of the exercise of the deductive faculty, there are some particularly worthy of notice, such as the following.—There is no beginning or change of existence without a cause.—Matter and mind have uniform and permanent laws.—Every quality supposes a subject, a real existence, of which it is a quality.—Means, conspiring together to produce a certain end, imply intelligence.

CHAPTER III.

CONSCIOUSNESS.

§ 123. Consciousness the 2d source of internal knowledge; its nature.

THE second source of that knowledge which, in distinction from sensations and external perceptions, is denominated Internal, is CONSCIOUSNESS. By the common usage of the language, the term Consciousness is appropriated to express the way or method in which we obtain the knowledge of those objects which belong to the mind itself, and which do not, and cannot exist independently of some mind. Imagining and reasoning are terms expressive of real objects of thought; but evidently they cannot be supposed to exist, independently of some mind which imagines and reasons. Hence every instance of consciousness may be regarded as embracing in itself the three following distinct notions at least; viz., (1.) The idea of self or of personal existence, which we possess, not by direct consciousness, but by suggestion, expressed in English by the words SELF, MYSELF, and the personal pronoun I; (2.) Some quality, state, or operation of the mind, whatever it may be; and (3.) A relative perception of possession, appropriation, or belonging to. For instance, a person says, I AM CONSCIOUS OF LOVE, OR OF ANGER, OR OF PENITENCE. Here the idea of SELF, or of personal existence, is expressed by the pronoun I; there is a different mental state, and expressed by its appropriate term, that of the affection of ANGER, &c.; the phrase, CONSCIOUS OF, expresses the feeling of relation, which instantaneously and necessarily recognises the passion of anger as the attribute or property of the subject of the proposition. And in this case, as in all others where we apply the term under consideration, consciousness does not properly extend to anything which has an existence extraneous to the conscious object or soul itself.

§ 124. Further remarks on the proper objects of consciousness.

As there are some things to which Consciousness, as the term is usually employed, relates, and others to which it does not, it is proper to consider it in this respect more fully.—(1.) As to those thoughts which may have arisen, or those emotions which may have agitated us in times past, we cannot with propriety be said to be conscious of them at the present moment, although we may be conscious of that present state of mind which we term the *recollection* of them.—(2.) Again, Consciousness has no direct connexion with such objects, whether material or immaterial, as exist at the present time, but are external to the mind, or, in other words, have an existence independent of it.

For instance, we are not, strictly speaking, conscious of any material existence whatever; of the earth which we tread, of the food which nourishes us, of the clothes that protect, or of anything else of the like nature with which we are conversant; but are conscious merely of the effects they produce within us, of the sensations of taste, of heat and cold, of resistance and extension, of hardness and softness, and the like.

(3.) This view holds also in respect to immaterial things, even the mind itself. We are not directly conscious, using the term in the manner which has been explained, of the existence even of our own mind, but merely of its qualities and operations, and of that firm belief or knowledge of its existence, necessarily attendant on those operations.

§ 125. Consciousness a ground or law of belief.

Consciousness, it may be remarked here, is to be regarded as a ground or law of belief; and the belief attendant on the exercise of it, like that which accompanies the exercise of Original Suggestion, is of the highest kind. It appears to be utterly out of our power to avoid believing, beyond a doubt, that the mind experiences certain sensations, or has certain thoughts, or puts forth particular intellectual operations, whenever, in point of fact, that is the case. We may be asked for the reason of this belief, but we have none to give, except that it is the result of an ultimate and controlling principle of our nature; and hence that nothing can ever prevent the convictions resulting from this source, and nothing can divest us of them.

Nor has the history of the human mind made known any instances that have even the appearance of being at variance with this view, except a few cases of undoubted insanity. A man may reason against Consciousness as a ground and law of belief, either for the sake of amusing himself or perplexing others; but when he not only reasons against it as such, but seriously and sincerely rejects it, it becomes quite another concern; and such a one has, by common consent, broken loose from the authority of his nature, and is truly and emphatically beside himself. It will be impossible to find a resting-place where such a mind can fix itself and repose; the best established truths, and the wildest and most extravagant notions, will stand nearly an equal chance of being either rejected or received; fancy and fact will be confounded and mingled together, and the whole mind will exhibit a scene of chaotic and irretrievable confusion.

§ 126. Instances of knowledge developed in consciousness.

It would be no easy task to point out the numerous states of mind, the ideas, and emotions, and desires, and volitions, which come within the range and cognizance of Consciousness; nor is there any special reason, connected with any object we have in view at present, why such a full enumeration should be attempted. A few instances will suffice to show how fruitful a source of experience and of knowledge this is.

(I.) All the various degrees of belief are matters of Consciousness. We are so constituted that the mind necessarily yields its assent in a greater or less degree when evidence is presented. These degrees of assent are exceedingly various and multiplied, although only a few of them are expressed by select and appropriate names; nor does it appear to be necessary for the ends of society, or for any other purpose, that it should be otherwise. Some of them are as follows: doubting, assenting, presumption, believing, disbelieving, probability, certainty, &c.

(II.) The names of all other intellectual acts and operations (not the names of the intellectual Powers, which, like the mind itself, are made known to us by Suggestion, and are expressed by a different class of terms, but simply of *acts* and *operations*) are expressive of the subjects of our Consciousness. Among others, the terms perceiving, thinking, attending, conceiving, remembering, comparing, judging, abstracting, reasoning, imagining.

(III.) Consciousness, considered as a source of knowledge, includes likewise all our emotions and desires, (everything, in fact, which really and directly comes within the range of the SENSITIVE or SENTIENT part of our nature,) as the emotions of the beautiful, the grand, the sublime, the ludicrous; the feelings of pleasure, and pain, and aversion, of hope and joy, of despondency and sadness, and a multitude of others.

(IV.) Here also originates our acquaintance with the complex emotions or passions. A man bestows a benefit upon us, and we are conscious of a new complex feeling which we call GRATITUDE. Another person does us an injury; and we are conscious of another and distinct feeling, which we call ANGER. In other words, we feel, we know that the passion exists, and that it belongs to ourselves; and it is the same of jealousy, hatred, revenge, friendship, sympathy, the filial and parental affections, love, &c.

(V.) All the moral and religious emotions and affections, regarded as subjects of internal knowledge, belong here; such as approval, disapproval, remorse, humility, repentance, religious faith, forgiveness, benevolence, the sense of dependence, adoration.—When we consider that the mind is constantly in action; that, in all our intercourse with our fellow-beings, friends, family, countrymen, and enemies, new and exceedingly diversified feelings are called forth; that every new scene in nature, and every new combination of events, have their appropriate results in the mind, it will be readily conjectured that this enumeration might be carried to a much greater extent. What has been said will serve to indicate some of the prominent sources for self-inquiry on this subject.

CHAPTER IV.

RELATIVE SUGGESTION OR JUDGMENT.

§ 127. Of the susceptibility of perceiving or feeling relations.

It is not inconsistent with the usage of our language to say, that the mind brings its thoughts together, and places them side by side, and compares them. Such are nearly the expressions of Mr. Locke, who speaks of the mind's bringing one thing *to* and setting it *by* another, and carrying its view from one to the other. And such is the imperfect nature of all arbitrary signs, that this phraseology will probably continue to be employed, although without some attention it will be likely to lead into error. Such expressions are evidently of material origin, and cannot be rightly interpreted in their application to the mind, without taking that circumstance into consideration. When it is said that our thoughts are brought together; that they are placed side by side, and the like, probably nothing more can be meant than this, that they are immediately successive to each other. And when it is further said that we compare them, the meaning is, that we perceive or feel their relation to each other in certain respects.

The mind, therefore, has an original susceptibility or power corresponding to this result; in other words, by which this result is brought about; which is sometimes known as its power of RELATIVE SUGGESTION, and at other times the same thing is expressed by the term JUDGMENT, although the latter term is sometimes employed with other shades of meaning.—"With the susceptibility of Relative Suggestion," says Dr. Brown, Lect. 51, "the faculty of *judgment*, as that term is commonly employed, may be considered as nearly synonymous; and I have accordingly used it as synonymous in treating of the different relations that have come under our review."

We arrive here, therefore, at an ultimate fact in our mental nature; in other words, we reach a principle so thoroughly elementary, that it cannot be resolved into any other. The human intellect is so made, so constituted, that, when it perceives different objects together, or has immediately successive conceptions of any absent objects of perception, their mutual relations are immediately felt by it. It considers them as equal or unequal, like or unlike, as being the same or different in respect to place and time, as having the same or different causes and ends, and in various other respects.

§ 128. Occasions on which feelings of relation may arise.

The occasions on which feelings of relation may arise are almost innumerable. It would certainly be no easy task to specify them all. Any of the ideas which the mind is able to frame, may, either directly or indirectly, lay the foundation of other ideas of relation, since they may, in general, be compared together; or if they cannot themselves be readily placed side by side, may be made the means of bringing others into comparison. But those ideas which are of an external origin are representative of objects and their qualities; and hence we may speak of the relations of things no less than of the relations of thought. And such relations are everywhere discoverable.

We behold the flowers of the field, and one is fairer than another; we hear many voices, and one is louder or softer than another; we taste the fruits of the earth, and one flavour is more pleasant than another. But these differences of sound, and brightness, and taste, could never be known to us without the power of perceiving relations. —Again, we see a fellow-being; and as we make him the subject of our thoughts, we at first think of him only as a man. But then he may, at the same time, be a father, a brother, a son, a citizen, a legislator; these terms express ideas of relation.

§ 129. Of the use of correlative terms.

Correlative terms are such terms as are used to express corresponding ideas of relation. They suggest the relations with great readiness, and, by means of them, the mind can be more steadily, and longer, and with less pain, fixed upon the ideas of which they are expressive. The words father and son, legislator and constituent, brother and sister, husband and wife, and others of this class, as soon as they are named, at once carry our thoughts beyond the persons who are the subjects of these relations to the relations themselves. Wherever, therefore, there are correlative terms, the relations may be expected to be clear to the mind.

§ 130. Of relations of identity and diversity.

The number of relations is very great; so much so, that it is found difficult to reduce them to classes; and probably no classification of them which has been hitherto proposed, exhausts them in their full extent. The most of those which it will be necessary to notice may be brought into the seven classes of relations of IDENTITY and DIVERSITY, of DEGREE, of PROPORTION, of PLACE, of TIME, of POSSESSION, and of CAUSE and EFFECT.

The first class of ideas of relation which we shall proceed to consider, are those of IDENTITY and DIVERSITY.—Such is the nature of our minds, that no two objects can be placed before us essentially unlike, without our having a perception of this difference. When, on the other hand, there is an actual sameness in the objects contemplated by us, the mind perceives or is sensible of their identity It is not meant by this that we are never liable to mistake; that the mind never confounds what is different, nor separates what is the same; our object here is merely to state the general fact.

Two pieces of paper, for instance, are placed before us, the one white and the other red; and we at once perceive, without the delay of resorting to other objects and bringing them into comparison, that the colours are not the same. We immediately and necessarily perceive a difference between a square and a circle, between a triangle and a parallelogram, between the river and the rude cliff that overhangs it, the flower and the turf from which it springs, the house and the neighbouring hill, the horse and his rider.

Whatever may be the appearance of this elementary perception at first sight, it is undoubtedly one of great practical importance. It has its place in all forms of réasoning, as the train of argument proceeds from step to step; and in Demonstrative reasoning in particular, it is evident, that without it we should be unable to combine together the plainest propositions.

§ 131. (II.) Relations of degree, and names expressive of them.

Another class of those intellectual perceptions which are to be ascribed to the Judgment, or what we term more explicitly the power of RELATIVE SUGGESTION, may properly enough be named perceptions of relations of Degree. Such perceptions of relation are found to exist in respect to all such objects as are capable of being considered as composed of parts, and as susceptible, in some respects, of different degrees.—We look, for instance, at two men; they are both tall; but we at once perceive and assert that one is taller than the other. We taste two apples; they are both sweet; but we say that one is sweeter than another. That is to say, we discover, in addition to the mere perception of the man and the apple, a relation, a difference in the objects in certain respects.

There are terms in all languages employed in the expression of such relations. In English a reference to the particular relation is often combined in the same term which expresses the quality. All the words of the comparative and superlative degrees, formed by merely altering the termination of the positive, are of this description, as whiter, sweeter, wiser, larger, smaller, nobler, kinder, truest, falsest, holiest, and a multitude of others. In other cases, (and probably the greater number,) the epithet expressive of the quality is combined with the adverbs *more* and *most, less* and *least.* But certainly we should not use such terms if we were not possessed of the power of relative suggestion. We should ever be unable to say of one apple that it is sweeter than another, or of one man that he is taller than another, without considering them in certain definite respects, and without perceiving certain relations. So that, if we had no knowledge of any other than relations of Degree, we should abundantly see the importance of the mental susceptibility under review, considered as a source of words and of grammatical forms in language.

§ 132. (III.) Of relations of proportion.

Among other relations which are discovered to us by the power of judgment or relative suggestion, are those of PROPORTION; a class of relations which are peculiar in this, that they are felt only on the presence of three or more objects of thought. They are discoverable particularly in the comparison of numbers, as no one proceeds far in numerical combinations without a knowledge of them. On examining the numbers two, three, four, twenty, twenty-seven, thirty-two, nine, five, eight, and sixteen, we feel certain relations existing among them; they assume a new aspect, a new power in the mental view. We perceive (and we can *assert,* in reference to that perception) that three is to nine as nine to twenty-seven; that two is to eight as eight to thirty-two; that four is to five as sixteen to twenty, &c.

And when we have once felt or perceived such relation actually existing between any one number and others, we ever afterward regard it as a property inseparable from that number, although the property had remained unknown to us until we had compared it with others. We attach to numbers, under such circumstances, a new attribute, a new power, the same as we do, under similar circumstances, to all the other subjects of our knowledge. There are many properties, for instance, of external bodies, which were not known to us at first, but, as soon as they are discovered, they are, of course, embraced in the general notion which we form of such bodies, and are considered as making a part of it. And pursuing the same course in respect to numbers, if, on comparing them with each other, we perceive certain relations never discovered before, the circumstance of their sustaining those relations ever afterward enters into our conception of them

§ 133. (IV.) Of relations of place or position.

Other feelings or perceptions of relation arise when we contemplate the place or position of objects. Our minds are so constituted, that such perceptions are the necessary results of our contemplations of the outward objects by which we are surrounded. Perhaps we are asked, What we mean by position or place? Without professing to give a confident answer, since it is undoubtedly difficult, by any mere form of words, fully to explain it, we have good grounds for saying that we cannot conceive of any body as having place, without comparing it with some other bodies. If, therefore, having two bodies fixed, or which maintain the same relative position, we can compare a third body with them, the third body can then be said to have place or position.

This may be illustrated by the chessmen placed on the chessboard. We say the men are in the same place, although the board may have been removed from one room to another. We use this language, because we consider the men only in relation to each other and the parts of the board, and not in relation to the room or parts of the room.—Again, a portrait is suspended in the cabin of a ship; the captain points to it, and says to a bystander, that it has been precisely in the same place this seven years. Whereas, in point of fact, it has passed from Europe to Africa, from Africa to America, and perhaps round the whole world. Still the speaker uttered no falsehood, because he spoke of the portrait, (and was so understood to speak of it,) in relation to the ship, and particularly the cabin; and not in relation to the parts of the world which the ship had visited.—Such instances show that place is relative.

Hence we may clearly have an idea of the place or position of all the different parts of the universe, considered separately, because they may be compared with other parts; although we are unable to form any idea of the place or position of the universe considered as a whole, because we have then no other body with which we can compare it. If it were possible for us to know all worlds and things at once, to comprehend the universe with a glance, we could not assert, with all our knowledge of it, that it is here, or there, or yonder, or tell where it would be.

But if place express a relative notion, then it follows that all words which involve or imply the place or position of an object are of a similar character. Such are the words high and low, superior and inferior, (when used in respect to the position of objects,) near and distant, above and beneath, further, nearer, hither, yonder, here, there, where, beyond, within, around, without, and the like.

§ 134. (V.) Of relations of time.

Another source of relative perceptions or judgments is TIME. Time holds nearly the same relation to duration as position does to space. The position or place of objects is but space marked out and limited; time, in like manner, is duration set off into distinct periods; and as our notions of the place of bodies are relative, so also are our conceptions of events considered as happening in time. It is true, that the notions of duration and space are in themselves original and absolute; they are made known to us by Original rather than by Relative Suggestion; but when they are in any way limited, and events are thereby contemplated in reference to them under the new forms of place and time, certain new conceptions arise which are relative.

All time is contemplated under the aspect of past, present, or future. We are able, chiefly in consequence of the revolutions of the heavenly bodies, to form a distinct notion of portions of time, a day, a month, a year, &c.; we can contemplate events, not only as existing at present, but as future or past. But always when we think or speak of events in time, (in other words, when we speak of the *date* of events,) there is a comparison and a perception of relation.

What, therefore, is the import of our language when we say, the independence of the North American colonies was declared July fourth, 1776.—The meaning of these expressions may be thus illustrated. We assume the present year, 1838, as a given period, and reckon back to the year *one*, which coincides with the birth of our Saviour; then the year 1776 expresses the distance between these two extremes, viz., one, and eighteen hundred thirty-eight. This seems to be all we learn when we say, the Independence of the United States was declared at the period above mentioned.—Again, we obviously mean the same thing, and convey the same idea, whether we say that the Saviour was born in the year ONE of the Christian era, or in the year 4004 from the creation of the world. But, in the last case, the year 4004 expresses the distance between these two extremes, viz., the beginning of the world and the present time; while, in the first instance, the event itself forms the beginning of the series.—So that all dates appear to be properly classed under the head of ideas of relation; and also all names whatever, which are in any way expressive of the time of events, as a second, a minute, day, week, hour, month, year, cycle, yesterday, to-morrow, to-day, &c.

§ 135. (VI.) Of ideas of possession.

Another class of relations may be called relations of POSSESSION.—Every one knows, that not unfrequently, in his examination of objects, there arises a new feeling, which is distinct from, and independent of, the mere conceptions of the objects themselves; and which, as it differs from other feelings of relation, may be termed the relation of possession or belonging to. This is one of the earliest feelings which human beings exercise. When we see the small child grasping its top and rattle with joy, and disputing the claims of another to a share in them, we may know that he has formed the notion of possession. It is not only formed in early life, but experience fully shows that it loses neither activity nor strength by the lapse of years.

The application of the Judgment, or that power by which we perceive the relations of things, is frequent in this particular form; and we find here a fruitful source of words. The whole class of possessive pronouns, which are to be found in all languages, have their origin here; such as MINE, THINE, YOUR, HIS, HER, &c. The relation of possession is imbodied also in the genitive case of the Greeks, Latins, Germans, and whatever other languages express relations in the same way; in the construct state of nouns in the Hebrew and the other cognate dialects; and in the preposition OF, which is the substitute for the genitive termination in English, and the articles DE, DU, DE'L, and DE LA in French.

The verbs TO BE in English, ESSE in Latin, ETRE in French, (and the same may undoubtedly be said of the corresponding verb of existence in all languages,) are often employed to express the relation of possession or belonging to. To say that the rose is red or the orange yellow, is as much as to say that the qualities of yellowness and redness are the possession of, or belong to, the rose and orange. But it will be observed, that the relation is not indicated by the name of the subject, nor by the epithet expressive of its quality, but by the verb which connects the subject and predicate. And similar remarks will apply to some other verbs.

This class of relations is involved in many complex terms, which imply definite qualities and affections of mind, as friend, enemy, lover, hater, adorer, worshipper These terms not only indicate certain individuals, to whom they are applied, but assert the existence of certain mental affections as their characteristics, and as belonging to them.

§ 136. (VII.) Of relations of cause and effect.

There are relations also of Cause and Effect. We will not delay here to explain the origin of the notions of cause and effect, any further than to say that the notion of cause, as it first exists in the mind, includes nothing more than invariable antecedence. When the antecedence to the event, or the sequence of whatever kind, is our own volition (and probably in two other cases, see § 118,) we have the new idea of POWER. The idea of invariable antecedence, therefore, which of course supposes some sequence, when it is combined with that of Power, constitutes the full notion of CAUSE. When the sequence is found invariably to follow, and its existence cannot be ascribed to anything else, it is called the EFFECT. Accordingly, men usually give the name of *events*, of *occurrences*, or *facts*, to those things which from time to time fall under their notice, when they are considered in themselves. They are the *mere* facts, the mere events, and nothing more. But when, in the course of their further experience, such events are found to have certain invariable forerunners, they cease to apply these terms, and call them, in reference to their antecedents, EFFECTS. And, in like manner, the antecedents are called CAUSES, not in themselves considered, but in reference to what invariably comes after.

Cause and effect, therefore, have certainly a relation to each other; it is thus that they exist in the view of the mind and in the nature of things, however true it may be that men are unable to trace any *physical* connexion between them. We cannot conceive of a cause, if we exclude from the list of our ideas the correlative notion of effect, nor, on the other hand, do we call anything an effect without a reference to some antecedent. These two notions, therefore, involve or imply the existence of each other; that is, are relative.

§ 137. Of complex terms involving the relation of cause and effect.

The suggestion of the relation of Cause and Effect exists on occasions almost innumerable; and in all languages gives a character to a multitude of words. This relation is imbodied, for instance, in a multitude of names which are expressive of complex objects, such as printer, farmer, sculptor, warrior, writer, poet, manufacturer, painter.

This may be thus illustrated. When we look at any interesting piece of statuary, the sight of it naturally suggests its author. But when our mind is thus directed from the statue to the sculptor, it is evident we do not think of him as we do of a thousand others, but we combine with the conception of the individual a reference to what he has done. We unite with the mere complex notion of man that of a cause, and this combination evidently alters its character, making it relative instead of absolute.—In like manner, when we look at a fine portrait or historical painting, we are naturally reminded of the artist, whose ingenuity has been displayed in its proportions and colouring. But the word painter, which we apply to him, expresses not merely the man, but comprises the additional notion of the relation of cause, which he holds to the interesting picture before us.

§ 138. Connexion of relative suggestion with reasoning.

It may be profitable to notice here the connexion which relative suggestion has with reasoning in general. The suggestions of relation (or elementary judgments, as they may perhaps properly be called) are, in some respects, to a train of reasoning, what parts are to the whole. But they evidently do not of themselves include all the parts in a train of reasoning, and are distinguished by this peculiarity, that their office in a great measure is to connect together other subordinate parts in the train. In the combination of numbers, and in the various applications of demonstrative reasoning, the relations of PROPORTION and the relations of IDENTITY and DIVERSITY, (otherwise called of AGREEMENT and DISAGREEMENT,) find a conspicuous place. Moral reasoning embraces all kinds of relations, those of degree, time, place, possession, and cause and effect, as well as of agreement and disagreement, and of proportion. Relative feelings, sometimes of one kind and sometimes of another, continually unfold themselves as the mind advances in argument. So that, although there are elements in reasoning besides perceptions of relation, it is evident that it cannot advance independently of their did. Facts may be accumulated, having close and decisive relations to the points to be proved, but those facts can never be so bound together as to result in any decisive conc usion, without a perception and knowledge of the relat.ons.

CHAPTER V.

ASSOCIATION. (I.) PRIMARY LAWS

§ 139. Reasons for considering this subject here.

In giving an account of the internal origin of knowledge, we might be expected to proceed directly from Relative Suggestion to a consideration of the Reasoning power, which is one of the most effective and fruitful sources of intellectual perception. By means of this power, we are enabled to combine and compare the ample materials furnished by ORIGINAL SUGGESTION, CONSCIOUSNESS, and RELATIVE SUGGESTION, and thus to develope in the mind new elements of thought, and to cast light on the darkened places in the field of truth. But there are powers of the mind, subordinate to the reasoning power, and essential to its action, which may with propriety be first considered; particularly Association and Memory. Other persons, perhaps, in examining the various parts of the mind, would propose for the consideration of these powers some other place; but we see no valid objection to considering them here. On the contrary, they have comparatively so little to do with what has gone before, and so much to do with what comes after, and, in particular, are so essential to every process of ratiocination, that this seems to be their appropriate position. As association is presupposed and involved in memory as well as in reasoning, we naturally begin with that principle first.

§ 140. Meaning of association and illustrations.

Our thoughts and feelings follow each other in a regular train. Of this statement no one needs any other proof than his individual experience. We all know, not only that our minds are susceptible of new states, but, what is more, that this capability of new states is not fortuitous, but has its laws. Therefore we not only say that our thoughts and feelings succeed each other, but that this antecedence and sequence is in a *regular* train

To this regular and established consecution of the states of the mind, we give the name of MENTAL ASSOCIATION.

Illustrations of this important principle, which exerts an influence over the emotions and desires as well as over the thoughts, are without number. Mr. Hobbes relates, in his political treatise of the Leviathan, that he was once in company where the conversation turned on the English Civil War. A person abruptly asked, in the course of the conversation, What was the value of a Roman denarius? Such a question, so remote from the general direction of the conversation, had the appearance not only of great abruptness, but of impertinence. Mr. Hobbes says, that, on a little reflection, he was able to trace the train of thought which suggested the question. The original subject of discourse naturally introduced the history of King Charles; the king naturally suggested the treachery of those who surrendered him up to his enemies; the treachery of these persons readily introduced to the mind the treachery of Judas Iscariot; the conduct of Judas was associated with the thirty pieces of silver, and, as the Romans occupied Judea at the time of the crucifixion of the Saviour, the pieces of silver were associated with the Roman denarii.

"When I was travelling through the wilds of America," says the eloquent Chateaubriand, "I was not a little surprised to hear that I had a countryman established as a resident at some distance in the woods. I visited him with eagerness, and found him employed in pointing some stakes at the door of his hut. He cast a look towards me, which was cold enough, and continued his work; but, the moment I addressed him in French, he started at the recollection of his country, and the big tear stood in his eye. These well-known accents suddenly roused, in the heart of the old man, all the sensations of his infancy."* —Such illustrations, which appeal to every one's consciousness in confirmation of their truth, show what association is.

§ 141. Of the general laws of association.

In regard to Association, all that we know is the fact

* Chateaubriand's Recollections of Italy, England, and America

that our thoughts and feelings, under certain circumstances, appear together and keep each other company. We do not undertake to explain *why* it is that association, in the circumstances appropriate to its manifestation, has an existence. We know the simple fact; and if it be an ultimate principle in our mental constitution, as we have no reason to doubt that it is, we can know nothing more.

Association, as thus understood, has its laws. By the Laws of association we mean no other than the general designation of those circumstances under which the regular consecution of mental states which has been mentioned occurs. The following may be named as among the Primary or more important of those laws, although it is not necessary to take upon us to assert either that the enumeration is complete, or that some better arrangement of them might not be proposed, viz., RESEMBLANCE, CONTRAST, CONTIGUITY in time and place, and CAUSE and EFFECT.

§ 142. Resemblance the first general law of association.

New trains of ideas and new emotions are occasioned by Resemblance; but when we say that they are occasioned in this way, all that is meant is, that there is a new state of mind immediately subsequent to the perception of the resembling object. Of the efficient cause of this new state of mind under these circumstances, we can only say, the Creator of the soul has seen fit to appoint this connexion in its operations, without our being able, or deeming it necessary, to give any further explanation. A traveller, wandering in a foreign land, finds himself, in the course of his sojournings, in the midst of aspects of nature not unlike those where he has formerly resided, and the fact of this resemblance becomes the antecedent to new states of mind. There is distinctly brought before him the scenery which he has left, his own woods, his waters, and his home.—The enterprising Lander, in giving an account of one of his excursions in Africa, expresses himself thus. "The foliage exhibited every variety and tint of green, from the sombre shade of the melancholy yew to the lively verdure of the poplar and young oak. For myself, I was delighted with the agreeable ramble; and imagined that I could distinguish among the notes of the songsters of the grove, the swelling strains of the English skylark and thrush, and the more gentle warbling of the finch and linnet. It was indeed a brilliant morning, teeming with life and beauty; and recalled to my memory a thousand affecting associations of sanguine boyhood, when I was thoughtless and happy."

The result is the same in any other case, whenever there is a resemblance between what we now experience and what we have previously experienced. We have been acquainted, for instance, at some former period, with a person whose features appeared to us to possess some peculiarity; a breadth and openness of the forehead, an uncommon expression of the eye, or some other striking mark; to-day we meet a stranger in the crowd by which we are surrounded, whose features are of a somewhat similar cast, and the resemblance at once vividly suggests the likeness of our old acquaintance.

Nor is the association which is based upon resemblance limited to objects of sight. Objects which are addressed to the sense of hearing are recalled in the same way.

> "How soft the music of those village bells,
> Falling at intervals upon the ear.
> With easy force it opens all the cells
> Where memory slept. Wherever I have heard
> A kindred melody, the scene recurs,
> And with it all its pleasures and its pains."

§ 143. Of resemblance in the effects produced.

Resemblance operates, as an associating principle, not only when there is a likeness or similarity in the things themselves, but also when there is a resemblance in the *effects* which are produced upon the mind.—The ocean, for instance, when greatly agitated by the winds, and threatening every moment to overwhelm us, produces in the mind an emotion similar to that which is caused by the presence of an angry man who is able to do us harm. And, in consequence of this similarity in the effects produced, it is sometimes the case that they reciprocally bring each other to our recollection.

Dark woods, hanging over the brow of a mountain,

cause in us a feeling of awe and wonder, like that which we feel when we behold approaching us some aged person, whose form is venerable for his years, and whose name is renowned for wisdom and justice. It is in reference to this view of the principle on which we are remarking, that the following comparison is introduced in Akenside's Pleasures of the Imagination:

"Mark the sable woods,
That shade sublime yon mountain's nodding brow,
With what religious awe the solemn scene
Commands your steps! As if the reverend form
Of Minos or of Numa should forsake
The Elysian seats, and down the embowering glade
Move to your pausing eye."

As we are so constituted that all nature produces in us certain effects, causes certain emotions similar to those which are caused in us in our intercourse with our fellow-beings, it so happens that, in virtue of this fact, the natural world becomes living, animated, operative. The ocean is in *anger;* the sky *smiles;* the cliff *frowns;* the aged woods are *venerable;* the earth and its productions are no longer a dead mass, but have an existence, a soul, an agency.—We see here, in part, the foundation of metaphorical language; and it is here that we are to look for the principles by which we are to determine the propriety or impropriety of its use.

§ 144. Contrast the second general or primary law.

CONTRAST is another law or principle by which our successive mental states are suggested; or, in other terms, when there are two objects, or events, or situations of a character precisely opposite, the idea or conception of one is immediately followed by that of the other. When the discourse is of the *palace* of the king, how often are we reminded in the same breath of the *cottage* of the peasant! And thus it is that wealth and poverty, the cradle and the grave, and hope and despair, are found, in public speeches and in writings, so frequently going together, and keeping each other company. The truth is, they are connected together in our thoughts by a distinct and operative principle; they accompany each other, certainly not because there is any resemblance in the things thus associated, but in consequence of their very marked contrariety. Darkness reminds of light, heat of cold, friendship of enmity; the sight of the conqueror is associated with the memory of the conquered, and, when beholding men of deformed and dwarfish appearance, we are at once led to think of those of erect figure or of Patagonian size. Contrast, then, is no less a principle or law of association than resemblance itself.

Count Lemaistre's touching story, entitled, from the scene of its incidents, THE LEPER OF AOST, illustrates the effects of the principle of association now under consideration. Like all persons infected with the leprosy, the subject of the disease is represented as an object of dread no less than of pity to others, and, while he is an outcast from the society of men, he is a loathsome spectacle even to himself. But what is the condition of his mind? What are the subjects of his thoughts? The tendencies of his intellectual nature prevent his thinking of wretchedness alone. His extreme misery aggravates itself by suggesting scenes of ideal happiness, and his mind revels in a paradise of delights merely to give greater intensity to his actual woes by contrasting them with imaginary bliss —"I represent to myself continually," says the Leper "societies of sincere and virtuous friends; families blessed with health, fortune, and harmony. I imagine I see them walk in groves greener and fresher than these, the shade of which makes my poor happiness; brightened by a sun more brilliant than that which sheds its beams on me; and their destiny seems to me as much more worthy of envy in proportion as my own is the more miserable."

Association by CONTRAST is the foundation of the rhetorical figure of Antithesis. In one of the tragedies of Southern we find the following antithetic expressions:

> "Could I forget
> What I have been, I might the better bear
> What I am destined to. I am not the first
> That have been wretched; but to think how much
> I have been happier."

Here the present is placed in opposition with the past, and happiness is contrasted with misery; not by a cold and strained artifice, as one might be led to suppose, but by the natural impulses of the mind, which is led to associate together things that are the reverse of each other

§ 145. Contiguity the third general or primary law.

Those thoughts and feelings which have been connected together by nearness of time and place, are readily suggested by each other; and, consequently, contiguity in those respects is rightly reckoned as another and third primary law of our mental associations. When we think of Palestine, for instance, we very readily and naturally think of the Jewish nation, of the patriarchs, of the prophets, of the Saviour, and of the apostles, because Palestine was their place of residence and the theatre of their actions. So that this is evidently an instance where the suggestions are chiefly regulated by proximity of place. When a variety of acts and events have happened nearly at the same period, whether in the same place or not, one is not thought of without the other being closely associated with it, owing to proximity of time. If, therefore, the particular event of the crucifixion of the Saviour be mentioned, we are necessarily led to think of various other events which occurred about the same period, such as the treacherous conspiracy of Judas, the denial of Peter, the conduct of the Roman soldiery, the rending of the vail of the temple, and the temporary obscuration of the sun.

The mention of Egypt suggests the Nile, the Pyramids, the monuments of the Thebais, the follies and misfortunes of Cleopatra, the battle of Aboukir. The mention of Greece is associated with Thermopylæ and Salamis, the Hill of Mars, and the Vale of Tempe, Ilissus, the steeps of Delphi, Lyceum, and the "olive shades of Academus." These, it will be noticed, are associations on the principle of contiguity in PLACE. But if a particular event of great interest is mentioned, other events and renowned names, which attracted notice at the same period, will eagerly cluster around it. The naming of the AMERICAN REVOLUTION, *for instance, immediately fills the mind with recollections of Washington, Franklin, Morris, Greene, Jay,* and many of their associates, whose fortune it was to enlist their exertions in support of constitutional rights, not merely in the same country, (for that circumstance alone might not have been sufficient to have recalled them,) but *at the same period of time.*

It is generally supposed, and not without reason for it, that the third primary law of mental association is more extensive in its influence than any others. It has been remarked with truth, that proximity in time and place forms the basis of the whole calendar of the great mass of mankind. They pay but little attention to the arbitrary eras of chronology; but date events by each other, and speak of what happened at the time of some dark day, of some destructive overflow of waters, of some great eclipse, of some period of drought and famine, of some war or revolution.

§ 146. Cause and effect the fourth primary law.

There are certain facts or events which hold to each other the relation of invariable antecedence and sequence. That fact or event to which some other one sustains the relation of constant antecedence, is, in general, called *an effect.* And that fact or event to which some other one holds the relation of invariable sequence, has, in general, the name of a *cause.* Now there may be no resemblance in the things which reciprocally bear this relation; there may be no contrariety; and it is by no means necessary that there should be contiguity in time or place, as the meaning of the term contiguity is commonly understood. There may be CAUSE and EFFECT without any one or all of these circumstances. But it is a fact which is known to every one's experience, that, when we think of the cause in any particular instance, we naturally think of the effect, and, on the contrary, the knowledge or recollection of the effect brings to mind the cause.—And in view of this well-known and general experience, there is good reason for reckoning CAUSE and EFFECT among the primary principles of our mental associations. What we here understand by principles or laws will be recollected, viz., The general designation of those circumstances under which the regular consecution of mental states occurs.

It is on the principle of Cause and Effect, that, when we see a surgical instrument, or any engine of torture, we have a conception of the pain which they are fitted to occasion. And, on the contrary, the sight of a wound, inflicted however long before, suggests to us the idea of the instrument by which it was made. Mr. Locke relates an incident, which illustrates the statements made here, of a man who was restored from a state of insanity by means of a harsh and exceedingly painful operation "The gentleman who was thus recovered, with great sense of gratitude and acknowledgment, owned the cure all his life after, as the greatest obligation he could have received; but, whatever gratitude and reason suggested to him, he could never bear the sight of the operator; that image brought back with it the idea of that agony which he suffered from his hands, which was too mighty and intolerable for him to endure."—The operation of the law of Cause and Effect, in the production of new associations, seems to be involved in the following characteristic passage of Shakspeare, Henry IV., 2d pt., act i ·

> "Yet the first bringer of unwelcome news
> Hath but a losing office; and his tongue
> Sounds ever after as a sullen bell,
> Remember'd knolling a departed friend."

CHAPTER VI.

ASSOCIATION. (II.) SECONDARY LAWS.

§ 147. Secondary laws, and their connexion with the primary.

THE subject of Association is not exhausted in the enumeration and explanation of its Laws which has thus far been given. Besides the PRIMARY LAWS, which have fallen under our consideration, there are certain marked and prominent circumstances, which are found to exert, in a greater or less degree, a modifying and controlling influence over the more general principles. As this influence is of a permanent character, and not merely accidental and temporary, the grounds or sources of it are called, by way of distinction, SECONDARY LAWS.—These are four in number, viz., lapse of Time, degree of co-existent Feeling, repetition or Habit, and original or constitutional Difference in character.

It must at once be obvious, that these principles, although holding a subordinate rank, give an increased range and power to the PRIMARY laws. It is not to be inferred from the epithet by which they are distinguished, that they are, therefore, of a very minor and inconsiderable importance. On the contrary, human nature without them, as far as we are capable of judging, would have assumed a sort of fixed and inflexible form, instead of presenting those pleasing and almost endless diversities it now does.—The primary laws are the great national roads along which the mind holds its course; the secondary are those cross-roads that intersect them from time to time, and thus afford an entrance into, and a communication with, the surrounding country; and yet all have a connexion with each other; and with all their turnings and intersections, concur at last in the ultimate destination.

§ 148. Of the influence of lapse of time.

The first of the four secondary laws which we shall consider, is LAPSE OF TIME. Stated more particularly, the law is this: Our trains of thought and emotion are more or less strongly connected and likely to be restored, according as the lapse of time has been greater or less.

Perhaps no lapse of time, however great, will utterly break the chain of human thought, and cause an entire inability of restoring our former experiences; but it appears evident from observation, as much so as observation renders evident in almost any case, that every additional moment of intervening time weakens, if it do not break and sunder, the bond that connects the present with the past, and diminishes the probability of such a restoration. We remember many incidents, even of a trifling nature, which occurred to-day, or the present week, while those of yesterday or of last week are forgotten. But if the increased period of months and years throws itself between the present time and the date of our past experiences, our ancient joys, regrets, and sufferings, then how unfrequent is their recurrence, and how weak and shadowy they appear! Increase the lapse of time a little further, and a dark cloud rests on that portion of our history; less substantial than a dream, it utterly eludes our search, and becomes to us as if it never had been.

There is, however, an apparent exception to this law which should be mentioned. The associated feelings of old men, which were formed in their youth and the early part of manhood, are more readily revived than those of later origin.—On this state of things in old men, two remarks are to be made. The FIRST is, that the law under consideration fully and unfailingly maintains itself in the case of aged persons, whenever the time is not extended far back. Events which happened but a few hours before are remembered, while there is an utter forgetfulness of those which happened a few weeks or even days before. So far as this, the law operates in old men precisely as in others. The SECOND remark is, that the failure of its operation in respect to the events of youth, is caused, not by an actual inability in the secondary law before us, to blot out and diminish here as in other cases, but by the greater power of the combined action of two other laws, viz., Co-existent feeling, and Repetition or habit. Our early life, as a general statement, was the most deeply interesting, and is the most frequently recurred to; and in this way its recollections become so incorporated with the mind as to hold a sort of precedence over our more recent experiences, and thrust them from their proper place.

§ 149. Secondary law of repetition or habit.

Another secondary law is REPETITION; in other words, successions of thought are the more readily suggested in proportion as they are the more frequently renewed. If we experience a feeling once, and only once, we find it difficult to recall it after it has gone from us; but repeated experience increases the probability of its recurring. Every schoolboy who is required to commit to memory, puts this law to the test, and proves it. Having read a sentence a number of times, he finds himself able to repeat it out of book, which he could not do with merely reading it once.

The operation of this law is seen constantly in particlar arts and professions. If men be especially trained up to certain trades, arts, or sciences, their associations on those particular subjects, and on everything connected with them, are found to be prompt and decisive. We can but seldom detect any hesitancy or mistake within the circle where their minds have been accustomed to operate, because every thought and process have been recalled and repeated thousands of times. With almost everything they see or hear, there is a train of reflection, connecting it with their peculiar calling, and bringing it within the beaten and consecrated circle. Every hour, unless they guard against it, hastens the process which threatens to cut them off, and insulate them from the great interests of humanity, and to make them wholly professional.

"Still o'er those scenes their memory wakes,
And fondly broods with miser care;
Time but the impression stronger makes;
As streams their channels deeper wear."

§ 150. Of the secondary law of co-existent emotion.

A third secondary law is CO-EXISTENT EMOTION.—It may be stated in other words as follows: The probability that our mental states will be recalled by the general laws, will in part depend on the depth of feeling, the degree of interest, which accompanied the original experience of them.

Why are bright objects more readily recalled than faint or obscure? It is not merely because they occupied more distinctly our perception, but because they more engaged our attention and interested us, the natural consequence of that greater distinctness. Why do those events in our personal history, which were accompanied with great joys and sorrows, stand out like pyramids in our past life, distinct to the eye, and immoveable in their position, while others have been swept away and cannot be found? Merely because there were joy and sorrow in the one case, and not at all, or only in a slight degree, in the other; because the sensitive part of our nature combined itself with the intellectual; the Heart gave activity to the operations of the Understanding.

We learn from the Bible that the Jews, in their state of exile, could not forget Jerusalem, the beloved and beautiful City And why not? How did it happen that, in their Captivity, they sat down by the rivers of Babylon, wept when they remembered Zion, and hung their harps on the willows? It was because Jerusalem was not only an object of thought, but of feeling. They had not only known her gates and fountains, her pleasant dwelling-places and temples, but had loved them. The Holy City was not a lifeless abstraction of the head; but a sacred and delightful image, engraven in the heart. And hence it was, that, in their solitude and sorrow, she arose before them so distinctly, "The morning star of memory."

§ 151. Original difference in the mental constitution.

The fourth and last secondary law of association is ORIGINAL DIFFERENCE IN THE MENTAL CONSTITUTION.—This Law, it will be noticed, is expressed in the most general terms; and is to be considered, therefore, as applicable both to the Intellectual and the Sensitive part of man. It requires, accordingly, to be contemplated in two distinct points of view.

The law of original difference in the mental constitution is applicable, in the FIRST place, to the Intellect, properly and distinctively so called; in other words, to the comparing, judging, and reasoning part of the soul. That there are differences in men intellectually, it is presumed will hardly be doubted, although this difference is perceptible in different degrees, and in some cases hardly perceptible at all. And these original or constitutional peculiarities reach and affect the associating principle, as well as other departments of intellectual action. The associations of the great mass of mankind (perhaps it may be entirely owing in some cases to the accidental circumstance of a want of education and intellectual developement) appear to run exclusively in the channel of Contiguity in time and place. They contemplate objects in their nearness and distance, in their familiar and outward exhibitions, without examining closely into analogies and differences, or considering them in the important relation of cause and effect. But not unfrequently we find persons whose minds are differently constructed, who exhibit a higher order of perception. But even in these cases we sometimes detect a striking difference in the application of their intellectual powers. One person, for instance, has from childhood exhibited a remarkable command of the relations and combinations of numbers; another exhibits, in like manner, an uncommon perception of uses, adaptations, and powers, as they are brought together, and set to work in the mechanic arts; another has the power of generalizing in an uncommon degree, and, having obtained possession of a principle in a particular case, which may appear to others perfectly and irretrievably insulated, he at once extends it to hundreds and thousands of other cases. In no one of these instances does the Associating power operate in precisely the same way, but exhibits in each a new aspect or phasis of action.

It it is perhaps unnecessary to delay here, for the purpose of confirming what has now been said by a reference to the history of individuals. A slight acquaintance with literary history will show that diversities of intellect, such as have been alluded to, and founded too in a great degree on peculiarities of the associating principle, have been frequent. How often had the husbandman seen the apple fall to the ground without even asking for the cause? But when Newton saw the fall of an apple, he not only asked for the cause, but, having conjectured it, he at once perceived its applicability to everything in like circumstances around him, to all the descending bodies on the earth's surface. And this was not all. Immediately expanding the operations of the principle which he had detected, from the surface of the earth to the stars of heaven, he showed its universality, and proved that the most distant planet is controlled by the same great law which regulates the particles of dust beneath our feet.—Here was a mind, not merely great by toil, but constitutionally great and inventive; a mind which was regulated in its action, not by the law of mere contiguity in time and place, but by the more effective associating principles of Analogy, and of Cause and Effect.

§ 152. The foregoing law as applicable to the sensibilities.

The law under consideration holds good, in the SECOND

place, in respect to original differences of emotion and passion, or, as it is more commonly expressed, of disposition. It will help to make us understood if we allude briefly in this part of the subject to two different classes of persons. One of the descriptions of men which we have now in view is composed of those, for such are undoubtedly to be found, who are of a pensive and melancholy turn. From their earliest life they have shown a fondness for seclusion, in order that they might either commune with the secrets of their own hearts, or hold intercourse, undisturbed by others, with whatever of impressiveness and sublimity is to be found in the works of nature. The other class are naturally of a lively and cheerful temperament. If they delight in nature, it is not in solitude, but in the company of others. While they seldom throw open their hearts for the admission of troubled thoughts, they oppose no obstacle to the entrance of the sweet beams of peace, and joy, and hope.

Now it is beyond question that the primary laws of association are influenced by the constitutional tendencies manifest in these two classes of persons; that is to say, in the minds of two individuals, the one of a cheerful, the other of a melancholy or gloomy disposition, the trains of thought will be very different. This difference is finely illustrated in those beautiful poems of Milton, L'ALLEGRO and IL PENSEROSO. L'ALLEGRO, or the cheerful man, finds pleasure and cheerfulness in every object which he beholds. The great sun puts on his amber light, the mower whets his scythe, the milkmaid sings,

> "And every shepherd tells his tale
> Under the hawthorn in the dale."

But the man of a melancholy disposition, IL PENSEROSO, chooses the evening for his walk, as most suitable to the temper of his mind; he listens from some lonely hillock to the distant curfew, and loves to hear the song of that "sweet bird,

> "That shun'st the noise of folly,
> Most musical, most melancholy."

Further: Our trains of suggested thoughts will be modified by those temporary feelings, which may be regarded as exceptions to the more general character of our dispositions. The cheerful man is not always cheerful, nor is the melancholy man at all times equally sober and contemplative. They are known to exchange characters for short periods, sometimes in consequence of good or ill health, or of happy or adverse fortune, and sometimes for causes which cannot be easily explained. So that our mental states will be found to follow each other with a succession, varying not only with the general character of our temper and dispositions, but with the transitory emotions of the day or hour.

All the laws of association may properly be given here in a condensed view. The PRIMARY or general laws are RESEMBLANCE, CONTRAST, CONTIGUITY in time and place, and CAUSE and EFFECF. Those circumstances which are found particularly to modify and control the action of these, are termed SECONDARY laws, and are as follows: Lapse of time, Repetition or habit, Co-existent feeling and Constitutional difference in mental character.

CHAPTER VII.

MEMORY.

§ 153. Remarks on the general nature of memory.

In the further prosecution of our subject, we naturally proceed from Association to the examination of the Memory, inasmuch as the latter necessarily implies the antecedent existence of the former, and in its very nature is closely allied to it. In reference to the great question of the Origin of human Knowledge, the Memory, as has already been intimated, is to be considered a source of knowledge, rather in its connexion with other mental susceptibilities than *in itself*. It does not appear how we could form any abstract ideas, based upon a knowledge of objects and classes of objects, without the aid of memory; and it is well known, that its presence and action is essentially involved in all the exercises of the reasoning power and of the imagination. Without delaying however, on its connexion with the origin of knowledge we shall proceed to consider the susceptibility itself, both in its general nature and in some of its peculiarities.

Memory is that power or susceptibility of the mind by which those conceptions are originated which are modified by a perception of the relation of past time. Accordingly, it is not a simple, but complex action of the intellectual principle, implying, (1.) a conception of the object; (2.) a perception of the relation of priority in its existence. That is, we not only have a conception of the object, but this conception is attended with the conviction that it underwent the examination of our senses, or was in some way perceived by us at some former period.

When we imagine that we stand in the midst of a forest or on the top of a mountain, but remain safe all the while at our own fireside, these pleasing ideas of woods, and of skies painted over us, and of plains under our feet, are mere conceptions. But when with these insulated conceptions we connect the relation of time, and they gleam upon our souls as the woods, plains, and mountains of our youthful days, then those intellectual states, which were before mere conceptions, become REMEMBRANCES. And the power which the mind possesses of originating these latter complex states, is what usually goes under the name of the power or faculty of MEMORY.

§ 154. Of memory as a ground or law of belief.

Memory, as explained in the preceding section, is a ground or law of Belief. So far as we have no particular reason to doubt that the sensations and perceptions in any given case are correctly reported in the remembrance, the latter controls our belief and actions not less than those antecedent states of mind on which it is founded. Such is the constitution of the human mind.—It will be noticed, that, in asserting the natural dependence of belief on memory, we guard it by an express limitation. It is only when we have no reason to doubt of our antecedent experiences being correctly reported in the remembrances, that our reliance on them is of the highest kind

Every man knows, from a species of internal feeling whether there be grounds for doubting his memory in any particular case or not; for the same Consciousness which gives him a knowledge of the *fact* of memory, gives him a knowledge of the *degree* also in which it exists; viz., whether in a high degree or low, whether distinct or obscure. If it be the fact that he finds reason for suspecting its reports, his reliance will either be diminished in proportion to this suspicion, or he will take means, if he be able to, to remove the grounds of such suspicion.

It cannot reasonably be anticipated, that any objection will be made to the doctrine of a reliance on memory, with the limitation which has now been mentioned Without such reliance, our situation would be no better, at least, than if we had been framed with an utter inability to rely on the Senses or on Testimony; we could hardly sustain an existence; we certainly could not derive anything in aid of that existence from the experience of the past.

§ 155. Of differences in the strength of memory.

The ability to remember is the common privilege of all, and, generally speaking, it is possessed in nearly equa degrees. To each one there is given a sufficient readiness in this respect; his power of remembrance is such as to answer all the ordinary purposes of life. But, although there is, in general, a nearly equal distribution of this power, we find a few instances of great weakness, and other instances of great strength of memory.

It is related by Seneca of the Roman orator Hortensius, that, after sitting a whole day at a public sale, he gave an account, from memory, in the evening, of all things sold, with the prices and the names of the purchasers; and this account, when compared with what had been taken in writing by a notary, was found to be exact in every particular.

The following is an instance of strength of memory somewhat remarkable.—An Englishman, at a certain time, came to Frederic the Great of Prussia, for the express purpose of giving him an exhibition of his power of recollection. Frederic sent for Voltaire, who read to the king a pretty long poem which he had just finished. The Englishman was present, and was in such a position that he could hear every word of the poem; but was concealed from Voltaire's notice. After the reading of the poem was finished, Frederic observed to the author that the production could not be an original one, as there was a foreign gentleman present who could recite every word of it. Voltaire listened with amazement to the stranger, as he repeated, word for word, the poem which he had been at so much pains in composing; and, giving way to a momentary freak of passion, he tore the manuscript in pieces. A statement was then made to him of the circumstances under which the Englishman became acquainted with his poem, which had the effect to mitigate his anger, and he was very willing to do penance for the suddenness of his passion by copying down the work from a second repetition of it by the stranger, who was able to go through with it as before.

A considerable number of instances of this description are found in the recorded accounts of various individuals; but they must be considered as exceptions to the general features of the human mind, the existence of which it is difficult to explain on any known principles. They are probably original and constitutional traits; and, if such be the case, they necessarily preclude any explanation further than what is involved in the mere statement of that fact. There are, however, some diversities and peculiarities of memory, less striking, perhaps, than those just referred to, which admit a more detailed notice

§ 156. Of circumstantial memory, or that species of memory which is based on the relations of contiguity in time and place.

There is a species of memory, more than usually obvious and outward in its character, which is based essentially upon the relations of Contiguity in time and place.—In the explanation of this form or species of memory, it may be proper to recur a moment to the explanations on the general nature of memory which have already been given. It will be kept in mind, that our remembrances are merely conceptions modified by a perception of the relation of past time. Removing, then, the modification of past time, and the remaining element of our remembrances will be conceptions merely. Our conceptions, it is obvious, cannot be called up by a mere voluntary effort, because to will the existence of a conception necessarily implies the actual existence of the conception already in the mind. They arise in the mind, therefore, in obedience to the influence of some of those principles of ASSOCIATION which have already been considered. And Memory, accordingly, will assume a peculiarity of aspect corresponding to the associating principle which predominates. If it be based, for instance, on the law of Contiguity, as it will deal chiefly with mere facts, and their outward incidents and circumstances, without entering deeply into their interior nature, it will be what may be described, not merely as an obvious and practical, but, in particular, as a *circumstantial* memory. If it be based chiefly on the other principles, it may be expected to exhibit a less easy and flexible, a less minute and specific, but a more philosophical character.

That species of memory which is founded chiefly on the law of contiguity, and which is distinguished by its specificalness or circumstantiality, will be found to prevail especially among uneducated people, not merely artisans and other labouring classes, but among all those, in whatever situation of life, who have either not possessed, or possessing, have not employed, the means of intellectual culture. Every one must have recollected instances of the great readiness exhibited by these persons, in their recollection of facts, places, times, names, specific arrangements in dress and in buildings, traditions, and local incidents. In their narrations, for instance, of what has come within their knowledge, they will, in general, be found to specify the time of events; not merely an indefinite or approximated time, but the identical year, and month, and day, and hour. In their description of persons and places, and in their account of the dress and equipage of persons, and of the localities and incidents of places, they are found to be no less particular.

§ 157. Illustrations of specific or circumstantial memory.

The great masters of human nature (Shakspeare among

others) have occasionally indicated their knowledge of this species of memory. Mrs. Quickly, in reminding Falstaff of his promise of marriage, discovers her readiness of recollection in the specification of the great variety of circumstances under which the promise was made. Her recollection in the case was not a mere general remembrance of the solitary fact, but was, in the manner of a witness in a court of justice, circumstantial.—"Thou didst swear to me on a parcel-gilt goblet, sitting in my Dolphin chamber, at the round table, by a sea-coal fire, on Wednesday in Whitsun week, when the prince broke thy head for likening him to a singing man of Windsor."—The coachman in Cornelius Scriblerus gives an account of what he had seen in Bear Garden: "Two men fought for a prize; one was a fair man, a sergeant in the guards; the other black, a butcher; the sergeant had red trousers, the butcher blue; they fought upon a stage about four o'clock, and the sergeant wounded the butcher in the leg."

§ 158. Of philosophic memory, or that species of memory which is based on other relations than those of contiguity.

There is another species of memory, clearly distinguishable from the CIRCUMSTANTIAL memory, which may be described as the Philosophic. This form of memory, relying but seldom on the aids of mere Contiguity, is sustained chiefly by the relations of Resemblance, Contrast, and Cause and Effect. The circumstantial memory, which deals almost exclusively with minute particulars, and especially with those which are accessible by the outward senses, admirably answers the purpose of those persons in whom it is commonly found. But mere contiguity in time and place, which is almost the sole principle that binds together facts and events in the recollection of those whose powers are but imperfectly developed, possesses comparatively little value in the estimation of the philosopher He looks more deeply into the nature of things. Bestowing but slight attention on what is purely outward and incidental, he detects with a discriminating eye the analogies and oppositions, the causes and consequences of events. It would seem that the celebrated Montaigne was destitute, perhaps in a more than common degree, of that form of reminiscence which we have proposed to designate as the circumstantial memory. He says on a certain occasion of himself, "I am forced to call my servants by the names of their employments, or of the countries where they were born, for I can hardly remember their proper names; and if I should live long, I question whether I should remember my own name." But it does not appear, notwithstanding his inability to remember names and insulated facts, especially if they related to the occurrences of common life, that he had much reason to complain of an absolute want of memory. His writings indicate his cast of mind, that he was reflective and speculative; and he expressly gives us to understand, that he was much more interested in the study of the principles of human nature than of outward objects. Accordingly, the result was such as might be expected, that his memory was rather philosophical than circumstantial, and more tenacious of general principles than of specific facts.

§ 159. Illustrations of philosophic memory.

A man whose perceptions are naturally philosophic, and whose remembrances consequently take the same turn, may not be able to make so rapid and striking advances in all branches of knowledge, as a person of a different intellectual bias. Almost every department of science presents itself to the student's notice under two forms, the practical and theoretical; its facts and its rules of proceeding on the one hand, and its principles on the other. The circumstantial memory rapidly embraces the practical part, seizing its facts and enunciating its rules with a promptness of movement and a show of power which throws the philosophic memory quite into the shade. But it is otherwise when they advance into the less obvious and showy, but more fertile region of analogies, classification, and principles.—On this topic Mr. Stewart has some pertinent remarks. "A man destitute of genius," [that is to say, in this connexion, of a naturally philosophic turn of mind,] "may, with little effort, treasure up in his memory a number of particulars in chemistry or natural history, which he refers to no principle, and from which he deduces no conclusion; and from his facility in acquiring this stock of information, may flatter himself with the belief that he possesses a natural taste for these branches of knowledge. But they who are really destined to extend the boundaries of science, when they first enter on new pursuits, feel their attention distracted, and their memory overloaded with facts, among which they can trace no relation, and are sometimes apt to despair entirely of their future progress. In due time, however, their superiority appears, and arises in part from that very dissatisfaction which they at first experienced, and which does not cease to stimulate their inquiries, till they are enabled to trace, amid a chaos of apparently unconnected materials, that simplicity and beauty which always characterize the operations of nature."

§ 160. Of that species of memory called intentional recollection.

There is a species or exercise of the memory known as INTENTIONAL RECOLLECTION, the explanation of which renders it proper briefly to recur again to the nature of memory in general.—The definition of MEMORY which has been given, is, that it is the power or susceptibility of the mind, by which those conceptions are originated, which are modified by the perception of the relation of past time. This definition necessarily resolves memory, in a considerable degree at least, into Association. But it will be recollected, that our trains of associated thought are not, in the strict sense, voluntary; that is, are not *directly* under the control of the WILL. They come and depart (we speak now exclusively of their *origination*) without its being possible for us to exercise anything more than an INDIRECT power over them. It follows, from these facts, that our remembrances also, which may be regarded in part as merely associated trains, are not, in the strict sense, voluntary; or, in other words, it is impossible for us to remember in consequence of merely choosing to remember. To will or to choose to remember anything, implies that the thing in question is already in the mind; and hence there is not only an impossibility resulting from the nature of the mind, but also an absurdity, in the idea of calling up thought by a mere direct volition. Our chief power, therefore, in quickening and strengthening the memory, will be found to consist in our skill in applying and modifying the various principles or laws of association. And this brings us to an explanation of what is called INTENTIONAL MEMORY or RECOLLECTION.

§ 161. Nature of intentional recollection.

Whenever we put forth an exercise of intentional memory, or make a formal attempt to remember some circumstance, it is evident that the event in general, of which the circumstance, when recalled, will be found to be a part, must have previously been an object of attention. That is, we remember the great outlines of some story, but cannot in the first instance give a complete account of it, which we wish to do. We make an effort to recall the circumstances not remembered in two ways.—We may, in the *first* place, form different suppositions, and see which agrees best with the general outlines; the general features or outlines of the subject being detained before us, with a considerable degree of permanency, by means of some feeling of desire or interest. This method of restoring thoughts is rather an inference of reasoning than a genuine exercise of memory.

We may, in the *second* place, merely delay upon those thoughts which we already hold possession of, and revolve them in our minds; until, aided by some principle of association, we are able to lay hold of the particular ideas for which we were searching. Thus, when we endeavour to recite what we had previously committed to memory, but are at a loss for a particular passage, we repeat a number of times the concluding words of the preceding sentence. In this way, the sentence which was forgotten is very frequently recalled.

§ 162. Instance illustrative of the preceding statements.

The subject of the preceding section will perhaps be more distinctly understood, in connexion with the following illustration. Dr. Beattie informs us, that he was himself acquainted with a clergyman, who, on being attacked with a fit of apoplexy, was found to have forgotten all the transactions of the four years immediately preceding the attack. And yet he remembered as well as ever what had happened before that period. The newspapers which were printed during the period mentioned were read with interest, and afforded him a great deal of amusement, being entirely new to him. It is further stated, that this individual recovered by degrees all he had lost; so as, after a while, to have nearly or quite as full a remembrance of that period as others. In this instance the power of the principles of association appears to have been at first completely prostrated by the disease, without any prospect of their being again brought into action, except by some assistance afforded them. This assistance, no doubt, was conversation, the renewed notice of various external objects addressed to the senses, and reading. By reading old newspapers, and by conversation in particular, he occasionally fell upon ideas which he had not only been possessed of before, but which had been associated with other ideas, forming originally distinct and condensed trains of thought. And thus whole series were restored.—Other series again were recovered by applying the methods of INTENTIONAL RECOLLECTION; that is, by forming suppositions and comparing them with the ideas already recovered, or by voluntarily delaying upon and revolving in mind such trains as were restored, and thus rousing up others. Such we can hardly doubt to have been, in the main, the process by which the person of whom we are speaking recovered the knowledge he had lost.

These views, in addition to what has now been said, may be illustrated also by what we sometimes observe in old men. Question them as to the events of early life, and at times they will be unable to give any answer whatever. But whenever you mention some prominent incident of their young days, or perhaps some friend on whom many associations have gathered, it will often be found that their memory revives, and that they are able to state many things in respect to which they were previously silent.

§ 163. Marks of a good memory.

The great purpose to which the faculty of memory is

subservient, is to enable us to retain the knowledge which we have from our experiences for future use. The prominent marks of a good memory, therefore, are these two, viz., tenacity in retaining ideas, and readiness in bringing them forward on necessary occasions.

First; of tenacity, or power of retaining ideas.—The impressions which are made on some minds are durable They are like channels worn away in stone, and names engraven in monumental marble, which defy the operation of the ordinary causes of decay, and withstand even the defacing touch of time. But other memories, which at first seemed to grasp as much, are destitute of this power of retention. The inscriptions made upon them are like characters written on the sand, which the first breath of wind covers over, or like figures on a bank of snow, which the sun shines upon and melts. The inferiority of the latter description of memory to the former must be obvious; so much so as to require no comment A memory whose power of retaining is greatly diminished, of course loses a great part of its value.

Second; of readiness, or facility in bringing forward what is remembered.—Some persons who cannot be supposed to be deficient in tenacity of remembrance, appear to fail in a confident and prompt command of what they remember. Some mistake has been committed in the arrangement of their knowledge; there has been some defect in the mental discipline; or for some other cause, whatever it may be, they often discover perplexity, and remember slowly and indistinctly. This is a great practical evil, which not only ought to be, but which can, in a great degree, be guarded against.

It is true, that so great readiness of memory cannot rationally be expected in men of philosophic minds as others, for the reason that they pay but little or no attention to particular facts, except for the purpose of deducing from them general principles. But it is no less true, that, when this want of readiness is such as to cause a considerable degree of perplexity, it must be regarded a great mental defect. And, for the same reason, a prompt command of knowledge is to be regarded a mental excellence.

§ 164. Directions or rules for the improvement of the memory.

In whatever point of view the memory may be contemplated, it must be admitted that it is a faculty always securing to us inestimable benefits. For the purpose of securing the most efficient action of this valuable faculty, and particularly that tenacity and readiness which have been spoken of, the following directions may be found worthy of attention.

(I.) *Never be satisfied with a partial or half-acquaintance with things.*—There is no less a tendency to intellectual than to bodily inactivity; students, in order to avoid intellectual toil, are too much inclined to pass on in a hurried and careless manner. This is injurious to the memory. "Nothing," says Dugald Stewart, "has such a tendency to weaken, not only the powers of invention, but the intellectual powers in general, as a habit of extensive and various reading without reflection." Always make it a rule fully to understand what is gone over. Those who are determined to grapple with the subject in hand, whatever may be its nature, and to become master of it, soon feel a great interest; truths, which were at first obscure, become clear and familiar. The consequence of this increased clearness and interest is an increase of attention; and the natural result of this is, that the truths are very strongly fixed in the memory.

(II.) *We are to refer our knowledge, as much as possible, to general principles.*—To refer our knowledge to general principles is to classify it; and this is perhaps the best mode of classification. If a lawyer or merchant were to throw all his papers together promiscuously, he could not calculate on much readiness in finding what he might at any time want. If a man of letters were to record in a commonplace book all the ideas and facts which occurred to him, without any method, he would experience the greatest difficulty in applying them to use. It is the same with a memory where there is no classification. Whoever fixes upon some general principles, whether political, literary, or philosophical, and collects facts in illustration of it, will find no difficulty in remembering them, however numerous; when, without such general principles, the recollection of them would have been extremely burdensome.

(III.) *Consider the nature of the study, and make use of those helps which are thus afforded.*—This rule may be illustrated by the mention of some departments of science. Thus, in acquiring a knowledge of geography, the study is to be pursued as much as possible with the aid of good globes, charts, and maps. It requires a great effort of memory, and generally an unsuccessful one, to recollect the relative extent and situation of places, the numerous physical and political divisions of the earth, from the book. The advantages of studying geography with maps, globes, &c., are two. (1.) The form, relative situation, and extent of countries become, in this case, ideas, or, rather, conceptions of *sight ;* such conceptions (§ 60) are very vivid, and are more easily called to remembrance than others.

(2.) Our remembrances are assisted by the law of contiguity in place, (§ 145,) which is known to be one of the most efficient aids. When we have once, from having a map or globe before us, formed an acquaintance with the general visible appearance of an island, a gulf, an ocean, or a continent, nothing is more easy than to remember the subordinate divisions or parts. Whenever we have examined, and fixed in our minds the general appearance or outlines of a particular country, we do not easily forget the situation of those countries which are contiguous.

We find another illustration of this rule in the reading of history.—There is such a multitude of facts in historical writings, that to endeavour to remember them all is fruitless; and, if it could be done, would be of very small advantage. Hence, in reading the history of any country, fix upon two or three of the most interesting epochs; make them the subject of particular attention; learn the spirit of the age, and the private life and fortunes of prominent individuals; in a word, study these periods not only as annalists, but as philosophers. When they are thus studied, the mind can hardly fail to retain them; they will be a sort of landmarks; and all the other events in the history of the country, before and afterward, will naturally arrange themselves in reference to them The memory will strongly seize the prominent periods, in consequence of the great interest felt in them; and the less important parts of the history of the country will be likely to be retained, so far as is necessary, by the aid of the principle of contiguity, and without giving them great attention.—Further, historical charts or genealogical trees of history are of some assistance, for a similar reason that maps, globes, &c., are in geography.

This rule for strengthening the memory will apply also to the more abstract sciences.—"In every science," says Stewart, (Elements, ch. vi., § 3,) "the ideas, about which it is peculiarly conversant, are connected together by some associating principle; in one science, for instance, by associations founded on the relation of cause and effect; in another, by the associations founded on the necessary relations of mathematical truths."

§ 165. Further directions for the improvement of the memory.

(IV.) *The order in which things are laid up in the memory should be the order of nature.*—In nature everything has its appropriate place, connexions, and relations. Nothing is insulated, and wholly cut off, as it were, from everything else; but whatever exists or takes place falls naturally into its allotted position within the great sphere of creation and events. Hence the rule, that knowledge, as far forth as possible, should exist mentally or subjectively in the same order as the corresponding objective reality exists. The laws of the mind will be found in their operation to act in harmony with the laws of external nature. They are, in some sense, the counterparts of each other. We might illustrate the benefits of the application of this rule by referring to almost any well-digested scientific article, historical narration, poem, &c. But perhaps its full import will be more readily understood by an instance of its utter violation.

A person was one day boasting, in the presence of Foote, the comedian, of the wonderful facility with which he could commit anything to memory, when the modern Aristophanes said he would write down a dozen lines in prose which he could not commit to memory in as many minutes. The man of great memory accepted the challenge; a wager was laid, and Foote produced the following.—"So she went into the garden, to cut a cabbage-leaf to make an apple-pie; and at the same time a great she-bear coming up the street, pops its head into the shop. What, no soap? So he died, and she very imprudently married the barber; and there were present the Piciniunies, and the Joblillies, and the Garyulies, and the grand Panjandrum himself, with the little round button at the top; and they all fell to playing catch as catch can, till the gunpowder ran out of the heels of their boots."—The story adds that Foote won the wager. And it is very evident that statements of this description, utterly disregarding the order of nature and events, must defy, if carried to any great length, the strongest memory.

(V.) *The memory may be strengthened by exercise.*—Our minds, when left to sloth and inactivity, lose their vigour; but when they are kept in exercise, and, after performing what was before them, are tasked with new requisitions, it is not easy to assign limits to their ability. This seems to be a general and ultimate law of our nature. It is applicable equally to every original susceptibility, and to every combination of mental action. In repeated instances we have had occasion to refer to its results, both on the body and the mind. The power of perception is found to acquire strength and acuteness by exercise. There are habits of conception and of association as well as of perception; and we shall be able to detect the existence and operation of the same great principle, when we come to speak of reasoning, imagination, &c. As this principle applies equally to the memory, we are able to secure its beneficial results by practising that repetition or exercise on which they are founded.

§ 166. Of observance of the truth in connexion with memory

Another help to the memory, which has seldom been noticed, and certainly not so much as its importance demands, is the conscientious and strict observance of the truth.—It will be found, on inquiry, that those who are scrupulous in this respect will be more prompt and exact in their recollections, within the sphere of what they undertake to remember, than others. A man of this description may possibly not remember so *much* as others; for the same conscientiousness, which is the basis of his veracity, would instinctively teach him to reject from his intellectual storehouse a great deal of worthless trash. But within the limits which, for good reasons, undoubtedly, he sets to his recollections, he will be much more exact, much more to be relied on, provided there is no original or constitutional ground of difference. It has been suggested in regard to Dr. Johnson, that his rigid attention to veracity, his conscientious determination to be exact in his statements, was the reason, in a considerable degree, that his memory was so remarkably tenacious and minute. And the suggestion is based in sound philosophy. If a man's deep and conscientious regard for the truth be such that he cannot, consistently with the requisitions of his moral nature, repeat to others mere vaguenesses and uncertainties, he will naturally give such strict and serious attention to the present objects of inquiry and knowledge, that they will remain in his memory afterward with remarkable distinctness and permanency.

CHAPTER VIII.

DURATION OF MEMORY.

§ 167. Restoration of thoughts and feelings supposed to be forgotten.

Before quitting the subject of Memory, there is another point of view not wholly wanting in interest, in which it is susceptible of being considered; and that is the permanency or duration of its power to call up its past experiences. It is said to have been an opinion of Lord Bacon, that no thoughts are lost; that they continue virtually to exist; and that the soul possesses within itself laws which, whenever fully brought into action, will be found capable of producing the prompt and perfect restoration of the collected acts and feelings of its whole past existence.

This opinion, which other able writers have fallen in with, is clearly worthy of examination, especially when we consider that it has a practical bearing, and involves important moral and religious consequences. Some one will perhaps inquire, Is it possible, is it in the nature of things, that we should be able to recall the millions of little acts and feelings which have transpired in the whole course of our lives? Let such an inquirer be induced to consider, in the first place, that the memory has its fixed laws, in virtue of which the mental exercises are recalled; and that there can be found no direct and satisfactory proof of such laws ever wholly ceasing to exist. That the operation of those laws appears to be weakened, and is in fact weakened, by lapse of time, is admitted; but while the frequency, promptness, and strength of their action may be diminished in any assignable degree, the laws themselves yet remain. This is the view of the subject which at first obviously and plainly presents itself; and, we may venture to add, is recommended by common experience.

It is known to every one, that thoughts and feelings sometimes unexpectedly recur which had slumbered in forgetfulness for years. Days, and months, and years have rolled on; new scenes and situations occupy us; and all we felt, and saw, and experienced in those former days and years, appears to be clothed in impenetrable darkness. But suddenly some unexpected event, the sight of a waterfall, of a forest, of a house, a peculiarly pleasant or gloomy day, a mere change of countenance, a word, almost anything we can imagine, arouses the soul, and gives a new and vigorous turn to its meditations. At such a moment we are astonished at the novel revelations which are made, the recollections which are called forth, the resurrections of withered hopes and perished sorrows, of scenes and companionships that seemed to be utterly lost.

> "Lulled in the countless chambers of the brain,
> Our thoughts are linked by many a hidden chain.
> Awake but one, and lo, what myriads rise!
> Each stamps its image as the other flies."

This is, perhaps, a faint exhibition of that perfect restoration of thought which Bacon and other philosophic minds have supposed to be possible. But if the statement be correct, it is undoubtedly one circumstance among others in support of that sentiment, although of subordinate weight.

§ 168. Mental action quickened by influence on the physical system.

The ability of the mind to restore its past experiences, depends, in some degree, on the state of the physical system. It is well known that there is a connexion existing between the mind and the body, and that a reciprocal influence is exercised. It is undoubtedly true, that the mental action is ordinarily increased or diminished, according as the body is more or less affected. And may not the exercise of the laws of memory be quickened, as well as the action of other powers? While it is admitted that an influence on the body exerts an influence on the mind, may it not be true that this general influence sometimes takes the particular shape of exciting the recollection, and of restoring long-past events?

There are various facts having a bearing on this inquiry, and which seem to show that such suggestions are not wholly destitute of foundation.—It appears, for instance, from the statements of persons who have been on the point of drowning, but have been rescued from that situation, that the operations of their minds were peculiarly quickened. In this wonderful activity of the mental principle, the whole past life, with its thousand minute incidents, has almost simultaneously passed before them, and been viewed as in a mirror. Scenes and situations long gone by, and associates not seen for years, and perhaps buried and dissolved in the grave, came rushing in upon the field of intellectual vision in all the activity and distinctness of real existence.

If such be the general experience in cases of this kind, it confirms a number of important views; placing beyond doubt that there is a connexion between the mind and body; that the mental operation is susceptible of being quickened; and that such increase of action may be attributable, in part at least, to an influence on the body. The proximate cause of the great acceleration of the intellectual acts, in cases of drowning, appears to be (as will be found to be the fact in many other similar cases) an affection of the brain. That is to say; in consequence of the suspension of respiration, the blood is prevented from readily circulating through the lungs, and hence becomes accumulated in the brain. It would seem that the blood is never thrown into the brain in unusual quantities without being attended with unusual mental affections.

§ 169 Other instances of quickened mental action, and of a restoration of thoughts.

The doctrine which has been proposed, that the mental action may be quickened, and that there may be a restoration or remembrance of all former thoughts and feelings, is undoubtedly to be received or rejected in view of facts. The only question in this case, as in others, is, What is truth? And how are we to arrive at the truth?

If the facts which have been referred to be not enough to enable one to form an opinion, there are others of a like tēndency, and in a less uncertain form. A powerful disease, while at some times it prostrates the mind, at others imparts to it a more intense action. The following passage from a recent work (although the cause of the mental excitement, in the instance mentioned in it, is not stated) may properly be appealed to in this connexion.—"Past feelings, even should they be those of our earliest moments of infancy, never cease to be under the influence of the law of association, and they are constantly liable to be renovated, even to the latest period of life, although they may be in so faint a state as not to be the object of consciousness.

"It is evident, then, that a cause of mental excitement may so act upon a sequence of extremely faint feelings, as to render ideas, of which the mind had long been previously unconscious, vivid objects of consciousness. Thus it is recorded of a female in France, that while she was subjected to such an influence, the memory of the Armorican language, which she had lost since she was a child, suddenly returned."*

§ 170. Effect on the memory of a severe attack of fever.

We may add here the following account of the mental

* Hibbert's Philosophy of Apparitions, part iv., chapter v.

affections of an intelligent American traveller. He was travelling in the State of Illinois, and suffered the common lot of visitants from other climates, in being taken down with a bilious fever.—" As very few live," he remarks, " to record the issue of a sickness like mine, and as you have requested me, and as I have promised to be particular, I will relate some of the circumstances of this disease. And it is in my view desirable, in the bitter agony of such diseases, that more of the symptoms, sensations, and sufferings should be recorded than have been; and that others in similar predicaments may know that some before them have had sufferings like theirs, and have survived them.

" I had had a fever before, and had risen and been dressed every day. But in this, with the first day, I was prostrated to infantile weakness, and felt with its first attack that it was a thing very different from what I had yet experienced. Paroxysms of derangement occurred the third day, and this was to me a new state of mind. That state of disease in which partial derangement is mixed with a consciousness generally sound, and a sensibility preternaturally excited, I should suppose the most distressing of all its forms. At the same time that I was unable to recognise my friends, I was informed *that my memory was more than ordinarily exact and retentive, and that I repeated whole passages in the different languages, which I knew with entire accuracy. I recited, without losing or misplacing a word, a passage of poetry, which I could not so repeat after I had recovered my health,*' &c.*

§ 171. Approval and illustrations of these views from Coleridge.

An opinion favourable to the doctrine of the durability of memory, and the ultimate restoration of thought and feeling, is expressed in the BIOGRAPHIA LITERARIA of Coleridge, in an article on the Laws of association. In confirmation of it, the writer introduces a statement of certain facts which became known to him in a tour in Germany in 1798, to the following effect.

In a Catholic town of Germany, a young woman of

* Flint's Recollections of the Valley of the Mississippi, letter xiv

four or five-and-twenty, who could neither read nor write, was seized with a nervous fever, during which she was incessantly talking Greek, Latin, and Hebrew, with much pomp and distinctness of enunciation. The case attracted much attention, and many sentences which she uttered, being taken down by some learned persons present, were found to be coherent and intelligible, each for itself, but with little or no connexion with each other. Of the Hebrew only a small portion could be traced to the Bible; the remainder was that form of Hebrew which is usually called Rabbinic. Ignorant, and simple, and harmless, as this young woman was known to be, no one suspected any deception; and no explanation could for a long time be given, although inquiries were made for that purpose in different families where she had resided as a servant.

Through the zeal, however, and philosophical spirit of a young physician, all the necessary information was in the end obtained. The woman was of poor parents, and at nine years of age had been kindly taken to be brought up by an old Protestant minister, who lived at some distance. He was a very learned man; being not only a great Hebraist, but acquainted also with Rabbinical writings, the Greek and Latin Fathers, &c. The passages which had been taken down in the delirious ravings of the young woman, were found by the physician precisely to agree with passages in some books in those languages which had formerly belonged to him. But these facts were not a full explanation of the case. It appeared, on further inquiry, that the patriarchal Protestant had been in the habit for many years of walking up and down a passage of his house, into which the kitchen door opened, and to read to himself with a loud voice out of his favourite books. This attracted the notice of the poor and ignorant domestic whom he had taken into his family; the passages made an impression on her memory; and although probably for a long time beyond the reach of her recollection when in health, they were at last vividly restored, and were uttered in the way above mentioned, in consequence of the feverish state of the physical system, particularly of the brain.

From this instance, and from several others of the

same kind, which Mr. Coleridge asserts can be brought up, he is inclined to educe the following positions or inferences.—(1.) Our thoughts may, for an indefinite time, exist in the same order in which they existed originally, and in a latent or imperceptible state.—(2.) As a feverish state of the brain (and, of course, any other peculiarity in the bodily condition) cannot create thought itself, nor make any approximation to it, but can only operate as an excitement or quickener to the intellectual principle, it is therefore probable, that all thoughts are, in themselves, imperishable.—(3.) In order greatly to increase the power of the intellect, he supposes it would require only a different organization of its material accompaniment.—(4.) And, therefore, he concludes the book of final judgment, which the Scriptures inform us will at the last day be presented before the individuals of the human race, may be no other than the investment of the soul with a *celestial* instead of a *terrestrial* body ; and that this may be sufficient to restore the perfect record of the multitude of its past experiences. He supposes it may be altogether consistent with the nature of a living spirit, that heaven and earth should sooner pass away, than that a single act or thought should be loosened and effectually struck off from the great chain of its operations.—In giving these conclusions, the exact language of the writer has not been followed, but the statement made will be found to give what clearly seems to have been his meaning.

§ 172. Application of the principles of this chapter to education.

Whether the considerations which have been brought forward lead satisfactorily to the conclusion of the duration of memory, and of the possible restoration of all mental exercises, must of course be submitted to each one's private judgment. But on the supposition that they do, it must occur to every one, that certain practical applications closely connect themselves with this subject. —The principle in question has, among other things, a bearing on the education of the young ; furnishing a new reason for the utmost circumspection in conducting it The term EDUCATION, in its application to the human mind is very extensive; it includes the example and advice of parents, and the influence of associates, as well as more direct and formal instruction. Now if the doctrine under consideration be true, it follows that a single remark of a profligate and injurious tendency, made by a parent or some other person in the presence of a child, though forgotten and neglected at the time, may be suddenly and vividly recalled some twenty, thirty, or even forty years after. It may be restored to the mind by a multitude of unforeseen circumstances, and even those of the most trifling kind; and even at the late period when the voice that uttered it is silent in the grave, may exert a most pernicious influence. It may lead to unkindness; it may be seized and cherished as a justification of secret moral and religious delinquencies; it may prompt to a violation of public laws; and in a multitude of ways conduct to sin, to ignominy, and wretchedness. Great care, therefore, ought to be taken, not to utter unadvised, false, and evil sentiments in the hearing of the young, in the vain expectation that they will do no hurt, because they will be speedily and irrecoverably lost.

And, for the same reason, great care and pains should be taken to introduce truth into the mind, and all correct moral and religious principles. Suitably impress on the mind of a child the existence of a God, and his parental authority; teach the pure and benevolent outlines of the Redeemer's character, and the great truths and hopes of the Gospel; and these instructions form essential links in the grand chain of memory, which no change of circumstances, nor lapse of time, nor combination of power, can ever wholly strike out. They have their place assigned them; and though they may be concealed, they cannot be obliterated. They may perhaps cease to exercise their appropriate influence, and not be recalled for years; the pressure of the business and of the cares of life may have driven them out from every prominent position, and buried them for a time. But the period of their resurrection is always at hand, although it may not be possible for the limited knowledge of man to detect the signs of it. Perhaps, in the hour of temptation to crime, they come forth like forms and voices from the dead, and with more than their original freshness and power; perhaps, in the hour of misfortune, in the prison-house, or in the land of banishment, they pay their visitations, and impart a consolation which nothing else could have supplied; they come with the angel tones of parental reproof and love, and preserve the purity and check the despondency of the soul.

§ 173. Connexion of this doctrine with the final judgment and a future life

There remains one remark more, of a practical nature, to be made.—The views which have been proposed in respect to the ultimate restoration of all mental experiences, may be regarded as in accordance with the Divine Word. It may be safely affirmed, that no mental principle which, on a fair interpretation, is laid down in that sacred book, will be found to be at variance with the common experience of mankind. The doctrine of the Bible, in respect to a future judgment, may well be supposed to involve considerations relative to man's intellectual and moral condition. In various passages they explicitly teach that the Saviour in the last day shall judge the world, and that all shall be judged according to the deeds done in the body, whether they be good or whether they be evil. But an objection has sometimes been raised of this sort, that we can never feel the justice of that decision without a knowledge of our whole past life on which it is founded, and that this is impossible. It was probably this objection that Mr. Coleridge had in view, when he proposed the opinion, that the clothing of the soul with a celestial instead of a terrestrial body, would be sufficient to restore the perfect record of its past experiences.

In reference to this objection to the scriptural doctrine of a final judgment, the remark naturally presents itself, that it seems to derive its plausibility chiefly from an imperfect view of the constitution of the human mind. It is thought that we cannot be conscious of our whole past life, because it is utterly forgotten, and is, therefore, wholly irrecoverable. But the truth seems to be, that nothing is *wholly* forgotten; the probability that we shall be able to recall our past thoughts may be greatly diminished, but it does not become wholly extinct The power of reminiscence slumbers, but does not die. At the Judgment-day, we are entirely at liberty to suppose, from what we know of the mind, that it will awake, that it will summon up thought and feeling from its hidden recesses and will clearly present before us the perfect form and representation of the past.

"Each fainter trace that memory holds
So darkly of departed years,
In one broad glance the soul beholds,
And all that was, at once appears."

CHAPTER IX.

REASONING

§ 174. Reasoning a source of ideas and knowledge.

Leaving the consideration of the memory, we are next to examine the power of Reasoning; a subject of inquiry abundantly interesting in itself, and also in consequence of its being one of the leading and fruiful sources of Internal knowledge. For our knowledge of the operations of this faculty, we are indebted, as was seen in a former chapter, to Consciousness, which gives us our direct knowledge of all other mental acts. But it will be remarked, that Reasoning is not identical with, or involved in, Consciousness. If consciousness give us a knowledge of the act of reasoning, the reasoning power, operating within its own limits and in its own right, gives us a knowledge of other things. It is a source of perceptions and knowledge which we probably could not possess in any other way.

Without the aid of Original Suggestion, it does not appear how we could have a knowledge of our existence; without Consciousness, we should not have a knowledge of our mental operations; without Relative Suggestion or Judgment, which is also a distinct source of knowledge, there would be no Reasoning; and, unassisted by Reasoning, we could have no knowledge of the relations of those things which cannot be compared without the aid of intermediate propositions. The reasoning power therefore, is to be regarded as a new and distinct fountain of thought, which, as compared with the other sources of knowledge just mentioned, opens itself still further in the recesses of the Internal Intellect; and as it is later in its developement, so it comes forth with proportionally greater efficiency. Accordingly, Degerando, in his treatise entitled *De la Generation des Connoissances*, expressly and very justly remarks, after having spoken of judgment or Relative Suggestion as a distinct source of knowledge; "The Reasoning faculty also serves to enrich us with ideas; for there are many relations so complicated or remote, that one act of judgment is not sufficient to discover them. A series of judgments or process of reasoning is therefore necessary."—But we would not be understood to limit the results of reasoning, considered as a distinct source of knowledge, to a few simple conceptions, such as the discovery, in a given case, of the mere relation of agreement or disagreement. It sustains the higher office of bringing to light the great principles and hidden truths of nature; it reveals to the inquisitive and delighted mind a multitude of fruitful and comprehensive views, which could not otherwise be obtained; and invests men, and nature, and events with a new character.

§ 175. Definition of reasoning, and of propositions.

Reasoning may be defined the mental process or operation whereby we deduce conclusions from two or more propositions premised.—A train of reasoning may be regarded, therefore, as a *whole;* and, as such, it is made up of separate and subordinate parts. These elementary parts are usually termed PROPOSITIONS; and before we can proceed with advantage in the further consideration of reasoning, it is necessary to go into a brief explanation of them.

A PROPOSITION has been defined to be a verbal representation of some perception, act, or affection of the mind. —Accordingly, when we speak of a Proposition, we are usually understood to mean some mental perception or combination of perceptions, expressed and laid out before us in words. Although such seems to be the ordinary meaning of the term, we may admit the possibility of propositions existing wholly in the mind, without being expressed in words. Mr. Locke expressly speaks of mental propositions, or those states of mind where two or more ideas are combined together previous to their being imbodied and set forth in the forms of language.

The parts of the proposition are, (1.) The SUBJECT, or that concerning which something is either asserted or denied, commanded or inquired. (2.) The PREDICATE, or that which is asserted, denied, commanded, or inquired concerning the subject. (3.) The COPULA, by which the two other parts are connected.—In these two propositions,

Cæsar was brave,
Men are fallible,

Men and *Cæsar* are the subjects; *fallible* and *brave* are the predicates; *are* and *was* are the copulas.

Propositions have been divided, (1.) Into SIMPLE, or those whose subject and predicate are composed of single words, as in this:

Benevolence is commendable.

(2.) Into COMPLEX, or those where the subject and predicate consist of a number of words, as in this:

Faithfulness in religion is followed by peace of mind.

(3.) Into modal, where the copula is qualified by some word or words, representing the manner or possibility of the agreement or discrepancy between the subject and predicate, as in these:

Men of learning *can* exert an influence;
Wars *may* sometimes be just.

PROPOSITIONS, more or less involved, are necessary parts in every process of reasoning. They may be compared to the separate and disjointed blocks of marble which are destined to enter into the formation of some edifice; the completed process of reasoning is the edifice, the propositions are the materials.

§ 176. Process of the mind in all cases of reasoning.

Leaving the consideration of its subordinate parts or elements, we are further to consider the general nature of reasoning; in other words, we are to examine the character of the complex mental process involved in that term. The definition given of reasoning, it will be remembered, was, that it is the mental process by which we deduce conclusions from two or more propositions premised. Hence there will be in every such process a succession of propositions, never less than two, and often a much greater number. The propositions often follow each other with much regularity; and hence not unfrequently we consider the arrangement of them as entirely arbitrary. This is a mistaken supposition. It is true, when a number of ideas or propositions are presented nearly at the same time, the mind puts forth a volition, or exercises choice, in selecting one idea or proposition in preference to another. But the ideas or propositions from which the choice is made, and without the presence of which it could not be made, are not brought into existence by a direct volition, and, therefore, mere arbitrary creations; but are suggested by the laws of association

§ 177. Illustration of the preceding statement.

As an illustration of what has been said, we will suppose an argument on the justice and expediency of capital punishments in ordinary cases. The disputant first denies, in general terms, the right which social combinations have assumed of capitally punishing offences of a slight nature. But, before considering the cases he has particularly in view, he remarks on the right of capital punishment for murder; he admits, we will suppose, that the principle of self-defence gives such a right. He then takes up the case of stealing, and contends that we have no right to punish the thief with death, because no such right is given by the laws of nature; for, before the formation of the civil compact, the institution of property, as a matter of civil and judicial regulation, was not known. He then considers the nature of civil society, and contends that, in the formation of the social compact, no such extraordinary power as that of putting to death for stealing, or other crimes of similar aggravation, could have been implied in that compact, because it never was possessed by those who formed it, &c.

Here is an argument, made up of a number of propositions, and carried on, as may be supposed, to a very considerable length. And in this argument, as in all others, every proposition is, in the first instance, suggested by the laws of association; it is not at all a matter of arbitrary volition. The disputant first states the inquiry in general terms; he then considers the particular case of murder; the crime of theft is next considered; and this is examined, first, in reference to natural law, and afterward in reference to civil law.—And this consecution of propositions takes place in essentially the same way as when the sight of a stranger in the crowd suggests the image of an old friend, and the friend suggests the village of his residence, and the village suggests an ancient ruin in its neighbourhood, and the ruin suggests warriors and battles of other days.—It is true that other propositions may have been suggested at the same time, and the disputant may have had his choice between them, but this was all the direct voluntary power which he possessed.

§ 178. Grounds of the selection of propositions.

A number of propositions are presented to the mind by the principles of association; the person who carries on the process of reasoning makes his selection among them. But it is reasonable to inquire, How it happens that there is such a suitableness or agreement in the propositions, as they are successively adopted into the train of reasoning? And this seems to be no other than to inquire into the circumstances under which the choice of them is made, or the grounds of the selection.

Let it be considered, then, that in all arguments, whether moral or demonstrative, there is some general subject on which the evidence is made to bear; there is some point in particular to be examined. In reference to these general outlines we have a prevailing and permanent desire. This desire is not only a great help in giving quickness and strength to the laws of association, but exercises also a very considerable indirect influence in giving an appropriate character to the thoughts which are suggested by those laws Hence the great body of the propositions which are at such times brought up, will be found to have a greater or less reference to the general subject. These are all very rapidly compared by the mind with those outlines in regard to which its feelings of desire are exercised, or with what we usually term *the point to be proved.*—Here the mind, in the exercise of that susceptibility of feelings of relation which we have already seen it to possess, immediately discovers the suitableness or want of suitableness, the agreement or want of agreement, of the propositions presented to it, to the general subject. This perception of agreement or disagreement, which is one of those relative feelings of which the mind is, from its very nature, held to be susceptible, exists as an ultimate fact in our mental constitution. All that can profitably be said in relation to it, is the mere statement of the fact, and of the circumstances under which it is found to exist.—Those propositions which are judged by the mind, in the exercise of that capacity which its Creator has given it, to possess a congruity or agreement with the general subject or point to be proved, are permitted by it to enter in, as continuous parts of the argument. And in this way a series of propositions rises up, all having reference to one ultimate purpose, regular, appropriate, and in their issue laying the foundation of the different degrees of assent.—This explanation will apply not only to the supposed argument in the last section, which is an instance of moral reasoning, but will hold good essentially of all other instances, of whatever kind. The difference in the various kinds of reasoning consists less in the mental process than in the nature of the subjects compared together, and in the conditions attending them.

§ 179. Reasoning implies the existence of antecedent or assumed propositions.

In attempting to give some explanation of the reasoning power, it is to be remarked further, that reasoning, both in its inception and its prosecution, has this characteristic, that it necessarily proceeds, in a great degree, upon assumptions. As every deductive process implies a comparison of propositions, there must, of course, be some propositions given, by the aid of which the comparison is prosecuted. There must be something assumed as known, by means of which to find out what is unknown. Accordingly, assumed propositions (either those which are known to be true, or, for the purposes of argument, are regarded as such) are always found at the commencement of the series; and they are also introduced frequently in its progress, particularly in Moral reasoning But the propositions which are assumed are not always expressed; especially those which, from the circumstance of their being representative of elementary convictions of the understanding, are denominated PRIMARY TRUTHS.

"In every process of reasoning," says Abercrombie, "we proceed by founding one step upon another which has gone before it; and when we trace such a process backward, we must arrive at certain truths which are recognised as fundamental, requiring no proof and admitting of none."

§ 180. Further considerations on this subject.

But when we say that reasoning proceeds upon assumptions, it does not necessarily follow that it proceeds upon propositions which are unknown or doubtful. The propositions which are referred to, are assumed in reference to the reasoning power, and not in reference to other sources of knowledge which the understanding possesses besides reasoning. Whatever things are known by Original Suggestion, whatever are known by Consciousness, or by the direct communication of the Senses, or by undoubted Memory or Testimony, as they cannot be made clearer by reasoning, but fully command our belief of themselves, are at once adopted by reasoning into its own processes, and employed as helps in eliciting the remote and unperceived truths which it is in search of. But, as has been intimated, this adoption is not always a formal and acknowledged one, but often silently and by implication. No one would think of formally and repeatedly enunciating, as he advances in an argument, the truth of his own existence or of his personal identity; and not much more would he think of enunciating that every effect has its cause, or that nature is uniform in her operations, or that a combination of means conspiring to a particular end indicates intelligence; truths which are so essential and familiar to the human intellect, that we daily base the most important conclusions upon them, while, at the same time, we scarcely think of their existence.

§ 181. Of differences in the power of reasoning.

The faculty of reasoning exists in different individuals in very different degrees. There is the same diversity here which is found to exist in respect to every other mental susceptibility and mental process. In some persons it is not even powerful enough to meet the ordinary exigencies of life, and hardly rescues its possessor from the imputation of idiocy; in others, it elevates human nature and bestows extraordinary grasp and penetration. And between the extremes of extraordinary expansion and marked imbecility, there are multitudes of distinct grades, almost every possible variety.

This difference depends on various causes.—(1.) It will depend, in the first place, on the amount of knowledge which the reasoner possesses. No man can permanently sustain the reputation of great ability in argument without having previously secured a large fund of knowledge as its basis. And we may add, that no man can reason well on any given subject, unless he has especially prepared himself in reference to that subject. All reasoning implies a comparison of ideas; or, more properly, a comparison of propositions, or of facts stated in propositions. Of course, where there is no knowledge on any given subject, where there is no accumulation of facts, there can be no possibility of reasoning; and where the knowledge is much limited, the plausibility and power of the argument will be proportionally diminished.

That many persons speak on subjects which are proposed to them without having made any preparation, cannot be denied; but there is a vast difference between noisy, incoherent declamation and a well-wrought argument, made up of suitable propositions, following each other with a direct and satisfactory reference to the conclusion. In every case of reasoning, the mind passes successively along the various topics involved in the argument; and, in so doing, is governed by the principles of association, as we have already had occasion to notice But what opportunity can there possibly be for the operation of these principles, when the mind is called to fasten itself upon a subject, and to decide upon that subject, without any knowledge of those circumstances which may be directly embraced in it, or of its relations and tendencies ?

(2.) The power of reasoning will depend, in the second place, on the power of attention and memory. There are some persons who seem to have no command of the ATTENTION. Everything interests them slightly, and nothing in a high degree. They are animated by no strong feeling ; and enter into no subject requiring long-continued and abstract investigation with a suitable intensity of ardour. A defective remembrance of the numerous facts and propositions which come under review is the natural consequence of this. And this necessarily implies a perplexed and diminished power of ratiocination.

(3.) A third ground of difference is diversity in the susceptibility of feeling relations. The remark has already been made, (§ 138,) that facts may be accumulated having close and decisive relations to the points to be proved, but that they can never be so bound together as to result in any conclusion, without a perception or feeling of those relations. But it is well known, whatever it may be owing to, that the relations of objects are much more readily and clearly perceived by some than by others. As, therefore, every train of reasoning implies a succession or series of relative perceptions, a defect in the power of relative suggestion necessarily implies a defect in the reasoning power. And, on the other hand, a great quickness and clearness in the perception of relations is necessarily attended (other things being equal) with an augmented efficiency of reasoning.

§ 182. Of habits of reasoning.

But whatever may be the mental traits that render, in particular cases, the reasoning power more or less efficient, its efficacy will undoubtedly depend, in a great degree, on Habit.—The effect of frequent practice, resulting in what is termed a HABIT, is often witnessed in those who follow any mechanic calling, where we find that what was once done with difficulty comes in time to be done with great ease and readiness. The muscles of such persons seem to move with a kind of instinctive facility and accuracy in the performance of those works to which they have been for a long time addicted.

There is a similar effect of frequent practice in the increase of quickness and facility in our mental operations; and certainly as much so in those which are implied in reasoning as in any others. If, for instance, a person has never been in the habit of going through geometrical demonstrations, he finds his mind very slowly and with difficulty advancing from one step to another; while, on the other hand, a person who has so often practised this species of argumentation as to have formed a habit, advances forward from one part of the train of reasoning to another with great rapidity and delight. And the result is the same in any process of moral reasoning. In the prosecution of any argument of a moral nature, there is necessarily a mental perception of the congruity of its several parts, or of the agreement of the succeeding proposition with that which went before. The degree of readiness in bringing together propositions, and in putting forth such perceptions, will greatly depend on the degree of practice.

§ 183. Of reasoning in connexion with language or expression.

Language is the great instrument of reasoning. There may indeed be a deductive process which is purely mental; but, in point of fact, this is seldom the case. In the use of language, it is worthy of notice, that there is often a want of correspondence between the purely mental process in reasoning and the outward verbal expression of it. When persons are called upon to state their arguments suddenly and in public debate, they often commit errors which are at variance with the prevalent opinion of their good sense and mental ability. This is particularly true of men who are chiefly engaged in the ordinary business of life, or are in any situation where there is a constant call for action. The conclusions at which such persons arrive may be supposed to be generally correct, but they frequently find themselves unable to state clearly and correctly to others the process of reasoning by which they arrived at them.—Oliver Cromwell, the famous English Protector, is said to have been a person to whom this statement would well apply. The complicated incidents of his life, and the perplexities of his situation, and his great success, sufficiently evince that he possessed a clear insight into events, and was in no respect deficient in understanding; but when he attempted to express his opinions in the presence of others, and to explain himself on questions of policy, he was confused and obscure. His mind readily insinuated itself into the intricacies of a subject; and while he could assert with confidence that he had arrived at a satisfactory conclusion, he could not so readily describe either the direction he had taken, or the involutions of the journey.—"All accounts," says Mr Hume, "agree in ascribing to Cromwell a tiresome, dark, unintelligible elocution, even when he had no intention to disguise his meaning; yet no man's actions were ever, in such a variety of difficult cases, more decisive and judicious."

§ 184. Illustration of the foregoing section.

Such instances are not unfrequent. Mr. Stewart somewhere mentions the case of an English officer, a friend of Lord Mansfield, who had been appointed to the government of Jamaica. The officer expressed some doubts of his competency to preside in the court of chancery. Mansfield assured him that he would not find the difficulty so great as he imagined.—"Trust," said he, "to your own good sense in forming your opinions, but beware of stating the grounds of your judgments. The judgments will probably be right; the arguments will infallibly be wrong."

The perplexity, which is so often experienced by men engaged in active life, in giving a prompt and correct verbal expression to the internal trains of thought, is probably owing in part to a want of practice of that kind, and in part to certain mental habits, which they have been led, from their situation, to form and strengthen. In a thousand emergencies they have been obliged to act with quickness, and, at the same time, with caution; in other words, to examine subjects, and to do it with expedition. In this way they have acquired exceeding readiness in all their mental acts. The consequence of this is, that the numerous minute circumstances, involved more or less in all subjects of difficult inquiry, are passed in review with such rapidity, and are made in so very small a degree the objects of separate attention, that they vanish and are forgotten. Hence these persons, although the conclusion to which they have come be satisfactory, are unable to state to others all the subordinate steps in the argument. Everything has once been distinctly and fairly before their own minds, although with that great rapidity which is always implied in a HABIT; but their argument, as stated in words, owing to their inability to arrest and imbody all the evanescent processes of thought, appears to others defective and confused.

CHAPTER X.

DEMONSTRATIVE REASONING.

§ 185. Of the subjects of demonstrative reasoning.

IN the remarks which have hitherto been made, the subject of reasoning has been taken up in the most general point of view. The considerations that have been proposed are applicable, in the main, to reasoning in all its forms. But it is necessary, in order to possess a more full and satisfactory conception of this subject, to examine it under the two prominent heads of Moral and Demonstrative.

There are various particulars in which moral and demonstrative reasoning differ from each other; the consideration of which will suggest more fully their distinctive nature. Among other things, DEMONSTRATIVE reasoning differs from any other species of reasoning in the subjects about which it is employed. The subjects are abstract ideas, and the necessary relations among them. Those ideas or thoughts are called abstract which are representative of such qualities and properties in objects as can be distinctly examined by the mind separate from other qualities and properties with which they are commonly united. And there may be reckoned, as coming within this class of subjects, the properties of numbers and of geometrical figures; also extension, duration, weight, velocity, forces, &c., so far as they are susceptible of being accurately expressed by numbers or other mathematical signs. But the subjects of moral reasoning, upon which we are to remark hereafter more particularly, are matters of fact, including their connexion with other facts, whether constant or variable, and all attendant circumstances.—That the exterior angle of a triangle is equal to both the interior and opposite angles, is a truth which comes within the province of demonstration. That Homer was the author of the Iliad, that Xerxes invaded Greece, &c., are inquiries belonging to moral reasoning.

§ 186. Use of definitions and axioms in demonstrative reasoning.

In every process of reasoning, there must be, at the commencement of it, something to be proved; there must also be some things, either known or taken for granted as such, with which the comparison of the propositions begins. The preliminary truths in demonstrative reasonings are involved in such definitions as are found in all mathematical treatises. It is impossible to give a demonstration of the properties of a circle, parabola, ellipse, or other mathematical figure, without first having given a definition of them. DEFINITIONS, therefore, are the facts assumed, the FIRST PRINCIPLES in demonstrative reasoning, from which, by means of the subsequent steps, the conclusion is derived.—We find something entirely similar in respect to subjects which admit of the application of a different form of reasoning. Thus, in Natural Philosophy, the general facts in relation to the gravity and elasticity of the air may be considered as first principles. From these principles in Physics are deduced, as consequences, the suspension of the mercury in the barometer, and its fall when carried up to an eminence.

We must not forget here the use of axioms in the demonstrations of mathematics. Axioms are certain self-evident propositions, or propositions the truth of which is discovered by intuition, such as the following: "Things equal to the same, are equal to one another;" "From equals take away equals, and equals remain." We generally find a number of them prefixed to treatises of geometry, and other treatises involving geometrical principles; and it has been a mistaken supposition, which has long prevailed, that they are at the foundation of geometrical and of all other demonstrative reasoning. But axioms, taken by themselves, lead to no conclusions. With their assistance alone, the truth, involved in propositions susceptible of demonstration, would have been beyond our reach.

But axioms are by no means without their use, although their nature may have been misunderstood. They are properly and originally intuitive perceptions of the truth; and whether they be expressed in words, as we generally find them, or not, is of but little consequence, except as a matter of convenience to beginners, and in giving instruction. But those intuitive perceptions which are always implied in them are essential helps; and if by their aid alone we should be unable to complete a demonstration, we should be equally unable without them. We begin with definitions; we compare together successively a number of propositions; and these intuitive perceptions of their agreement or disagreement, to which, when expressed in words, we give the name of axioms, attend us at every step.

§ 187. The opposites of demonstrative reasonings absurd.

In demonstrations we consider only one side of a question; it is not necessary to do anything more than this. The first principles in the reasoning are given; they are not only supposed to be certain, but they are assumed as such; these are followed by a number of propositions in succession, all of which are compared together; if the conclusion be a demonstrative one, then there has been a clear perception of certainty at every step in the train. Whatever may be urged against an argument thus conducted is of no consequence; the opposite of it will always imply some fallacy. Thus, the proposition that the three angles of a triangle are *not* equal to two right angles, and other propositions, which are the opposite of what has been demonstrated, will always be found to be false, and also to involve an absurdity; that is, are inconsistent with, and contradictory to, themselves.

But it is not so in Moral Reasoning And here, therefore, we find a marked distinction between the two great forms of ratiocination. We may arrive at a conclusion on a moral subject with a great degree of certainty; not a doubt may be left in the mind; and yet the opposite of that conclusion may be altogether within the limits of possibility. We have, for instance, the most satisfactory evidence that the sun rose to-day, but the opposite *might* have been true, without any inconsistency or contradiction, viz., That the sun did not rise. Again, we have no doubt of the great law in physics, that heavy bodies descend to the earth in a line directed towards its centre. But we can conceive of the opposite of this without involving any contradiction or absurdity. In other words, they might have been subjected, if the Creator had so determined, to the influence of a law requiring them to move in a different direction. But, on a thorough examination of a demonstrative process, we shall find ourselves unable to admit even the *possibility* of the opposite.

§ 188. Demonstrations do not admit of different degrees of belief.

When our thoughts are employed upon subjects which come within the province of moral reasoning, we yield different degrees of assent; we form opinions more or less probable. Sometimes our belief is of the lowest kind: nothing more than mere presumption. New evidence gives it new strength; and it may go on, from one degree of strength to another, till all doubt is excluded, and all possibility of mistake shut out.—It is different in demonstrations; the assent which we yield is at all times of the highest kind, and is never susceptible of being regarded as more or less. This results, as must be obvious on the slightest examination, from the nature of demonstrative reasoning.

In demonstrative reasonings we always begin with

certain first principles or truths, either known or taken for granted; and these hold the first place, or are the foundation of that series of propositions over which the mind successively passes until it rests in the conclusion. In mathematics, the first principles, of which we here speak are the definitions.

We begin, therefore, with what is acknowledged by all to be true or certain. At every step there is an intuitive perception of the agreement or disagreement of the propositions which are compared together. Consequently, however far we may advance in the comparison of them, there is no possibility of falling short of that degree of assent with which it is acknowledged that the series commenced.—So that demonstrative certainty may be judged to amount to this. Whenever we arrive at the last step, or the conclusion of a series of propositions, the mind, in effect, intuitively perceives the relation, whether it be the agreement or disagreement, coincidence or want of coincidence, between the last step or the conclusion, and the conditions involved in the propositions at the commencement of the series; and, therefore, demonstrative certainty is virtually the same as the certainty of intuition. Although it arises on a different occasion, and is, therefore, entitled to a separate consideration, there is no difference in the degree of belief.

§ 189. Of the use of diagrams in demonstrations.

In conducting a demonstrative process, it is frequently the case that we make use of various kinds of figures or diagrams.—The proper use of diagrams, of a square, circle, triangle, or other figure which we delineate before us, is to assist the mind in keeping its ideas distinct, and to help in comparing them together with readiness and correctness. They are a sort of auxiliaries, brought in to the help of our intellectual infirmities, but are not absolutely necessary; since demonstrative reasoning, wherever it may be found, resembles any other kind of reasoning in this most important respect, viz., in being a comparison of our ideas.

In proof that artificial diagrams are only auxiliaries, and are not essentially necessary in demonstrations it may be remarked, that they are necessarily all of them imperfect. It is not within the capability of the wit and power of man to frame a perfect circle, or a perfect triangle, or any other figure which is perfect. We might argue this from our general knowledge of the imperfection of the senses; and we may almost regard it as a matter determined by experiments of the senses themselves, aided by optical instruments. "There never was," says Cudworth, "a straight line, triangle, or circle, that we saw in all our lives, that was mathematically exact; but even sense itself, at least by the help of microscopes, might plainly discover much unevenness, ruggedness, flexuosity, angulosity, irregularity, and deformity in them."*

Our reasonings, therefore, and our conclusions, will not apply to the figures before us, but merely to an imagined perfect figure. The mind can not only originate a figure internally and subjectively, but can ascribe to it the attribute of perfection. And a verbal statement of the properties of this imagined perfect figure is what we understand by a DEFINITION, the use of which, in this kind of reasoning in particular, has already been mentioned

---

CHAPTER XI.

MORAL REASONING.

§ 190. Of the subjects and importance of moral reasoning.

MORAL REASONING, which is the second great division or kind of reasoning, concerns opinions, actions, and events; embracing, in general, those subjects which do not come within the province of demonstrative reasoning. The subjects to which it relates are often briefly expressed, by saying that they are *matters of fact;* nor would this definition, concise as it is, be likely to give an erroneous idea of them.

Skill in this kind of reasoning is of great use in the formation of opinions concerning the duties and the gen

* Treatise concerning Immutable Morality, bk. iv., ch iii.

eral conduct of life. Some may be apt to think, that those who have been most practised in demonstrative reasoning can find no difficulty in adapting their intellectual habits to matters of mere probability. This opinion is not altogether well founded. Although that species of reasoning has a favourable result in giving persons a command over the attention, and in some other respects, whenever exclusively employed it has the effect, in some degree, to disqualify them for a correct judgment on those various subjects which properly belong to moral reasoning.—The last, therefore, which has its distinctive name from the primary signification of the Latin MORES, viz., *manners, customs,* &c., requires a separate consideration.

§ 191. Of the nature of moral certainty.

Moral reasoning causes in us different degrees of assent, and in this respect differs from demonstrative. In demonstration there is not only an immediate perception of the relation of the propositions compared together; but, in consequence of their abstract and determinate nature, there is also a knowledge or absolute certainty of their agreement or disagreement. In moral reasoning the case is somewhat different.—In both kinds we begin with certain propositions, which are either known or regarded as such. In both there is a series of propositions successively compared. But in moral reasoning, in consequence of the propositions not being abstract and fixed, and, therefore, often uncertain, the agreement or disagreement among them is, in general, not said to be known, but *presumed;* and this presumption may be more or less, admitting a great variety of degrees. While, therefore, one mode of reasoning is attended with knowledge, the other can properly be said to produce, in most cases, only judgment or opinion.—But the probability of such judgment or opinion may sometimes arise so high as to exclude all reasonable doubt. And hence we then speak as if we possessed certainty in respect to subjects which admit merely of the application of moral reasoning. Although it is possible that there may be some difference between the belief attendant on demonstration and that produced by the highest probability, the effect on our feelings is, at any rate, essentially the same. A man who should doubt the existence of the cities of London and Pekin, although he has no other evidence of it than that of testimony, would be considered hardly less singular and unreasonable than one who might take it into his head to doubt of the propositions of Euclid.—It is this very high degree of probability which we term *moral certainty.*

§ 192. Of reasoning from analogy.

MORAL REASONING admits of some subordinate divisions; and of these, the first to be mentioned is reasoning from *analogy.*—The word analogy is used with some vagueness, but, in general, denotes a resemblance, either greater or less.—Having observed a consistency and uniformity in the operations of the physical world, we are naturally led to presume that things of the same nature will be affected in the same way, and will produce the same effects; and also that the same or similar effects are to be attributed to like causes. ANALOGICAL REASONING, therefore, is that mental process by which unknown truths or conclusions are inferred from the resemblance of things.

The argument by which Sir Isaac Newton establishes the truth of universal gravitation is of this sort. He proves that the planets, in their revolutions, are deflected towards the sun in a manner precisely similar to the deflection of the earth towards the same luminary; and also that there is a similar deflection of the moon towards the earth, and of a body projected obliquely at the earth's surface towards the earth's centre. Hence he infers by analogy, that all these deflections originate from the same cause, or are governed by one and the same law, viz., *the power of gravitation.* There are a variety of subjects, both speculative and practical, in respect to which we may reason in this way, and sometimes with considerable satisfaction. It is nevertheless true, that much care is necessary in arguments drawn from this source, especially in scientific investigations. The proper use of analogical reasoning in scientific inquiries seems to be, merely to illustrate and confirm truths which are susceptible of proof from other sources of evidence, either by casting a direct additional light or by answering objections

§ 193. Of reasoning by induction.

We now come to another method of moral reasoning, viz., by induction. *Inductive reasoning* is the inferring of general truths from particular facts that have fallen under our observation. Our experience teaches us that nature is governed by uniform laws; and we have a firm expectation, (whether it be an original principle of our constitution, or whatever may be the origin of it,) that events will happen in future, as we have seen them happen in times past. With this state of mind we are prepared to deduce inferences by induction.

When a property has been found in a number of subjects of the same kind, and nothing of a contradictory nature appears, we have the strongest expectation of finding the same property in all the individuals of the same class; in other words, we come to the conclusion that the property is a general one. Accordingly, we apply a magnet to several pieces of iron; we find, in every instance, a strong attraction taking place; and we conclude, although we have made the experiment with only a small number of the masses of iron actually in existence, that it is a property of iron to be thus affected by that substance, or that all iron is susceptible of magnetical attraction. This is a conclusion drawn by induction

The belief which attends a well-conducted process of inductive reasoning bears a decided character; it is moral probability of the highest kind, or what is sometimes termed moral certainty; and is at least found to be sufficient for all practical purposes. We obtain all the general truths relating to the properties and laws of material objects in this way.

And we thus not only acquire a knowledge of material objects, but apply the same inductive process also in the investigation of laws which govern the operations of the mind. It is by experience, or observing what takes place in a number of individuals, that we are able to infer the general law of association, viz., when two or more ideas have existed in the mind in immediate succession, they are afterward found to be mutually suggested by each other. It is the same in ascertaining other general laws of the mind

S 2

§ 194. Of combined or accumulated arguments.

When a proposition in geometry is given to be demonstrated, it sometimes happens that two or more solutions may be offered leading to the same end. The theorem or the problem is one and the same, as also the conclusion; but there may be more than one train of reasoning, more than one series of intermediate steps connecting the proposition which is to be investigated with the result. But as the conclusion in each of these different cases is certain, it does not strengthen it, although it may gratify curiosity to resort to a different and additional process.

It is not thus in moral reasoning. The great difference between the two kinds of reasoning, as before observed, is not so much in the mental process as in the subjects about which they are employed. Now, as the subjects in moral reasoning are not of a purely abstract nature, and are, therefore, often attended with uncertainty, our belief, when we arrive at the conclusion, is not always of the highest kind. More frequently it is some inferior degree of probability. Hence, in any moral inquiry, the more numerous the series of arguments which terminates in a particular conclusion, the stronger will be our belief in the truth of that conclusion.

Thus we may suppose a question to arise, Whether the Romans occupied the island of Great Britain at some period previous to the Saxon conquest? In reference to this inquiry a number of independent arguments may be brought forward. (1.) The testimony of the Roman historians. (2.) The remains of buildings, roads, and encampments, which indicate a Roman origin. (3.) The coins, urns, &c., which have been discovered. Although these arguments are independent of each other, they all bear upon the same conclusion; and, being combined together, they very essentially increase the strength of our belief.

CHAPTER XII.

PRACTICAL DIRECTIONS IN REASONING.

§ 195. Rules relating to the practice of reasoning.

VARIOUS directions have been given by writers on Logic, (which, it may be remarked here, is only another name for whatever concerns the nature, kinds, and applications of Reasoning,) the object of which is to secure the more prompt, accurate, and efficient use of the reasoning power. It is but natural to suppose, that some of these dialectical rules are of greater, and others of less value. Such as appeared to be of the least questionable importance, are brought together and explained in this chapter; nor will this occasion any surprise, when it is recollected that it has been the object of this work throughout, not only to ascertain what the mental operations are, but, by practical suggestions from time to time, to promote what is of a good, and prevent what is of a hurtful tendency in such operations.

The directions now referred to have, of course, a more intimate connexion with Moral than with Demonstrative reasoning; but this is a circumstance which enhances rather than diminishes their worth. The occasions which admit and require the application of moral reasoning, being inseparable from the most common occurrences and exigences of life, are much more numerous than those of demonstrative reasoning.

§ 196. Of being influenced in reasoning by a love of the truth.

(I.) The first direction in relation to reasoning which will be given, concerns the feelings with which it is proper to be animated. It is this. In all questions which admit of discussion, and on which we find ourselves at variance with the opinions of others, *we are to make truth our object.*—The opposite of a desire of the truth is a wish to decide the subject of dispute in one way rather than another, independently of a just consideration of the evidence. The foundation of such a preference of one result to another are, in general, the prejudices of interest and passion; and these are the great enemies of truth. Whenever we are under their influence, we form a different estimation of testimony, and of other sources of evidence, from what we should do under other circumstances; and at such times they can hardly fail to lead us to false results.—This rule is important on all occasions of reasoning whatever, but particularly in public debate; because at such times the presence of others and the love of victory combine with other unpropitious influences to induce men to forget or to disregard the claims which truth is always entitled to enforce.

§ 197. Care to be used in correctly stating the subject of discussion.

(II.) Another rule in the prosecution of an argument is, that the question under debate is to be fairly and correctly stated. The matter in controversy may be stated in such a way as to include, in the very enunciation of it, something taken for granted, which must necessarily lead to a decision in favour of one of the opponents. But this amounts to begging the question, a species of fallacy or sophism upon which we shall again have occasion to remark.—Sometimes the subject of discussion is stated so carelessly, that the true point at issue is wholly left out. It may be proper, therefore, in many cases, to adopt the practice of special pleaders, and first to ascertain all the points in which the opponents agree, and those in which they differ. And then they can hardly fail of directing their arguments to what is truly the subject of contention.

In order that there may not be a possibility of misunderstanding here, dialecticians should aim to have clear ideas of everything stated in the question which has an intimate connexion with the point at issue. Subordinate parts of the question, and even particular words, are to be examined. If, for instance, the statement affirm or deny anything in regard to the qualities or properties of material bodies, it is incumbent upon us to possess as clear ideas as possible, both of the object in general, and of those properties or qualities in particular. Similar remarks will apply to other subjects of inquiry of whatever kind.

§ 198. Consider the kind of evidence applicable to the subject.

(III.) As one subject clearly admits of the application of one species of evidence, while another as clearly requires evidence of a different kind, we are thence enabled to lay down this rule, viz., We are to consider what kind of evidence is appropriate to the question under discussion.

When the inquiry is one of a purely abstract nature, and all the propositions involved in the reasoning are of the same kind, then we have the evidence of Intuition or intuitive perception; and the conclusion, for reasons already mentioned, is certain.—In the examination of the properties of material bodies, we depend originally on the evidence of the Senses; which gives a character and strength to our belief, according to the circumstances under which the objects are presented to them.—In judging of those facts in events and in the conduct of men which have not come under our own observation, we rely on Testimony. This source of belief causes probability in a greater or less degree, according as the testimony is from one or more, given by a person who understands the subject to which it relates, or not, &c.—And again, some subjects admit of the evidence of Induction, and in respect to others we have no other aids than the less authoritative reasonings from Analogy. In other cases, the evidence is wholly made up of various incidental circumstances, which are found to have relation to the subject in hand, and which affect the belief in different degrees and for various causes.

And hence, as the sources of belief, as well as the belief itself, have an intimate connexion with the subject before us, they ought to be taken into consideration. The evidence should be appropriate to the question. But if the question admit of more than one kind of evidence, then all are entitled to their due weight.

§ 199. Reject the aid of false arguments or sophisms.

(IV.) There is a species of false reasoning which we call a SOPHISM. A sophism is an argument which contains some secret fallacy under the general appearance of correctness. The aid of such arguments, which are cal culated to deceive, and are, in general, inconsistent with a love of the truth, should be rejected.

(1.) IGNORATIO ELENCHI, or misapprehension of the question, is one instance of sophism. It exists when, from some misunderstanding of the terms and phrases that are employed, the arguments advanced do not truly apply to the point in debate. It was a doctrine, for instance, of some of the early philosophic teachers of Greece, that there is but *one principle of things.* Aristotle, under standing by the word principle what we commonly express by the word ELEMENT, attempted to show the contrary, viz., that the elements are not one, but many; thus incurring the imputation of IGNORATIO ELENCHI; for those who held the doctrine which was thus subjected to his animadversion, had reference, not to the forms, but the *cause* of things; not to any doctrine of elementary material particles, but to the intellectual origin, the creative mind, the Supreme Being, whom, as the PRINCIPLE, (that is, as the beginning and the support of things,) they maintained to be one.*

(2.) PETITIO PRINCIPII, or begging of the question, is another instance of sophism. This sophism is found whenever the disputant offers, in proof of a proposition, the proposition itself in other words. The following has been given as an instance of this fallacy in reasoning:—A person attempts to prove that God is eternal, by maintaining that his existence is without beginning and without end. Here the proof which is offered, and the proposition itself which is to be proved, are essentially the same.—When we are told that opium causes sleep, because it has a soporific quality, or that grass grows by means of its vegetative power, the same thing is repeated in other terms.—This fallacy is very frequently practised; and a little care in detecting it would spoil many a fine saying, as well as deface many an elaborate argument. What is called *arguing in a circle* is a species of sophism very nearly related to the above. It consists in making two propositions reciprocally prove each other.

(3.) NON CAUSA PRO CAUSA, or the assignation of a false

* La Logique ou L'art de Penser, (Port Royale,) part iii., chap. xix

cause.—People are unwilling to be thought ignorant; rather than be thought so, they will impose on the credulity of their fellow-men, and sometimes on themselves, by assigning false causes of events. Nothing is more common than this sophism among illiterate people; pride is not diminished by deficiency of learning, and such people, therefore, must gratify it by assigning such causes of events as they find nearest at hand. Hence, when the appearance of a comet is followed by a famine or a war, they are disposed to consider it as the cause of those calamities. If a person have committed some flagrant crime, and shortly after suffer some heavy distress, it is no uncommon thing to hear the former assigned as the direct and the sole cause of the latter. This was the fallacy which historians have ascribed to the Indians of Paraguay, who supposed the baptismal ceremony to be the cause of death, because the Jesuit missionaries, whenever opportunity offered, administered it to dying infants, and to adults in the last stage of disease.

(4.) Another species of sophistry is called FALLACIA ACCIDENTIS.—We fall into this kind of false reasoning whenever we give an opinion concerning the general nature of a thing from some accidental circumstance. Thus, the Christian religion has been made the pretext for persecutions, and has, in consequence, been the source of much suffering; but it is a sophism to conclude that it is, on the whole, not a great good to the human race, because it has been attended with this perversion. Again, if a medicine have operated in a particular case unfavourably, or, in another case, have operated very favourably, the universal rejection or reception of it, in consequence of the favourable or unfavourable result in a particular instance, would be a hasty and fallacious induction of essentially the same sort. That is, the general nature of the thing is estimated from a circumstance which may be wholly accidental.

§ 200. Fallacia equivocationis, or the use of equivocal terms and phrases

(V.) It is a further direction of much practical importance, that the reasoner should be careful, in the use of language, to express everything with plainness and precision; and, especially, never attempt to prejudice the cause of truth, and snatch a surreptitious victory by the use of an equivocal phraseology. No man of an enlarged and cultivated mind can be ignorant that multitudes of words in every language admit of diversities of signification. There are found also in all languages many words, which sometimes agree with each other, and sometimes differ in signification, according to the connexion in which they appear, and their particular application. There is, therefore, undoubtedly an opportunity, if any should be disposed to embrace it, of employing equivocal terms, equivocal phrases, and perplexed and mysterious combinations of speech, and thus hiding themselves from the penetrating light of truth, under cover of a mist of their own raising.

No man, whose sole object is truth and justice, will resort to such a discreditable subterfuge. If, in reasoning, he finds himself inadvertently employing words of an equivocal signification, it will be a first care with him to guard against the misapprehensions likely to result from that source. He will explain so precisely the sense in which he uses the doubtful terms, as to leave no probability of cavilling and mistake.

§ 201. Of the sophism of estimating actions and character from the circumstance of success merely.

(VI.) The foregoing are some of the fallacies in reasoning which have found a place in writers of Logic. To these might be added the fallacy or sophism to which men are obviously so prone, of judging favourably of the characters and the deeds of others from the mere circumstance of success. Those actions which have a decidedly successful termination are almost always applauded, and are looked upon as the result of great intellectual forecast; while, not less frequently, actions that have an unsuccessful issue are not only stigmatized as evil in themselves, but as indicating in their projector a flighty and ill-balanced mind.—The fallacy, however, does not consist in taking the issues or results into consideration, which are undoubtedly entitled to their due place in estimating the actions and characters of men, but in too much limiting our view of things, and forming a favourable or unfavourable judgment from the mere circumstance of good or ill success alone.

While there is no SOPHISM more calculated to lead astray and perplex, there is none more common than this; so much so, that it has almost passed into a proverb, that a hero must not only be brave, but *fortunate*. Hence it is that Alexander is called Great because he gained victories and overran kingdoms; while Charles XII. of Sweden, who the most nearly resembles him in the characteristics of bravery, perseverance, and chimerical ambition, but had his projects cut short at the fatal battle of Pultowa, is called a madman.

"Machiavel has justly animadverted," says Dr. Johnson, "on the different notice taken by all succeeding times of the two great projectors Catiline and Cæsar. Both formed the same project, and intended to raise themselves to power by subverting the commonwealth. They pursued their design, perhaps, with equal abilities and equal virtue; but Catiline perished in the field, and Cæsar returned from Pharsalia with unlimited authority; and from that time, every monarch of the earth has thought himself honoured by a comparison with Cæsar; and Catiline has never been mentioned but that his name might be applied to traitors and incendiaries."

§ 202. Of adherence to our opinions.

Whenever the rules laid down have been followed, and conclusions have been formed with a careful and candid regard to the evidence presented, those opinions are to be asserted and maintained with a due degree of confidence. It would evince an unjustifiable weakness to be driven from our honest convictions by the effrontery, or even by the upright though misguided zeal, of an opponent. Not that a person is to set himself up for infallible, and to suppose that new accessions of evidence are impossible, or that it is an impossibility for him to have new views of the evidence already examined. But a suitable degree of stability is necessary in order to be respected and useful; and, in the case supposed, such stability can be exhibited without incurring the charge, which is sometimes thrown out, of doggedness and intolerance.

It is further to be observed, that we are not always to relinquish judgments which have been formed in the way pointed out, when objections are afterward raised which we cannot immediately answer. The person thus attacked can, with good reason, argue in this way: I have once examined the subject carefully and candidly; the evidence, both in its particulars and in its multitude of bearings, has had its weight; many minute and evanescent circumstances were taken into view by the mind, which have now vanished from my recollection; I therefore do not feel at liberty to alter an opinion thus formed, in consequence of an objection now brought up, which I am unable to answer, but choose to adhere to my present judgment, until the whole subject, including this objection, can be re-examined.—This reasoning would in most cases be correct, and would be entirely consistent with that love of truth and openness to conviction which ought ever to be maintained.

§ 203. Effects on the mind of debating for victory instead of truth.

By way of supporting the remarks under the first rule we here introduce the subject of contending for victory merely. He who contends with this object, takes every advantage of his opponent which can subserve his own purpose. For instance, he will demand a species of proof or a degree of proof which the subject in dispute does not admit; he gives, if possible, a false sense to the words and statements employed by the other side; he questions facts which he himself fully believes and everybody else, in the expectation that the opposite party is not furnished with direct and positive evidence of them. In a word, wherever an opening presents, he takes the utmost advantage of his opponent, however much against his own internal convictions of right and justice.

Such a course, to say nothing of its moral turpitude, effectually unsettles that part of our mental economy which concerns the grounds and laws of belief. The practice of inventing cunningly devised objections against arguments known to be sound, necessarily impairs the influence which such arguments ought to exert over us. Hence the remark has been made with justice, that persons who addict themselves to this practice frequently end in becoming skeptics. They have so often perplexed, and apparently overthrown what they felt to be true, that they at last question the existence of any fixed ground of belief in the human constitution, and begin to doubt of everything.

This effect, even when there is an undoubted regard for the truth, will be found to follow from habits of ardent disputation, unless there be a frequent recurrence to the original principles of the mind which relate to the nature and laws of belief. The learned Chillingworth is an instance. The consequences to which the training up of his vast powers to the sole art of disputation finally led, are stated by Clarendon.—"Mr. Chillingworth had spent all his younger time in disputations, and had arrived at so great a mastery that he was inferior to no man in those skirmishes; but he had, with his notable perfection in this exercise, contracted such an irresolution and habit of doubting, that, by degrees, he became confident of nothing. Neither the books of his adversaries nor any of their persons, though he was acquainted with the best of both, had ever made great impression on him. All his doubts grew out of himself, when he assisted his scruples with all the strength of his own reason, and was then too hard for himself."

CHAPTER XIII.

IMAGINATION.

§ 204. Imagination an intellectual rather than a sensitive process.

Leaving the subject of reasoning, we next proceed to the consideration of the Imagination; which, as well as the reasoning power, obviously comes under the general head of the Intellect rather than of the Sensibilities. It is true, we are apt to associate the exercises of the heart with those of the imagination, and undoubtedly we have some reason for doing so; but in doing this we are liable not merely to associate, but to identify and confound them. But they are, in fact, essentially different. An exercise of the Imagination, *in itself considered*, is purely an intellectual process. The process may, indeed, be stimulated and accelerated by a movement of the sensibilities; there may be various extraneous influences operating either to increase or to diminish its vivacity and energy; but the process itself, considered separately from contingent circumstances, is wholly intellectual. So that he who possesses a creative and well-sustained imagination, may be said, with no small degree of truth, to possess a powerful intellect, whatever torpidity may characterize the region of the affections.

§ 205. The imagination closely related to the reasoning power.

The imagination is not only entitled to be ranked under the general head of the Intellect, in distinction from the Sensibilities; but it is to be remarked further, which may perhaps have escaped the notice of some, that it possesses, especially in the process or mode of its action, a close affinity with the reasoning power. It is a remark ascribed to D'Alembert, whose great skill in the mathematics would seem to justify his giving an opinion on such a subject, that the imagination is brought into exercise in geometrical processes; which is probably true, so far as some of the mental acts involved in imagination, such as association and the perception of relations, are concerned. And, in illustration of his views, he intimates, in the same connexion, that Archimedes the geometrician, of all the great men of antiquity, is best entitled to be placed by the side of Homer.* Certain it is, that, in some important respects, there is an intimate relationship between the powers in question, the deductive and imaginative. They both imply the antecedent exercise of the power of abstraction; they are both occupied in framing new combinations of thought from the elements already in possession; they both put in requisition, and in precisely the same way, the powers of association and relative suggestion. But, at the same time, they are separated from each other and characterized by the two circumstances, that their objects are different, and that they

* Stewart's Historical Dissertation.—Prefatory Remarks.

operate, in part, on different materials. Reasoning, as it aims to give us a knowledge of the truth, deals exclusively with facts more or less probable. Imagination, as it aims chiefly to give pleasure, is at liberty to transcend the limits of the world of reality, and, consequently, often deals with the mere conceptions of the mind, whether they correspond to reality or not. Accordingly, the one ascertains what is true, the other what is possible; the office of the one is to inquire, of the other to create; reasoning is exercised within the limits of what is known and actual, while the appropriate empire of the imagination is the region of the conjectural and conceivable.

§ 206. Definition of the power of imagination.

Without delaying longer upon the subject, which, however, is not without its importance, of the place which imagination ought to occupy in a philosophical classification of the mental powers, we next proceed to consider more particularly what imagination is, and in what manner it operates.—Imagination is a complex exercise of the mind, by means of which various conceptions are combined together, so as to form new wholes. The conceptions have properly enough been regarded as the materials from which the new creations are made; but it is not until after the existence of those mental acts which are implied in every process of the imagination, that they are fixed upon, detained, and brought out from their state of singleness into happy and beautiful combinations.

Our conceptions have been compared to shapeless stones, as they exist in the quarry, "which require little more than mechanic labour to convert them into common dwellings, but that rise into palaces and temples only at the command of architectural genius." That rude and little more than mechanic effort, which converts the shapeless stones of the quarry into common dwellings, may justly be considered, when divested of its metaphorical aspect, a correct representation of this mental property as it exists among the great mass of mankind; while the architectural genius which creates palaces and temples is the well-furnished and sublime imagination of poets, painters, and orators.

We speak of imagination as a complex mental operation, because it implies, in particular, the exercise of the power of association in furnishing those conceptions which are combined together; also the exercise of the power of relative suggestion, by means of which the combination is effected.

§ 207. Process of the mind in the creations of the imagination.

It may assist us in more fully understanding the nature of imagination, if we endeavour to examine the intellectual operations of one who makes a formal effort at writing, whether the production he has in view be poetical or of some other kind.—A person cannot ordinarily be supposed to sit down to write on any occasion whatever, whether it involve a higher or lesser degree of the exercise of the imagination, without having some general idea of the subject to be written upon already in the mind. The general idea, or the subject in its *outlines*, must be supposed to be already present. He accordingly commences the task before him with the expectation and the desire of developing the subject more or less fully, of giving to it not only a greater continuity and a better arrangement, but an increased interest in every respect. As he feels interested in the topic which he proposes to write upon, he can, of course, by a mere act of the will, although he might not have been able in the first instance to have originated it by such an act, detain it before him for a length of time.

Various conceptions continue, in the mean while, to arise in the mind, on the common principles of association; but, as the general outline of the subject remains fixed, they all have a greater or less relation to it. And partaking in some measure of the permanency of the outline to which they have relation, the writer has an opportunity to approve some and to reject others, according as they impress him as being suitable or unsuitable to the nature of the subject. Those which affect him with emotions of pleasure, on account of their perceived fitness for the subject, are retained and committed to writing; while others, which do not thus affect and interest him, soon fade away altogether.—Whoever carefully notizes the operations of his own mind, when he makes an effort at composition, will probably be well satisfied that this account of the intellectual process is very near the truth.

§ 208. Further remarks on the same subject.

The process, therefore, stated in the most simple and concise terms, is as follows. We first think of some subject. With the original thought or design of the subject, there is a coexistent desire to investigate it, to adorn it, to present it to the examination of others. The effect of this desire, followed and aided as it naturally is at such times by an act of the will, is to keep the general subject in mind; and, as the natural consequence of the exercise of association, various conceptions arise, in some way or other related to the general subject. Of some of these conceptions we approve in consequence of their perceived fitness to the end in view, while we reject others on account of the absence of this requisite quality of agreeableness or fitness.

For the sake of convenience and brevity we give the name of IMAGINATION to this complex state or series of states of the mind. It is important to possess a single term expressive of the complex intellectual process; otherwise, as we so frequently have occasion to refer to it in common conversation, we should be subjected, if not properly to a circumlocution, at least to an unnecessary multiplication of words. But while we find it so much for our convenience to make use of this term, we should be careful and not impose upon ourselves, by ever remembering that it is the name, nevertheless, not of an original and independent faculty, which of itself accomplishes all that has been mentioned, but of a complex or combined action of a number of faculties.

§ 209. Illustration from the writings of Dr. Reid.

Dr. Reid (Essay iv., ch. iv.) gives the following graphical statement of the selection which is made by the writer from the variety of his constantly arising and departing conceptions.—" We seem to treat the thoughts, that present themselves to the fancy in crowds, as a great man treats those [courtiers] that attend his levee. They are all ambitious of his attention. He goes round the circle, bestowing a bow upon one, a smile upon another, asks a short question of a third, while a fourth is honoured with a particular conference; and the greater part have no particular mark of attention, but go as they came. It is true, he can give no mark of his attention to those who were *not there;* but he has a sufficient number for making a choice and distinction."

§ 210. Grounds of the preference of one conception to another.

A question after all arises, On what principle is the mind enabled to ascertain that congruity or incongruity, fitness or unfitness, agreeably to which it makes the selection from its various conceptions? The fact is admitted, that the intellectual principle is successively in a series of different states, or, in other words, that there are successive conceptions or images, but the inquiry still remains, Why is one image in the group thought or known to be more worthy than any other image, or why are any two images combined together in preference to any two others?

The answer is, it is owing to no secondary law, but to an instantaneous and original suggestion of fitness or unfitness. Those conceptions which, by means of this original power of perceiving the relations of things, are found to be suitable to the general outlines of the subject, are detained. Those images which are perceived to possess a peculiar congruity and fitness for each other, are united together, forming new and more beautiful compounds. While others, although no directly voluntary power appears to be exercised over either class, are neglected and soon become extinct. But no account of this vivid feeling of approval or disapproval, of this very rapid perception of the mutual congruity of the images for each other or for the general conception of the subject, can be given, other than this, that with such a power the original author of our intellectual susceptibilities has been pleased to form us. This is our nature; here we find one of the elements of our intellectual efficiency; without it we might still be intellectual beings, but it would be with the loss both of the reasoning power and of the imagination.

§ 211 Illustration of the subject from Milton

What has been said can perhaps be made plainer, by considering in what way Milton must have proceeded in forming his happy description of the Garden of Eden He had formed, in the first place, some general outlines of the subject; and as it was one which greatly interested his feelings, the interest which was felt tended to keep the outlines steadily before him. If the feeling of interest was not sufficient to keep the general subject before the mind, he could hardly fail to detain it there by adding the influence of a direct and decisive act of the will Then the principles of association, which are ever at work, brought up a great variety of conceptions, having a relation of some kind to those general features; such as conceptions of rocks, and woods, and rivers, and green leaves, and golden fruit.

The next step was the exercise of that power which we have of perceiving relations, which we sometimes denominate the Judgment, but more appropriately the susceptibility or power of Relative Suggestion. By means of this he was at once able to determine, whether the conceptions which were suggested were suitable to the general design of the description and to each other, and whether they would have, when combined together to form one picture, a pleasing effect. Accordingly, those which were judged most suitable were combined together as parts of the imaginary creation, and were detained and fixed by means of that feeling of interest and those acts of the will which were at first exercised towards the more prominent outlines merely; while others speedily disappeared from the mind. And thus arose an imaginary landscape, glowing with a greater variety and richness of beauty, more interesting and perfect, in every respect, than we can ever expect to find realized in nature.

§ 212. The creations of imagination not entirely voluntary.

From the explanation which has been given of the operations of the power under consideration, it will be seen that, in its action, it is subject to limitations and restrictions. The opinion, that even persons of the most ready and fruitful imagination can form new imaginary creations whenever they choose, by a mere volition, however widely it may have prevailed, does not appear to be well founded. In accordance with what may be regarded as the common opinion, we will suppose, as an illustration of what we mean, that a person wills to imagine a sea of melted brass, or an immense body of liquid matter which has that appearance. The very expressions, it will be noticed, are nugatory and without meaning, since the sea of brass which the person wills to conceive of or imagine, is, by the very terms of the proposition, already present to his thoughts. Whatever a person wills, or, rather, professes to will to imagine, he has, in fact, already imagined; and, consequently, there can be no such thing as imaginations which are exclusively the result of a direct act of the will. So that the powers of invention, although the influence of the indirect and subordinate action of the will may be considerable, must be aroused and quickened to their highest efforts in some other way.

And this view admits of some practical applications. Men of the greatest minds (great, we mean, in the walks of literature) are kept in check by the principles which are involved in the exercise of imagination. Genius, whatever capabilities we may attribute to it, has its laws. And it is true, in regard to every standard work of the imagination, that it is the result, not of an arbitrary and unexplainable exercise of that power, but of a multitude of circumstances, prompting and regulating its action; such as the situation in life, early education, domestic habits, associates, reading, scenery, religion, and the influence of local superstitions and traditionary incidents. These are like the rain and sunshine to the earth, without which it necessarily remains in its original barrenness, giving no signs of vivification and beauty. In the matter of creative power, Bunyan will bear a comparison, undoubtedly, with Walter Scott; but Scott, in the situation in which he was placed, and with the habits of thought and feeling which he cherished, could not have written the Pilgrim's Progress; nor could Bunyan, on the other hand, have written the Heart of Mid Lothian; not because either of them was destitute of the requisite degree of imagination, but because the creations of the imagination always have a relation to circumstances, and are not the result of a purely arbitrary act of the will.

§ 213. Illustration of the statements of the preceding section.

It would be an easy matter, and not without interest, to illustrate this fact in the operations of the mind by a reference to the private history of those individuals from whom the great works of literature have originated. But, as this does not come within our plan, we will refer merely to a single instance.—Moore relates, in his life of Lord Byron, that on a certain occasion he found him occupied with the history of Agathon, a romance by Wieland And, from some remarks made at the time, he seems to be of opinion that Byron was reading the work in question as a means of furnishing suggestions to, and of quickening, his own imaginative powers. He then adds, "I am inclined to think it was his practice, when engaged in the composition of any work, to excite his vein by the perusal of others on the same subject or plan, from which the slightest hint caught by his imagination, as he read, was sufficient to kindle there such a train of thought as, but for that spark, had never been awakened."

This is said of a distinguished poet. Painting is an art kindred with poetry; and both are based on the imagination. Accordingly, the remarks which have been made apply also to painting, and, indeed, to every other art which depends essentially on the imaginative power. "Invention," says Sir Joshua Reynolds, "is one of the great marks of genius; but, if we consult experience, we shall find that it is by being conversant with the inventions of others that we learn to invent, as by reading the thoughts of others we learn to think. It is in vain for painters or poets to endeavour to invent without materials on which the mind may work, and from which invention must originate. Nothing can come of nothing. Homer is supposed to have been possessed of all the learning of his time; and we are certain that Michael Angelo and Raffaelle were equally possessed of all the knowledge in the art which had been discovered in the works of their predecessors."*

* Discourses before the Royal Academy, vi.

§ 214. On the utility of the faculty of the imagination.

We have proceeded thus far in endeavouring to explain the nature of imagination; and we here turn aside from this general subject, for the purpose of remarking on the utility of this power. And this appears to be necessary, since there are some who seem disposed to prejudice its claims in that respect. They warmly recommend the careful culture of the memory, the judgment, and the reasoning power, but look coldly and suspiciously on the imagination, and would rather encourage a neglect of it. But there is ground for apprehending that a neglect of this noble faculty in any person who aspires to a full developement and growth of the mind, cannot be justified, either by considerations drawn from the nature of the mind itself, or by the practical results of such a course.

In speaking on the utility of the imagination, it is certainly a very natural reflection that the Creator had some design or purpose in furnishing men with it, since we find universally that he does nothing in vain. And what design could he possibly have, if he did not intend that it should be employed, that it should be rendered active, and trained up with a suitable degree of culture? But if we are thus forced upon the conclusion that this faculty was designed to be rendered active, we must further suppose that its exercise was designed to promote some useful purpose. And such, although it has sometimes been perverted, has been the general result.

Nowhere is the power of imagination seen to better advantage than in the Prophets of the Old Testament. If it be said that those venerable writers were inspired, it will still remain true that this was the faculty of the mind which inspiration especially honoured by the use which was made of it. And how many monuments may every civilized nation boast of in painting, architecture, and sculpture, as well as in poetry, where the imagination, in contributing to the national glory, has, at the same time, contributed to the national happiness! Many an hour it has beguiled by the new situations it has depicted, and the new views of human nature it has disclosed; many a pang of the heart it has subdued, either by introducing us to greater woes which others have suffered, or by intoxicating the memory with its luxuriance and lulling it into a forgetfulness of ourselves; many a good resolution it has cherished, and subtending, as it were, a new and wider horizon around the intellectual being, has filled the soul with higher conceptions, and inspired it with higher hopes. Conscious of its immortal destiny, and struggling against the bounds that limit it, the soul enters with joy into those new and lofty creations which it is the prerogative of the imagination to form; and they seem to it a congenial residence. Such are the views which obviously present themselves on the slightest consideration of this subject; and it is not strange, therefore, that we find in the writings of no less a judge than Addison, some remarks to this effect, that a refined imagination "gives a man a kind of property in everything he sees, and makes the most rude, uncultivated parts of nature administer to his pleasures; so that he looks upon the world, as it were, in another light, and discovers in it a multitude of charms that conceal themselves from the generality of mankind.'

§ 215. Importance of the imagination in connexion with reasoning.

In remarking on the subject of the utility of the imagination, there is one important point of view in which it is capable of being considered; that of the relation of the imagination to the other intellectual powers. And, among other things, there is obviously ground for the remark, that a vigorous and well-disciplined imagination may be made subservient to promptness, and clearness, and success in reasoning. The remark is made, it will be noticed, on the supposition of the imagination being well disciplined, which implies that it is under suitable control; otherwise it will rather encumber and perplex than afford aid.

Take, for instance, two persons, one of whom has cultivated the reasoning power exclusive of the imagination. We will suppose him to possess very deservedly the reputation of an able and weighty dialectician; but it will be obvious to the slightest observation, that there is, in one respect, a defect and failure; there is an evident want of selection and vivacity in the details of his argument. He cannot readily appreciate the relation which the hearer's mind sustains to the facts which he wishes to present; and accordingly, with much expense of patience on their part, he laboriously and very scrupulously takes up and examines everything which can come within his grasp, and bestows upon everything nearly an equal share of attention. And hence it is, that many persons who are acknowledged to be learned, diligent, and even successful in argument, at the same time sustain the reputation, which is by no means an enviable one, of being dull, tiresome, and uninteresting.

Let us now look a moment at another person, who is not only a man of great powers of ratiocination, but has cultivated his imagination, and has it under prompt and judicious command. He casts his eye rapidly over the whole field of argument, however extensive it may be, and immediately perceives what facts are necessary to be stated and what are not; what are of prominent, and what of subordinate importance; what will be easily understood and possess an interest, and what will be difficult to be appreciated, and will also lose its due value from a want of attraction. And he does this on the same principles and in virtue of the same mental training which enables the painter, architect, sculptor, and poet, to present the outlines of grand and beautiful creations in their respective arts. There is a suitableness in the different parts of the train of reasoning; a correspondence of one part to another; a great and combined effect, enhanced by every suitable decoration, and undiminished by any misplaced excrescence, which undoubtedly implies a perfection of the imagination in some degree kindred with that which projected the group of the Laocoon, crowned the hills of Greece with statues and temples, and lives in the works of renowned poets. The debater, who combines the highest results of reasoning with the highest results of the imagination, throws the light of his own splendid conceptions around the radiance of truth; so that brightness shines in the midst of brightness, like the angel of the Apocalypse in the sun.

CHAPTER XIV

DISORDERED INTELLECTUAL ACTION.

(I.) EXCITED CONCEPTIONS OR APPARITIONS.

§ 216. Disordered intellectual action as connected with the body.

HAVING completed our examination of the Intellect so far as it presents itself to our notice in its more frequent and regular action, we now propose to conclude the subject, by giving some instances of intellectual states which appear to take place in violation of its ordinary principles. Whatever anticipations we might have been disposed to form A PRIORI, in relation to the action of the mind, it is a matter abundantly confirmed by painful experience and observation, that its operations are not always uniform; and that, in some cases, as we shall have occasion to see, it exhibits an utter and disastrous deviation from the laws which commonly regulate it. The causes of these deviations it may not be easy always, and in all respects, to explain; but it is well understood, that they are frequently connected with an irregular and diseased condition of the body.

The mind, it will be recollected, exists in the threefold nature or threefold division of the Intellect, the Sensibilities, and the Will. The action of the Will depends upon the antecedent action of the Sensibilities; and that of the sensitive nature is based upon the antecedent action of the Intellect. The action of the Intellect or Understanding is twofold, External and Internal. And we have already endeavoured, on a former occasion, to show, that the developement of the External Understanding is first in the order of time, as it is obviously first in the order of nature. It is here, so far as the mind is concerned, that we find the commencement of action; but it is well understood, and seems to be entirely undeniable, that all the action which takes place here, takes place in connexion with bodily action. The External intellect does not act, nor is it capable of acting, although the mind is so constituted that the movement of all the other parts depends upon movement here, without the antecedent affection of the outward or bodily senses. And hence the intellect generally, and particularly the External intellect, is unfavourably affected, as a general thing in connexion with a disordered state of the bodily system.

§ 217. Of excited conceptions and of apparitions in general.

The fact that disordered intellectual action is closely connected with a disordered state of the body, will aid, in some degree, in the explanation of the interesting subject of EXCITED CONCEPTIONS OR APPARITIONS. Conceptions, the consideration of which is to be resumed in the present chapter, are those ideas which we have of any absent object of perception. In their ordinary form they have already been considered in a former part of this Work. (See chapter viii., part i.) But they are found to vary in degree of strength; and hence, when they are at the highest intensity of which they are susceptible, they may be denominated vivified or EXCITED CONCEPTIONS. They are otherwise called, particularly when they have their origin in the sense of sight, APPARITIONS.

Apparitions, therefore, are appearances, which seem to be external and real, but which, in truth, have merely an interior or subjective existence; they are merely vivid or excited conceptions. Accordingly, there may be apparitions, not only of angels and departed spirits, which appear to figure more largely in the history of apparitions than other objects of sight; but of landscapes, mountains, rivers, precipices, festivals, armies, funeral processions, temples; in a word, of all visual perceptions which we are capable of recalling.—Although there are excited conceptions both of the hearing and the touch, and sometimes, though less frequently, of the other senses, which succeed in reaching and controlling our belief with unreal intimations, those of the sight, in consequence of the great importance of that organ and the frequency of the deceptions connected with it, claim especial attention

§ 218. Of the less permanent excited conceptions of sight.

Excited conceptions, which are not permanent, but

have merely a momentary, although a distinct and real existence, are not uncommon. In explanation of these, there are two things to be noticed.—(I.) They are sometimes the result of the natural and ordinary exercise of that power of forming conceptions, which all persons possess in a greater or less degree. We notice them particularly in children, in whom the conceptive or imaginative power, so far as it is employed in giving existence to creations that have outline and form, is generally more active than in later life. Children, it is well known, are almost constantly projecting their inward conceptions into outward space, and erecting the fanciful creations of the mind amid the realities and forms of matter, beholding houses, men, towers, flocks of sheep, clusters of trees, and varieties of landscape in the changing clouds, in the wreathed and driven snow, in the fairy-work of frost, and in the embers and flickering flames of the hearth. This at least was the experience of the early life of Cowper, who has made it the subject of a fine passage in the poem of the Task.

> "Me oft has fancy, ludicrous and wild,
> Soothed with a waking dream of houses, towers,
> Trees, churches, and strange visages expressed
> In the red cinders, while, with poring eye,
> I gazed, myself creating what I saw."

Beattie too, after the termination of a winter's storm places his young Minstrel on the shores of the Atlantic to view the heavy clouds that skirt the distant horizon.

> "Where mid the changeful scenery ever new,
> Fancy a thousand wondrous forms descries,
> More wildly great than ever pencil drew,
> Rocks, torrent, gulfs, and shapes of giant size,
> And glittering cliffs on cliffs, and fiery ramparts rise."

(II.) Again, excited conceptions, which are not permanent, are frequently called into existence in connexion with some anxiety and grief of mind, or some other modification of mental excitement. A person, for instance, standing on the seashore, and anxiously expecting the approach of his vessel, will sometimes see the image of it, and will be certain, for the moment, that he has the object of his anticipations in view, although, in truth, there is no vessel in sight. That is to say, the conception, idea, or image of the vessel, which it is evidently in the power of every one to form who has previously seen one, is rendered so intense by feelings of anxiety, as to be the same in effect as if the real object were present, and the figure of it were actually pictured on the retina.—It is in connexion with this view that we may probably explain a remark in the narrative of Mrs. Howe's captivity, who in 1775 was taken prisoner, together with her seven children, by the St. Francois Indians. In the course of her captivity, she was at a certain time informed by the Indians that two of her children were no more; one having died a natural death, and the other being knocked on the head. "I did not utter many words," says the mother, "but my heart was sorely pained within me, and *my mind exceedingly troubled with strange and awful ideas*, [meaning conceptions, or images.] I often imagined, for instance, that I *plainly saw* the naked carcasses of my children hanging upon the limbs of trees, as the Indians are wont to hang the raw hides of those beasts which they take in hunting."

§ 219. Of the less permanent excited conceptions of sound

In regard to excited conceptions of sound, (we may remark incidentally, as we intend to confine ourselves chiefly to those of sight,) they are not, as was seen in a former part of this Work, (§ 60,) so easily called into existence, and so vivid, as visual conceptions. Consequently, we have grounds for making a distinction, and for saying that only one of the remarks made in reference to the less permanent excited conceptions of sight will apply to those of sound. In other words, excited conceptions of sound (those which appear and depart suddenly, without any permanent inconvenience to the subject of them) originate in connexion with a greater or less degree of mental excitement.—Persons, for instance, sitting alone in a room, are sometimes interrupted by the supposed hearing of a voice, which calls to them. But, in truth, it is only their own internal conception of that particular sound, which, in consequence of some peculiar mental state, happens at the moment to be so distinct, as to control their belief and impose itself upon them for a reality. This is probably the whole mystery of what Boswell has related as a singular incident in the life of Dr. Johnson, that while at Oxford he distinctly heard his mother call him by his given name, although she was at the very time in Litchfield.—The same principle explains also what is related of Napoleon. Previously to his Russian expedition, he was frequently discovered half reclined on a sofa, where he remained several hours, plunged in profound meditation. Sometimes he started up convulsively, and with an ejaculation. Fancying he heard his name, he would exclaim, Who calls me? These are the sounds, susceptible of being heard at any time in the desert air, which started Robinson Crusoe from his sleep, when there was no one on his solitary island but himself:

> "The airy tongues, that syllable men's names,
> On shores, in desert sands, and wildernesses."

§ 220. First cause of permanently vivid conceptions or apparitions. Morbid sensibility of the retina of the eye.

We have been led to see, particularly in a former chapter, (§ 64,) as well as in the preceding part of this, that our conceptions or renovated ideas may be so vivid as to affect our belief for a short time hardly less powerfully than the original perceptions. But as in the cases referred to there was not supposed to be an unsound or disordered state of the body, this extreme vividness of conception was exceedingly transitory. There are other cases of a comparatively permanent character, which are deserving of a more particular notice in the history of our mental nature. These last always imply a disordered state of the body, which we were led to see in the last chapter is often attended with very marked effects on the mind.

In attempting to give an explanation of the origin of permanently vivid conceptions, the first ground or cause of them which we shall notice is an unnatural and morbid sensibility of the retina of the eye, either the whole of the retina or only a part. This cause, it is true, is in some degree conjectural, in consequence of the retina being so situated as to render it difficult to make it a subject of observation and experiment. But knowing, as we do, that the nervous system generally is liable to be diseased, and that the disease of a particular portion is commonly productive of results having relation to the object or uses of that portion, we may for this reason, as well as for what we know directly and positively of the occasionally disordered affections of the optic nerve, give it a place in the explanations of the subject before us. In order to understand the applicability of this cause of permanently vivid conceptions or apparitions, it is necessary to keep in mind, that, in conceptions of visible objects, there is probably *always* a slight sympathetic affection of the retina of the eye, analogous to what exists when the visible object is actually present. In a perfectly healthy state of the body, including the organ of visual sense, this affection of the retina is of course very slight But, under the influence of a morbid sensibility, the mere conceptions of the mind may at times impart such an increased activity to the whole or a part of the retina, as to give existence to visual or spectral illusions.

There is an account given in a foreign Medical Journal (the Medico-chirurgical Repertory of Piedmont) of a young lady, who attended for the first time the music of an orchestra, with which she was exceedingly pleased. She continued to hear the sounds distinctly and in their order for weeks and months afterward, till her whole system becoming disordered in consequence of it, she died. Now we naturally suppose, in this case, that the nerve of the tympanum of the ear, which, both in a physiological point of view and in its relation to the mind, corresponds to the retina of the eye, continued actually to vibrate or reverberate with the sound, although she was no longer within hearing of it. In other words, it was diseased; it had become morbidly sensitive, and in this state was a source of action to itself, independently of any outward cause. And as the mental state or sensation of sound depends upon the actual condition of the auditory nerve, independently of the outward causes which may have been instrumental in producing that particular condition, we see how the sounds, which she at first heard for a few hours, continued for a number of months after to be generated and repeated.—And so in regard to the optic nerve. It may be so morbidly sensitive, that the mere conception of a man or of some other visible object may affect it as really and in the same way as if the man were actually present to the sight. And if so, the individual who is subject to this morbid affection has the power in himself of originating and sustaining the representation or pictures of objects, although no such objects are present. In other words, as these results depend upon the state of his physical system and not upon volition, he is properly said to be subject to Apparitions.—We will only add, in confirmation of what has been said, that in one of the most interesting cases of spectral illusions or apparitions which has been published, the person who was the subject of them expressly states, that for some hours preceding their occurrence she had a peculiar feeling in the eyes, which was relieved as soon as they had passed away.*

§ 221. Second cause of permanently excited conceptions or apparitions Neglect of periodical blood-letting.

But there are other causes of the mental states under consideration, which, in some respects at least, are not so closely and exclusively connected with the eye. One is the neglect of periodical blood-letting. The doctrine, that permanently excited conceptions or apparitions are attendant on a superabundance of blood, occasioned by this neglect, seems to be illustrated and confirmed by the actual and recorded experience of various individuals, as in the following instance.

Nicolai, the name of the individual to whom the statements here given relate, was an inhabitant of Berlin, a celebrated bookseller, and naturally a person of a very vivid imagination. He was neither an ignorant man, nor superstitious; a fact which some undoubtedly will esteem it important to know. The following account of the apparitions which appeared to him is given in his own words.—"My wife and another person came into my apartment in the morning, in order to console me, but I was too much agitated by a series of incidents, which had

* Brewster's Natural Magic, letter iii.

most powerfully affected my moral feeling, to be capable of attending to them. On a sudden I perceived, at about the distance of ten steps, a form like that of a deceased person. I pointed at it, asking my wife if she did not see it. It was but natural that she should not see anything; my question, therefore, alarmed her very much, and she immediately sent for a physician. The phantom continued about eight minutes. I grew at length more calm, and, being extremely exhausted, fell into a restless sleep, which lasted about half an hour. The physician ascribed the apparition to a violent mental emotion, and hoped there would be no return; but the violent agitation of my mind had in some way disordered my nerves, and produced further consequences, which deserve a more minute description.

"At four in the afternoon, the form which I had seen in the morning reappeared. I was by myself when this happened, and, being rather uneasy at the incident, went to my wife's apartment, but there likewise I was persecuted by the apparition, which, however, at intervals disappeared, and always presented itself in a standing posture. About six o'clock there appeared also several walking figures, which had no connexion with the first. After the first day the form of the deceased person no more appeared, but its place was supplied with many other phantasms, sometimes representing acquaintances, but mostly strangers; those whom I knew were composed of living and deceased persons, but the number of the latter was comparatively small. I observed the persons with whom I daily conversed did not appear as phantasms, these representing chiefly persons who lived at some distance from me.

"These phantasms seemed equally clear and distinct at all times and under all circumstances, both when I was by myself and when I was in company, as well in the day as at night, and in my own house as well as abroad; they were, however, less frequent when I was in the house of a friend, and rarely appeared to me in the street. When I shut my eyes, these phantasms would sometimes vanish entirely, though there were instances when I beheld them with my eyes closed, yet, when they disappeared on such occasions, they generally returned when

I opened my eyes. I conversed sometimes with my physician and my wife of the phantasms which at the moment surrounded me; they appeared more frequently walking than at rest, nor were they constantly present. They frequently did not come for some time, but always reappeared for a longer or shorter period, either singly or in company, the latter, however, being most frequently the case. I generally saw human forms of both sexes, but they usually seemed not to take the smallest notice of each other, moving as in a market-place, where all are eager to press through the crowd; at times, however, they seemed to be transacting business with each other. I also saw, several times, people on horseback, dogs, and birds. All these phantasms appeared to me in their natural size, and as distinct as if alive, exhibiting different shades of carnation in the uncovered parts, as well as different colours and fashions in their dresses, though the colours seemed somewhat paler than in real nature. None of the figures appeared particularly terrible, comical, or disgusting, most of them being of an indifferent shape, and some presenting a pleasing aspect. The longer these phantoms continued to visit me, the more frequently did they return, while, at the same time, they increased in number about four weeks after they had first appeared I also began to hear them talk; these phantoms sometimes conversed among themselves, but more frequently addressed their discourse to me; their speeches were commonly short, and never of an unpleasant turn. At different times there appeared to me both dear and sensible friends of both sexes, whose addresses tended to appease my grief, which had not yet wholly subsided: their consolatory speeches were, in general, addressed to me when I was alone. Sometimes, however, I was accosted by these consoling friends while I was engaged in company and not unfrequently while real persons were speaking to me. These consolatory addresses consisted sometimes of abrupt phrases, and at other times they were regularly executed."

§ 222. Methods of relief adopted in this case.

These are the leading facts in this case, so far as the

mere appearance of the apparitions is concerned. But as Nicolai, besides possessing no small amount of acquired knowledge, was a person of a naturally philosophic turn of mind, he was able to detect and to assign the true cause of his mental malady.—He was, it is to be remembered, in the first place, a person of very vivid fancy, and hence his mind was the more likely to be affected by any disease of the body. A number of years before the occurrences above related, he had been subject to a violent vertigo, which had been cured by means of leeches; it was his custom to lose blood twice a year, but previously to the present attack, this evacuation had been neglected. Supposing, therefore, that a mental disorder might arise from a superabundance of blood and some irregularity in the circulation, he again resorted to the application of leeches. When the leeches were applied, no person was with him besides the surgeon; but, during the operation, his chamber was crowded with human phantasms of all descriptions. In the course of a few hours, however, they moved around the chamber more slowly; their colour began to fade, until, growing more and more obscure, they at last dissolved into air, and he ceased to be troubled with them afterward.*

§ 223. Third cause of excited conceptions. Attacks of fever.

In violent attacks of fever there are sometimes excited conceptions, particularly those which have their origin in the sense of sight, and are known, by way of distinction, under the name of Apparitions. The conceptions which the sick person has, become increased in vividness, until the mind, seeming to project its own creations into the exterior space, peoples the room with living and moving phantoms. There is a statement illustrative of this view in the fifteenth volume of Nicholson's Philosophical Journal, a part of which will be here repeated. The fever in this instance, of which an account is given by the patient himself, was of a violent character, originating in some deep-seated inflammation, and at first affecting the memory, although not permanently.

* Memoir on the appearance of Spectres or Phantoms occasioned by Disease, with Psychological Remarks, read by Nicolai to the Royal Society of Berlin on the 28th of February, 1799; as quoted by Hibbert, pt. i., ch. i.

"Being perfectly awake," says this person, "in full possession of memory, reason, and calmness, conversing with those around me, and seeing, without difficulty or impediment, every surrounding object, I was entertained and delighted with a succession of faces, over which I had no control, either as to their appearance, continuance or removal.

"They appeared directly before me, one at a time, very suddenly, yet not so much so but that a second of time might be employed in the emergence of each, as if through a cloud or mist, to its perfect clearness. In this state each face continued five or six seconds, and then vanished, by becoming gradually fainter during about two seconds, till nothing was left but a dark opaque mist, in which almost immediately afterward appeared another face. All these faces were in the highest degree interesting to me for beauty of form, and for the variety of expression they manifested of every great and amiable emotion of the human mind. Though their attention was invariably directed to me, and none of them seemed to speak, yet I seemed to read the very soul which gave animation to their lovely and intelligent countenances. Admiration and a sentiment of joy and affection when each face appeared, and regret upon its disappearance, kept my mind constantly riveted to the visions before it; and this state was interrupted only when an intercourse with the persons in the room was proposed or urged," &c.—The apparitions which this person experienced were not limited to phantasms of the human countenance; he also saw phantasms of books, and of parchment and papers containing printed matter. Nor were these effects exclusively confined to ideas received from the sense of sight; at one time he seemed to himself to hear musical sounds. That is, his conceptions of sound were so exceedingly vivid, it was in effect the same as if he had really heard melodious voices and instruments

§ 224. Fourth cause of apparitions and other excited conceptions. Inflammation of the brain.

Apparitions, and excited conceptions in general, exist, in the fourth place, in consequence of inflammations and other diseases of the brain.—We may infer, from certain passages which are found in his writings, that Shakspeare had some correct notions of the influence of a disordered condition of the brain on the mental operations. We allude, among others, to the passage where, in explanation of the apparition of the dagger which appeared to Macbeth, he says,

> "A dagger of the mind, a false creation,
> Proceeding from the heat-oppressed brain."

Whether the seat, or appropriate and peculiar residence of the soul, be in the brain or not, it seems to be certain, that this part of the bodily system is connected, in a very intimate and high degree, with the exercises of the mind, particularly with perception and volition. Whenever therefore, the brain is disordered, whether by a contusion or by a removal of part of it, by inflammation or in other ways, the mind will in general be affected in a greater or less degree.—It may indeed be said, that the immediate connexion, in the cases which we now have reference to, is not between the mind and the substance of the brain, but between the mind and the blood which is thrown into that part of the system. It is, no doubt, something in favour of this notion, that so large a portion of the sanguineous fluid finds a circulation there; it being a common idea among anatomists, that at least one tenth of all the blood is immediately sent from the heart into the brain, although the latter is in weight only about the fortieth part of the whole body. It is to be considered also, that the effects which are wrought upon the mind by the nitrous oxide and the febrile miasma gas are caused by an intermediate influence on the blood. On the other hand, it may be said that there cannot be a great acceleration of the blood's motion or increase of its volume, without a very sensible effect on the cerebral substance. And, therefore, it may remain true, that very much may be justly attributed to the increase of quantity and motion in the blood, and still the brain be the proximate cause of alterations in the states of the mind.

§ 225. Facts having relation to the 4th cause of excited conceptions.

But here we stand in need of facts, as in all other parts

of this investigation. The following statement, selected from a number of others not less authenticated, can be relied on.*—A citizen of Kingston-on-Hull had a quarrel with a drunken soldier, who attempted to enter his house by force at an unseasonable hour. In this struggle the soldier drew his bayonet, and, striking him across the temples, divided the temporal artery. He had scarcely recovered from the effects of a great loss of blood on this occasion, when he undertook to accompany a friend in his walking-match against time, in which he went forty-two miles in nine hours. He was elated by his success, and spent the whole of the following day in drinking, &c.

The result of these things was an affection, probably an inflammation, of the brain. And the consequence of this was the existence of those vivid states of mind which are termed apparitions. Accordingly, our shopkeeper (for that was the calling of this person) is reported to have seen articles of sale upon the floor, and to have beheld an armed soldier entering his shop, when there was nothing seen by other persons present. In a word, he was for some time constantly haunted by a variety of spectres or imaginary appearances; so much so, that he even found it difficult to determine which were real customers and which were mere phantasms of his own mind. The remedy in this case was blood-letting, and some other methods of cure which are practised in inflammations of the brain. The restoration of the mind to a less intense and more correct action was simultaneous with that of the physical system.

§ 226. Fifth cause of apparitions. Hysteria.

It is further to be observed, that people are not unfrequently affected with apparitions in the paroxysms of the disease known as HYSTERIA or hysterics.—For the nature of this disease, which exists under a variety of forms, and is of a character so peculiar as to preclude any adequate description in the narrow limits we could properly allot to it, the reader is referred to such books as treat of medical subjects. This singular disease powerfully agitates the mind; and its effects are as various as they are stri-

* See the Edinburgh Medical and Surgical Journal, vol. vi., p. 288

king. When the convulsive affections come on, the patient is observed to laugh and cry alternately, and altogether without any cause of a rational or moral nature; so that he has almost the appearance of fatuity, or of being delirious. But apparitions or intensely vivid conceptions are among its most striking attendants. The subjects of it distinctly see every description of forms; trees, houses, men, women, dogs, and other inferior animals, balls of fire, celestial beings, &c. We can, without doubt, safely refer to the experience of those who have been much conversant with instances of this disease, in confirmation of this.

The existence of the states of mind under consideration might, without much question, be found, on further examination, to connect itself with other forms of disease The subject is certainly worthy, whether considered in relation to science or to human happiness, of such further developements as it is capable of receiving.

CHAPTER XV.

DISORDERED INTELLECTUAL ACTION.

(II.) INSANITY.

§ 227. Meaning of the term insanity.

In illustration of the general subject of disordered intellectual action, we proceed, in the next place, to the consideration of that more decided internal mental derangement which is known as INSANITY. The term Insanity, etymologically considered, indicates simply a want of soundness or want of health. In its application to the mind, it indicates an unsound or disordered state of the mental action; generally, however, of a more decided and deeply seated nature than that form of disordered intellect which has already been considered under the head of APPARITIONS.

As the mind is complicated in its structure, existing, as it were, in various departments and subdivisions of departments, the disordered action, which we now propose to consider, may pervade either the whole mind, or exist exclusively in some one of its departments. Accordingly, Insanity may be regarded either as partial or total; involving either the whole mind, or only a part. The method which we propose to pursue in the investigation of the subject, is to consider it in connexion with the powers of the mind separately, as affording, on the whole, the most satisfactory view. And it is proper to add here, that we examine it at present only so far as it may naturally be supposed to exist in connexion with the Intellect, leaving the consideration of it, as it is occasionally found to exist in the Sensibilities, to a more appropriate place.

§ 228. Of disordered or alienated sensations.

Beginning with the External Intellect, the power which first presents itself to our notice is Sensation. It is well known that all the outward senses are liable to be disordered, and, as the inward sensation corresponds to the condition of the outward or bodily organ, a disordered or irregular movement of the organ of sense necessarily communicates itself to the inward or mental state. A regular or healthy sensation always has reference to some outward cause, (we mean here outward, even in reference to the organ of sense,) but a disease in the bodily organ disturbs this relation, and necessarily gives to the inward mental state the character, as compared with other sensations, of being unreal, visionary, and deceptive. Not unreal and deceptive in itself, but because it intimates a relation which is obliterated, and tends to force upon our belief an outward cause which has no existence.

There are diseased or disordered visual sensations, existing in connexion with a morbid condition of the visual organ; but as this view of the subject was necessarily involved, in some degree, in what has already been said on the subject of excited conceptions or Apparitions, it is not necessary to enlarge upon it here. There are also diseased or disordered sensations of touch. A single instance, out of multitudes like it, will serve both to illustrate and to confirm the remark. In the Natural Magic of Dr.

Brewster is an account of a lady (the case which we have already had occasion to refer to) who was subject to spectral illusions, of whom it is expressly said, in connexion with her remarkable mental affections, that she possesses "a naturally morbid imagination, so strongly affecting her corporeal impressions, that the story of any person having suffered severe pain by accident or otherwise will occasionally produce acute twinges in the corresponding part of her person. An account, for instance, of the amputation of an arm, will produce an instantaneous and severe sense of pain in her own arm." There are also (and we might apply the statement to all the senses without exception) diseased or disordered sensations of hearing. The celebrated Mendelsohn was frequently subject to the attacks of a violent species of catalepsis. And it happened, if he had recently heard any lively conversation, a loud voice apparently repeated to him, while in the fit, the particular words, which had been distinguished from others by being pronounced with an emphatic and raised tone of voice, and "in such a manner that his ear reverberated with the sound."

§ 229. Of disordered or alienated external perception.

We naturally proceed from sensation to a power closely connected with it, that of External Perception. Indeed, what has been said of sensation will apply, in a considerable degree, to the last-mentioned power, because sensation naturally precedes perception, and is always involved in it. But perception, while it involves sensation, implies also something more, something additional; it involves the reference of the inward mental state to the outward cause or object, and not unfrequently implies also acts of comparison, by which it distinguishes one cause from another. And particularly is this the case in respect to those perceptions which are designated as ACQUIRED perceptions, in order to distinguish them from ORIGINAL. So that, in view of what has been said, it would seem to be the fact, in the first place, that, when our sensations are disordered, our perceptions will be so likewise. But this is not all. In consequence of some interior cause, such as an inability to attend to a thing for any length of time, or incapacity of instituting comparisons, disordered and false external perceptions will sometimes exist when there appears to be no unsoundness in the sensations.

Agreeably to these views, we find that persons, in whom the power of external perception is disordered from the first of the two causes just referred to, sometimes have perceptions of colour which do not accord with those of mankind generally, being entirely unable, for instance, to distinguish blue from green. Other persons, again, have no distinct perception of minute sounds, and take no more pleasure in the harmonies of a musical composition of truly great merit, than they do in the most discordant screams. When the disordered action of the perceptive power originates from the second cause, the subjects of it are apt to confound times, persons, and places. They mistake, for instance, their friends and relations for others, and are at a loss as to the place where they are, although they may have been in it hundreds of times before. They exhibit particularly this species of alienated perception when they attempt to read a book. They no doubt see the letters no less than others, but the action of the mind, in other respects, not being such as to permit them to dwell upon them, and compare and combine them into words, they are unable to read; it is, at least, exceedingly difficult.

§ 230. Disordered state or insanity of original suggestion.

When we pass from the External to the Internal intellect, from the region of sensation and external perception to the interior domain of Original Suggestion, to the convictions involved in Consciousness, to the important powers of Relative Suggestion, Memory, and Reasoning, we are introduced, indeed, to a higher order of mental action, but we find no exemption from those disorders to which the human mind, in all its great departments, is occasionally exposed.—In regard to Original Suggestion, which comes first in order, a power which deals with original ideas and principles merely, without professing to ascertain the relations existing among them, it must be admitted that it does not give so frequent and decided indications of disordered action as we find elsewhere. Nevertheless, this is sometimes the case. The conviction, for instance, not only that we exist, but that we have personal identity; that we are now what we have been in times past in all that constitutes us rational and accountable beings, is obviously essential to a sound mind. But this elementary and important conviction, which obviously does not rest upon judgment nor the deductions of reasoning, but upon the higher basis of ORIGINAL SUGGESTION, is sometimes annulled, either in whole or in part. To this head, so far as the conviction of the identity of the mind is concerned, we may refer the interesting case of the Rev. Simon Browne, an English clergyman, who fully believed, for many years before his death, that he had entirely lost his rational part or soul, and was the possessor merely of a corporeal or animal life, such as is possessed by the brutes. He was a man of marked ability, both in conversation and writing; and this, too, on all subjects not connected with his malady, after his partial alienation. But so entirely was he convinced of the absence, and of the probably actual extinction of his soul, that, in a valuable work which he dedicated to the Queen of England, he speaks of it in the dedication as the work of one who "was once a man; of some little name; but of no worth, as his present unparalleled case makes but too manifest; for, by the immediate hand of an avenging God, his very thinking substance has, for more than seventeen years, been gradually wasting away, till it is wholly perished out of him, if it be not utterly come to nothing."*

§ 231. Unsoundness or insanity of consciousness.

The basis of the various convictions or judgments of Consciousness, as that term is defined and illustrated by writers, is the antecedent idea and belief of personal identity. If this last conviction, therefore, be lost, as in the case mentioned in the last section, all that is involved in Consciousness goes with it. It is the business of Consciousness to connect the acts of the mind with the mind itself; to consolidate them, as it were, into one. But if, in our full belief, our mind is destroyed; if self or personality is obliterated, then it is clearly no longer within the

* Conolly's Indications of Insanity, ch. x.

power of consciousness to recognise our various acts of perception and reasoning as having a home and agency in our own bosoms. Self is destroyed; and the mental acts which are appropriate to self are mere entities, floating about, as it were, in the vacuities of space, without the possibility of being assigned to any locality or ascribed to any cause. The instance, therefore, mentioned in the preceding section, which may be regarded as of a mixed kind, (that is to say, showing a perplexed action, both of Original Suggestion and Consciousness,) will serve to illustrate what is said here.—Another instance, not less striking, is that of a celebrated watchmaker of Paris, who became insane during the period of the French Revolution. This man believed that he and some others had been beheaded, but that the heads were subsequently ordered to be restored to the original owners. Some mistake, however, as the insane person conceived, was committed in the process of restoration, in consequence of which he had unfortunately been furnished with the head of one of his companions instead of his own. He was admitted into the hospital Bicêtre, "where he was continually complaining of his misfortune, and lamenting the fine teeth and wholesome breath he had exchanged for those of very different qualities."

Instances also have probably, from time to time, occurred, in which, although the conviction of personality and personal identity has remained, yet in the fixed belief of the insane person the bond of connexion between the mind and its powers has been dissolved; and the memory perhaps, or the reasoning, or the imagination, which once belonged to himself, has been transferred by some mysterious agency to an intellect more favoured than his own.

§ 232. Insanity of the judgment or relative suggestion.

Pursuing this subject in its connexion with the powers of the Internal Intellect in the order in which they presented themselves to our notice in the Second Part of this Division, and which seems to be essentially the order of nature, we next proceed to Relative Suggestion. The power of Relative Suggestion, like that of Original Suggestion, is exceedingly simple in its action, being limited to the mere matter of perceiving relations; but it is different in this respect, that while mental disorder but seldom reaches original suggestion, there is scarcely an instance of decidedly disordered intellect, in which relative suggestion (that is to say, JUDGMENT in its simplest form) is not affected in a greater or less degree. And this seems to be unavoidable. For relations always imply the existence of something else, of other objects. And if mistakes, in consequence of a wrong mental action in other respects, exist in regard to those other things, whatever they may be, they necessarily either annul or greatly perplex the results of the power by which such relations are perceived.—Besides this, the power in its own nature, and independently of perplexities from other sources, is liable to be, and is in fact, sometimes disordered. But as this subject is closely connected with that of reasoning, and as they reciprocally throw light upon each other, we shall say nothing further here.

§ 233. Disordered or alienated association. Light-headedness

The laws of the mind, the great principles which regulate its action, as well as its mere perceptions or states, may be disordered; for instance, the law of association The irregular action of this important principle of our intellectual nature is sometimes greater, at others less. There is one of the slighter forms of mental alienation from this cause, which may be termed LIGHT-HEADEDNESS; otherwise called by Pinel, demence, and by Dr. Rush, dissociation. Persons subject to this mental disease are sometimes designated as "flighty," "hair-brained;" and when the indications of it are pretty decided, as a "little cracked."—Their disorder seems chiefly to consist in a deficiency of the ordinary power over associated ideas. Their thoughts fly from one subject to another with great rapidity; and, consequently, one mark of this state of mind is great volubility of speech and almost constant motion of the body. This rapid succession of ideas and attendant volubility of tongue are generally accompanied with forgetfulness in a greater or less degree. And as the subject of this form of derangement is equally incapable of checking and reflecting upon his present ideas, and of recalling the past, he constantly forms incorrect judgments of things. Another mark which has been given is a diminished sensibility to external impressions.

§ 234. Illustrations of this mental disorder.

Dr. Rush, in his valuable work on the Diseases of the Mind, has repeated the account which an English clergyman who visited Lavater, the physiognomist, has given of that singular character. It accurately illustrates this mental disorder.—"I was detained," says he, "the whole morning by the strange, wild, eccentric Lavater, in various conversations. When once he is set agoing, there is no such thing as stopping him till he runs himself out of breath. He starts from subject to subject, flies from book to book, from picture to picture; measures your nose, your eye, your mouth, with a pair of compasses; pours forth a torrent of physiognomy upon you; drags you, for a proof of his dogma, to a dozen of closets, and unfolds ten thousand drawings; but will not let you open your lips to propose a difficulty; and crams a solution down your throat before you have uttered half a syllable of your objection.

"He is as meager as the picture of famine; his nose and chin almost meet. I read him in my turn, and found little difficulty in discovering, amid great genius, unaffected piety, unbounded benevolence, and moderate learning, much caprice and unsteadiness; a mind at once aspiring by nature and grovelling through necessity; an endless turn to speculation and project; in a word, a clever, flighty, good-natured, necessitous man."

§ 235. Of partial insanity or alienation of the memory.

Among other exhibitions of partial insanity, using the terms in the manner already explained, we may include some of the more striking instances of weakened and disordered memory. Every other part of the intellect may be sound and regular in its action, (for it will be recollected that we confine ourselves here to the disorders of the INTELLECT, without anticipating those of the Sensibilities and the Will,) the powers of perception, of association, of imagination, of reasoning, at least so far as they are able to act independent of the memory, while the action of the latter power is either essentially obliterated, or is the subject of strange and unaccountable deviations. From the plan of this work, we are obliged to content ourselves with the briefest possible notices; and can therefore only refer to one or two instances in illustration of what has been said. The instances of weakened and perverted memory are of three kinds; (1.) those where there is a general prostration, caused in various ways, such as grief and old age; (2.) those where there is a sudden and entire prostration extending to particular subjects, or through a particular period of time, generally caused by some sudden and violent affection of the body; and, (3.) those where there is not so much an inordinate weakness or obliteration of the power under consideration, as a singularly perverse and irregular action of it.—It is probably not necessary to say anything of the first class. Of the second class is the case mentioned by Dr. Beattie, of a gentleman who, in consequence of a violent blow on the head, lost his knowledge of Greek, but did not appear to have lost anything else. Another instance is that mentioned by Dr. Abercrombie, of a lady who, in consequence of a protracted illness, lost the recollection of a period of about ten or twelve years; but spoke with perfect consistency of things as they stood before that time. Of the third class is the case of a man who always called tobacco a hogshead; and of another man who, when he wanted coals put upon his fire, always called for paper, and when he wanted paper, called for coals; and of another, who could not be made to understand the name of an object if it was spoken to him, but understood it perfectly when it was written. These three cases will be found more particularly detailed in Dr. Abercrombie's Inquiries into the Intellectual Powers. A case perhaps still more interesting is found in Dr. Conolly's Indications of Insanity, as follows:

"A gentleman of considerable attainments, after long-continued attention to various subjects, found himself incapable of writing what he sat down to write; and, wishing to write a check, could get no farther than the first two words; he found that he wrote what he did not mean to write, but by no effort could he write what he intended. This impairment of his memory and attention lasted about half an hour, during which time his external senses were not impaired, but the only ideas which he had were such as the imagination dictated, without order and without object. He knew also, during this time, that when he spoke, the words he uttered were not the words he wished to utter. When he recovered, he found that in his attempt to write the check, he had, instead of the words 'fifty dollars, being one half year's rate,' put down 'fifty dollars through the salvation of Bra.'"

§ 236. Of the power of reasoning in the partially insane.

It will be noticed, so far as we have gone in the examination of the subject of insanity, that we have considered the powers of the mind separately. Probably every power of the mind, but particularly those of the intellect, may become more or less disordered. Having considered sensation, perception, original suggestion, consciousness, judgment, association, and memory, we propose, as coming next in order, to examine the subject in its connexion with the reasoning power.—In some cases of insanity there is a total inability of reasoning. There is no power of attention, no power of comparison, and, of course, no ability in the mind to pass from the premises of an argument to the conclusion. We have already had occasion to refer to the power of relative suggestion, by means of which comparisons are instituted. Whenever this power is disordered and fails to perform its office, such is the close connexion between it and reasoning, the operations of the latter are disturbed also. In such cases the inability to reason is total; that is to say, it extends to all subjects alike. But it is more frequently the case, that the alienation of reasoning is not so extensive, but exists chiefly in relation to certain subjects, in respect to which the belief is affected. When the train of reasoning leads the person within the range of those particular subjects, whatever they are, we at once discover that the intellect is disordered. And this view has led to the common remark, which is obviously well founded, that the more common form of insane or alienated reason does not consist so much in the mode of connecting propositions, and in the conclusions drawn from them, as in the premises. The insane person believes, for instance, that he is a king. Accordingly, he reasons correctly in requiring for himself the homage suited to a king, and in expressing dissatisfaction on account of its being withheld; but he commits an essential error in the premises, which assume that he actually possesses that station.

§ 237. Instance of the above form of insanity of reasoning.

We have an instance of the form of insanity just mentioned in the character of Don Quixote. Cervantes represents the hero of his work as having his naturally good understanding perverted by the perusal of certain foolish, romantic stories, falsely purporting to be a true record of knights and deeds of chivalry. These books, containing the history of dwarfs, giants, necromancers, and other preternatural extravagance, were zealously perused, until the head of Don Quixote was effectually turned by them. Although he was thus brought into a state of real mental derangement, it was limited to the extravagances which have been mentioned. We are expressly informed, that, in all his conversations and replies, he gave evident proofs of a most excellent understanding, and never "lost the stirrups" except on the subject of chivalry. On this subject he "was crazed."—Accordingly, when the barber and curate visited him on a certain occasion, the conversation happened to turn on what are termed reasons of state, and on modes of administration; and Don Quixote spoke so well on every topic, as to convince them that he was quite sound, and had recovered the right exercise of his judgment. But something being unadvisedly said about the Turkish war, the knight at once remarked, with much solemnity and seriousness, that his majesty had nothing to do but to issue a proclamation, commanding all the knights-errant in Spain to assemble at his court on a certain day; *and, although not more than half a dozen should come, among these one would be found who would alone be sufficient to overthrow the whole Turkish power.*

When the subject of conversation turned upon war,

which had so near a connexion with shields, and lances, and all the associations of chivalry, it came within the range of his malady, and led to the absurd remark which showed at once the unsoundness of his mind, notwithstanding the sobriety and good sense which he had just before exhibited.

§ 238. Partial mental alienation by means of the imagination.

Men of sensibility and genius, by giving way to the suggestions of a melancholy imagination, sometimes become mentally disordered. Not that we are authorized to include these cases as among the more striking forms of insanity; they in general attract but little notice, although sources of exquisite misery to the subjects of them. But such are the extravagant dreams in which they indulge; such are the wrong views of the character and actions of men, which their busy and melancholy imaginations are apt to form, that they cannot be reckoned persons of truly sound minds. These instances, which are not rare, it is difficult fully to describe; but their most distinguishing traits will be recognised in the following sketch from Madame de Staël's Reflections on the Character and Writings of Rousseau.

After remarking that he discovered no sudden emotions, but that his feelings grew upon reflection, and that he became impassioned in consequence of his own meditations, she adds as follows.—"Sometimes he would part with you with all his former affection; but if an expression had escaped you which might bear an unfavourable construction, he would recollect it, examine it, exaggerate it, perhaps dwell upon it for a month, and conclude by a total breach with you. Hence it was that there was scarce a possibility of undeceiving him; for the light which broke in upon him at once was not sufficient to efface the wrong impressions which had taken place so gradually in his mind. It was extremely difficult, too, to continue long on an intimate footing with him. A word, a gesture, furnished him with matter of profound meditation; he connected the most trifling circumstances like so many mathematical propositions, and conceived his conclusions to be supported by the evidence of demonstration

"I believe," she further remarks, "that imagination was the strongest of his faculties, and that it had almost absorbed all the rest. He dreamed rather than existed, and the events of his life might be said more properly to have passed in his mind than without him: a mode of being, one should have thought, that ought to have secured him from distrust, as it prevented him from observation; but the truth was, it did not hinder him from attempting to observe; it only rendered his observations erroneous. That his soul was tender, no one can doubt after having read his works; but his imagination sometimes interposed between his reason and his affections, and destroyed their influence; he appeared sometimes void of sensibility; but it was because he did not perceive objects such as they were. Had he seen them with our eyes, his heart would have been more affected than ours"

§ 239. Insanity or alienation of the power of belief.

The action of the various intellectual powers which have been brought to view in this chapter, terminates in the causation or production of Belief. In regard to that particular state of the intellect which is denominated belief, it is obvious that, in a sound mind, it has a natural and determinate relation to all the various intellectual susceptibilities, both External and Internal. This relation is sometimes disturbed; and the belief exists in a position altogether unsustained by the evidence which is presented. There are three classes of persons in whom this state of mind, or, in other words, the faculty or susceptibility of belief, if we may be permitted so to call it, appears to be disordered.—(1.) The first class are those who seem incapable of believing anything which they are required to receive on the testimony of others. They must see it with their own eyes; they must hear it, or handle it for themselves; they must examine it by square, rule, and compass. They remind one of the Savage, who complained, when something was proposed for his belief, "that it would not believe for him." The causes of this singular inability are worthy of more inquiry than has hitherto been expended upon them. When it is very great, it is a mark of the approach or actual existence of idiocy.–

(2) There is another class of persons, who plainly snow a derangement of this power by their readiness to believe everything. No matter how incongruous or improbable a story is, it is received at once. They take no note of dates, characters, and circumstances; and, as they find nothing too improbable to believe, they find nothing too strange, marvellous, and foolish to report. This state of mind is frequently an accompaniment of light-headedness.—(3.) There are other cases, where the alienation of belief is not general, but particular. There is nothing peculiar and disordered in its ordinary action, but only in respect to particular facts. That is, certain propositions, which are erroneous and absurd, are received by the disordered persons as certain; and nothing can convince them of the contrary. One believes himself to be a king; another, that he is the prophet Mohammed; and various other absurdities are received by them as undoubtedly true. On all other subjects they appear to be rational; but the alienation or insanity of belief is evident as soon as their cherished errors are mentioned.

MENTAL PHILOSOPHY.

DIVISION SECOND.

THE SENSIBILITIES.

SENTIENT OR SENSITIVE STATES OF THE MIND.

SENTIMENTS.

INTRODUCTION

CLASSIFICATION OF THE SENSIBILITIES.

§ 240. Reference to the general division of the whole mind.

It will be recollected that we proposed, as the basis of our inquiries, the general division of the mind into the Intellect, the Sensibilities, and the Will. These great departments of the mind are not only generically distinct; but the difference between them is so clear and marked, it is surprising they should have been so often confounded together. They are not only different in their nature, a fact which is clearly ascertained by Consciousness, in its cognizance of their respective acts, but are separated from each other, as all observation shows, by the relations which they respectively sustain. The Intellect or Understanding comes first in order, and furnishes the basis of action to the other great departments of the mind. It is this portion of the mind which we have endeavoured to examine, and which we are now about to leave for the purpose of advancing into departments of our mental nature, which, considered in reference to the Intellect, may be regarded as occupying a more remote and interior position.

§ 241. The action of the sensibilities implies that of the intellect.

The action of the Sensibilities is subsequent in time to that of the Intellective nature. As a general thing, there is, and can be, no movement of the sensibilities; no such thing as an emotion, desire, or feeling of moral obligation, without an antecedent action of the intellect. If we are pleased or displeased, there is necessarily before the mind some object of pleasure or displeasure; if we exercise the feeling of desire, there must necessarily be some object desired, which is made known to us by an action of the intellect. So that if there were no intellect, or if the intellectual powers were entirely dormant and inactive there would be no action of the emotive part of our nature and of the passions.

And we may not only say, in general terms, that the action of the sensibilities implies the antecedent action of the intellect, but may even assert more specifically, (making allowance for those constitutional differences which pervade every part of the mental structure,) that the activity of the sensibilities will be nearly in *proportion* to that of the intellect. In other words, on all subjects which are calculated to excite any interest at all, those who have the broadest and most satisfactory views will be likely to feel more intensely than others; the sensibilities expanding and exerting themselves in conformity with the expanded and energetic action of the perceptive and cognitive powers.

§ 242. Division of the sensibilities into natural or pathematic, and moral.

As we pass onward from the percipient and cognitive nature to the distinct and more remote region of the emotions and passions, it seems proper, before we enter more minutely into the various inquiries which may be expected to present themselves, to consider whether the department of the Sensibilities itself is not susceptible of being resolved into some subordinate yet important divisions. In accordance with this suggestion, our first remark is, that the Sensibilities, when subjected to a careful examination, will clearly be found to separate themselves into the great divisions of the Natural or Pathematic, and the Moral. These leading departments will be found to run, if we may be allowed the expression, in two separate channels, which, although they are, for the most part, parallel with each other, are, nevertheless, essentially and sufficiently distinct; each being characterized by its own attributes and by its appropriate results. Our examination of the Sensibilities will accordingly proceed upon the basis of this division.

In reference to the use of the term Pathematic, as applicable to the states of mind embraced in one of these great divisions, it is proper to observe, that it appears to have been formed from its Greek original, and first used by Sir James Mackintosh. He repeatedly speaks of that part of our nature which includes the emotions and passions, as *unnamed;* and, in the progress of his discussions, appears at times to be embarrassed for the want of suitable English words to express it. Under these circumstances he proposes the term in question, which, in its etymological import, is applicable to any state of mind which involves emotion, desire, or passion.

§ 243. The moral and natural sensibilities have different objects.

The Natural and Moral Sensibilities appear to take, fundamentally, different views of the objects in respect to which they are called into exercise. The one considers objects chiefly as they have a relation to ourselves; the other, as they relate to all possible existences. The one looks at things in the aspect of their desirableness; the other fixes its eye on the sublime feature of their rectitude. The one asks what is GOOD; the other, what is RIGHT.

Obliterate from man's constitution his Conscience, (what may be called, if we may be allowed the expression, the *moralities* of his nature,) and you at once strike from the mind one half of its motives to action; for, in respect to everything which is considered by us desirable to be done, the question always recurs, is it *right* to be done? At one time, on the supposition of an entire erasure of the moral sensibilities, all his movements are dictated by the suggestions and cravings of the appetites. At other times, he covets knowledge, or seeks society, or indulges in the refinements of the arts; but it will be found in these instances, as well as when he is under the influence of the appetites, that pleasure is still his object, and that he is disappointed in not securing it. And even in his higher moods of action, when raised, in some degree, above the influence of the subordinate propensities, his movements will always be based on calculations of interest; and although the various suggestions which influence his conduct may have an extensive range, they will never fail to revolve within the limits of a circle, the centre of which is HIMSELF. It is his moral nature, and that alone, which places him beyond the limits of this circle, and enables him, on suitable occasions, to act with exclusive reference to God, his fellow-men, and the universe.

§ 244. The moral sensibilities higher in rank than the natural.

And such being the objects of these two great departments of our nature, it is not surprising that they do not hold the same place in our estimation. There is obviviously a sort of graduation in the feelings of regard and honour which we attach to different parts of the mind We at once, as it were instinctively, regard some as higher than others. We may not be able always to tell why it is so; but such is the fact. We never hesitate, for instance, to assign a lower place to the instincts than to the appetites; and, on the other hand, we always allot to the appetites, in the graduation of our regard, a place below that of the affections. And, entirely in accordance with this general fact, we find it to be the case, that the moral sensibilities excite within us higher sentiments of regard; in other words, hold, in our estimation of them, a higher rank than the appetites, propensities, and passions, which constitute the leading divisions of our pathematic nature.

The moral sensibility appears to occupy, in respect to the other great division of our sensitive nature, the position of a consultative and judicial power; it not only stands above it, and over it, in our estimation, but actually is so, viz., in the exercise of a higher authority; it keenly scrutinizes the motives of action; it compares emotion with emotion, desire with desire; it sits a sort of arbitress, holding the scales of justice, and dispensing such decisions as are requisite for the due regulation of the empire of the passions.

§ 245. The moral sensibilities wanting in brutes.

It will, perhaps, throw additional light upon the distinction which we assert to exist in the Sensibilities, if we call to recollection here that the natural or pathematic sensibilities exist in brute animals essentially the same as in man. Brute animals are susceptible of various emotions. They have their instincts, appetites, propensities, and affections, the same as human beings have, and, perhaps, even in a higher degree. They rush with eagerness in the pursuit of whatever is calculated to gratify their appetites, and are deeply interested in everything that is addressed to the natural affections. They are pleased and displeased; they have their prepossessions and aversions; they love and hate with as much vehemence, at least, as commonly characterizes human passion.

But if we look for the other and more elevated portion of the sensibilities, viz., the Moral Sensibilities, it is not there. And here, we apprehend, is the great ground of distinction between men and the brutes. The latter, as well as human beings, appear to understand what is good, considered as addressed simply to the natural affections; but man has the higher knowledge of moral as well as of natural good. The brute, as well as man, knows what is desirable, considered in the light of the natural appetites and passions; but man enjoys the infinitely higher prerogative of knowing what is worthy of pursuit, considered in the light of moral and conscientious perceptions

§ 246. Classification of the natural sensibilities.

Beginning, in the examination of the interesting subject before us, with the Natural or Pathematic sensibilities, we shall find this portion of our sensitive nature resolving itself into the subordinate divisions of the Emotions and Desires. These two classes of mental states follow each other in the order in which they have been named; the Emotions first, which are exceedingly numerous and various; and then the Desires, embracing, under the latter term, the Appetites, Propensities, and Affections. This is not only the order in succession or time, but it is also the order in nature.

In other words, and stated more particularly, such is the constitution of the human mind, that, when we pass from the region of the Intellect to that of the Sensibilities, we first find ourselves (and there is no other possible position which, in the first instance, we can occupy) in the domain of the EMOTIONS. We are at first pleased or displeased, or have some other emotion in view of the thing, whatever it is, which has come under the cognizance of the intellect. And emotions, in the ordinary process of mental action, are followed by Desires. As we cannot be pleased or displeased without some antecedent perception or knowledge of the thing which we are pleased or displeased with, so we cannot desire to possess or avoid anything, without having laid the foundation of such de sire in the existence of some antecedent emotion. And this is not only the matter of fact which, as the mind is actually constituted, is presented to our notice, but we cannot well conceive how it could be otherwise. To desire a thing which utterly fails to excite within us the least emotion of pleasure, seems to be a sort of solecism or absurdity in nature; in other words, it seems to be impossible, from the nature of things, under any conceivable circumstances. At any rate, it is not possible, as the mind is actually constituted, whatever might have been the fact if the mind had been constituted differently.

§ 247. Classification of the moral sensibilities.

If we look at the conscientious or Moral sensibilities, we find that they divide themselves in a manner entirely analogous to the division which is found to exist in the Natural. The first class of mental states which presents itself to our notice under this general head, is that of moral Emotions; corresponding in the place which they occupy in relation to the Intellect, as well as in some other respects, to the natural emotions. The moral emotions are followed by another class of moral feelings, which may be designated as Obligatory feelings, or feelings of moral obligation; which hold the same relation to the moral emotions which the Desires do to the natural emotions. If we had not moral emotions, (that is to say, feelings of moral approval and disapproval,) it would not be possible for us to feel under moral obligation in any case whatever; the latter state of the mind being obviously dependent on the former.—It will be noticed, that in this place we scarcely do more than simply state the fact of this subordinate classification, without entering into minute explanations. The precise relation which the two departments of our moral nature sustain to each other will be more fully stated and clearly understood, when, in their proper place, they come particularly under examination

THE SENSIBILITIES.

PART FIRST.

NATURAL OR PATHEMATIC SENSIBILITIES.

NATURAL OR PATHEMATIC SENTIMENTS.

CLASS FIRST.

EMOTIONS OR EMOTIVE STATES OF THE MIND

CHAPTER I.

NATURE OF THE EMOTIONS.

§ 248. We have a knowledge of emotions by consciousness.

In prosecuting the examination of the Sensibilities, in accordance with the plan which has been marked out in the Introduction, we begin with the Emotions. It is, of course, implied in the arrangement we have made, which assigns them a distinct place, that this class of mental states has a nature and characteristics of its own, in virtue of which they are distinguished from all others. At the same time, it cannot be denied that it is extremely difficult to explain by mere words what that precise nature is. We do not suppose, indeed, that any one is ignorant of what is meant when we have occasion to speak of an emotion, whether it be an emotion of melancholy, of cheerfulness, of surprise, or of some other kind. But, whatever may be the fact as to our knowledge, it is unquestionable that we are unable to give a verbal explanation of them, *in themselves considered.*

In this respect they are like all other states of the mind, which are truly simple. The fact of their entire simplicity necessarily renders them undefinable; because a definition implies a separation of the thing defined into parts. So that we are dependent for a knowledge of the interior and essential nature of emotions, not upon verbal explanations and definitions, which are inadequate to the communication of such knowledge, but upon Consciousness. It is a species of knowledge which the soul reveals to itself by its own act, directly and immediately. While, therefore, we do not profess to define emotions, in any proper and legitimate sense of defining, we may commend them without impropriety to each one's internal examination. And certainly we may rely upon the intimations which consciousness, when properly interrogated, can hardly fail to disclose in this case as well as in others

§ 249. The place of emotions, considered in reference to other mental acts

Although, in attempting to give some idea of Emotions, we are obliged, for a knowledge of them, in themselves considered, to refer each one to his own consciousness, we may nevertheless mention some circumstances which throw an indirect light on them; and, at any rate, render more clear to our perception the relation which they sustain to other mental states. The first circumstance which we propose to indicate has reference to the position which they occupy; (of course it will be understood that we mean their position, not in the material sense of the term, but in time or succession.) It will be found, on examination, to be the fact, as we have already had occasion to suggest, that Emotions always occupy a place between intellections or acts of the intellect and the desires, if they are natural emotions; and between intellections and feelings of moral obligation, if they are moral emotions. That they are subsequent to intellections, we believe must be abundantly clear. It is as obvious as any axiom of geometry, that we cannot have any feeling, any emotion, in respect to that, whatever it is, which we have no knowledge of.

In regard to the Desires, it is true, that, like the emotions, they are subsequent to the perceptive and cognitive acts; but it is well understood that they are not in *immediate* proximity with them. It is perfectly obvious, that no act of perception or of cognition in any shape can lay the foundation for a desire, unless the object of perception is pleasant to us; in other words, unless it excites within us pleasant emotions. For, whenever we speak of a thing as pleasant to us, we certainly involve the fact that we have pleasant emotions in view of it.—Nor, furthermore, can any perceptive or intellectual act lay the foundation for Obligatory feelings (that is to say, feelings of moral obligation) without the intervention and aid of moral emotions. It may be regarded as self-evident, that we never could feel under moral obligation to do or not to do a thing, unless the thing to be done or not to be done had first excited within us an emotion of approval or disapproval. So that the desires, and those feelings in the moral sensibilities which correspond to them, are based upon emotions, as really as the emotions are based upon intellections. In the order of nature, therefore, emotions are found in the place which has now been allotted them, and they are found nowhere else; being always and necessarily posterior to a knowledge of the things to which they relate; and, on the other hand, antecedent, by an equally strict natural necessity, to the other states of mind which have been mentioned.

§ 250. The character of emotions changes so as to conform to that of perceptions.

It is important to impress upon the recollection, that the order of succession, in fact and in nature, is precisely that which has been stated, viz., intellections, emotions, and desires in the case of the natural sensibilities, and obligatory feelings in the case of the moral sensibilities. The two last mentioned being followed immediately, as their natural results, by acts of the will, which terminate and complete the entire process of mental action. But as we must take them and examine them in their order, we say further, in regard to the Emotions, which is the topic before us at present, that the fact of their subsequence to intellections and of their being based upon them is confirmed by the circumstance of their always changing or varying in precise accordance with the perceptive or intellective acts. If it were otherwise, (that is to say, if they had any other foundation than intellective acts) how does it happen that these changes so uniformly take place?

We are looking, for instance, on some extended landscape; but are so situated that the view of certain objects is interrupted, and, of course, the relations of the whole are disturbed. At such a time the emotions we have are far from being pleasant; perhaps they are decidedly unpleasant. But as soon as our imperfect perceptions are corrected, as soon as we are able to embrace the portions which were previously thrust out of view, and thus restore the interrupted proportions and harmony of the whole scenery, our emotions change at once, and we experience the highest pleasure.—Again, if we look at a painting which has come from the hand of some master of his art, we are distinctly conscious at first sight of a pleasing emotion; but we examine it further, and make ourselves acquainted with a number of things less prominent than others, but still decidedly showing the skill of the painter, which escaped our first view, and we are conscious of a distinct change in that emotion. It becomes more decided, more full, in precise conformity with the increased knowledge which we have obtained of the merit which the picture actually possesses. And it is so, if no unusual disturbing influence is interposed, in every other case, showing not only the intimate but proximate connexion between the emotions and the intellective acts, and the dependence of the former on the latter.

§ 251. Emotions characterized by rapidity and variety.

When we assert that the position of emotions is between intellections on the one hand, and desires and obligations on the other, we imply, of course, that there is a real and marked distinction between them and the latter mental states. And this distinction exists. If consciousness gives us a knowledge of emotions, the same consciousness can hardly fail to give a knowledge of the mental states that are subsequent to them; and the difference of knowledge, resulting from these different acts of consciousness, involves necessarily a difference in the things known.

(1.) Among other things, if we consult our consciousness for the purpose of ascertaining the comparative nature of the mental states in question, we shall undoubtedly be led to notice that the emotions, as compared with the others, are generally more prompt and rapid in their origin, as well as more evanescent. They arise and depart on the surface of the mind, swelling and sinking almost instantaneously, like the small waves and ripples that play upon the scarcely agitated surface of a summer's lake, and which have no sooner arrested the eye of the beholder than they are gone. The desires and feelings of obligation not only arise subsequently and more slowly, but obviously possess a greater tenacity and inflexibility of nature

When a strong desire or a decided sentiment of duty has once entrenched itself in the soul, it is well known that it is comparatively difficult to dislodge it.

(2.) There is another circumstance involved in the distinction between them. The emotions have less unity in kind; in other words, are more various. Desires and obligations, although liable, like other mental states, to be modified by peculiar circumstances, are, in themselves considered, always one and the same. But of emotions we find many varieties, such as the emotions of cheerfulness and joy, of melancholy and sorrow, of shame, of surprise, astonishment, and wonder. We have furthermore the emotions, differing from all others, of the ludicrous, the emotions of beauty and sublimity, also the moral emotions of approval and disapproval, and some others. —If the reader will bear these statements in mind, taken in connexion with some things to be said hereafter, he will feel less objection, than he might otherwise have felt, to the general and subordinate classifications which we have thought ourselves authorized to make. These divisions we hold to be fundamental. They are necessarily involved, as we apprehend, in a thorough and consistent knowledge of the mind. Important points, for instance, in the doctrine of the Will, will be found to depend upon distinctions which are asserted to exist in the sensibilities. It is desirable, therefore, that the grounds of such distinctions should be understood, so that they may not only be above rejection, but above doubt.

CHAPTER II.

EMOTIONS OF BEAUTY.

§ 252. Characteristics of emotions of beauty.

We do not profess to enter into an examination of every possible emotion. They are so various and multiplied, it would be difficult to do it; nor would any important object be answered. Proceeding on the principle of selecting those which, either in themselves, or by reason of their relation to the arts and to human conduct, appear to be most interesting and important, we shall begin with emotions of Beauty.—We have already had occasion to remark, that all emotions are undefinable. This remark is applicable to those under consideration as well as others. Of the emotions of beauty it will be as difficult to give a definition, so as to make them clearer to any one's comprehension than they already are, as to define the simple sensations of colour, sound, or taste. We find in them, however, these two marks or characteristics.

(1.) The emotion of beauty, in the first place, is always a pleasing one. We never give the name to one which is painful, or to any feeling of disgust. Whenever, therefore, we speak of an emotion of beauty, we imply, in the use of the terms, some degree of satisfaction or pleasure. All persons, the illiterate as well as the scientific, use the phrase with this import.—(2.) We never speak of emotions of beauty, to whatever degree may be our experience of inward satisfaction, without referring such emotions to something external. The same emotion, which is called satisfaction or delight of mind when it is wholly and exclusively internal, we find to be termed an emotion of beauty if we are able to refer it to something without, and to spread its charms around any external object.

§ 253. Of what is meant by beautiful objects.

There are many objects which excite the emotion of beauty; that is, when the objects are presented, this emotion, in a greater or less degree, immediately exists. These objects we call beautiful.—There are other objects which, so far from exciting pleasant emotions within us, are either indifferent, or cause feelings of a decidedly opposite character; so that we speak of them as deformed or disgusting. If there were no emotions, pleasant or unpleasant, excited by either of these classes, or if the emotions which they cause were of the same kind, we should apply to them the same epithets. So that the ground of distinction, which, in speaking of these different objects, we never fail to make, appears to exist in our own feelings. In other words, we call an object BEAUTIFUL, because it excites within us pleasant emotions, which, in the circumstances of the case, we cannot well ascribe to any other cause. And when we prefer to say, in other terms, that an object has beauty, we obviously mean the same thing, viz., that the object has a trait or quality (perhaps we may find it difficult to explain precisely what it is) which causes these emotions.

§ 254. Of the distinction between beautiful and other objects

In view of what has been said, we may venture to make two remarks.—(I.) Every beautiful object has something in itself which truly discriminates it from all other objects. This something, this peculiar trait, whatever it is, lays the foundation for those results in the human mind, which, on being experienced, authorize us to speak of the object as beautiful. This is clear, not only from what, on a careful examination, we shall frequently find in the objects themselves, but also from the fact, that the operations of the mind always have their appropriate causes. If the mind experiences a pleasant emotion in view of a certain object, it is because there is something in the object which has a determinate and permanent relation to that particular mental state which distinguishes it from other objects. If it were not for that distinctive trait in the object, the human mind is so constituted that it could not have experienced the corresponding emotion

(II.) Beautiful objects are distinguished from all others, not only by something in themselves, certain original and inherent traits characteristic of them, but also, and perhaps still more, by a superadded trait, a species of borrowed effulgence, derived and reflected back from the mind itself. When we contemplate a beautiful object, we are pleased; we are more or less happy. We naturally connect this emotion of pleasure with the object which is its cause; and we have been in the habit of doing this, no doubt in most instances unconsciously to ourselves, from early life. The consequence is, the association between the inward delight and the outward cause becomes so strong, that we are unable to separate them; and the objects, additional to their own proper qualities appear to be surrounded, and to beam out with an effulgence which comes from the mind.

§ 255. Grounds or occasions of emotions of beauty various.

The next remark which we have to make on the subject of Beauty is, that the objects by which it is occasioned are not always the same, but are very various; differing from each other not only in their general nature, but also in their subordinate incidents. Accordingly, we may with propriety regard the term BEAUTY not so much a particular as a *general* or *common* name, expressive of numerous emotions, which always possess the characteristic of being pleasant, and are in every respect always the same in nature, but which may differ from each other both in the occasions of their origin, and also in the degree or intensity in which they exist.

(I.) In regard to the occasions on which they arise, we may remark more particularly, that emotions of beauty are felt, and frequently in a very high degree, in the contemplation of material objects that are addressed to the sense of sight, such as woods, waters, cultivated fields, and the visible firmament. We look abroad upon nature, in the infinite variety of her works, as she is exhibited in the depths below and in the heights above, in her shells and minerals, in her plants, and flowers, and trees, in her waters, and her stars, and suns; and we find the mind kindling at the sight; fountains of pleasure are suddenly opened within us; and we should do violence to our mental structure if we did not pronounce them beautiful.

(II.) Again, emotions of beauty are felt in the contemplation of intellectual and moral objects. In other words, mind, as well as matter, furnishes the occasion on which they arise. Whenever we discover intelligence, wisdom, truth, honour, magnanimity, benevolence, justice, or other traits of a mind acting as it was created and designed to act, we have a foundation laid for emotions of beauty.—The human countenance, considered merely as a material object, and as presenting nothing more than outline and colour, is undoubtedly beautiful; but becomes more so when it distinctly indicates to us intelligence and amiability.

(III.) But emotions of beauty are not exclusively limited to these occasions. Feelings, which not only bear the same name, but are truly analogous in kind, exist also on the contemplation of many other things.—The sentiment or feeling of beauty exists, for instance, when we are following out a happy train of reasoning; and hence the mathematician, who certainly has a delightful feeling analogous to what we experience in contemplating many works of nature, speaks of a *beautiful* theorem.—The connoisseur in music applies the term *beautiful* to a favourite air; the lover of poetry speaks of a beautiful song; and the painter discovers beauty in the design and in the colouring of his pictures. We also apply the term beauty to experiments in the different departments of physics; especially when the experiment is simple, and results in deciding a point which has occasioned doubt and dispute. We speak of it, and, as we suppose, with a degree of propriety, as a beautiful experiment.

So that all nature, taking the word in a wide sense, is the province of beauty; the intellectual and the sensitive, as well as the material world. We do not, however, mean by this to descend into particulars, and to say that everything which exists within the range of these departments is beautiful; but merely that from none of the great departments of nature are the elements of beauty excluded.

§ 256. All objects not equally fitted to cause these emotions.

From what has been said, it must be evident that there is a correspondence between the mind and the outward objects which are addressed to it.—This has already been clearly seen in respect to the sensations and external perceptions; and it is not less evident in respect to that part of our nature which we are now attending to. The mind, and the external world, and the external circumstances of our situation, are reciprocally suited to each other. Hence, when we ascribe the quality of beauty to any object, we have reference to this mutual adaptation. An object is ordinarily called beautiful when it has agreeable qualities; in other words, when it is the cause or antecedent of the emotion of beauty. However it might appear to other beings, it would not have the character of beauty to us, if there were not a sort of correspondence, an adaptedness to each other, between our mental constitution and such outward object.

But no one can be ignorant that not all objects cause the emotions in question; and of those which possess this power, some have it in a greater, and some in a less degree. This brings us to a very important inquiry. It is no unreasonable curiosity which wishes to know, Why the effect is so limited, and why all objects are not embraced in it? Why different objects cause the same emotion in different degrees? And why the same objects produce a diversity of emotions in different individuals, and even in the same individual at different times?

§ 257. A susceptibility of emotions of beauty an ultimate principle of our mental constitution.

In answering these questions, something must be taken for granted; there must be some starting point, otherwise all that can be said will be involved in inextricable confusion. That is, we must take for granted that the mind has an original susceptibility of such emotions. Nor can we suppose there can be any objection to a concession which is warranted by the most general experience. We all know that we are created with this susceptibility, because we are all conscious of having had those emotions which are attributed to it. And if we are asked how or why it is that the susceptibility at the bottom of these feelings exists, we can only say that such was the will of the Being who created the mind, and that this is one of the original or ultimate elements of our nature.

Although the mind, therefore, is originally susceptible of emotions of beauty, as every one knows; still it is no less evident, from the general arrangements we behold, both in physical and in intellectual nature, that these emotions have their fixed causes or antecedents. We have seen that these causes are not limited to one class or kind, but are to be found under various circumstances; in the exercises of reasoning, in the fanciful creations of poetry, in musical airs, in the experiments of physics, in the forms of material existence, and the like. Perhaps we may assert, as a general statement, (that is to say, in a great number or majority of cases,) these objects cannot be presented to the mind, and the mind be unmoved by it; it contemplates them, and it necessarily has a feeling of delight, of a greater or less degree of strength, which authorizes us in characterizing them as beautiful.

In asserting that this is correct as a *general statement*, it is implied that some objects do not originally cause these emotions. And hence we are led to enter into more particular inquiries, having reference to this difference, in what may be called, in the phraseology of some recent writers, the ÆSTHETIC power of objects. Accordingly, our purpose, in the remarks which are to follow, is to point out some of those objects, and forms and qualities of objects, which seem from their very nature, and in distinction from other objects which do not have this power fitted to create within us the feelings under consideration

§ 258. Remarks on the beauty of forms.—The circle.

In making that selection of those objects and qualities of objects which we suppose to be fitted, in the original constitution of things, to cause within us pleasing emotions of themselves, independently of any extraneous aid, we cannot profess to speak with certainty. The appeal is to the general experience of men; and all we can do is to give, so far as it seems to have been ascertained, the results of that experience. Beginning, therefore, with material objects, we are justified by general experience in saying that certain dispositions or forms of matter are beautiful; for instance, the CIRCLE.

We rarely look upon a winding or serpentine form without experiencing a feeling of pleasure; and on seeing a circle, this pleasure is heightened. Hence Hogarth, who, both by his turn of mind and by his habits of life, has claims to be regarded as a judge, expressly lays it down in his Analysis of Beauty, that those lines which have most variety in themselves contribute most towards the production of beauty; and that the most beautiful line by which a surface can be bounded is the waving or serpentine, or that which constantly, but imperceptibly, deviates from the straight line. This, which we frequent ly find in shells, flowers, and other pleasing natural productions, he calls the line of beauty.

§ 259. Original or intrinsic beauty.—The circle.

It is necessary, in examining the subject of beauty, to look at it in two points of view, viz., as Intrinsic and as Associated. In the remarks which we may have occasion to make in this chapter, we have reference exclusively to what may be denominated Original or Intrinsic beauty; by which we mean that which is founded in the nature of the object, independently of accidental or merely accessory circumstances.—Accordingly, it is this form of beauty which we ascribe to the CIRCLE. Those objects which are circular, or approach that form, exhibiting a constantly varying outline, have in themselves, and on account of this configuration, a degree, and not unfrequently a *high* degree, of beauty. The bending stem of the tulip, the curve of the weeping willow, the windings of the ivy, the vine wreathing itself around the elm, the serpentine river, are highly pleasing. The vast circular expanse of the visible sky, when seen in a cloudless night, is a beautiful object, independently of the splendour that is spread over it by its brilliant troops of stars. The arch of the rainbow, expanding its immense curve over our heads, could hardly fail to be regarded as an object of great beauty, even if nothing but the form and outline were presented to our vision, without the unrivalled lustre of its colours. And the same of other instances, scattered in profusion through the works of nature, but too numerous to be mentioned here.

§ 260. Of the beauty of straight and angular forms.

Although the circular or constantly varying outline is thought, more than any other, to excite the delightful emotions under consideration, we are not to suppose that the power of beauty is excluded from other forms. In examining the works of nature, it is hardly necessary to say that we find numerous instances of straight and angular forms, as well as of the serpentine and winding, although perhaps less frequently. It can hardly be doubted that these forms, as they are operated upon and moulded in nature's hands, possess more or less beauty. It is almost a matter of supererogation to attempt to illustrate this statement to those who have a heart and eye open to the great variety of her works, which on every side are presented to our notice. Her forms, either original or in their combinations, are without number; and if it be true that beauty does not claim a relationship with all, it is equally so that it is not restricted to one, or even a small portion of them. The intertwining shrubbery, which spreads itself abroad upon the ground, emits, if we may be allowed the expression, its sparkles and gleams of beauty around our feet. The elm, which rises upward towards the heavens, and forms its broad and green arch over our heads, is radiant with beauty also, although it is exceedingly diverse in its appearance. We readily admit, for we cannot well do otherwise without violence to the suggestions of our nature, that the curve of the weeping willow possesses beauty. But, at the same time, we are not prepared to assert that the solitary palm-tree is absolutely destitute of it, although it displays, as it rises on the bosom of the desert, nothing but a tall, straight, branchless trunk, surmounted at the top, like a Corinthian column, by a single tuft of foliage.

"There are an infinite number of the feebler vegetables," says Mr. Alison, "and many of the common grasses, the forms of which are altogether distinguished by angles and straight lines, and where there is not a single curvature through the whole; yet all of which are beautiful." He ascribes in another place a high degree of beauty to the knotted and angular stem of the balsam. And remarks also, in regard to the myrtle, that it is "generally reckoned a beautiful form, yet the growth of its stem is perpendicular, the junctions of its branches form regular and similar angles, and their direction is in straight or angular lines."

§ 261. Of square, pyramidal, and triangular forms.

The remarks of the last section, going to show that beauty is not limited to circular forms, is confirmed by what we observe in the works of art as well as of nature. The square, for instance, although we do not sup pose it presents very high claims, comes in for a share of notice. On account of its practical convenience, and also for the reason of its being more entirely within the reach of human skill than some other forms, it is frequently introduced into architecture; generally with a pleasing effect, and sometimes with a high degree of beauty.

In the Gothic architecture, the pyramidal, a form still further removed from any relationship with the circle, has a conspicuous place, and when properly combined with other forms, gives a decided pleasure. Hogarth, in illustration of his remark, that variety has a great share in producing beauty, explicitly observes, that the pyramid, which gradually diminishes from its basis to its point, is a beautiful form. And it is in consequence of being so regarded that we find it so frequently employed, not only as a characteristic feature in the order of architecture just referred to, but in steeples, sepulchral monuments, and other works of art.

Triangular forms also are not without beauty Mr. Alison states, that the forms of Grecian and Roman furniture, in their periods of cultivated taste, were almost universally distinguished by straight or angular lines. What is there, he inquires, more beautiful than the form of the ancient tripod? "The feet gradually lessening to the end, and converging as they approach it; the plane of the table placed, with little ornament, nearly at right angles to the feet; and the whole appearing to form an imperfect triangle, whose base is above. There is scarcely in such a subject a possibility of contriving a more angular form, yet there can be none more completely beautiful."

In connexion with these statements, it is proper to add a single explanatory remark. We have much reason to believe that the emotion will be stronger in all cases in proportion as the beautiful object is distinctly and immediately embraced by the mind. It may be asserted, with undoubted good reason, that the square form has a degree of beauty as well as the circle, although it is generally conceded that it has less. But it is a matter of inquiry, whether the difference in this respect is owing so much to the original power of the forms themselves, as to the circumstance just alluded to. In other words, whether it be not owing to the fact, that the circle, being more simple, makes a more direct, entire, and decided impression; whereas the attention is divided among the sides and angles of the square and other similar figures.

§ 262. Of the original or intrinsic beauty of colours.

We proceed to remark, as we advance in the further consideration of this interesting subject, that we experience emotions of beauty in beholding the colours, as well as in contemplating the outlines or forms of bodies. The doctrine which we hold is, that some colours of themselves, independently of the additional interest which may subsequently be attached to them in consequence of certain associations, are fitted to excite within us those feelings of pleasure which authorize us in this, as well as in other analogous cases, to speak of the cause of them as beautiful. In other words, there are some colours which possess, as we suppose, an original or intrinsic beauty.—In support of this opinion, we are merely able to allude to some of the various considerations which naturally present themselves, without entering into that minute exposition of them which would be admissible in a treatise professedly and exclusively devoted to the subject before us.

(1.) The pleasure which results from the mere beholding of colours may be observed in very early life. It is in consequence of this pleasing emotion that the infant so early directs its eyes towards the light that breaks in from the window, or which reaches the sense of vision from any other source. It is pleasing to see with what evident ecstasy the child rushes from flower to flower, and compares their brilliancy. Casting his eyes abroad in the pursuit of objects that are richly variegated, he pauses to gaze with admiration on every tree that is most profusely loaded with blossoms, or that is burdened with fruit of the deepest red and yellow. It is because he is attracted with the brightness of its wings that he pursues the butterfly with a labour so unwearied, or suspends his sport to watch the wayward movements of the humming-bird.

(2.) The same results are found also, very strikingly and generally, among all savage tribes. The sons of the forest are not so wholly untutored, so wholly devoid of natural sensibility, that they will not sometimes forget the ardour of the chase in the contemplation of the flowers which bloom in the neighbourhood of their path. Seeing how beautiful the fish of their lakes and rivers, the bird of their forests, and the forest tree itself, are rendered by colours, they commit the mistake of attempting to render their own bodies more beautiful by artificial hues. They value whatever dress they may have in proportion to the gaudiness of its colours; they weave rich and variegated plumes into their hair; and as they conjectured, from his scarlet dress, that Columbus was the captain of the Spaniards, so they are wont to intimate and express their own rank and dignity by the splendour of their equipments.

(3.) And the same trait which has been so often noticed in Savages, may be observed also, though in a less degree, among the uneducated classes in civilized communities. In persons of refinement, the original tendency to receive pleasing emotions from the contemplation of colours seems to have, in a measure, lost its power, in consequence of the developement of tendencies to receive pleasure from other causes. In those, on the contrary, who have possessed less advantages of mental culture, and whose sources of pleasure may in consequence be supposed to lay nearer to the surface of the mind, this tendency remains undiminished. Coloured objects generally affect them with a high degree of pleasure; so much so that the absence of colour is not, in their estimation, easily compensated by the presence of any other qualities. We cannot well suppose that there is any intermediate influence between the beautiful object and the mind, of which this pleasure is the product; but must rather conclude, in the circumstances of the case, that the presence of the object, and that only, is the ground of its existence

§ 263. Further illustrations of the original beauty of colours.

We may derive additional proof of the fact that colours are of themselves fitted to cause emotions of beauty from what we learn in the case of those persons who have been blind from birth, but in after life have suddenly been restored by couching, or in some other way—"I have couched," says Dr. Wardrop,* speaking of James Mitchell, "one of his eyes successfully; and he is much amused with the visible world, though he mistrusts information gained by that avenue. One day I got him a new and *gaudy* suit of clothes, which delighted him beyond description. It was the most interesting scene of sensual gratification I ever beheld."

But this person, it appears, had some faint notions of light and colours previous to the operation by which his powers of vision were more fully restored. And the facts, stated in connexion with his exercise of this imperfect vision, are equally decisive in favour of the doctrine under consideration. The statements to which we refer are as follows.—"At the time of life when this boy began to walk, he seemed to be attracted by bright and dazzling colours; and though everything connected with his history appears to prove that he derived little information from the organ, yet he received from it much sensual gratification. He used to hold between his eye and luminous objects such bodies as he found to increase, by their interposition, the quantity of light; and it was one of his chief amusements to concentrate the sun's rays by means of pieces of glass, transparent pebbles, or similar substances, which he held between his eye and the light, and turned about in various directions. These too he would often break with his teeth, and give them that form which seemed to please him most. There were other modes by which he was in the habit of gratifying this fondness for light. He would retire to any outhouse or to any room within his reach, shut the windows and doors, and remain there for some considerable time, with his eyes fixed on some small hole or chink which admitted the sun's rays, eagerly watching them. He would also, during the winter nights, often retire to a dark corner of the room and kindle a light for his amusement. On these occasions, as well as in the gratification of his other senses, his countenance and gestures displayed a most interesting avidity and curiosity."

* As quoted by Mr. Stewart in his account of Mitchell

The conclusion which we deduce from these sources of proof is, that colours are fitted, from our very constitution, to produce within us emotions of beauty.

§ 264. Of sounds considered as a source of beauty.

We next propose to inquire into the application of these principles in respect to sounds. And here also we have reason to believe that they hold good to a certain extent; in other words, that certain sounds are pleasing of themselves; and are hence, agreeably to views already expressed, termed BEAUTIFUL.—In proceeding, however, to the consideration of beauty as it exists in connexion with sounds, it may be proper to recur to the remark which was made near the commencement of the chapter, that the sources or grounds of beauty, although the emotions they excite within us are all of essentially the same kind, are very various. In view of what was there said, we do not feel at liberty to doubt, as some may be disposed to do, whether there is beauty in sounds, merely because sounds are obviously altogether different from some other objects which constitute sources of beauty, such as colours or forms. It is not the intention of nature that the empire of the beautiful shall be limited in this manner. On the contrary, if certain sounds have something within them, which from its very nature is calculated to excite within us pleasing emotions, they are obviously distinguished by this circumstance from other sounds, and furnish a sufficient reason for our regarding them and speaking of them as BEAUTIFUL.

(1.) In asserting, however, that there is an original beauty in sounds, we do not wish to be understood as saying that all sounds, of whatever kind, possess this character. There are some sounds which, in themselves considered, are justly regarded as indifferent, and others as positively disagreeable. No one would hesitate in pronouncing the discordant creaking of a wheel, the filing of a saw, the braying of the ass, the scream of a peacock, or the hissing of a serpent, to be disagreeable. There are other sounds, such as the bleating of the lamb, the lowing of the cow, the call of the goat, and other notes and cries of animals, which appear to be, in themselves, entirely indifferent. We are aware that they are sometimes spoken of as beautiful; nor is it necessary to deny that they are sometimes heard with a high degree of pleasure. But we regard the beauty in this case as rather associated than intrinsic; the result rather of accessory circumstances than of the thing itself. The happy remarks of Mr. Alison, going to show the nature of the beauty which is ordinarily felt at such times, will be read with interest.

"The bleating of a lamb is beautiful in a fine day in spring; in the depth of winter it is very far from being so. The lowing of a cow at a distance, amid the scenery of a pastoral landscape in summer, is extremely beautiful; in a farmyard it is absolutely disagreeable. The hum of the beetle is beautiful in a fine summer evening, as appearing to suit the stillness and repose of that pleasing season: in the noon of day it is perfectly indifferent. The twitter of the swallow is beautiful in the morning, and seems to be expressive of the cheerfulness of that time; at any other hour it is quite insignificant. Even the song of the nightingale, so wonderfully charming in the twilight or at night, is altogether disregarded during the day; in so much so, that it has given rise to the common mistake that this bird does not sing but at night"

§ 265. Illustrations of the original beauty of sounds.

(2.) Other sounds, those which are properly termed musical, have a beauty which is original or intrinsic, and not merely accessory. It is true that different nations have different casts or styles of music, modified by the situation and habits of the people; but everything that can properly be called music, whatever occasional or accidental modification it may assume, is in its nature more or less beautiful. Musical sounds, independently of their combinations and expression, are characterized in a way which distinguishes them from all others; viz., by the circumstance of their possessing certain mathematical proportions in their times of vibration Such sounds please us originally; in other words, whenever, in all ordinary circumstances, they are heard, they please naturally and necessarily.—We are aware that attempts have sometimes been made to explain the pleasure which is received from musical sounds, as well as from those of a different character, on the doctrine of association. But there are various difficulties in this explanation, some of which will now be referred to.

(1.) In the first place, we are led to expect, from the analogy of things which we witness in other cases, that we shall find, in the human heart also, an original sensibility to the beautiful in the matter under consideration. We refer now to what we frequently notice in the lower animals; and although we do not claim that very much weight should be attached to this view of the subject, it certainly furnishes some matter for reflection. Why should brute animals be originally pleased with musical sounds, and man, whom we may well suppose to have as much need of this pleasure, be naturally destitute of the capability of receiving it? In regard to brute animals, (we do not say all, but many of them,) there is no possible question as to the fact involved in this inquiry Through all the numberless varieties which they exhibit, from the mouse, of which Linnæus says with strict truth, "DELECTATUR MUSICA," to the elephant on the banks of the Niger, that responds with his unwieldy dance to the rude instrument of the untutored African, they yield their homage to the magic of sweet sounds. To attempt to explain the pleasure they receive on the ground of association would be difficult, perhaps ridiculous. The simple fact is, that they listen and are delighted. It is the sound, and nothing but the sound, which excites the joy they exhibit. So great is the acknowledged power of music over many brute animals, that the classical traditions which celebrate the achievements of the early poets and musicians scarcely transcend the bounds of truth.

> "For Orpheus' lute was strung with poets' sinews,
> Whose golden touch could soften steel and stones,
> Make tigers tame, and huge leviathans
> Forsake unsounded deeps to dance on sands."

(2.) In the second place, children, at an early period of life, before they have had an opportunity of connecting associations with them to any great extent, are highly pleased with musical sounds. This is a fact which we cannot suppose has escaped the notice of any one. Let a wandering musician suddenly make his appearance in a country village, with his fife, bagpipe, or hand-organ, (instruments which are not supposed to possess the highest claims to musical power,) and it is surprising to see with what an outburst of joy the sound is welcomed to the heart of childhood. Delighted countenances cluster at the windows; and merry groups, that just before made the streets ring with their noise, suddenly leave their sports, and rush with a new and delighted impulse to the presence of the strolling minstrel. This is universally the fact; and when we consider the early age at which it takes place, it seems to be inconsistent with any other view than that which ascribes to sounds of a certain character an original or intrinsic attraction.

(3.) We witness, furthermore, the same result in Savage tribes, when they first become acquainted with the instruments of music, however simple or imperfect they may be, which have been fabricated by European skill. It is said of the native inhabitants of this country, that they frequently purchased of the Spaniards, when they first came to America, small bells; and when they hung them on their persons, and heard their clear musical sounds responding to the movement of their dances, they were filled with the highest possible delight. At a later period in the history of the country, it is related by one of the Jesuit missionaries, that once coming into the company of certain ignorant and fierce Indians, he met with a rude and menacing reception, which foreboded no very favourable termination. As it was not his design, however, to enter into any contention if it could possibly be avoided, he immediately commenced playing on a stringed instrument; their feelings were softened at once; and the evil spirit of jealousy and anger, which they exhibited on his first approach to them, fled from their minds."*—We cannot suppose it necessary to multiply instances to the same effect.

* See Irving's Life and Voyages of Columbus, ch. ix.—London Quarterly Review, vol. xxvi., p. 287.

§ 266. Further instances of the original beauty of sounds.

(4.) In the fourth place, deaf persons, who have been suddenly restored to the sense of hearing, and also persons who, in consequence of their peculiar situation, have never heard musical sounds till a certain period of their life, and have therefore been unable, in either case, to form associations with such sounds, either pleasant or unpleasant, have been found, on hearing them for the first time, to experience a high degree of pleasure.—So far as we have been able to learn, we believe this to be the fact. At the same time, as instances of this kind seldom occur, and are still less frequently recorded, we do not profess to rely upon the statement as universally true, with an entire degree of confidence. The circumstances which are related of Caspar Hauser, on hearing musical sounds for the first time, are one of the few instances in point. The statement is as follows.—"Not only his mind, but many of his senses, appeared at first to be in a state of stupor, and only gradually to open to the perception of external objects. It was not before the lapse of several days that he began to notice the striking of the steeple clock and the ringing of the bells. This threw him into the greatest astonishment, which at first was expressed only by his listening looks and by certain spasmodic motions of his countenance; but it was soon succeeded by a stare of benumbed meditation. Some weeks afterward the nuptial procession of a peasant passed by the tower, with a band of music, close under his window. He suddenly stood listening, motionless as a statue; his countenance appeared to be transfigured, and his eyes, as it were, to irradiate his ecstasy; his ears and eyes seemed continually to follow the movements of the sounds as they receded more and more; and they had long ceased to be audible, while he still continued immoveably fixed in a listening posture, as if unwilling to lose the last vibrations of these, to him, celestial notes, or as if his soul had followed them and left his body behind it in torpid insensibility."*

§ 267. The permanency of musical power dependent on its being intrinsic

On the subject of the original or intrinsic beauty of cer-

* Life of Caspar Hauser, ch. iii.

tain sounds, one other remark remains to be made here. —It will be recollected, that the doctrine which we are opposing is, that all the power which musical sounds have, considered as a source of beauty, is wholly resolvable into association. If this be true, then it seems to be the proper business of professed composers of music to study the nature and tendency of associations rather than of sounds. The common supposition in this matter undoubtedly is, that the musical composer exercises his invention and taste, in addition to the general conception or outline of his work, in forming perfect chords, varied modulation, and accurate rythm. This is a principal, not the only one, but a principal field of his labours; the theatre on which his genius is especially displayed; and without these results of chord, modulation, and rythm, it is certain that his efforts will fail to please. But if the doctrine which we are opposing be true, would it not be the fact, that he could bring together the most harsh and discordant sounds, and compose, by means of them, the great works of his art, provided he took the pains to cover their deformity by throwing over them some fascinating dress of association? But we presume it will not be pretended that mere association possesses this power as a general thing, even in the hands of genius.—Furthermore, we do not hesitate to say, that from the nature of the case, the musical genius which composes its works for immortality must deal chiefly with the elements and essentialities of things, and not with the mere incidents and accessories. Permanency in the works of art, of course, implies a corresponding permanency in their foundation. Associations are correctly understood to be, from their very nature, uncertain and changeable, while the beauty of some musical compositions (we speak but the common sentiment of mankind in saying it) is imperishable; a fact which seems to be inconsistent with its being founded on an unfixed and evanescent basis.

§ 268. Of motion as an element of beauty.

Motion also, a new and distinct object of contemplation, has usually been reckoned a source of the beautiful, and very justly.—A forest or a field of grain, gently waved by the wind, affects us pleasantly. The motion of a winding river pleases; and this, not only because the river is serpentine, but because it is never at rest. We are delighted with the motion of a ship as it cleaves the sea under full sail. We look on as it moves like a thing of life, and are pleased without being able to control our feelings, or to tell why they exist. And the waves, too, around it, which are continually approaching and departing, and curling upward in huge masses, and then breaking asunder into fragments of every shape, present a much more pleasing appearance than they would if profoundly quiet and stagnant.

With what happy enthusiasm we behold the foaming cascade, as it breaks out from the summit of the mountain and dashes downward to its base! With what pleasing satisfaction we gaze upon a column of smoke ascending from a cottage in a wood; a trait in outward scenery which landscape painters, who must certainly be accounted good judges of what is beautiful in the aspects of external nature, are exceedingly fond of introducing. It may be said in this case, we are aware, that the pleasure arising from beholding the ascending smoke of the cottage is caused by the favourite suggestions which are connected with it, of rural seclusion, peace, and abundance. But there is much reason to believe that the feeling would be, to some extent, the same, if it were known to ascend from the uncomfortable wigwam of the Savage, from an accidental conflagration, or from the fires of a wandering horde of gipsies.—And if motion, on the limited scale on which we are accustomed to view it, be beautiful, how great would be the ecstasy of our feelings if we could be placed on some pinnacle of the universe, and could take in at one glance the regular and unbroken movement of the worlds and systems of infinite space.

§ 269. Explanation of the beauty of motion from Kaimes.

The author of the Elements of Criticism, who studied our emotions with great care, has the following explanations on this subject.—"Motion is certainly agreeable in all its varieties of quickness and slowness; but motion long continued admits some exceptions. That degree of continued motion which corresponds to the natural course of our perceptions is the most agreeable. The quickest motion is for an instant delightful; but it soon appears to be too rapid: it becomes painful by forcibly accelerating the course of our perceptions. Slow, continued motion becomes disagreeable for an opposite reason, that it retards the natural course of our perceptions.

"There are other varieties in motion, besides quickness and slowness, that make it more or less agreeable: regular motion is preferred before what is irregular; witness the motion of the planets in orbits nearly circular: the motion of the comets in orbits less regular is less agreeable.

"Motion uniformly accelerated, resembling an ascending series of numbers, is more agreeable than when uniformly retarded: motion upward is agreeable by the elevation of the moving body. What then shall we say of downward motion regularly accelerated by the force of gravity, compared with upward motion regularly retarded by the same force? Which of these is the most agreeable? This question is not easily solved.

"Motion in a straight line is no doubt agreeable: but we prefer undulating motion, as of waves, of a flame, of a ship under sail: such motion is more free and also more natural. Hence the beauty of a serpentine river"

CHAPTER III.

ASSOCIATED BEAUTY.

§ 270. Associated beauty implies an antecedent or intrinsic beauty.

THE views on the subject of beauty, which we think it important to enforce, involve the positions, FIRST, that there is an original or intrinsic beauty; and SECOND, that there is a beauty dependent on association.—In opposition to those persons who may be disposed to maintain that no object is beautiful of itself, but that all its beauty depends on association, we wish, in this connexion, to introduce what we regard as an important remark of Mr

Stewart "The theory," he remarks, "which resolves the *whole* effect of beautiful objects into Association, must necessarily involve that species of paralogism, to which logicians give the name of *reasoning in a circle*. It is the province of association to impart to one thing the disagreeable or the agreeable effect of another; but association can never account for the *origin* of a class of pleasures different in kind from all the others we know. If there was nothing originally and intrinsically pleasing or beautiful, the associating principle would have no materials on which it could operate."*

This remark, if it be true, appears to be decisive on the subject before us. And that it is true, we think must appear from the very nature of association. What we term association, it will be recollected, does not so much express a state of the mind, a thought, a feeling, a passion, as it does a principle or law of the mind; in other words, the circumstance under which a new state of mind takes place. Association, therefore, as Mr. Stewart intimates, does not of itself originate or create anything; but acts in reference to what is already created or originated. Something must be given for it to act upon. If it imparts beauty to one object, it must find it in another. If the beauty exists in that other object in consequence of association, it must have been drawn from some other source still more remote. If, therefore, association merely takes the beauty on its wings, if we may be allowed the expression, and transfers it from place to place, there must, of necessity, be somewhere an original or intrinsic beauty, which is made the subject of such transfer.

§ 271. Objects may become beautiful by association merely.

In accordance with what has thus far been said on this whole subject, it will be kept in mind, that some of the forms, of which matter is susceptible, are pleasing of themselves and originally; also that we are unable to behold certain colours, and to listen to certain sounds, and gaze upon particular expressions of the countenance, and to contemplate high intellectual and moral excellence, without emotions in a greater or less degree delightful

* Essay on the Beautiful, chapter vi.

At the same time, it must be admitted, that in the course of our experience we find a variety of objects, that seem, as they are presented to us, to be unattended with any emotion whatever; objects that are perfectly indifferent. And yet these objects, however wanting in beauty to the great mass of men, are found to be invested in the minds of some with a charm, allowedly not their own. These objects, which previously excited no feelings of beauty, may become beautiful to us in consequence of the associations which we attach to them. That is to say, when the objects are beheld, certain former pleasing feelings peculiar to ourselves are recalled.

The lustre of a spring morning, the radiance of a summer evening, may of themselves excite in us a pleasing emotion; but as our busy imagination, taking advantage of the images of delight which are before us, is ever at work and constantly forming new images, there is, in combination with the original emotion of beauty, a superadded delight. And if, in these instances, only a part of the beauty is to be ascribed to association, there are some others where the whole is to be considered as derived from that source.

Numerous instances can be given of the power of association, not only in heightening the actual charms of objects, but in spreading a sort of delegated lustre around those that were entirely uninteresting before. Why does yon decaying house appear beautiful to me, which is indifferent to another? Why are the desolate fields around it clothed with delight, while others see in them nothing that is pleasant? It is because that house formerly detained me as one of its inmates at its fireside, and those fields were the scenes of many youthful sports. When I now behold them after so long a time, the joyous emotions which the remembrance of my early days calls up within me, are, by the power of association, thrown around the objects which are the cause of the remembrances.

§ 272. Further illustrations of associated feelings.

He who travels through a well-cultivated country town, cannot but be pleased with the various objects which he oeholds; the neat and comfortable dwellings; the meadows, that are peopled with flocks and with herds of cattle; the fields of grain, intermingled with reaches of thick and dark forest. The whole scene is a beautiful one; the emotion we suppose to be partly original; a person, on being restored to sight by couching for the cataract, and having had no opportunity to form associations with it, would witness it for the first time with delight. But a considerable part of the pleasure is owing to the associated feelings which arise on beholding such a scene; these dwellings are the abode of man; these fields are the place of his labours, and amply reward him for his toil; here are contentment, the interchange of heartfelt joys, and "ancient truth."

Those who have travelled over places that have been signalized by memorable events, will not be likely to suspect us of attributing too great a share of our emotions to association. It is true, that, in a country so new as America, we are unable to point so frequently as a European might do to places that have witnessed achievements and sufferings of such a character as to become sacred in a nation's memory. But there are some such consecrated spots. With whatever emotion or want of emotion the traveller may pass by other places of our wild and stormy coast, he would do violence to the finest impulses of the heart if he did not stop at the Rock of Plymouth, the landing-place of the Pilgrim Fathers. Not because there is anything in the scenery, either of the ocean or the land, which presents claims upon him more imperative, or so much so as that of some other places. But there is a moral power, the spirit of great achievements hovering around the spot, (explainable on the principles of association and on them alone,) which spreads itself over the hard features of the soil, and illuminates the bleakness of the sky, and harmonizes what would be otherwise rugged and forbidding into a scene of touching loveliness and beauty.

The powerful feeling which exists on visiting such a spot, whether we call it an emotion of beauty or sublimity, or give it a name expressive of some intermediate grade, is essentially the same with that which is caused in the bosom of the traveller when he looks for the first time upon the hills of the city of Rome. There are other cities of greater extent, and washed by nobler rivers, than the one which is before him; but upon no others has he ever gazed with such intensity of feeling. He beholds what was once the mistress of the world; he looks upon the ancient dwelling-place of Brutus, of Cicero, and of the Cæsars. The imagination is at once peopled with whatever was noble in the character and remarkable in the achievements of that extraordinary nation; and there is a strength, a fulness of emotion, which would never have been experienced without the accession of those great and exciting remembrances.—It is in connexion with the principles of this chapter, and in allusion to places of historical renown, that Rogers, in his Pleasures of Memory, has said, with equal philosophical truth and poetical skill:

> "And hence the charms historic scenes impart;
> Hence Tiber awes, and Avon melts the heart;
> Aerial forms in Tempe's classic vale,
> Glance through the gloom, and whisper in the gale;
> In wild Vaucluse with love and Laura dwell,
> And watch and weep in Eloisa's cell."

§ 273. Instances of national associations.

The influence of association in rousing up and in giving strength to particular classes of emotions, may be strikingly seen in some national instances.—Every country has its favourite tunes. These excite a much stronger feeling in the native inhabitants than in strangers. The effect on the Swiss soldiers of the Ranz des Vaches, their national air, whenever they happen to hear it in foreign lands, has often been mentioned. So great was this effect, that it was found necessary in France to forbid its being played in the Swiss corps in the employment of the French government. The powerful effect of this song cannot be supposed to be owing to any peculiar merits in the composition; but to the pleasing recollections which it ever vividly brings up to the minds of the Swiss, of mountan life, of freedom, and of domestic pleasures.

The English have a popular tune called Belleisle March. Its popularity is said to have been owing to the circumstance that it was played when the English army marched into Belleisle, and to its consequent association with remembrances of war and of conquest. And it will be found true of all national airs, that they have a charm for the natives of the country, in consequence of the recollections connected with them, which they do not possess for the inhabitants of other countries.

We have abundant illustrations of the same fact in respect to colours. The purple colour has acquired an expression or character of dignity, in consequence of having been the common colour of the dress of kings; among the Chinese, however, yellow is the most dignified colour, and evidently for no other reason than because yellow is that which is allotted to the royal family. In many countries, black is expressive of gravity, and is used particularly in seasons of distress and mourning; and white is a cheerful colour. But among the Chinese white is gloomy, because it is the dress of mourners; and in Spain and among the Venetians black has a cheerful expression, in consequence of being worn by the great.

Many other illustrations to the same purpose might be brought forward. The effect of association is not unfrequently such as to suppress and entirely throw out the original character of an object, and to substitute a new one in its stead. Who has not felt, both in man and woman, that a single crime, that even one unhappy deed of meanness or dishonour, is capable of throwing a darkness and distortion over the charms of the most perfect form? The glory seems to have departed; and no effort of reasoning or of imagination can fully restore it.

§ 274. The sources of associated beauty coincident with those of human happiness.

It would be a pleasing task to point out more particularly some of the sources of associated beauty, if it were consistent with the plan which we propose to follow. But it has been our object throughout to give the sketch or outline of a system, rather than indulge in minuteness of specification. And as to the subject which we now allude to, it could hardly be expected that we should attempt to explain it extensively, much less exhaust it, when we consider that the sources of associated beauty are as wide and as numerous as the sources of man's happiness.

The fountains of human pleasure, connected with the senses, the intellect, the morals, and the social and religious relations, are exceedingly multiplied. And whenever the happiness we experience, from whatever source it may proceed, is brought into intimacy with a beautiful object, we generally find that the beauty of the object is heightened by that circumstance. In other cases, the association is so strong, that a beauty is shed upon objects which are confessedly destitute of it in themselves.—It is enough, therefore, to say, that the sources of associated beauty are necessarily as wide as the unexplored domain of human joy.

§ 275. Summary of views in regard to the beautiful.

As the subject of emotions of beauty is one of no small difficulty, it may be of advantage to give here a brief summary of some of the prominent views in respect to it.

(1.) Of emotions of beauty it is difficult to give a definition, but we notice in them two marks or characteristics.—They imply, first, a degree of pleasure, and secondly, are always referred by us to external objects as their cause.

(2.) Every beautiful object has something in itself, which discriminates it from other objects that are not beautiful. On this ground we may with propriety speak of beauty in the object. At the same time, a superadded lustre is reflected back upon it from the mind; and this too, whether the beauty be original or associated.

(3.) The feeling which we term an emotion of beauty is not limited to natural scenery, but may be caused also by the works of art, by the creations of the imagination, and by the various forms of intellectual and moral nature, so far as they can be presented to the mind. All these various objects and others may excite within us feelings of pleasure, and the mind, in its turn, may reflect back upon the objects the lustre of its own emotions, and thus increase the degree of their beauty.

(4.) There is in the mind an original susceptibility of emotions in general, and of those of beauty in particular; and not only this, some objects are found in the constitution of things to be followed by these feelings of beauty, while others are not; and such objects are spoken of as being originally beautiful. That is, when the object is presented to the mind, it is of itself followed by emotions of beauty, without being aided by the influence of accessory and contingent circumstances.

(5.) Without pretending to certainty in fixing upon those objects, to which what is termed original or intrinsic beauty may be ascribed, there appears to be no small reason in attributing it to certain forms, to sounds of a particular character, to bright colours, to some varieties of motion, and, we may add, to intellectual and moral excellence, whenever it can be made a distinct object of per ception.

(6.) Many objects, which cannot be considered beautiful of themselves, become such by being associated with a variety of former pleasing and enlivening recollections; and such as possess beauty of themselves may augment the pleasing emotions from the same cause. Also much of the difference of opinion which exists as to what objects are beautiful and what are not, is to be ascribed to difference of association.—These are some of the prominent views resulting from inquiries into this subject.

CHAPTER IV.

EMOTIONS OF SUBLIMITY

§ 276. Connexion between beauty and sublimity.

Those emotions which, by way of distinction, we designate as SUBLIME, are a class of feelings which have much in common with emotions of beauty; they do not appear to differ so much in nature or kind as in degree. Wher we examine the feelings which are embraced under these two designations, we readily perceive that they have a progression; that there are numerous degrees in point of intensity; but the emotion, although more vivid in one case than the other, and mingled with some foreign elements, is, for the most part, essentially the same. So that it is by no means impossible to trace, in a multitude of cases, a connexion even between the fainter feelings of beauty and the most overwhelming emotions of the sublime.

This progression of our feelings, from one that is gentle and pleasant to one that is powerful, and even painful, has been illustrated in the case of a person who is supposed to behold a river at its first rise in the mountains, and to follow it as it winds and enlarges in the subjacent plains, and to behold it at last losing itself in the expanse of the ocean. For a time, the feelings which are excited within him, as he gazes on the prospect, are what are termed emotions of beauty. As the small stream which had hitherto played in the uplands, and amid foliage that almost hid it from his view, increases its waters, separates its banks to a great distance from each other, and becomes the majestic river, his feelings are of a more powerful kind. We often, by way of distinction, speak of the feelings existing under such circumstances as emotions of grandeur. At last it expands and disappears in the immensity of the ocean: the vast illimitable world of billows flashes in his sight. Then the emotion, widening and strengthening with the magnitude and energy of the objects which accompany it, becomes sublime.—Emotions of sublimity, therefore, chiefly differ, at least in most instances, from those of beauty in being more vivid.

§ 277. The occasions of the emotions of sublimity various.

As the emotions of sublimity are simple, they are consequently undefinable. Nevertheless, as they are the direct subjects of our consciousness, we cannot be supposed to be ignorant of their nature. It may aid, however, in rendering our comprehension of them more distinct and clear in some respects, if we mention some of the occasions on which they arise.—But, before proceeding to do this, it is proper to recur a moment to a subject more fully insisted on in the chapter on Beauty, but which also properly has a place here. We have reference to the unquestionable fact, that the occasions of sublime emotions are not exclusively one; in other words, are not found in a single element merely, as some persons may be likely to suppose, but, like those of beauty, are multiplied and various. The measure of the sublimity of the object is the character of the emotion which it excites; and if the sublime emotion exists, as unquestionably it does on various occasions, this of itself is decisive as to the remark which has been made. Accordingly, the proper object before us, in the first instance, seems to be to indicate some of these occasions.

§ 278. Great extent or expansion an occasion of sublimity

In endeavouring to point out some of the sources of sublimity, our first remark is, that the emotion of the sublime may arise in view of an object which is characterized by vast extent or expansion; in other words, by the attribute of mere horizontal amplitude. Accordingly, it is with entire propriety that Mr. Stewart makes a remark to this effect, that a Scotchman, who had never witnessed anything of the kind before, would experience an emotion approaching to sublimity on beholding, for the first time, the vast plains of Salisbury and Yorkshire in England. Washington Irving also, in a passage of the Alhambra, has a remark to the same purport. "There is something," he observes, "in the sternly simple features of the Spanish landscape, that impresses on the soul a feeling of sublimity. The immense plains of the Castiles and La Mancha, extending as far as the eye can reach, derive an interest from their very nakedness and immensity, and have something of the solemn grandeur of the ocean."

In regard to the ocean, one of the most sublime objects which the human mind can contemplate, it cannot be doubted that one element of its sublimity is the unlimited expanse which it presents.

§ 279. Great height an element or occasion of sublimity.

Mere height, independently of considerations of expansion or extent, appears also to constitute an occasion of the sublime. Every one has experienced this, when standing at the base of a very steep and lofty cliff, hill, or mountain. When, in the silence of night, we stand under the clear, open sky, we can hardly fail, as we look upward, to experience a sublime emotion, occasioned partly by the immensity of the object, but also in part by its vast height. Travellers have often spoken of the sublime emotion occasioned by viewing the celebrated Natural Bridge in Virginia from the bottom of the deep ravine over which it is thrown. This bridge is a single solid rock, about sixty feet broad, ninety feet long, and forty thick. It is suspended over the head of the spectator, who views it from the bottom of the narrow glen, at the elevation of two hundred and thirty feet; an immense height for such an object. It is not in human nature to behold, without strong feeling, such a vast vault of solid limestone, springing lightly into the blue upper air, and remaining thus outstretched, as if it were the arm of the Almighty himself, silent, unchangeable, eternal.

§ 280. Of depth in connexion with the sublime.

It is a circumstance confirmatory of the view, that it is impossible to resolve the grounds of sublimity into a single occasion or element, that we find the depth as well as the height of things, the downward as well as the upward, the antecedent and cause of this emotion. We are doubtful, however, whether depth is so decisively, as it is certainly not so frequently a cause, as elevation or height; which last, on account of its frequent connexion with their existence, has given the name to this class of feelings But others may think differently. Mr. Burke has the following passage on this point.—"I am apt to imagine, that height is less grand than depth; and that we are more struck at looking down from a precipice than looking up at an object of equal height; but of that I am not very positive."

But, however this may be, there is no doubt that sublime emotions may arise from this cause. When we are placed on the summit of any high object, and look downward into the vast opening below, it is impossible not to be strongly affected. The sailor on the wide ocean, when, in the solitary watches of the night, he casts his eye upward to the lofty, illuminated sky, has a sublime emotion: and he feels the same strong sentiment stirring within him when, a moment afterward, he thinks of the vast, unfathomable abyss beneath him, over which he is suspended by the frail plank of his vessel

§ 281. Of colours in connexion with the sublime.

The colours also, as well as the form of bodies, may, to a limited extent, furnish the occasion of sublime emotions. The lightning, when at a distance it is seen darting to the earth in one continuous chain of overpowering brightness; the red meteor shooting athwart the still, dark sky; the crimson Aurora Borealis, which occasionally diffuses the tints of the morning over the hemisphere of midnight, are sublime objects; and, although there are other elements which unite in forming the basis of the sublime emotion, it is probably to be ascribed, in part, to the richness and vividness of colours. What object is more sublimely impressive than the contrasted hues of the mingling fires and smoke of a burning volcano? Darkness, particularly, is an element of the sublime. When the clouds are collecting together on some distinct and distant portion of the sky, how intently the eye fixes itself on those masses which wear the visage of the deepest gloom! Forests, and frowning cliffs, and mountains, and the wide ocean itself, and whatever other objects are susceptible of sublimity, are rendered still more sublime by the shades and darkness that are sometimes made to pass over them. The poets of all countries have represented the Deity, the most sublime object of contemplation, as enthroned in the midst of darkness.—" He bowed the heavens also, and came down; and *darkness was under his feet.* He made *darkness* his secret place; his pavilion round about were *dark* waters, and *thick clouds* of the skies."

§ 282. Of sounds as furnishing an occasion of sublime emotions.

We find another element of the sublime in sounds of a certain description. There are some cries and voices of animals which are usually regarded as sublime. The roar of the lion, not only in the solitudes of his native deserts, but at all times, partakes of the character of sublimity. The human voice, in combination with a suitable number of other voices, is capable of uttering sublime sounds; and does, in fact, utter them in performing many of the works of the great masters and composers of music There is no small degree of sublimity in the low, deep murmur of the organ, independently of the moral and religious associations connected with it. It is presumed no one will doubt, that the trumpet, in the hands of a skilful performer, is capable of originating sublime sounds. Almost every one must have noticed a peculiarly impressive sound sent forth by a large and compact forest of pines, when waved by a heavy wind, which obviously has the same character. The heavy and interminable sound of the ocean, as it breaks upon the shore, is sublime; and hardly less so the ceaseless voice of the congregated waters of some vast cataract. To these instances may be added the sound of a cannon, not only when it comes from the field of battle, but at any time; and still more the mighty voice of thunder. The latter sound is often mentioned in the Scriptures, in connexion with the attributes of the Supreme Being, and apparently for the purpose of heightening the idea of his sublimity. "The Lord also thundered in the heavens, and the Highest gave his voice."—"The voice of the Lord is upon the waters; the God of glory thundereth."

We leave this part of the subject with introducing a remark from Coleridge, which goes to confirm the general doctrine of the sublimity of some sounds. He had been saying something of the scenery of the lake of Ratzeburg, when he adds: "About a month ago, before the thaw came on, there was a storm of wind. During the whole night, such were the thunders and howlings of the breaking ice, that they left a conviction on my mind that there are sounds more sublime than any sight *can* be, more absolutely suspending the power of comparison, and more utterly absorbing the mind's self-consciousness in its total attention to the object working upon it."*

§ 283. Of motion in connexion with the sublime.

It will be noticed, from the train of thought which has been pursued, that there is a close analogy between beauty and sublimity, not only in the feelings which are originated, but also in the occasions of their origin. As the sentiments of beauty were found to be connected not only with the forms of objects, but also with colours and

* The Friend, Am. ed., page 323

sounds, so also are those of sublimity. And furthermore, as we found beauty connecting itself with certain kinds of motion, we find motion the basis likewise, in some of its modifications, of emotions of the sublime.

We often experience, for instance, emotions of sublimity in witnessing objects that move with great swiftness. This is one source of the feelings we have at beholding bodies of water rushing violently down a cataract. For the same reason, although there are undoubtedly other elements of the emotions we feel, the hurricane, that hastens onward with irresistible velocity, and lays waste whatever it meets, is sublime. And here also we find a cause of part of that sublime emotion which men have often felt, on seeing at a distance the electric fluid darting from the cloud to the earth, and at witnessing the sudden flight of a meteor.

§ 284. Indications of power accompanied by emotions of the sublime.

The contemplation of mental objects, as well as of material, may be attended with this species of emotion. Power, for instance, is an attribute of mind, and not of matter, and the exhibition of it is frequently sublime. It is hardly necessary to say, in making this remark, that power is not anything which is addressed directly to the outward senses; but is rather presented to the mind as an object of inward suggestion. Nevertheless, the causes of this suggestion may exist in outward objects; and, whenever this is the case, the feelings with which we contemplate such objects are generally increased. In other words, whatever sublimity may characterize an object, if, in addition to its other sublime traits, it strongly suggests to us the idea of power, the sublime feeling is more or less heightened by this suggestion.

Nothing can be more sublime than a volcano, throwing out from its bosom clouds, and burning stones, and immense rivers of lava. And it is unquestionable, that the sublime emotion is attributable, in part, to the overwhelming indications of power which are thus given. An earthquake is sublime; not only in its mightier efforts of destruction, but hardly less so in those slighter tremblings and heavings of the earth, which indicate the foot steps of power rather than of ruin. The ocean, greatly agitated with a storm, and tossing the largest navies as in sport, possesses an increase of sublimity, on account of the more striking indications of power which it at such a time gives. The shock of large armies also, which concentrates the most terrible exhibition of human energy, is attended with an increased sublimity for the same reason. But in all these instances, as in most others, the sublime emotion cannot be ascribed solely to one cause; something is to be attributed to vast extent; something to the original effect of the brilliancy or darkness of colours; and something to feelings of dread and danger.

§ 285. Of the original or primary sublimity of objects.

If there be a connexion between the beautiful and sublime; if beauty, grandeur, and sublimity are only names for various emotions, not so much differing in kind as in degree, essentially the same views which were advanced in respect to beauty will hold here. It will follow, if the contemplation of some objects is attended with emotions of beauty, independently of associated feelings; or, in other words, if they have a primary or original beauty, that there are objects also originally sublime. Hence we may conclude, that whatever has great height, or great depth, or vast extent, or other attributes of the sublime, will be able to excite in us emotions of sublimity of themselves, independently of the subordinate or secondary aid arising from any connnected feelings.

§ 286. Considerations in proof of the original sublimity of objects.

It may be inferred, that there is such primary or original sublimity in some objects, not only in view of the connexion which has been stated to exist between the beautiful and sublime, but because it is no doubt agreeable to the common experience of men. But, in resting the proposition (where undoubtedly it ought to rest) on experience, we must inquire, as in former chapters, into the feelings of the young. And this for the obvious reason, that, when persons are somewhat advanced in age, it is difficult to separate the primary from the secondary or associated sublimity. They have then become inextricably mingled together.—Now take a child, and place him suddenly on the shores of the ocean, or in full sight of darkly wooded mountains of great altitude, or before the clouds, and fires, and thunders of volcanoes; and, in most cases, he will be filled with sublime emotions; his mind will swell at the perception; it will heave to and fro like the ocean itself in a tempest. His eye, his countenance, his gestures, will indicate a power of internal feeling, which the limited language he can command is unable to express. This may well be stated as a fact, because it has been frequently noticed by those who are competent to observe.

Again, if a person can succeed in conveying to a child, by means of words, sublime ideas of whatever kind, similar emotions will be found to exist, although generally in a less degree than when objects are directly presented to the senses.

There is an incident in the life of Sir William Jones which will serve to illustrate this statement. "In his fifth year, as he was one morning turning over the leaves of a Bible in his mother's closet, his attention was forcibly arrested by the sublime description of the angel in the tenth chapter of the Apocalypse; and the impression which his imagination received from it was never effaced. At a period of mature judgment, he considered the passage as equal in sublimity to any in the inspired writers, and far superior to any that could be produced from mere human compositions; and he was fond of retracing and mentioning the rapture which he felt when he first read it." The passage referred to is as follows. "And I saw another mighty angel come down from heaven, clothed with a cloud; and a rainbow was upon his head, and his face was as it were the sun, and his feet as pillars of fire."*

§ 287. Influence of association on emotions of sublimity.

Granting, therefore, that sublime emotions are in part original, still it is unquestionably true that a considerable share of them is to be attributed to association. As an illustration, we may refer to the effects of sounds. When

* Teignmouth's Life of Sir William Jones, Am. ed., page 14.

a sound suggests ideas of danger, as the report of artillery and the howling of a storm; when it calls up recollections of mighty power, as the fall of a cataract and the rumbling of an earthquake, the emotion of sublimity which we feel is greatly increased by such suggestions. Few simple sounds are thought to have more of sublimity than the report of a cannon; but how different, how much greater the strength of feeling than on other occasions, whenever we hear it coming to us from the fields of actual conflict! Many sounds, which are in themselves inconsiderable, and are not much different from many others to which we do not attach the character of sublimity, become highly sublime by association. There is frequently a low, feeble sound preceding the coming of a storm, which has this character.

> "Along the woods, along the moorish fens,
> Sighs the sad genius of the coming storm,
> Resounding long in fancy's listening ear."
>
> THOMPSON'S *Winter*.

It is sometimes the case, that people, whose sensibilities are much alive to thunder, mistake for it some common sounds, such as the noise of a carriage or the rumbling of a cart. While they are under this mistake they feel these sounds as sublime; because they associate with them all those ideas of danger and of mighty power which they customarily associate with thunder. The hoot of the owl at midnight is sublime chiefly by association; also the scream of the eagle, heard amid rocks and deserts. The latter is particularly expressive of fierce and lonely independence; and both are connected in our remembrance with some striking poetical passages.

CHAPTER V.

EMOTIONS OF THE LUDICROUS.

§ 288. General nature of emotions of the ludicrous.

IN prosecuting the general subject of emotions, we are next to consider another well-known class, which are of a character somewhat peculiar, viz., *emotions of the ludicrous*

It is difficult to give a precise definition of this feeling, although the same may be said of it as in respect to emotions of beauty, that it is a pleasant or delightful one. But the pleasure which we experience receives a peculiar modification, and one which cannot be fully conveyed in words, in consequence of our perception of some incongruity in the person or thing which is the cause of it.—In this case, as in many other inquiries in mental philosophy, we are obliged to rely chiefly on our own consciousness and our knowledge of what takes place in ourselves

§ 289. Occasions of emotions of the ludicrous.

It may, however, assist us in the better understanding of them, if we say something of the occasions on which the emotions of the ludicrous are generally found to arise. And, among other things, it is exceedingly clear, that this feeling is never experienced, except when we notice something, either in thoughts, or in outward objects and actions, which is unexpected and uncommon. That is to say, whenever this emotion is felt, there is always an unexpected discovery by us of some new relations.—But then it must be observed, that the feeling in question does not necessarily exist in consequence of the discovery of such new relations merely. Something more is necessary, as may be very readily seen.

Thus we are sometimes, in the physical sciences, presented with unexpected and novel combinations of the properties and qualities of bodies. But whenever we discover in those sciences relations in objects, which were not only unknown, but unsuspected, we find no emotion of ludicrousness, although we are very pleasantly surprised. Again, similes, metaphors, and other like figures of speech imply in general some new and unexpected relations of ideas. It is this trait in them which gives them their chief force. But when employed in serious compositions, they are of a character far from being ludicrous.

Hence we infer, that emotions of ludicrousness do not exist on the discovery of new and unexpected relations, unless there is at the same time a perception, or supposed perception, of some incongruity or unsuitableness. Such perception of unsuitableness may be expected to give to the whole emotion a new and specific character, which every one is acquainted with from his own experience, but which, as before intimated, it is difficult to express in words.

§ 290. Of what is understood by wit.

The subject of emotions of the ludicrous is closely connected with what is termed Wit. This last-named subject, therefore, which it is of some importance to understand, naturally proposes itself for consideration in this place. In regard to WIT, as the term is generally understood at the present time, there is ground to apprehend, that an emotion of the ludicrous is always, in a greater or less degree, experienced in every instance of it.

This being the case, we are led to give this definition, viz.: WIT consists in suddenly presenting to the mind an assemblage of related ideas of such a kind as to occasion feelings of the ludicrous.—This is done in a variety of ways; and, among others, in the two following.

§ 291. Of wit as it consists in burlesque or in debasing objects

The first method which wit employs in exciting the feelings of the ludicrous, is by debasing those things which are grand and imposing; especially those which have an appearance of greater weight, and gravity, and splendour than they are truly entitled to. Descriptions of this sort are termed burlesque.

An attempt to lessen what is truly and confessedly serious and important, has, in general, an unpleasant effect, very different from that which is caused by true wit. And yet it is the case, that objects and actions truly great and sublime may sometimes be so coupled with other objects, or be represented in such new circumstances, as to excite very different feelings from what they would otherwise.

In the practice of burlesque, as on all other occasions of wit, there is a sudden and uncommon assemblage of related ideas. Sometimes this assemblage is made by means of a formal comparison. Take, as an instance, the following comparison from Hudibras:

"And now had Phœbus in the lap
Of Thetis taken out his nap;
And, like a lobster boiled, the morn
From black to red began to turn."

We find illustrations of burlesque also in those instances where objects of real dignity and importance are coupled with things mean and contemptible, although there is no direct and formal comparison made. As in this instance from the above-mentioned book:

"For when the restless Greeks sat down
So many years before Troy-town,
And were renowned, as Homer writes,
For well-soled boots no less than fights."

In these instances we have related ideas. In the first, there is undoubtedly an analogy between a lobster and the morning, in the particular of its turning from dark to red. But however real it may be, it strikes every one as a singular and unexpected resemblance. In the other passage, it is not clear that Butler has done anything more than Homer, in associating the renown of the Greeks with their boots as well as their valour. But to us of the present day the connexion of ideas is hardly less uncommon and singular, not to say incongruous, than in the former.

§ 292. Of wit when employed in aggrandizing objects.

The second method which wit employs in exciting emotions of the ludicrous, is by aggrandizing objects which are in themselves inconsiderable. This species of wit may be suitably termed *mock-majestic* or *mock-heroic.* While the former kind delights in low expressions, this is the reverse, and chooses learned words and sonorous combinations. In the following spirited passage of Pope, the writer compares dunces to gods, and Grub-street to heaven:

"As Berecynthia, while her offspring vie
In homage to the mother of the sky,
Surveys around her in the bless'd abode
A hundred sons, and every son a god;
Not with less glory mighty Dulness crowned,
Shall take through Grub-street her triumphant round;
And her Parnassus glancing o'er at once,
Behold a hundred sons, and each a dunce."

In this division of wit are to be included those instances where grave and weighty reflections are made on mere trifles. In this case, as in others, the ideas are in some respects related, or have something in common; but the grouping of them is so singular and unexpected, that we cannot observe it without considerable emotion

> "My galligaskins, that have long withstood
> The winter's fury and encroaching frosts,
> By time subdued, (*what will not time subdue!*)
> A horrid chasm disclose."

But it is not to be supposed that wit is limited to the methods of assembling together incongruous ideas which have just been referred to. A person of genuine wit excites emotions of the ludicrous in a thousand ways, and which will be so diverse from each other, that it will be found exceedingly difficult to subject them to any rules

§ 293. Of the character and occasions of humour.

Closely connected with the general subject of ludicrous emotions and of wit, is that of Humour. It is well known that we often apply the terms *humour* and *humorous* to descriptions of a particular character, whether written or given in conversation, and which may be explained as follows.

It so happens that we frequently find among men what seems to us a disproportion in their passions; for instance, when they are noisy and violent, but not durable. We find inconsistencies, contradictions, and disproportions in their actions. They have their foibles, (hardly any one is without them,) such as self-conceit, caprice, foolish partialities, and jealousies.—Such incongruities in feeling and action cause an emotion of surprise, like an unexpected combination of ideas in wit. Observing them, as we do, in connexion with the acknowledged high traits and responsibilities of human nature, we can no more refrain from an emotion of the ludicrous, than we can on seeing a gentleman of fine clothes and high dignity making a false step and tumbling into a gutter. A person who can seize upon these specialities in temper and conduct, and set them forth in a lively and exact manner, is called a man of humour; and his descriptions are termed humorous descriptions.

§ 294. Of the practical utility of feelings of the ludicrous.

It is not impossible that the feelings which we have examined in this chapter may have the appearance, to some minds, of being practically useless. If this were the fact, it would be at variance with the economy of the mind in other respects; which gives evidence everywhere that its original tendencies are ingrafted upon it for some practical ends. But it is not so. The feeling of the ludicrous (or, as it is sometimes called, the sense of ridicule) is attended with results which, although they may not be perfectly obvious at first, will be found, on a little examination, to be of no small moment. It is entirely clear, that it constitutes one of the important guides and aids which nature has appointed of human conduct. Scarcely any one is willing to undergo ridicule, even in its milder and more acceptable forms; much less to subject himself to the "world's dread laugh." And many persons would be less attentive to the decencies and proprieties of personal conduct, and of the intercourse of life, than they are in fact, were it not for the fear of this species of retribution. It is true it is not powerful enough, nor is it the appropriate instrument to attack the more marked depravities incident to our nature, the strongholds of its sin; but it is unquestionably an effective and useful agent in its application to whatever is mean, incongruous, and unseemly.—See, in connexion with this subject, Campbell's Philosophy of Rhetoric, bk. i., ch. iii., and Beattie on Laughter and Ludicrous Compositions.

CHAPTER VI.

INSTANCES OF OTHER SIMPLE EMOTIONS.

§ 295. Emotions of cheerfulness, joy, and gladness.

UNDER the general head of Emotions there are many other simple feelings which merit some attention. Although they are, perhaps, not less essential to our nature, and not less important than those which have been already attended to, we do not find so many difficulties in their examination, and but a few remarks will be wanting to explain them.

We begin with the emotion of *cheerfulness.* Of the nature of this feeling none can be supposed to be ignorant. It exists, in a greater or less degree, throughout the whole course of our life. It is seen in the benignant looks, and is heard in the garrulity of old age; it sheds its consolations over the anxieties and toils of manhood, and reigns with a sort of perpetual spring in youth.

The words *joy* and *delight* express a high degree of cheerfulness; the feeling is the same; the difference is in its greater intensity. The word *gladness* is nearly synonymous with these last, but seems to be applied particularly when the joy is of a more sudden and less permanent character.

§ 296. Emotions of melancholy, sorrow, and grief.

While there are many things in life which are fitted to make us cheerful and happy, every one must know that for wise purposes a degree of bitterness is mingled in our cup, and that circumstances occur from time to time which are of an opposite tendency. And these prove to us occasions of melancholy, which is the name of another specific simple emotion.

There are different degrees of this emotion, as well as of that of cheerfulness. We sometimes express the very slightest degree of it by the words uneasiness or discontent. When the feeling of melancholy is from any circumstance greatly increased, we usually give it the name of *sorrow;* so that sorrow seems to hold nearly the same relation to melancholy that joy does to cheerfulness.

The word *grief* also has nearly the same relation to sorrow that gladness has to joy. As far as the mere feeling is concerned which they represent, the two words grief and sorrow may be regarded as synonymous with each other; with this exception, that the term grief is commonly employed when the sorrow exists suddenly and with great strength. Hence grief sometimes shows itself by external signs, and even in frantic transports; while sorrow, even when it is deeply rooted, is more tacit, enduring, and uncommunicative.

§ 297. Emotions of surprise, astonishment, and wonder.

Whenever anything novel and unexpected presents itself to our notice, whether in nature or in ordinary events, we experience a new simple emotion, distinct from any which has hitherto been mentioned, which we call a feeling of *surprise.*— The word *astonishment,* which we frequently use, does not express a different emotion, but the same emotion in a different degree. When the feeling is exceedingly strong, it seems to suspend, for a time, the whole action of the mind; and we say of a person in such a situation, not merely that he is surprised, but is astonished or amazed.

When the facts or events which occasion the surprise are of such a singular and complicated character as to induce us to dwell upon them for a length of time, the feeling arising is then often called *wonder.* It is not, however, a different emotion from what we ordinarily call surprise, but the same emotion, modified by different circumstances.

It may be added here, that this emotion is highly important to our preservation, security, and improvement. It is in new circumstances, in untried and unexplored situations, that we are particularly required to be upon our guard, since we know not what effects may attend them, nor whether these effects may prove good or evil to us. Happily for us, the emotion of surprise and astonishment which we experience at such times is very vivid, so much so as to arrest for a time both our perceptions and our conduct, and to compel us to pause and consider where we are and what is to be done.

§ 298. Emotions of dissatisfaction, displeasure, and disgust.

There is another emotion which approaches very near to the feeling of melancholy, and still slightly differs from it, which we express by the term *dissatisfaction.* It is a painful feeling, though only in a small degree; but its nature, like that of other simple emotions, cannot be fully understood, except by a reference to the testimony of our own inward experience.

When from any circumstance the emotion of dissatisfaction exists in an increased degree, we often express this difference, although the nature of the feeling remains the same, by another term, that of *displeasure.*

There appear to be other forms of the simple feeling of dissatisfaction. The feeling of *disgust* is the emotion of dissatisfaction, existing in an increased degree, but under such circumstances as to distinguish it, in the view of our consciousness, from the feeling of displeasure. The latter feeling approximates more closely to an emotion of hostility to the cause of it than the former. The terms are sometimes used together, and yet not as perfectly synonymous; as when we say, that, on a certain occasion, we were both displeased and disgusted.

§ 299. Emotions of diffidence, modesty, and shame.

There is an emotion, often indicated outwardly by a half-averted look, and shyness, and awkwardness of manner, expressed by the term *diffidence.* An interesting modification of this feeling, as we suppose it to be, is *modesty;* differing from diffidence perhaps slightly in kind or nature, but probably only in degree. Although this feeling attracts but little notice in the genealogy of our mental operations, and occupies but a small space in its description, it is important in its results. It combines its influences in connexion with the natural desire of regard or esteem, in keeping men in their place, and in thus sustaining that propriety of conduct, and those gradations of honour and of duty, which are so essential to the existence and the happiness of society.

A higher degree of this mental state is *shame.* When we find ourselves involved in any marked improprieties of conduct, this feeling exists; characterized outwardly by a downcast eye and a flushed countenance. It is not, however, exclusively attendant upon guilt; although guilt, among other consequences flowing from it, is in part punished in this way. But it seems to be, rather, an appropriate punishment, attendant on those minor violations of decency and order which may exist without an infringement on morals.

§ 300. Emotions of regard, reverence, and adoration.

Different from all the feelings which have now been

mentioned is the emotion of regard or respect, which, in its simplest form, at least, we exercise towards the great mass of our fellow-beings. The mere fact that they are creatures of God, and are possessed of intellectual and moral powers like our own, is deemed sufficient to lay the foundation of the exercise of this feeling towards them.

When we observe in any individuals marked traits of mental excellence, as wisdom, truth, and justice, especially when these traits are expanded and exalted by great age, the feeling of respect which we exercise in ordinary cases is heightened into *reverence*. Every country can boast of a few such men, the just objects of the deepened regard of reverence; and the eyes of successive generations have been turned with the same deep feelings towards those who are scattered along in various places in the long tract of history.

When the reverence or veneration is free from every inferior intermixture; in other words, when the object of it is regarded as without weakness, and possessed of every possible perfection, it then becomes *adoration;* a homage of the soul so pure and exalted that it properly belongs only to the Supreme Being. The wisdom of the wisest men is often perplexed with errors; the goodness of the best of men is marred by occasional infirmities; how much deeper, therefore, and purer, and more elevated, will be our sentiments of veneration, when directed towards Him whose wisdom never fails, and who is not only just and kind in his administrations, but the original and inexhaustible source of beneficence and rectitude!

We conclude here the examination of the Emotions. We would not pretend that this part of our sentient nature has been fully explored in the views which have been taken; but would hope that so much has been said as to throw some satisfactory light upon it, and to leave us at liberty to turn to another class of subjects.

THE SENSIBILITIES.

PART FIRST

NATURAL OR PATHEMATIC SENSIBILITIES.

NATURAL OR PATHEMATIC SENTIMENTS.

CLASS SECOND

THE DESIRES.

CHAPTER I.

NATURE OF DESIRES.

§ 301. Of the prevalence of desire in this department o the mind.

We now proceed to enter upon a separate portion of the Natural or Pathematic Sensibilities, distinguished from that which has hitherto received our attention by the possession of its appropriate nature, and by sustaining its distinct and appropriate relations. The characteristic element of this region of the Natural Sensibilities, that which in fact constitutes the basis of its existence, is the state of mind, distinct from all others, which we denominate DESIRE. This state of mind not only stands at the threshold of the department which we now enter upon, but diffuses abroad its influence, and runs through, and gives a character to, all the subordinate divisions into which this part of the Pathematic nature will be found to resolve itself. No appetite, no propensity, or affection exists in fact, nor can we suppose it possible for them to exist, exclusively of any intermixture of the ingredient of DESIRE.—It is for this reason that we denominate this portion of the sensitive nature Desires, as we called the other Emotions; and as we sometimes speak of the EMOTIVE sensibilities, so we might, with no impropriety, speak of the DESIROUS OR DESIRING sensibilities.

§ 302. The nature of desires known from consciousness.

As DESIRES occupy so prominent a place in those principles of the mind which we now propose to give some account of, it is proper to delay here, in order briefly to attempt some explanation of their nature. And, in doing this, we are obliged, in the first place, to repeat the remark already often made, that we must turn the acts of the mind inward upon itself, and consult the intimations of our own consciousness. We do not suppose that any definition of desire, inasmuch as it is obviously a simple state of the mind, could possibly throw any such light upon it as to preclude the necessity of an internal reference. It is the light of the mind, if we will but turn our eyes to behold it, and that alone, which can truly indicate what may be called the essentiality of its nature.--At the same time, while we must obviously consult consciousness for a knowledge of its distinctive character, we may probably render our conceptions of it more distinct and perfect, by considering some of the circumstances or incidents of its origin, and some of the relations it sustains.

§ 303. Of the place of desires in relation to other mental states

It is important to possess a well-settled and definite idea of the place of Desires, considered in relation to other mental states; especially as a thorough understanding of this point throws light upon the important subject of the philosophy of the Will.—(1.) And the first remark to be made here is, that desires never follow, in direct and *immediate* sequence, to intellections or the cognitive acts of the mind. There is a distinct department or portion of the mind, *located,* if we may be permitted to use that expression, between the intellect and the mental states under consideration. It requires no further proof than the simple statement itself when we say that we never desire a thing, simply because we perceive it or have a knowledge of it. The mere perception of a thing is of itself no adequate reason why we should make the thing an object of pursuit. There must obviously be some intermediate state of the mind, existing as the proximate and causative occasion of desires, viz., an *emotion.* Accordingly, the prerequisite condition to desire is some antecedent feeling, generally of a pleasurable nature, which intervenes between the desire, and the perception or knowledge of the desired object.

(2.) In illustration of what has been said, it is the fact, that, whenever we desire the presence or possession of an object, it is because we are in some way pleased with it. Whenever, on the other hand, we desire its removal from our presence, it is because we are in some way displeased with it. And these expressions, indicative of pleasure or displeasure, obviously involve the existence of that distinct state of the mind which we denominate an

EMOTION; a state of feeling entirely different both from the perception of the object which goes before such emotion, and the desire of the object which follows after it. Accordingly, we may feel at liberty to state, in general terms, that no man ever desired an object, or could by any possibility desire it, in regard to which he had experienced no emotion, but had always been in a state of perfect indifferency. Such, in the matter under consideration, is obviously the fixed law of the mind

§ 304. The desires characterized by compara .ve fixedness and permanency.

There is one mark or trait attending the feelings under consideration which appears to be worthy of notice. We refer to the fact, that the desires, as compared with the emotions, appear to possess a greater degree of fixedness or permanency. It is well known that our emotions rapidly go and come; sinking and rising on the mind's surface like the unfixed waves of a troubled sea. But the desires, which are subsequent to them in the time of their origin, and may be regarded as produced in, and as emerging from, the troubled waters of emotion, evidently exhibit less facility and elasticity of movement. Having once entered their allotted position, although they are not absolutely immoveable, they occupy it with so much pertinacity as to render it proper to regard this as one of their characteristics.

There certainly can be no great effort necessary in understanding the statement which has been made; and no great difficulty, as we suppose, in recognising and substantiating its truth. Take, for instance, the case of a man who is an exile in a foreign land, or of the unfortunate individual who is unjustly condemned to the occupancy of a prison; and they will assuredly tell you, that the desires they have to see once more the light of heaven, their native land, and the countenances of their friends, sustains itself in their bosoms with a pertinacity which defies all change; and that they might as well rend away the fibres of the heart itself, as to separate from it a feeling so deeply rooted.—We give this as an illustration; but it is more or less so in every case where the desires have decidedly fixed themselves upon any interesting topic.

§ 305. Desires always imply an object desired.

An additional characteristic of Desires is, that they always have an object, generally a distinct and well-defined one; and cannot possibly exist without it. To speak of a desire, without involving the idea of an object desired, would be an anomaly in language. They differ in this respect from emotions; which, although they have their antecedent causes or occasions, do not possess, in their own nature, a prospective or anticipative bearing, but terminate in themselves. Desires, on the contrary, are always pointing onward to what is to be hereafter. And this is probably one reason of their greater degree of fixedness or permanency. The desires lean upon the objects which they have in view, as a sort of pillar of support; they may be said, with strict truth at the bottom of the expression, to cling around it as the vine encircles and rests itself upon the elm; and, of course, are not left loose and fluttering, which is substantially the case with the states of mind which immediately precede them, at the mercy of every passing wind.

§ 306. The fulfilment of desires attended with enjoyment.

As a general thing, it may be said of the emotions that they are either pleasant or painful, although, in some instances, even of those feelings it might not be easy to predicate distinctly and confidently either the one or the other. And this last statement is true particularly of the desires; which, although they exist distinctly and well-defined in the view of the mind's consciousness, and constitute a powerful motive to action, can hardly be said, for the time being, to involve, in their own nature, either pleasure or its opposite. At any rate, we find it difficult, in ordinary cases, distinctly to detect either of these traits.

But, however this may be, there is still another characteristic circumstance, which aids in distinguishing them from other mental states. It is this. Every desire, when the object towards which it is directed is attained, is attended with a degree of pleasure. It is absolutely inseparable from the nature of desire, that the acquisition of the object of its pursuit, whether that object be good or evil, will be followed by the possession of some enjoyment. Sometimes the enjoyment is very great, at others less; varying generally with the intensity of the desire.

§ 307. Of variations or degrees in the strength of the desires.

There is this further statement to be made in reference to the Desires, applicable, however, to a multitude of other states of the mind, that they exist *in different degrees*. As a general thing, they will be found to exist in a greater or less degree, in accordance with the greater or less vividness and strength of the antecedent emotions. The original cause, however, of these variations, making allowance for some occasional constitutional differences, is to be sought for in the intellect or understanding. The more distinctly we perceive or understand a thing, the more distinct and vivid, we may reasonably expect, will be our emotions. And as the Desires are based upon the emotions as the antecedent occasion or ground of their existence, they may, in like manner, be expected to exhibit, as has already been intimated, a vividness and strength, corresponding, in a very considerable degree, to that of the feelings which preceded them.—It will be noticed, that we do not speak here of the permanency of desires, which is a very different thing, but simply of their intensity or strength for the time being.

§ 308. Tendency to excite movement an attribute of desire.

We shall conclude this notice of the nature of desire with remarking that there is one other characteristic attribute which particularly distinguishes it, and which undoubtedly must enter as an element into every perfect delineation of it. Such is the nature of desire, that it is of itself, in virtue of its own essence, a prompting, exciting, or, as Mr. Hobbes would term it, a *motive* state of the mind. In other words, its very existence involves the probability of action; it sets the mind upon the alert; it arouses the faculties, both mental and bodily, and places them in the attitude of movement.—It is true that the desire does not, in point of fact, always result in action. Before action can be consummated, another power, still more remote in the interior structure of the mind, must be consulted, that of the Will. If the Will decidedly opposes the desire, its tendency is, of course, frustrated in the object aimed at; but the tendency itself, although disappointed of its object, still remains. It is there, and cannot be otherwise than there, while the desire exists.

This important tendency does not exist, as a general thing, in other departments of the mind. It does not exist, for instance, in the cognitive or intellective part of the mind, in itself considered. If the intellect were insulated from the nature which is back of it, man would be a being of speculation merely, not of action. Nor does it exist in the emotions. If man were formed with the emotive sensibilities only, without the accompaniment of those ulterior sensibilities which are built upon them, he would be as unmoved and inoperative as if he were constituted with the single attribute of perceptivity. He would be like a ship anchored in the centre of the ocean, agitated and thrown up and down on the rising and falling billows, but wholly incapable of any movement in latitude or longitude. The tendency to excite movement, as an inherent or essential characteristic, exists in the desires, and nowhere else, except in the corresponding portion of the moral sensibilities, viz., the feelings of moral obligation. The tendency in question belongs to these two mental states alike.—It is the office of the Will, as a separate and relatively a higher part of our nature, to act in reference to this tendency, either in checking or aiding, in annulling or consummating it.

§ 309. Classification of this part of the sensibilities.

If we were called upon to consider the Desires in their simplest form only, we might perhaps feel at liberty to dismiss the subject with what has already been said. But the circumstance that they are subject to various modifications and combinations sets us upon a new field of inquiry of great extent and interest. The Desires are sometimes modified by being directed to particular ends. In other words, they are constituted with specific tendencies, from which they seldom vary. This is the case with the Instincts, properly so called; and probably not less so, in their original and unperverted action, with the Appetites. In regard to the Affections, a distinct class of the active or sensitive principles which come under this general head, it seems, as far as we can judge, to be the fact, that the DESIRES exist in a close and inseparable combination with certain emotions, and are thus made to assume an aspect which they would not otherwise possess. Accordingly, we have a basis, an ample and distinctly defined one, for a subordinate classification. And it is to the examination of the Desires, as they exist in this classification, that we now proceed; beginning with those which, in the gradations of regard we are naturally led to bestow upon them, are generally adjudged as lowest in point of rank, and proceeding upward to those which are higher. In accordance with this plan, they will present themselves to notice, and be made the subject of distinct consideration, in the order of the Instincts, the Appetites, the Propensities, and the Affections.

§ 310. *The principles, based upon desire, susceptible of a twofold operation.*

There is one important remark which is applicable to all the principles, with the exception of the Instincts, which now present themselves for examination. It is, that, with the exception just mentioned, they all have a twofold action, INSTINCTIVE and VOLUNTARY. This statement, of course, will not apply to the pure instincts; for the very idea of their being instincts, in the proper sense of the term, seems to imply an absolute exclusion of their being voluntary. But as we advance from the Instincts to the Appetites, and still upward to the Propensities and Affections, we find each and all of these important principles susceptible of being contemplated in this twofold aspect. Each, under circumstances of such a nature as to preclude inquiry and reflection, is susceptible of an instinctive action; and each, under other circumstances more favourable to the exercise of reasoning, is susceptible of a deliberate or voluntary action.—This remark is important in our estimate of these principles, considered in a moral point of view.

CHAPTER II.

INSTINCTS.

§ 311. Of instincts in man as compared with those of inferior animals.

In proceeding to examine that part of our sensitive constitution which is comprehended under the general name of Desires, we naturally begin with *instincts*, which are nothing more than desires, existing under a particular and definite modification.—It is generally conceded, that there are in our nature some strong and invariable tendencies to do certain things, without previous forethought and deliberation, which bear that name. The actions of men are not always governed by feelings founded on reasoning, but are sometimes prompted by quick and decisive impulses, which set themselves in array before reason has time to operate. It is from this circumstance that these mental tendencies or desires are termed instinctive; a word which implies, in its original meaning, a movement or action, whether mental or bodily, without reflection and foresight.

Although such instinctive tendencies are undoubtedly found in men, it must be admitted that they are less frequent, and, in general, less effective, than in the lower animals. And, in truth, it could not be expected to be otherwise, when we remember that the brute creation are wholly destitute of the powers of abstraction and of reasoning, or, at most, possess them only in a small degree. The provident oversight of the Supreme Being, without whose notice not a sparrow falleth to the ground, has met this deficiency by endowing them with instincts the most various in kind, and strikingly adapted to the exigences of their situation. We find the proofs of this remark in the nests of birds, in the ball of the silkworm, in the house of the beaver, in the return and flight of birds at their appointed seasons, and in a multitude of other instances.

§ 312. Illustrations of the instincts of brute animals.

It would be easy, by means of various interestin

to illustrate the nature of the instinctive principle.—The philosopher Galen once took a kid from its dead mother by dissection, and, before it had tasted any food, brought it into a certain room, having many vessels full, some of wine, some of oil, some of honey, some of milk, or some other liquor, and many others filled with different sorts of grain and fruit, and there laid it. After a little time the embryon had acquired strength enough to get up on its feet; and it was with sentiments of strong admiration that the spectators saw it advance towards the liquors, fruit, and grain, which were placed round the room, and, having smelt all of them, at last sup the milk alone. About two months afterward, the tender sprouts of plants and shrubs were brought to it, and, after smelling all of them and tasting some, it began to eat of such as are the usual food of goats.

The cells constructed by the united efforts of a hive of bees have often been referred to as illustrating the nature of instincts.—"It is a curious mathematical problem," says Dr. Reid, "at what precise angle the three planes which compose the bottom of a cell in a honey-comb ought to meet, in order to make the greatest saving or the least expense of material and labour. This is one of those problems belonging to the higher parts of mathematics, which are called problems of *maxima* and *minima*. It has been resolved by some mathematicians, particularly by the ingenious Mr. Maclaurin, by a fluxionary calculation, which is to be found in the Transactions of the Royal Society of London. He has determined precisely the angle required; and he found, by the most exact mensuration the subject could admit, that it is the very angle in which the three planes in the bottom of the cell of a honey-comb do actually meet.

"Shall we ask here, who taught the bee the properties of solids, and to resolve problems of maxima and minima? We need not say that bees know none of these things. They work most geometrically, without any knowledge of geometry; somewhat like a child, who, by turning the handle of an organ, makes good music without any knowledge of music. The art is not in the child, but in him who made the organ. In like manner when a bee makes its comb so geometrically, the geometry is not in the bee, but in that great Geometrician who made the bee, and made all things in number, weight, and measure."

§ 313. Instances of instincts in the human mind.

But it is not our design to enter particularly into the subject of the instincts of animals in this place, although this topic is undoubtedly one of exceeding interest both to the philosopher and the Christian. Such inquiries are too diverse and remote from our main object, which has particular, if not exclusive, reference to the economy of human nature. There are certain instinctive tendencies in man, as well as in the inferior animals; but they are few in number; and, compared with the other parts of his nature, are of subordinate importance. Some of them will now be referred to.

(I.) The action of respiration is thought, by some writers, to imply the existence of an instinct. We cannot suppose that the infant at its birth has learned the importance of this act by reasoning upon it; and he is as ignorant of the internal machinery which is put in operation, as he is of its important uses. And yet he puts the whole machinery into action at the very moment of coming into existence, and with such regularity and success that we cannot well account for it, except on the ground of an instinctive impulse.

(II.) "By the same kind of principle," says Dr. Reid, (Essays on the Active Powers, iii., chapter ii.,) "a new-born child, when the stomach is emptied, and nature has brought milk into the mother's breast, sucks and swallows its food as perfectly as if it knew the principles of that operation, and had got the habit of working according to them.

"Sucking and swallowing are very complex operations. Anatomists describe about thirty pairs of muscles that must be employed in every draught. Of those muscles, every one must be served by its proper nerve, and can make no exertion but by some influence communicated by the nerve. The exertion of all those muscles and nerves is not simultaneous. They must succeed each other in a certain order, and their order is no less necessary than the exertion itself.—This regular train of operations is carried on, according to the nicest rules of art, by the infant, who has neither art, nor science, nor experience, nor habit.

"That the infant feels the uneasy sensation of hunger, I admit; and that it sucks no longer than till this sensation be removed. But who informed it that this uneasy sensation might be removed, or by what means? That it knows nothing of this is evident, for it will as readily suck a finger, or a bit of stick, as the nipple."

(III.) The efforts which men make for self-preservation appear to be in part of an instinctive kind. If a man is in danger of falling from unexpectedly losing his balance, we say with much propriety that the instantaneous effort he makes to recover his position is instinctive. If a person is unexpectedly and suddenly plunged into a river, the first convulsive struggle which he makes for his safety seems to be of the same kind. His reasoning powers may soon come to his aid, and direct his further measures for his preservation; but his first efforts are evidently made on another principle. When a violent blow is aimed at one, he instinctively shrinks back, although he knew beforehand it would be aimed in sport, and although his reason told him there was no danger.

§ 314. Further instances of instincts in men.

(IV.) There is also a species of resentment which may properly be called instinctive. Deliberate resentment implies the exercise of reason, and is excited only by intentional injury. Instinctive resentment, on the other hand, operates whether the injury be intentional or not, and precisely as it does in the lower animals.

When we experience pain which is caused by some external object, this feeling arises in the mind with a greater or less degree of power, and prompts us to retaliate on the cause of it. A child, for instance, stumbles over a stone or stick of wood and hurts himself, and, under the impulse of instinctive resentment, violently beats the unconscious cause of its suffernig. Savages, when they have been struck by an arrow in battle, have been known to tear it from the wound, break, and bite it with their teeth, and dash it on the ground, as if the original design and impetus of destruction were in the arrow itself.—Similar views will apply, under certain circumstances, to many other active principles.

(V.) There is undoubtedly danger of carrying the doctrine of the instinctive tendencies of the human mind too far; but we may consider ourselves safe in adding to those which have been mentioned, the power of interpreting natural signs. Whenever we see the outward signs of rage, pity, grief, joy, or hatred, we are able immediately to interpret them. It is abundantly evident that children, at a very early period, read and decipher, in the looks and gestures of their parents, the emotions and passions, whether of a good or evil kind, with which they are agitated.

§ 315. Of the final cause or use of instincts.

Although the instincts, as a general statement, commend themselves less decisively to our regard and admiration than some other portions of the mind, they still have their important uses. It seems, in particular, to be the design of the instinctive part of our nature to aid and protect us in those cases where reason cannot come seasonably to our aid. According as the reasoning powers acquire strength, and prepare themselves more and more for the various emergencies to which we are exposed, the necessity of instinctive aids is proportionally diminished. But there are some cases which the reasoning power can never reach; and, consequently, our whole protection is in instinct.

It is evident, therefore, that they are a necessary part of our constitution; that they help to complete the mental system; and although of subordinate power and value in man, compared with the inferior animals, they still have their worth. As the reasoning power predominates in man, so instincts predominate in the lower animals; and as we do not expect to find the glory of reasoning in brutes, so we should not expect to discover the full excellence of instinctive powers in men; but should rather look for them in the insect and the worm, in the beasts of the field, and the fishes of the sea, and the fowls of the air, dwelling in them as a part of their nature, and blessing while they control and guide them.

CHAPTER III.

APPETITES.

§ 316. Of the general nature and characteristics of the appetites.

UNDER the general head of Desires, the subject of APPETITES seems next to propose itself for consideration. But as it is one of limited extent, and of subordinate importance in a metaphysical point of view, only a few remarks will be necessary. The arrangement, which brings the subject forward for discussion under the head of Desires, will recommend itself on a very little attention. The prominent appetites are those of HUNGER and THIRST; but the appetite of hunger is nothing more than the desire for food; the appetite for thirst is a desire for drink.

Nevertheless, they appear to be sufficiently distinguished from the other desires. They are not like the instincts, always gratified in a certain fixed and particular manner; nor are they like them in being wholly independent of the reasoning power. On the contrary, they may be restrained and regulated in some degree; and when it is otherwise, their demands may be quieted in various ways.

But without dwelling upon such considerations, the statement has been made with much appearance of reason, that they are characterized by these three things.—(1.) They take their rise from the body, and are common to men with the brutes.—(2.) They are not constant in their operation, but occasional.—(3.) They are accompanied with an uneasy sensation.

It may be remarked here, that the feeling of uneasiness now referred to appears always to precede the desire or appetite, and to be essential to it.

§ 317. The appetites necessary to our preservation, and not originally of a selfish character.

Although our appetites do not present much of interest, considered as parts of our mental economy, they have their important uses, in connexion with the laws and requirements of our physical nature.—"The appetites of hunger and thirst," says Stewart, "were intended for the preservation of the individual; and without them reason would have been insufficient for this important purpose. Suppose, for example, that the appetite of hunger had been no part of our constitution, reason and experience might have satisfied us of the necessity of food to our preservation; but how should we have been able, without an implanted principle, to ascertain, according to the varying state of our animal economy, the proper seasons for eating, or the quantity of food that is salutary to the body? The lower animals not only receive this information from nature, but are, moreover, directed by instinct to the particular sort of food that it is proper for them to use in health and in sickness. The senses of taste and smell, in the savage state of our species, are subservient, at least in some degree, to the same purpose.

"Our appetites can with no propriety be called *selfish*, for they are directed to their respective objects as ultimate ends, and they must all have operated, *in the first instance*, prior to any experience of the pleasure arising from their gratification. *After* this experience, indeed, the desire of enjoyment will naturally come to be combined with the appetite; and it may sometimes lead us to stimulate or provoke the appetite with a view to the pleasure which is to result from indulging it. Imagination, too, and the association of ideas, together with the social affections, and sometimes the moral faculty, lend their aid, and all conspire together in forming a complex passion, in which the animal appetite is only one ingredient. In proportion as this passion is gratified, its influence over the conduct becomes the more irresistible, (for all the *active* determinations of our nature are strengthened by habit,) till at last we struggle in vain against its tyranny. A man so enslaved by his animal appetites exhibits humanity in one of its most miserable and contemptible forms."*

§ 318. Of the prevalence and origin of appetites for intoxicating drugs

There are not only natural appetites, but artificial or

* Stewart's Philosophy of the Moral and Active Powers, bk i., ch. 1

acqured ones. It is no uncommon thing to find persons who have formed an appetite for ardent spirits, for tobacco, for opium, and intoxicating drugs of various kinds. It is a matter of common remark, that the appetite for inebriating liquors, in particular, is very prevalent, especially among Savage tribes.—And it may be proper briefly to explain the origin of such appetites.

Such drugs and liquors as have been referred to have the power of stimulating the nervous system, and by means of this excitement they cause a degree of pleasure. This pleasurable excitement is soon followed by a corresponding degree of languor and depression, to obtain relief from which resort is again had to the intoxicating draught or drug. This results not only in a restoration, but an exhilaration of spirits; which is again followed by depression and distress. And thus resort is had, time after time, to the strong drink, the tobacco, the opium, or whatever it is which intoxicates, until an appetite is formed so strong as to subdue, lead captive, and brutalize the subject of it. So that the only way to avoid the forming of such a habit, after the first erroneous step has been taken, is quietly to endure the subsequent unhappiness attendant on the pleasurable excitement of intoxication, till the system has time to recover itself, and to throw off its wretchedness by its own efforts.

§ 319. Of the twofold operation and the morality of the appetites.

In accordance with the remarks in the last section in the chapter on the Nature of desires, we may add here the general statement, that the operation of all the Appetites, of whatever kind, is twofold, INSTINCTIVE and VOLUNTARY. So far as they are directed to their objects as *ultimate* ends, without taking into consideration anything else, their operation is obviously analogous to that of the pure instincts. But after the first instance of their gratification, they may be instigated to subsequent action, not so much by a view of the ultimate object as of the pleasure accessory to its acquisition. And thus it sometimes happens, that their action, in view of the enjoyment before them, is turbulent and violent. Nevertheless, we may avail ourselves of the aid of other principles of the mind to subject them to a degree of restraint, to regulate, and, in a certain sense, to cultivate them. And, so far as this can be done, they are obviously susceptible of what may be called a VOLUNTARY action.

And here is the basis of the morality of the appetites. So far as they are susceptible of a merely instinctive action, they cannot be said to possess any moral character, either good or bad. They are greatly useful in their place; but, in a moral point of view, are to be regarded simply as innocent. It is only so far as they are voluntary, so far as they can be reached and controlled by the will, that they can, by any possibility, be morally good or evil, virtuous or vicious. So that virtue and vice, considered in relation to the appetites, is located, not in the appetites themselves in their intrinsic nature, but in their exercises; and in those exercises only which are subordinate to the influence of the will.

CHAPTER IV.

PROPENSITIES.

§ 320. General remarks on the nature of the propensities.

As we advance further in the examination of this portion of the natural or pathematic sensibilities, we meet with certain forms of Desire which are different from any we have hitherto attended to, and which accordingly require a distinct consideration. There is certainly no danger of their being confounded with the Instincts, inasmuch as they do not exhibit that fixedness and inflexibleness of action which is usually characteristic of those states of mind. They differ from the Appetites also, first, because they are much less dependent for their existence and exercise upon the condition of the body; and, secondly, because in that comparative estimation which is naturally attached to the different active principles of our nature, they confessedly hold a higher rank. At the same time they evidently, in the graduation of our regard, fall below the Affections, besides being distinguished from them in some other respects. Hence we may, with entire propriety, not only assign them a separate and distinct position, but shall find a convenience in designating them by a distinctive name.—Among the Propensities (for this is the name which we propose to attach to them) may be mentioned the principle of self preservation, or the desire of continued existence; curiosity, or the desire of knowledge; sociality, or the desire of society; self-love, or the desire of happiness; the desire of esteem, the propensity to imitate, and some others.

Although we have briefly indicated some of the circumstances which separate the Propensities from the other leading principles coming under this general head, it will be noticed that we have not attempted to give a statement of what they are in themselves. It is true, they are all based upon desire, and they all have some object. But whatever is intrinsic or specifically characteristic in their nature will be best learned from the considerations that will necessarily arise, as they pass successively under review.

§ 321. Principle of self-preservation, or the desire of continued existence.

The first of those original desires which we shall proceed to notice may be denominated the principle of SELF-PRESERVATION, or the desire of a continuance of existence.—The proof of the existence of such a desire is not only abundant in what we see around us, but is so intimate also to our own consciousness, that it can hardly be necessary to enter into details. "All that a man hath will he give for his life," was a sort of moral axiom in the earliest antiquity; and it stands as little in need of the verification of proof now as it did then. It is true that the principle may, in its practical operation, be overcome by the ascendant influence of other principles, by the mere desire of esteem, by the love of country, or by the sentiments of duty; but, although annulled in its results, it can hardly be said to be extinct in its nature. It still lingers, unextinguished and unextinguishable, in the foundations and depths of the mind. Even in cases of suicide, the desire of the extinction of life which is supposed to exist is not absolute but relative; the self-mur derer would still cling to existence if it could be possess ed separate from the evils which attend it; it is not life in itself considered, which he hates, but the variety of unpleasant circumstances, either actual or imagined, which are connected with it.

§ 322. Of the twofold action of the principle of self-preservation.

The principle of self-preservation, or desire of the continuance of existence, as well as the appetites, has a twofold operation, viz., INSTINCTIVE and VOLUNTARY. These two aspects or methods of its operation are to be carefully distinguished from each other. The instinctive operation takes place when life is threatened or endangered on some sudden and unexpected emergencies. When a person is in danger of falling, he instinctively puts forth his hand to sustain himself; when a blow is suddenly aimed at him, he instinctively makes an effort to ward it off; and the operation of this instinctive form of the desire is exceedingly rapid as well as effective. This instinctive action is highly important in all cases where an effort for self-preservation, based upon inquiry and reasoning, would come too late.—When the exercise of the desire under consideration exists in connexion with inquiry and reasoning, and, of course, is ultimately based upon decisions of the will, it is said to be VOLUNTARY. It is under the suggestions of this form of the principle in question that we are led to make all those prospective calculations and efforts which have particular reference to the continuance and protection of life. In either point of view, whether considered as instinctive or voluntary, it is a principle evidently adapted with great wisdom to man's situation and wants. It is practically a powerful motive to action; and in its voluntary exercise is always morally good, so far as it exists in entire conformity with the requisitions of an unperverted conscience.

§ 323. Of curiosity, or the desire of knowledge.

Another of the leading Propensive principles is CURIOSITY, or the desire of knowledge; in respect to which it scarcely admits of a doubt, that it is to be regarded as one of the implanted and original characteristics of our mental constitution. Although it must be acknowledged that this principle exists in very various degrees, from the weakest form of life and activity to almost irrepressible strength, yet a person utterly without curiosity would be deemed almost as strange and anomalous as a person without sensation. If curiosity be not natural to man, then it follows that the human mind is naturally indifferent to the objects that are presented to it, and to the discovery of truth: and that its progress in knowledge is naturally unattended with satisfaction; a state of things which could not be expected, and is not warranted by facts. On the contrary, we see the operation of this principle everywhere. When anything unexpected and strange takes place, the attention of all persons is immediately directed towards it; it is not a matter of indifference, but all are anxious to ascertain the cause.

There is at least one class of writers whose prospects of being read depend in a great measure on the workings of this principle; we refer to novelists and writers of romance. However commonplace may be their conceptions, and however uninteresting their style, if they lay the plan of their novel or romance with so much skill as strongly tc excite the curiosity, they can command readers. And this, undoubtedly, is the whole secret of success in a multitude of cases.

§ 324. Further illustrations of the principle of curiosity.

In further proof of the existence of this propensity as a natural or implanted one, it may be proper to refer to the whole class of the Deaf and Dumb, and to those unfortunate individuals who are blind as well as deaf and dumb These persons almost uniformly give the most striking indications of a desire to learn; it seems to glow in their countenance, to inspire their gestures, and to urge them on with a sort of violence in their inquiries. Certainly, if the principle of curiosity were not implanted, and did not exist in great strength, they would be entirely overcome by the multitude of discouragements with which they are encompassed.

Take, as an illustration, the case of James Mitchell, of

whom Mr. Stewart has given a minute and interesting account. Although this unfortunate boy was afflicted with the threefold deprivation of being deaf, sightless, and without the use of speech, he exhibited a considerable degree of mental activity. The principle of Curiosity, in particular, existed in great strength. He showed a strong desire to examine, and to obtain a knowledge of all objects that came within his reach. We find him exploring the ground inch by inch; we see him creeping on his hands and knees on bridges and the tops of houses; examining not only men, but dogs, horses, carriages, furniture, and musical instruments; standing by the side of shoemakers, tailors, and bricklayers, and intently curious to know the mode and the result of their labours.

But it is unnecessary to dwell upon these general considerations, or to refer to extraordinary instances, when we constantly witness in all infants and children the most ample proofs that the principle of curiosity is deeply implanted in the human mind. It seems to be their life; it keeps them constantly in motion; from morn till night it furnishes new excitements to activity and new sources of enjoyment. The poets, many of whom are entitled to the credit of an exact observance of human nature, have made this trait in infants and children the foundations of many striking passages, as in the following:

> "In the pleased infant see its power expand,
> When first the coral fills his little hand,
> Throned in his mother's lap, it dries each tear,
> As her sweet legend falls upon his ear;
> Next it assails him in his top's strange hum,
> Breathes in his whistle, echoes in his drum;
> Each gilded toy that doting love bestows,
> He longs to break, and every spring expose."

§ 325. Of the twofold operation and the morality of the principle of curiosity.

The innate principle or propensity of curiosity, like that of self-preservation, has its twofold action, INSTINCTIVE and VOLUNTARY.—An action which is purely instinctive is always directed towards its object as an *ultimate* end; it looks at the object itself, without regard to the good or evil which may be involved in it; it chooses and pursues it for its own sake It is in this way that the principle of curiosity operates in the first instance. This is its instinctive operation. And, so far as it thus operates, it is neither selfish nor benevolent; neither morally good nor evil; but simply innocent and useful.

It possesses also a VOLUNTARY action, founded upon a view of consequences, and implying the exercise of reflection. We may direct it to proper objects; we may stimulate its exercise by considerations of interest or of duty, we may restrain it when it becomes irregular and inordinate. And its action, so far as it exists under such circumstances, may, with entire propriety, be denominated voluntary. And, so far as it is of this character, morality is predicable of it; it may be either virtuous or vicious. If it be stimulated to action for good ends, and with a suitable regard to all other moral claims, its exercise is virtuous. If it have bad ends in view, or be put forth with such intensity as to violate other moral obligations, its exercise is vicious. It is in accordance with these views that Mr. Stewart remarks upon and disapproves the conduct of a certain ancient astronomer. It appears that, on a certain occasion, the astronomer was accused of indifference in respect to public transactions. He replied to the charge by the remark that *his* country was in the heavens; distinctly implying that he had deliberately merged the duties of the citizen in those of the astronomer, and that love to his country was essentially annulled by the higher love which he cherished for his chosen science. We obviously have here an instance of the inordinate exercise of the principle under consideration. It was not duly subordinated. It became so intense as to conflict, in the view of an enlightened conscience, with the proper exercise of other feelings, and with the discharge of other duties.

§ 326. Imitativeness, or the propensity to imitation.

Another of the original propensities of the human mind is the principle of Imitation, or the desire of doing as we see others do. We find the evidence of the existence of such a principle everywhere around us.—If this propensity be not natural, it will be difficult to account for what every one must have noticed in infancy and childhood

And we take this occasion to remark, that on this whole subject we shall refer particularly to the early periods of life. That is a time when human nature will be likely to show itself in its true features. And in respect to the principle now before us, it is certain that children are early found to observe with care what others do, and to attempt doing the like. They are greatly aided by this propensity in learning to utter articulate sounds. It is not without long-continued efforts, in which they are evidently sustained by the mere pleasure of imitation, that they acquire the use of oral language.

At a little later period of life, after having learned to articulate, and having become old enough to take part in juvenile sports, we find the same propensity at work. With the animation and formidable airs of jockeys, they bestride a stick for a horse, and try equestrian experiments; they conduct their small and frail carriages through courts and streets, and journey with their rude sledges from one hill-top to another. Ever busily engaged, they frame houses, build fortifications, erect waterworks, and lay out gardens in miniature. They shoulder a cane for a musket; practise a measured step and fierce look; and become soldiers, as well as gardeners and architects, before they are men.—But the operation of this propensity is not limited to children; men also do as their fathers have done before them; it often requires no small degree of moral courage to deviate from the line of precedents. Whether right or wrong, we generally feel a degree of safety, much greater than we should otherwise feel, so long as we tread in the path of others

§ 327. Practical results of the principle of imitation.

It may, perhaps, be supposed by some, whatever evidence may exist in favour of regarding the principle under consideration as an original one, that it has but a slight connexion with the advancement and the happiness of mankind. But it is a remark not unfrequently to be made in respect to the principles of the mind, that often results of great magnitude are found to connect themselves with elements in human nature that appeared in themselves exceedingly insignificant. Such, it is possible, may be the case here. We often speak of imitativeness as a principle which governs children; but are less willing to acknowledge, which is hardly less the fact, that it is a principle which governs men. We cannot doubt, from the reflection we have been able to bestow upon it, that the principle before us, whatever aspect it may present at first sight, was designed to be, and is in fact, one of the important supports of society; a source of knowledge, happiness, and power. If this principle were obliterated, the bond of union which now holds so closely together the two great divisions of society, the old and the young, would be greatly weakened; an event, in all points of view, much to be deplored. Not only in childhood, but in mature age, as we have already had occasion to intimate, we walk in the steps of our fathers, following in arts and in manners the same practices, and sustaining the same institutions; and it is desirable, as a general thing, that we should do so. And we do it, not merely because we suppose them to be clothed with the attribute of superior wisdom, but also because we are prompted, often unconsciously to ourselves, by the influence of this powerful principle. And it is in this way, partly at least, that generation is connected with generation; that the torch of experience, lighted in the preceding age, is made to shed its beams over that which follows; and that society, kept in the vicinity of the beaten track, is not subject to sudden and disastrous convulsions.

We would merely add, if this principle has such vast influence, as we have no doubt that it has, it is incumbent on every one carefully to consider the nature and tendency of the example which he sets. He who sets a bad example, either in domestic or in public life, is not only blasted and withered in himself, but almost necessarily leads on in his train a multitude of others to the same results of degradation and ruin. On the contrary, he who does good in his day and generation, infuses, whether he designs it or not, the effulgence of his example into a multitude of hearts which nature has opened for its reception; and thus, with better and higher results, lights them upward to happiness and glory.

§ 328. Of the natural desire of esteem.

Another important propensity, not resolvable into any thing else, but original, and standing on its own basis, is the *desire of esteem.*—In proof of the natural and original existence of this principle in the human mind, we are at liberty to appeal, as in the case of all the other propensities, to what we notice in the beginnings of life, and the first developements of the mental nature. Before children are capable of knowing the advantages which result from the good opinion of others, they are evidently mortified at expressions of neglect or contempt, and as evidently pleased with expressions of regard and approbation. As it is impossible satisfactorily to account for this state of things on the ground of its being the result of reasoning, experience, or interest, the only explanation left is, that this desire is a part of the connatural and essential furniture of the mind.

(II.) We may remark further, that the desire of esteem is found to exist very extensively and strongly in the more advanced periods of life. If we look at the history of nations and of individuals, how many men do we find who have been willing to sacrifice their life rather than forfeit the favourable opinion of others! When they have lost all besides, their health, their fortune, and friends, they cling with fondness to their good name; they point triumphantly to their unsullied reputation as a consolation in their present adversities, and the pledge of better things in time to come. This is especially true of those periods in the history of nations, when the original sentiments and traits of the people have not been corrupted by the introduction of the arts of luxury and refinement.

(III.) There is this consideration also, which has a bearing upon this topic.—We are sometimes in such a situation, that the favourable or unfavourable opinion of others can have no possible bearing, so far as we can judge, on our own personal interests. And further than this, the unfavourable sentiment which we suppose to exist is not responded to in a single instance out of the particular circle of those who indulge it. It exists there, and there alone; without the possibility of affecting injuriously either our property or general reputation. And yet it is difficult for us not to be affected unpleasantly; we feel as if the intentions of nature had been violated; as if some real wrong had been done us; as if we had been deprived of that which is obviously a right.—If this view of the subject is correctly stated, as we have reason to think it is, it goes strongly against the doctrine that the desire of esteem is based upon personal and interested considerations, and not upon the intrinsic nature of the mind.

(IV.) It is an additional proof in favour of the natural origin of this propensity, that it operates strongly in reference to the future. We not only wish to secure the good opinion of others at the present time, and in reference to present objects, but are desirous that it should be permanent, whether we shall be in a situation directly to experience any good effects from it or not. Even after we are dead, although we shall be utterly separated, both from the applauses and the reprobations of men, still we wish to be held in respectful and honourable remembrance. Fully convinced as we are that no human voice shall ever penetrate and disturb the silence of our tombs, the thought would be exceedingly distressing to us if we anticipated that our memories would be calumniated. We may attempt to reason on the folly of such feelings, but we find it impossible to annul the principles planted within us, and to stifle the voice of nature speaking in the breast.

§ 329. Of the desire of esteem as a rule of conduct.

The operation of this principle, when kept within its due and appropriate limits, is favourable to human happiness. It begins to operate at a very early period of life, long before the moral principles have been fully brought out and established; and it essentially promotes a decency and propriety of deportment, and stimulates to exertion. Whenever a young man is seen exhibiting an utter disregard of the esteem and approbation of others, the most unfavourable anticipation may be formed of him; he has annihilated one of the greatest restraints on an evil course which a kind Providence has implanted within us, and exposes himself to the hazard of unspeakable vice and misery. It is narrated of Sylla, the Roman Dictator, that, on a certain occasion, happening to see Julius Cæsar walking immodestly in the streets, he remarked to those around him that he foresaw in that young man many Mariuses; distinctly intimating, that a person so destitute of regard for the feelings and opinions of others, would be likely to take a course dictated by his sensuality or ambition, irrespective in a great degree of the admonitions of conscience and of considerations of the public good. A prediction founded in a knowledge of the principles of human nature, and abundantly verified by the result.

But while we distinctly recognise in the desire of esteem an innocent and highly useful principle, we are carefully to guard, on the other hand, against making the opinion of others the sole and ultimate rule of our conduct. Temporary impulses and peculiar local circumstances may operate to produce a state of public sentiment, to which a good man cannot conscientiously conform. In all cases where moral principles are involved, there is another part of our nature to be consulted. In the dictates of an enlightened Conscience, we find a code to which not only the outward actions, but the appetites, propensities, and affections, are amenable, and which infallibly prescribes the limits of their just exercise. To obey the suggestions of the desire of esteem, in opposition to the requisitions of conscience, would be to subvert the order of the mental constitution, and to transfer the responsibility of the supreme command to a mere sentinel of the outposts.

§ 330. Of the desire of possession.

We are so constituted, that we naturally and necessarily have not only a knowledge of objects, but of a multitude of relations which they sustain. And, among other things, we very early form a notion of the relation of POSSESSION. There are but few suggestions of the intellect with which the mind forms so early an acquaintance as with this. Whenever we see children, as we constantly do, contending with each other for the occupancy of a chair or the control of a rattle, we may be assured that they have distinctly formed the idea of possession. They know perfectly well what it is, although they cannot define it, and may possibly not be able to give a name to it Although there can, in reality, be no actual possession without involving the existence of a relation, since the fact or actuality of possession implies, on the one hand, an object which is possessed, and on the other a possessor; nevertheless, as the notion or idea of possession exists suggestively and abstractly in the mind, it is to be regarded as a single and definite object, distinctly perceptible in the mind's eye, and sustaining the same relation to the sensibilities as any other object or relation, either mental or material, which is susceptible of being intellectually represented. Of possession, as thus explained, existing as it were distinctly projected and imbodied in the light of the mental vision, all men appear to have a natural or implanted desire. The fact of its existence, either actual or possible, is revealed in the intellect; and the heart, with an instinctive impulse, corresponds to the perception of the intellect by yielding its complacency and love.

§ 331. Of the moral character of the possessory principle.

Although the desire of possession (the possessory principle, or propension, as it might be conveniently termed) has undoubtedly, like the other propensities, its instinctive action, yet its morality, that is to say, its moral character, depends wholly upon the features of its voluntary action. We are not disposed to speak, as some on a slight examination might be inclined to do, of the possessory principle as being, in a moral sense, an unmixed evil. So far as its action may be regulated, either in the form of restraint or of encouragement, by reason, reflection, and the control, either direct or indirect, of the will, (all of which is implied when we speak of its voluntary action,) just so far it is capable of being either right or wrong, reprehensible or meritorious. When acting independently of all comparison and reflection, it assumes the form of an instinct, is often in that form beneficial, and always innocent; when it usurps the authority due to other and higher principles, prompting us to look with an evil eye on the rightful possessions of another, and to grasp with an earnest and unholy seizure what does not belong to us, it becomes vicious; when, on the other hand, its action is the reverse of all this, prompted by upright motives, and adhering strictly to the line of rectitude, it is to be regarded as virtuous.

We apprehend it is impossible even to conceive of a being so far elevated in the scale of perception and feeling as to involve moral accountability, which shall be constituted on the principle of an entire exclusion of the possessory desire. If it desires its own existence and happiness, which we suppose to be a trait essential to every rational and accountable creature, it seems to follow, as a matter of course, that it will desire those attributes and gifts which are conducive to the preservation and perfection of such existence and happiness. What sin can there possibly be in desiring to expand the range of that existence, which in itself is such an invaluable good, provided it be done with a suitable regard to the relations and the claims of all other beings! So far from being a sin, it is, and must be, a duty. If it be not so, what shall be said of those passages of the Apostle Paul, not to mention other parts of Scripture of a similar import, where he directs the Corinthians not only to "covet to prophesy," but in general terms, "to covet earnestly the best gifts;" 1 Cor. xii., 31; xiv., 39.

§ 332. Of perversions of the possessory desire.

Although the propensity in question is susceptible, by possibility at least, of a virtuous exercise, there is too much reason to believe that its ordinary action is a perverted and vicious one. It is a great law of the mind, that the repetition of the exercise of the active principles increases their strength; and as the occasions of the exercise of the possessory principle are very numerous, it is the almost unavoidable result that it becomes inordinately strong. When this is the case, the otherwise innocent desire of possession assumes the form of the sin of Covetousness; a term which is universally understood to express an eagerness and intensity of acquisition that presses upon the domain of some other active principles, and is at variance with some of the claims of duty. This is undoubtedly one of the great sins which attach to human nature; too prevalent, it is to be feared, in the heart of every individual; and which receives in all parts of the Scriptures a decided and solemn rebuke.

When the possessory principle becomes, by further repetition, increased in the intensity of its action, it assumes the still more aggravated and guilty form of Avarice. In this form it not only loses that character of innocence which it originally possessed, but becomes exceedingly loathsome and abhorrent in the unperverted eye of moral purity.

§ 333. Of the desire of power.

Another of the original propensities is the desire of Power.—In regard to POWER, it is hardly necessary to say, that it is not an object directly addressed to, or cognizable by, the senses; but it is an attribute of mind, and is made known to us by an act of the Internal intellect; that is to say, of the intellect operating independently of a direct connexion with the senses. We do not see power as we see and extended object; nor do we touch it, nor is it an object of the taste or smell; but it is revealed to the mind by an act of Original Suggestion, on the occasions appropriate to that species of mental action. But, although it is not cognizable by the senses, it is as much a reality, as much an object of emotion and desire, as if that were the case. It stands out as distinctly perceptible to the mind's eye, as an extended and coloured body does to the bodily eye. This being the case, we may, with entire propriety of language, speak of the desire of power; for wherever there is an object, that object may, in possibility at least, be desired; but where there is no object before the mind, it is not possible for desire to exist.

These remarks are preparatory to what we have now to say, viz., that the desire of power is natural to the human mind; in other words, that the desire of power is an original principle of the mind.—In support of this view, which may perhaps fail at first sight to commend itself to the reception of the reader, the first remark we have to make is, that power in its own nature is a thing desirable. It cannot be doubted that power is in fact, and is to be regarded as, an essential attribute of all mental being.—Accordingly, if an intellectual and sentient existence is desirable, then power is desirable also, as being necessarily involved in such existence. The desire of existence, by common acknowledgment, is natural to us; the desire of happiness is natural also; and since there can be neither the one nor the other without power, it seems reasonable to think that the desire of power is essential to, and is implanted in, our nature.

There are various circumstances, obvious to every one's notice, which go to confirm this view of the subject. "The infant," says Mr. Stewart, "while still on the breast, delights in exerting its little strength on every object it meets with, and is mortified when any accident convinces it of its own imbecility. The pastimes of the boy are, almost without exception, such as suggest to him the idea of *power*. When he throws a stone or shoots an arrow, he is pleased with being able to produce an effect at a distance from himself; and while he measures with his eye the amplitude or range of his missile weapon, contemplates with satisfaction the extent to which his power has reached. It is on a similar principle that he loves to bring his strength into comparison with that of his fellows, and to enjoy the consciousness of superior prowess."

§ 334. Of the moral character of the desire of power.

If it be true that the desire of power is connatural to the human mind, it will probably be found, like other analogous principles, to possess a twofold action, INSTINCTIVE and VOLUNTARY. So far as its action is instinctive, we may suppose it to be innocent at least, and probably useful. So far as it is voluntary, the virtue or vice which attaches to it will depend upon its regulation. If it be kept in subordination to the dictates of an enlightened conscience, and to the feelings and duties we owe to the Supreme Being, its exercise is virtuous. If, on the contrary, it acquires inordinate strength, as it is very likely to do, and is excessive in its operation, pushing us forward to the pursuit of forbidden objects and the invasion of other's rights, it then becomes vicious.

When the desire of power becomes excessive, and exists and operates as a leading and predominant principle, we commonly denominate it Ambition. He who is under the influence of AMBITION, desires power; not because it assimilates him to his Maker, not because it affords him the increased means of usefulness, nor for any other reason which commends itself to a strictly virtuous mind; but simply because it administers to the gratification of an unrestrained and insatiable selfishness.

§ 335. Propensity of self-love, or the desire of happiness.

We proceed to explore this part of our sensitive nature still further, by adding, that the desire of enjoyment or happiness appears to be an original or connatural element of the mental constitution. No one will presume to assert that the desire of suffering is natural; that we ordinarily rejoice in the prospect of coming woes, and endure them with gladness of heart. Nor are there satisfactory grounds for the opinion that enjoyment and suffering are indifferent to the human mind, and that there is no choice to be had between them. Such a supposition would be contrary to the common experience and the most obvious facts. On the contrary, our own consciousness and what we witness in others effectually teach us, that the desire of happiness is as natural as that of knowledge or esteem, and even hardly less so, than it is to desire food and drink when we experience the uneasy sensations of hunger and thirst.

Under the instigation and guidance of this strong propensity, men not only flee from present evil and cling to present happiness, but, foreseeing the events of the future, they prepare raiment and houses, fill their granaries, in anticipation of a day of want, and take other measures for the prolonging of life, health, and comfort. It is kindly provided that they are not left, in taking precautions subservient to their preservation and well-being, to the suggestions and the law of reason alone, but are guided and kept in action by this decisive and permanent principle. And it is proper to add, that this desire operates not only in reference to outward and bodily comforts, but also in relation to inward consolations, the inspirations and solaces of religion in the present life, and the anticipated possession of that more glorious happiness which religious faith attaches to a future state of existence.

But it should ever be remembered, that the desire of our own happiness, like the other desires which have been mentioned, ought to be subjected to a suitable regulation. An enlightened conscience will explain under what conditions our personal welfare may be pursued, and in what cases, whether it relate to the present or the future, it should be subordinated to considerations of public benefit and of universal benevolence.

§ 336. Of selfishness as distinguished from self-love.

We cannot but suppose, for the reasons that have just been suggested, that the desire of happiness or propensity of personal good is an attribute of man's nature. This opinion is not only accordant with the suggestions of the light of nature, but is sanctioned by other and higher authority. The pursuit of our own happiness is obviously recognised in the Scriptures, and is urged upon us as a duty. While we are required to love our neighbour, it is nowhere said that we must perform this duty to the exclusion of a suitable regard for our own felicity. —The desire of happiness thus implanted in our own constitution, we denominate by a simple and expressive term, SELF-LOVE. But it cannot be denied that the import of the term is frequently misunderstood, and that the term itself is liable to erroneous applications.

This is owing to the fact that the principle is not always, and perhaps we should say, is not generally regulated and restrained as it ought to be; but frequently degenerates into a perversion which ought to be carefully distinguished from its innocent exercise. It is not self-love, but the *perversion* of self-love, which is properly called SELFISHNESS; and while self-love is always innocent, and, under proper regulations, is morally commendable, as being the attribute of a rational nature, and as being approved by God himself, SELFISHNESS, on the contrary, is always sinful, as existing in violation of what is due to others, and at variance with the will of God.—It is due to the cause of morals and religion, as well as of sound philosophy, to make this important distinction. Self-love is the principle which a holy God has given; selfishness is the loathsome superstructure which man, in the moments of his rebellion and sin, has erected upon it.

§ 337. Reference to the opinions of philosophical writers.

It would be easy to introduce passages in support of the greater part of the views of this chapter, if it were deemed necessary, from writers whose opinions are received with deference, and are justly entitled to be so. It appears from the recent work of Dr. Chalmers on the Moral and Intellectual Constitution of Man, that he regards the desire of possession (the possessory principle, as it may conveniently be designated) as connatural to the human mind. (Vol. i., ch. vi., § 8—13.) Mr. Stewart takes the same view in regard to the principle of self-love, or the desire of happiness. (Active and Moral Powers, bk. ii., chap. i.) On this important subject, which in some of its aspects is closely connected with the requisitions and appeals of revealed religion, we find the following explicit statement in Dr. Wardlaw's recently published treatise, entitled Christian Ethics.

" Self-love is an essential principle in the constitution of every intelligent creature; meaning by self-love the desire of its own preservation and well-being. By no effort of imagination can we fancy to ourselves such a creature constituted without this. It is an original law in the nature of every sentient existence. In man, it is true, in regard especially to the sources from which it has sought its gratification, it is a principle which, since his fall, has been miserably perverted and debased, degenerating, in ten thousand instances, into utter selfishness, and in all partaking of this unworthy taint. Between selfishness, however, and legitimate self-love, there is an obvious and wide discrepancy. The latter is not at all distinctive of our nature as degenerate, but was interwoven in its very texture as it came from the Creator's hand. The former is properly the corruption of the latter. It leads the creature, who is under its dominant influence, to prefer self to fellow-creatures and to God, so as to seek its own real or supposed advantage at the expense of the interests and the honour of both. So far, on the contrary, is self-love from being unwarrantable, that, in that part of God's law which prescribes our feeling and conduct towards our fellow-creatures, it is assumed as the standard measure of the commanded duty, 'Thou shalt love thy neighbour as THYSELF.' Take away self-love, or suppose it possible that the human heart should be divested of it, and you annihilate the command by rendering it unintelligible.

"There is not, assuredly, any part of the divine word, by which we are required, in any circumstances, to divest ourselves of this essential principle in our constitution. That word, on the contrary, is full of appeals to it, under every diversity of form. Such are all its threatenings, all its promises, all its invitations."

§ 338. The principle of sociality original in the human mind.

Sociality, or the desire of society, is another of the implanted propensities. Men naturally (not moved to it primarily by the influences of education or considerations of interest, but of themselves and *naturally*) have a desire of the company or society of their fellow-men; a tendency of the mind, expressed by the single term SOCIALITY or SOCIABILITY.—We are aware that the desire of society, as well as some of the other original propensions, has sometimes been regarded as a mere modification of Self-love. It is the fact, however, that, in its first operation, the desire of society acts instinctively, being directed to its object as an *ultimate* end, wholly irrespective of any pleasure which may subsequently be found attached to its attainment. It is one of the characteristics of Desire, as we have already seen, that the attainment of its object is attended with more or less pleasure. And this is as true of the successful issue of the principle of Sociality as of any other principle, involving as a part of its nature the desiring element. Accordingly, after the experience of pleasure attendant upon its successful exercise, even in a single instance, it is possible that its subsequent action may be prompted rather by a regard to the concomitant enjoyment than to the object which originally called it forth. Such an exercise of the principle under consideration may, with some appearance of propriety, be termed a *selfish* one; but this is rather a secondary than an original exercise; and does not so much indicate what the principle is by nature, as what it may become by subordinate or by perverting influences. In itself considered, it is innocent and highly useful; it may, indeed, after its first exercise, be indulged from a regard to personal or self-interested considerations; that is to say, from a regard to our own happiness or pleasure; but even the exercise of the principle from such considerations is not to be regarded, as some may suppose, as morally wrong, provided it is so regulated as not to conflict with the proper operation of other principles and with the claims of duty

§ 339. Evidence of the existence of this principle of sociality.

(I.) The existence of the propensity under consideration is shown, in the first place, by what we notice in the early periods of life. No one is ignorant that infants and very young children exhibit a strong attachment to their parents and others who tend upon them, and a desire for their company and uneasiness at their absence. When left alone, even for a very short time, they discover a great degree of unhappiness, which may sometimes be ascribed to fear, but more often to the mere sense of loneliness, and the desire for society.

When other infants and children are brought into their company whom they have never seen before, this propensity is at once shown in their smiles, their animated gestures, and sparkling eyes. And when they are old enough to go out and play in the streets, we find them almost always in groups. Their sports, their wanderings in fields and forests, their excursions in fishing and hunting, are all made in companies; and the privilege of amusing themselves in these ways, on the condition of not being allowed the attendance of others, would be deemed scarcely better than a punishment.

(II.) In the second place, this propensity, which shows itself with so much strength in children, continues to exist, and to give interesting and decisive proofs of its ex istence, in manhood and age. It is true, that those who are further advanced in years, from the circumstance of their finding greater resources in themselves, are in general more capable of supporting retirement and solitude than children But it is very evident, in the maturity as well as in the earlier periods of life, that man's proper element (that in which alone he can secure the developement of his powers and be happy) is society, in some shape and in some degree. Hence the frequency of family meetings, of social and convivial parties, of commemorative celebrations, of religious, literary, and political assemblies, which constantly occur in all communities throughout the world, and which seem to be almost as necessary as the air they breathe or their daily food.

§ 340. Other illustrations of the existence of this principle.

So strong is this principle, that men, if deprived of human society, will endeavour to satisfy its demands by forming a species of intimacy with the lower animals; a circumstance which seems to us decisively to evince not only the innate existence, but the great strength of the social tendency. Baron Trenck, for instance, in order to alleviate the wretchedness of his long and dreadful imprisonment, made the attempt, and was successful in it, to tame a mouse. The mouse, according to his account of him, would not only play around him and eat from his hand, but discovered extraordinary marks of sagacity as well as of attachment.

Mr. Stewart, in illustrating this very subject, makes the following statement.—"The Count de Lauzun was confined by Louis XIV. for nine years in the Castle of Pignerol, in a small room where no light could enter but from a chink in the roof. In this solitude he attached himself to a spider, and contrived for some time to amuse himself in attempting to tame it, with catching flies for its support, and with superintending the progress of its web. The jailer discovered his amusement and killed the spider; and the count used afterward to declare, that the pang he felt on the occasion could be compared only to that of a mother for the loss of a child."

More recently we find statements of a similar purport

in the interesting little work of Silvio Pellico, which gives an account of his Ten Years' Imprisonment.—"Being almost deprived of human society," he remarks, "I one day made acquaintance with some ants upon my window; I fed them; they went away, and, ere long, the place was thronged with these little insects, as if come by invitation. A spider, too, had weaved a noble edifice upon my walls, and I often gave him a feast of gnats and flies, which were extremely annoying to me, and which he liked much better than I did. I got quite accustomed to the sight of him; he would run over my bed, and come and take the precious morsels out of my hand."

On a certain occasion, after having been visited by some one who took a more than usual interest in his situation, he exclaims, "How strange, how irresistible is the desire of the solitary prisoner to behold some one of his own species! It amounts to almost a sort of *instinct*, as if to prevent insanity, and its usual consequence, the tendency to self-destruction. The Christian religion, so abounding in views of humanity, forgets not to enumerate among its works of mercy the visiting of the prisoner. The mere aspect of man, his look of commiseration, his willingness, as it were, to share with you, and bear a part of your heavy burden, even when you know he cannot relieve you, has something that sweetens your bitter cup."

§ 341. Relation of the social principle to civil society.

It is on such considerations that we maintain the principle which has now been the subject of examination, to be connatural to the human mind. If men are frequently found in a state of contention, jealous of each other's advancement, and seeking each other's injury, we are not to regard this as their natural position, but rather as the result, in many cases at least, of misapprehension. If they understood, in every case, the relative position of those with whom they contend, and especially, if they were free from all unfavourable influences from those who happen to be placed in positions of authority, the great mass of mankind would find the principle of sociality successfully asserting its claims against those causes of compulsion and strife which, for various reasons, too often exist

In concluding this subject, we may properly revert a moment to the strange notion of Mr. Hobbes, and those who think with him, that man is kept in society only by the fear of what he significantly calls the Leviathan; that is to say, of Civil Society in the exercise of force. These writers give us to understand, that it is the chain, the sword, and the fagot, which sustains the uniformity of the social position. We have no doubt that Civil Government, in its proper administration, has a favourable effect, even in the exercise of force. But, at the same time, it is a great and important fact, that Civil Society has a different, and, in all respects, a better foundation than this. It is based on the constitution of the mind itself; on the unfailing operations of the social principle It is true that the tendencies of this principle are sometimes temporarily annulled by counteracting and adverse influences; but the principle itself is never, in a sound mind, perfectly extinguished. There is philosophical truth, as well as poetical beauty, in the well-known expressions of Cowper:

> "Man in society is like a flower
> Blown in his native bed; 'tis there alone
> His faculties, expanded in full bloom,
> Shine out; there only reach their proper use."

CHAPTER V.

THE MALEVOLENT AFFECTIONS.

§ 342. Of the comparative rank of the affections.

It will be recollected, after some general remarks on the Nature of desire, we proposed to prosecute the examination of what may be called, in distinction from the emotive, the *desirous* portion of the Pathematic sensibilities, under the subordinate heads of the Instincts, the Appetites, the Propensities, and the Affections. Having examined, so far as seemed to be necessary for our purpose, the three first divisions, we are now prepared to proceed to the last.

The Affections are distinguished from the other forms of the desirous or propensive nature, besides other subordinate marks or characteristics which will naturally present themselves to our notice as they come separately under examination, in being, in the first place, more complex, and also by the circumstance of their sustaining a higher place in the graduation of our esteem and honour. —It may be difficult to explain how it happens, but it is unquestionably the fact, that there is a difference in the sentiments of esteem with which we contemplate different parts of our nature; some being regarded with higher, and some with less honour. In the graduation of our regard, it appears to be the fact, that we generally estimate the appetites as, in some degree, higher than the instincts, and the propensities as higher than either. To the Affections, especially the Benevolent affections, which occupy, in our estimation, a still more elevated position, we look with increased feelings of interest. They obviously stand at the head of the list; and when we shall have completed their examination, nothing more will remain to be said on the regular or ordinary action of the Natural Sensibilities.—We shall then be at liberty to proceed to another and still more important class of subjects

§ 343. Of the complex nature of the affections.

The Affections, unlike the Appetites and Propensities as they exist in their primitive or original developement, are not simple states of mind, but complex. Accordingly, the term AFFECTION denotes a state of mind, of which it is indeed true that some simple emotion is always a part, but which differs from any single simple emotion in being combined with some form of that state of the mind called DESIRE. "As to every sort of passion," says Kaimes, "we find no more in the composition but an emotion, pleasant or painful, accompanied with desire."

The affections are susceptible of being divided, although it may not be, in all respects, easy to carry the arrangement into effect in its detail, into the two classes of Benevolent and Malevolent. The malevolent affections, as a general thing, include a painful emotion, accompanied with a desire of evil to the unpleasant object The benevolent affections, on the contrary, include, for the most part, a pleasant emotion, accompanied with the desire of good to the pleasing object. But what distinguishes and characterizes the two classes, is probably not so much the nature of the emotion as the desire of good or evil which attends it.—It is on the basis of this division that we propose to proceed in the examination of this subject.

It is proper to remark here, that the term PASSIONS, in conformity with the authorized usage of language, is susceptible of being employed as entirely synonymous with AFFECTIONS. In this sense we shall sometimes have occasion to use it; although it is frequently the case that it is employed also as expressive, not merely of the existence of the affections, but as implying their existence in a raised or eminent degree.

§ 344. Of resentment or anger.

The first of the MALEVOLENT affections which we propose to consider (that which may be termed the foundation or basis of all the others) is Resentment or Anger. This affection, like all others, is of a complex nature, involving an unpleasant or painful emotion, accompanied with the desire of inflicting unpleasantness or pain on the object towards which it is directed. In its original or natural state, the desire appears to be, to some extent, the counterpart of the emotion; that is to say, having experienced an unpleasant or painful emotion, in consequence of the actual or supposed ill conduct of others, we naturally desire, in the exercise of the Resentment arising under such circumstances, a corresponding retribution of pain on the offending agent. But in saying that they are reciprocally counterparts, we do not feel at liberty to assert, although there seem to be grounds for such a suggestion, that they possess to each other a precise and *exact* correspondence.

There are various modifications of Resentment, so distinct from each other as easily to admit of a separate notice and to be entitled to a distinct name, such as Peevishness, Jealousy, and Revenge. These will be considered, although in as brief a manner as possible, in their proper place. It is necessary to remark a little more at length upon the passion now before us, which may be regarded as in some important sense the foundation and the place of origin to all the others.

§ 345. Illustrations of instinctive resentment.

The AFFECTIONS, agreeing in this respect with what has been said of the Appetites and Propensities, have a twofold action, instinctive and voluntary; operating, in the one case, suddenly and without thought; in the other, operating on reflection and with deliberate purpose of mind.—Accordingly, we proceed to remark, in the first place, on the instinctive form of resentment. The occasions on which this form of resentment arises or is liable to arise, are all cases of harm or suffering, whether such harm or suffering be caused intentionally or not. The harm which we experience is followed by the resentment at once; the rapidity of the retributive movement may be compared to that of a flash of lightning; quick as the operation of thought is universally allowed to be, there is no opportunity for its interposition between the harm which has been experienced and the resentment that follows. Under such circumstances it is, of course, impossible that the resentment should be regulated by the consideration whether the hurt which we have experienced was intentional or not. It is the harm, in itself considered, which arouses us, exclusive of any reference to the cirumstances under which it is inflicted.

We not unfrequently see instances of instinctive resentment corresponding to what has been said. It is under the influence of this form of resentment that the child who has been accidentally hurt by a stone or a billet of wood, wreaks a momentary anger upon the inanimate object; that the Savage breaks and fiercely tramples on the arrow which has wounded him; and that men, in the first moments of their suffering, almost universally discover a sudden and marked displeasure with the cause of it.

§ 346. Uses and moral character of instinctive resentment.

The object (or FINAL CAUSE, as it is sometimes termed) for which the principle of instinctive resentment is implanted in man, seems to be to furnish him with a degree of protection in the case of sudden and unforeseen attacks. The reasoning power is comparatively slow in its operation; and if the constitution of our nature were such as to require us always to wait for its results before acting, we might, in some cases, fail of that protection which an instinctive effort would have given. Hence the practical importance of this form of the principle under consideration.

It may be added, that instinctive resentment has no moral character. It is the glory of the moral nature, that it lays back, if we may be allowed the expressions, of the intellective nature; and that it does not, and cannot, act independently of the antecedent action, to a greater or less extent, of the intellect. In other words, the nature of conscience is such as to require as the basis of its action a knowledge of the thing and its relations, upon which it is about to pronounce its opinion; which knowledge can be acquired only by the perceptive and comparing acts of the intellect. But such is the rapidity of instinctive action, that it entirely excludes a suitable knowledge of the event which calls it forth; and as it in this way excludes the cognizance and authority of conscience, it cannot be said to have a moral character, either good or evil.

§ 347. Of voluntary in distinction from instinctive resentment.

The second, and, in a practical and moral point of view, the more important form of this affection is what may be denominated Voluntary Resentment. By inquiring into the cause of the resentment which we have instinctively experienced, and by suggesting reasons either for its increase or diminution, we are enabled to modify its action, and to impart to it the character of voluntariness and accountability.

The proper occasion of deliberate or Voluntary, in distinction from instinctive Resentment, is INJURY, as it stands distinguished from mere harm or hurt. That is to say Voluntary resentment, when exercised in accordance with the intentions of nature, takes into view, not only the harm or suffering which has been occasioned, but the motive or intention of the agent. The final cause or object of instinctive resentment is immediate protection; nor does it appear to have anything further in view. The final cause of voluntary resentment is not only protection, but justice In other words, while it aims to secure protection, it does not propose the attainment of that object, except in conformity with what is strictly proper and right. It always, therefore, in its appropriate and legitimate exercise, dispenses its retribution, not simply with a reference to the harm, loss, or suffering which has been endured, but chiefly with reference to the feelings which at the time existed in the mind of the agent or cause of the suffering

A moral character, accordingly, attaches only to the voluntary form of resentment. If there is an exact proportion between the resentment and its cause; in other words, if resentment precisely corresponds to what justice requires, it is right. But if it exceeds this just proportion, it is wrong. This statement is made on the supposition that we are considering the subject by the mere aid of the light of nature, exclusively of the Scriptures. If, under the Christian dispensation, we are required, for high and holy reasons peculiar to that dispensation, to subdue resentful feelings which otherwise might have been justly exercised, that circumstance evidently places the subject in a different light.

§ 348. Tendency of anger to excess, and the natural checks to it.

Few principles are more operative in man, in point of fact, than that of resentment. And although, reasoning on the principles of nature merely, without taking into view the duty of forgiveness inculcated in the Scriptures, we may justify its deliberate and voluntary exercise in many cases, it must be admitted, on the whole, that it is particularly liable to a perverted and excessive action. It is too frequently the fact, that man is found wreaking his anger on those who, on a full and candid examination of all the circumstances of the case, would be found entitled to no such treatment.

One cause of the frequency of excessive and unjustifiable resentment is to be found in the fact, that, in consequence of the suffering or loss we endure, our thoughts are wholly taken up with our own situation, and we find it very difficult to estimate properly either the facts or the motives of our supposed adversary's conduct. If we could turn away our thoughts from ourselves, so far as fully to understand all the circumstances of a proceeding which, in itself considered, we have found so injurious to us, we should frequently be willing to check the vehemence of our anger, if we did not wholly extinguish it.

Nature, however, has herself instituted some checks on the undue exercise of this passion.—First. The exercise of this passion is, in its very nature, painful. It is in this respect very different from the exercise of the benevolent affections, which is pleasant. So great is the pain attendant upon deliberate and protracted anger, that it is not uncommon to hear persons assert that they have themselves endured more suffering in their own minds than the gratification of their passions has caused to their opponents. Nature seems to have attached this penalty to the exercise of this passion, in order to remind men, at the most appropriate moment, of the necessity of keeping it in due subjection.

Second. Whenever our resentment passes the proper bounds, the feelings of the community, which were before in our favour, immediately turn against us. We are so constituted that we naturally desire the good opinion of others; and, consequently, the loss of their good opinion operates upon us as a punishment, and not unfrequently a severe one. Under the influence of the experience or the anticipation of this incidental retribution, it is not unfrequently the case, that men restrict within proper bounds those angry feelings, which, under other circumstances, they would probably have indulged to excess.

Third. The tendency of the indulgence of anger is to lower a man in his own estimation, and still more so in the estimation of others, who will be less ready to admit those mitigating circumstances that partially justify his feelings to himself. The mere outward signs of the angry passions give a shock to our sensibilities, and are hateful to us; while those of an opposite character beam upon the soul with the pleasantness of a tranquil morning's light. The smile of benevolence wins upon our affections; but the scowl of anger, whether it be directed against ourselves or others, fills us with pain and dread And, moreover, while the indulgence of anger tends, as a general thing, to degrade the subject of it in our view, we look with increased respect and honour on those who successfully resist its approaches, and are calm and forbearing amid insult and injury.

§ 349. Other reasons for checking and subduing the angry passions

In addition to those checks to the angry passions which nature herself seems to have furnished, it may be proper to mention a few considerations, drawn from reason and the Scriptures, which, if they have the weight they are entitled to, will tend to the same desirable result.—(1.) We should always keep in recollection, in the first place, that when the mind is much agitated by passion, it is rendered by that circumstance itself incapable, to a considerable degree, of correct judgment. Actions, considered as the indications of feeling and character, do not at such times appear to us in their true light. They are seen through an unfavourable medium, and represented unnaturally, with distorted and discoloured features. It is said to have been a saying of Socrates to his servant on a certain occasion, that he would beat him if he were not angry; a remark which seems to indicate that, in the opinion of the author of it, anger is a state of mind unfavourable to a correct judgment of the merit or demerit of the person towards whom it is directed.

(2.) We should consider, in the second place, even if we have no particular reason to distrust our powers of judging, that we may, by possibility at least, have mistaken the motives of the person whom we imagine to have injured us. Perhaps the oversight or crime which we allege against him, instead of being premeditated or intentional, was mere inadvertence. It is even possible that his intentions were favourable to us, instead of being, as we suppose, of a contrary character. And if it were otherwise; if the wrong done us were an intentional wrong, it is still possible that this hostile disposition may have originated from serious misconceptions in regard to our own character and conduct. And obviously the easiest and best way would be to correct these misconceptions, and thus to secure safety for the future, and, in all probability, recompense for the past.

(3.) There is another consideration which ought to prevent the indulgence of this passion and to allay its effects. It is, that all have offended against the Supreme Being, and stand in need of pardon from Him. If we ourselves were without sin; if we could boast of perfect purity of character, there might seem to be some degree of reasonableness in our exacting from others the full amount of what is due to perfect and inflexible rectitude. But the actual state of things is far different from this. Every one who knows his own heart must see and feel himself to be a transgressor. How unsuitably, therefore, to the circumstances of his own situation, does that man conduct who talks largely of satisfaction and revenge, when he is every moment dependent on the clemency and forgiveness of a Being whom he has himself so often sinned against.

In the fourth place, there are many passages of Scripture which expressly require us to subdue the malevolent passions, and to forgive the injuries which have called them into action. And this, we may here take occasion to remark, is one of the great and striking characteristics of the Gospel revelation. The doctrine, that we are to love and do good to our enemies, obviously distinguishes the Christian Code from every other; and gives to it, as compared with mere human systems, an inexpressible elevation. Its language is, "Ye have heard, it hath been said, thou shalt love thy neighbour and hate thine enemy. But I say unto you, love your enemies; bless them that curse you; do good to them that hate you, and pray for them which despitefully use you and persecute you."

§ 350. Modifications of resentment. Peevishness.

When, in all ordinary cases, the resentful feeling shows itself, we variously denominate it by the terms resentment, hostility, anger, hatred, indignation, and the like; but there are some modifications of the feeling, distinguished either by excess or diminution, or in some other way, which may be regarded as possessing a distinctive character. One of these is PEEVISHNESS OR FRETFULNESS; a species of malevolent passion which, probably with more frequency than its decided manifestations, interrupts the peace and happiness of life.

Peevishness differs from ordinary anger in being excited by very trifling circumstances, and in a strange facility of inflicting its effects on everybody and everything within its reach. The peevish man has met with some trifling disappointment, (it matters but little what it is,) and the serenity of whole days is disturbed; no smiles are to be seen; everything, whether animate or inanimate, rational or irrational, is out of place, and falls under the rebuke of this fretful being.—Anger, in its most marked and decided manifestations, may be compared to a thunder-shower, that comes dark and heavily, but leaves a clear sky afterward. But peevishness is like an obscure, drizzling fog; it is less violent, and lasts longer. In general, it is more unreasonable and unjust than violent anger, and would certainly be more disagreeable, were it not often, in consequence of being so disproportioned to its cause, so exceedingly ludicrous.

§ 351. Modifications of resentment. Envy.

One of the most frequent forms of resentment is Envy By this term we are accustomed to express that ill-will or hatred which has its rise from the contemplation of the superiority of another. Considered as a mere state of the mind, Envy is to be regarded as only one of the perversions of resentment; but, considered in respect to the occasions of its origin, it must be added that it is one of the most degrading and hateful perversions. There is no passion which is more tormenting in the experience, as might be expected from its hatefulness; and none which is more decisively condemned by the sentiments of justice.

If we are asked why it is that, on the mere contemplation of the more favourable situation, and the greater advancement of another, we experience such an odious perversion of a principle apparently good in itself, we shall probably find a reason in the irregular and inordinate action of the principle of Self-love. Men frequently become so intensely selfish, that they cannot admit others to an equal participation of what they enjoy, much less see them advanced to a higher situation, without a greater or less degree of repining and discontent. And it is this state of mind which is appropriately denominated Envy

§ 352. Modifications of resentment. Jealousy.

There are still other varieties of that Resentment or Hostility, which may be regarded, in some important sense, as the basis of the whole series of the Malevolent passions. Among these is Jealousy, which includes a painful emotion caused by some object of *love*, and attended with a desire of evil towards that object.—The circumstance which characterizes this passion, and constitutes its peculiar trait, is, that all its bitterness and hostility are inflicted on some one whom the jealous person loves. The feeling of suspicious rivalship which often exists between candidates for fame and power, is sometimes called jealousy, on account of its analogy to this passion.—There are various degrees of jealousy, from the forms of mere mistrust and watchful suspicion to its highest paroxysms. In general, the strength of the passion will be found to be in proportion to the value which is attached to the object of it; and is, perhaps, more frequently found in persons who have a large share of pride than in others. Such, in consequence of the habitual belief of their own superiority, are likely to notice many trifling inadvertencies, and to treasure them up as proofs of intended neglect, which would not have been observed by others, and certainly were exempt from any evil intention.

The person under the influence of this passion is incapable of forming a correct judgment of the conduct of the individual who is the object of it; he observes everything and gives it the worst interpretation; and circumstances which, in another state of the mind, would have been tokens of innocence, are converted into proof of guilt Although poetry, it is no fiction:

> "Trifles, light as air,
> Are to the jealous confirmation strong
> As proofs of holy writ."

Hence it is justly said to be the monster that "makes the meat it feeds on;" for it perseveringly broods over the slightest suggestion, even when made with the most sincere kindness, and rears up a shapeless and frightful form, which in turn nourishes the baleful passion from which is derived its own existence.

It may be remarked of this passion, that it is at times exceedingly violent. At one moment the mind is animated with all the feelings of kindness; the next, it is transported with the strongest workings of hatred, and then it is suddenly overwhelmed with contrition. Continually vacillating between the extremes of love and hatred, it knows no rest; it would gladly bring destruction on the object whom it dreads to lose more than any other, and whom at times it loves more than any other.

§ 353. Modifications of resentment. Revenge.

Another of the marked modifications of Resentment is REVENGE. By the spirit of revenge, as we sometimes express it, we generally understand a disposition not merely to return suffering for suffering, but to inflict a degree of pain on the person who is supposed to have injured us, beyond what strict justice requires. So that revenge seems to differ from resentment rather in degree than in kind; in other words, it is unrestrained or excessive resentment. It is true, however, that it generally implies something more than mere excess. It commonly exhibits the aspect of coolness and deliberateness in its designs; and is as persevering in the execution of its hostile plans as it is deliberate in forming them. If resentment, when properly regulated, may be considered, on the principles of nature, as morally right, revenge, which is the unrestrained or inordinate form of resentment, is always morally wrong. It is a passion which is not only greatly inconsistent with the due exercise of the other powers of the mind, but is equally condemned by enlightened conscience and the Scriptures.

§ 354. Nature of the passion of fear.

We conclude this review of this portion of the Affections with a single other notice. The passion of Fear, like the other passions or affections that have passed under examination, embraces both a simple emotion of pain, caused by some object which we anticipate will be injurious to us, and also additional to the painful emotion, the desire of avoiding such object or its injurious effects.—The question might suggest itself with some appearance of reason, whether Fear, in view of the definition just given, should be included under the general head of the Malevolent passions. And this is one of the cases referred to, in separating the Affections into the twofold division of the Benevolent and Malevolent, when it was remarked, it might not in all respects be easy to carry the arrangement into effect in its details. Nevertheless, the fact that we experience pain in viewing the object feared, accompanied with a desire of avoiding it, seems very clearly to involve the idea that it is an object of greater or less aversion. In other words, that we have more or less ill will towards it. It is certainly the case if the object is of such a nature that its presence is painful, that we can hardly be said to love it. So that, at least, it would seem to come more naturally under the head of the malevolent affections than under the other class.

But to return to the nature of the passion itself. The strength or intensity of fear will be in proportion to the apprehended evil. There is a difference of original susceptibility of this passion in different persons; and the amount of apprehended evil will consequently vary with the quickness of such susceptibility. But, whatever causes may increase or diminish the opinion of the degree of evil which threatens, there will be a correspondence between the opinion which is formed of it and the fearful passion.

When this passion is extreme, it prevents the due exercise of the moral susceptibility, and interrupts correct judgment of any kind whatever. It is a state of mind of great power, and one which will not bear to be trifled with. It may serve as a profitable hint to remark, that there have been persons thrown into a fright suddenly, and perhaps in mere sport, which has immediately resulted in a most distressing and permanent mental disorganization.—In cases where the anticipated evil is very great, and there is no hope of avoiding it in any way, the mind exists in that state which is called DESPAIR. But the consideration of this deplorable state of mind, so far as it may be necessary to meet the objects of the present Work, will more properly come under the head of Disordered or Alienated Sensibilities.

CHAPTER VI.

THE BENEVOLENT AFFECTIONS.

§ 355. Of the nature of love or benevolence in general.

WE proceed now to the consideration of the other great division of the Affections. As the original principle of Resentment is the basis of the Malevolent affections, so Love, in its more general form, appears to be at the foundation, as a general thing at least, of those which are termed, by way of distinction, Benevolent. The affection of Love, like the other affections, is a complex state of mind, embracing, FIRST, a pleasant emotion in view of the object; and, SECOND, a desire of good to that object. Hence there will always be found in the object some quality, either some excellence in the form, or in the relations sustained, or in the intellect, or in the moral traits, or in all combined, which is capable of exciting a pleasurable emotion. This emotion is the basis of the subsequent desire; but it is the strict and indissoluble combination of the two that constitutes the Affection properly so called.

It is proper to remark here that there are many modifications or degrees of this affection; such as the unimpassioned preference of friendly regard and esteem, the warmer glow of friendship in the more usual acceptation of the term, and the increased feeling of devoted attachment. There are not only differences in degree, but the affection itself, considered in respect to its nature simply, seems to be modified, and to be invested with a different aspect, according to the circumstances in which it is found to operate. The love which children feel for their parents is different in some respects from that which they feel for their brothers and sisters. The love of parents for their children possesses traits, difficult to be described in language, but recognisable by Consciousness, which distinguish it from their love to mankind generally, or their love to their country, or their friends. Hence we are enabled, in consistency with what is the fact in respect to them, to consider the Affections under different forms or heads, viz., the Parental affection, the Filial affection, the Fraternal affection, Humanity, or the love of the human race, Patriotism, or the love of country, Friendship, Gratitude, and Sympathy or Pity.

§ 356. Love, in its various forms, characterized by a twofold action.

Love, not only in its more general form, but in all the varieties which, in consequence of our situation and of the relations we sustain, it is made to assume, is characterized, like the opposite principle of resentment, by its twofold action. It is sometimes seen, particularly in parents and children, to operate INSTINCTIVELY; that is to say, without deliberation or forethought. At other times it is subjected to more or less of regulation, being either stimulated or repressed in its exercise by the facts and reflections which are furnished by reasoning; and then it is said to possess a deliberate or VOLUNTARY exercise.-This trait or characteristic, which pervades the whole series of the Natural or Pathematic sensibilities, has been so often referred to that it is unnecessary to delay upon it here.

§ 357. Of the parental affection.

The principle of benevolence, love, or good-will, which in its general form, has thus been made the subject of a brief notice, is susceptible, like the malevolent affection of Resentment, of various modifications. One of the most interesting and important of these modifications is the Parental Affection.—The view which we propose to take of this modification of benevolence or love is, that it is an original or implanted principle. In support of this view a number of things may be said.

(I.) It is supported, in the first place, by the consideration, that the relation between the parent and child is much more intimate and indissoluble than any other. The child, in the view of the parent, is not so much a distinct and independent being as a reproduction and continuance of himself He sees not only the reflection of his person and dispositions in his offspring, but of his hopes, joys, and prospects; in a word, of his whole being. Under such circumstances, it is almost impossible that the parental affection should be less deeply seated, less near to the root and bottom of the soul, than any other which can be named.

(II.) Such an affection seems, in the second place, to be required in order to enable parents to discharge effectually the duties which are incumbent upon them. The cares and troubles necessarily incidental to the parental relation, the daily anxieties, the nights of wakeful solicitude, the misgivings, the fears, and the sorrows without number, it would be impossible for human nature to support without the aid of an implanted principle.—And hence it is, that, in the ordering and constitution of nature, this principle rises in such inexpressible beauty upon the parental heart. It diffuses its light upon it, like a star upon a tempestuous ocean, and guides it forward in comparative safety.

(III.) In the third place, the acknowledged fact that this affection has an instinctive as well as a voluntary action, is a strong circumstance in favour of its being regarded as implanted. A purely voluntary affection cannot, from the nature of the case, be implanted, because it depends upon the Will; and will either exist or not exist, in accordance with the mere volitive determination. An instinctive affection cannot be otherwise than implanted, because, as it does not depend upon the will, it has no other support than in nature. Now, although this affection has a voluntary action, based upon inquiry and reason, it has also, at its foundation, an instinctive action, which is to be regarded as the work of the author of the mind himself. So that, although it is proper to accompany the statement with the remark that it has a twofold action, the affection, regarded as a whole, may justly be looked upon as an original or implanted one.

(IV.) In the fourth place, its universality is a circum

stance in favour of the view which has been taken. We should naturally expect, in regard to any affection not implanted, and which depends exclusively upon the decisions of the reason and the will, that there would be frequent failures in its exercise. We may even be confident that this would be the result. But the parental affection, in a mind not actually disordered, never fails. In all climes and countries, and among all classes of men, however debased by ignorance or perverted by the prevalence of vice, we may find the traces, and with scarcely an exception, the marked and distinct traces of this ennobling principle. There is no portion of the human race so degraded that it would not turn with abhorrence from the man that did not love his offspring.

§ 358. Illustrations of the strength of the parental affection

(V.) Another circumstance in favour of regarding the principle as an implanted one is its great strength. Secondary affections, or those which, by a process of association, are built upon others, are sometimes, it is true, exceedingly strong; but this is found to be the case only in particular instances, and not as a general trait. In respect to the affection before us, it is not found to be strong in one mind and weak in another, but is strong, excedingly strong, as a general statement, in all minds alike. It might be interesting to give some illustrations of this statement, as, in truth, scarcely any of the facts illustrative of the mind's action in its various departments are wholly destitute of interest. But, on this subject, such is the universal intensity of this affection, that they multiply on every side. He who has not noticed them has voluntarily shut his eyes to some of the most interesting exhibitions of human nature. So that a single incident of this kind, which will not fail to find a corroborative testimony in every mother's heart, will suffice.

"When the Ajax man-of-war took fire in the straits of Bosphorus in the year 1807, an awful scene of distraction ensued. The ship was of great size, full of people, and under the attack of an enemy at the time; the mouths of destruction seemed to wage in contention for their prey. Many of those on board could entertain no hopes of deliverance: striving to shun one devouring element, they were the victims of another. While the conflagration was raging furiously, and shrieks of terror rent the air, an unfortunate mother, regardless of herself, seemed solicitous only for the safety of her infant child. She never attempted to escape; but she committed it to the charge of an officer, who, at her earnest request, endeavoured to secure it in his coat; and, following the tender deposite with her eyes as he retired, she calmly awaited that catastrophe in which the rest were about to be involved. Amid the exertions of the officer in such an emergency, the infant dropped into the sea, which was no sooner discovered by the unhappy parent, than, frantic, she plunged from the vessel's side as if to preserve it; she sunk, and was seen no more."*

§ 359. *Of the filial affection.*

As a counterpart to the interesting and important affection which has thus been briefly noticed, nature has instituted the filial affection, or that affection which children bear to their parents. The filial affection, although it agrees with the parental in the circumstance of its being implanted or connatural in the human mind, differs from it in some of its traits.—It is understood, among other things, to possess less strength. And it is undoubtedly the fact, that it does not, as a general thing, flow forth towards its object with the same burning, unmitigated intensity. And this is just what we might expect, on the supposition that the human mind comes from an Author who possesses all wisdom. The great practical object for which the parental affection is implanted in the bosoms of parents, is to secure to their offspring that close attention and care which are so indispensable in the incipient stages of life. The responsibility which rests upon them in the discharge of their duties to their children, is, in the variety of its applications and in the aggregate of its amount, obviously greater than that which rests upon children in the discharge of their duty to their parents. Nothing could answer, so far as we are able to judge, the requisitions which are constantly made on the parent to

* Origin and Progress of the Passions, (Anonymous,) vol. i., p. 148

meet the child's condition of weakness, suffering, and want, and to avert its liabilities, both mental and bodily, to error, but the wakeful energy of a principle stronger even than the love of life. But it is different on the part of the children. As a general thing, no such calls of constant anxiety and watchfulness in the behalf of another are made upon them, at least in the early part of their life. Hence their love to their parents, although unquestionably strong enough for the intentions of nature, burns with a gentler ray.

§ 360. The filial affection original or implanted.

We took occasion, in the preceding section, to remark incidentally, that the filial affection, as well as the parental, is original or implanted, in distinction from the doctrine of its being of an associated or secondary formation It is not our purpose, however, to enter minutely into this inquiry; and yet there are one or two trains of thought having a bearing upon it which we are unwilling wholly to omit.—Our first remark is, that if the filial affection were wholly voluntary and not implanted; in other words, if it were based wholly on reason and reflection, there is no question that it would be extinguished much more frequently than it is in point of fact. But that mere reason and reflection are not the entire basis of the affection, seems to be evident from the fact that we continue to love our parents under circumstances when reason, if we consulted that alone, would probably pronounce them unworthy of love. Our parents, as is sometimes the case, may treat us with great and unmerited neglect; they may plunge into the commission of crimes; they may become degraded and despised in the eyes of the community; but they still have a pure and elevated place, which nature has furnished for them in their children's hearts.—This train of thought (which, it is proper to remark in passing, is equally applicable to parental love, and tends to confirm the views brought forward under that head) goes with no small weight to show that the affection before us has an instinctive or natural basis.

Our second remark, which is also equally applicable to the parental affection, is, that men, with scarcely an exception, show, by their judgments and treatment of this affection, that they regard it as constitutional or implanted. It is evident that they expect us to treat our parents with great forbearance and kindness under all circumstances. If another person should insult and injure us, public sentiment would probably justify us in inflicting some sort of punishment. But it would not justify us, under precisely the same circumstances of provocation, in inflicting punishment upon, or even showing marked disrespect to a parent, because it would be a violation of nature. Not merely the disapprobation, but the contempt and abhorrence of mankind, inflicted with scarcely the possibility of a failure, is the fearful penalty which nature has attached to a want of parental love, even when the conduct of the parent himself has been reprehensible.—This is evidently the work of nature. Men act in this case as their nature prompts them. But nature is never at variance with herself. If she in this way distinctly intimates that she requires us to love our parents at all times, in adversity and in prosperity, in honour and in degradation, in good and in evil report, it is obvious that she has not left the affection to mere reason and reflection, for it is impossible that love so unchangeable could be sustained in such a manner, but supports it upon an instinctive or constitutional basis.

We merely add, leaving it to the reader himself to make the application of the remark, that nearly all the considerations which were brought forward to show the connatural origin of the parental affection, might be properly adduced to show the same thing in the case of the filial affection.

§ 361. Illustrations of the filial affection.

Interesting instances of the results of the filial affection are to be found wherever there are men. And while it is admitted that there are some unfavourable tendencies in human nature, it is pleasant to contemplate it in an aspect so amiable and honourable. It is the fact, indeed, that children, as a general thing, do not appear to be willing to labour and suffer so much for parents as the parents do for the children. There are more frequent instances of a failure of filial than of parental love. Nevertheless, in all ages of the world, the filial affection has sustained itself in such a way as to bring honour to the Being that implanted it. Children have not only supported and consoled their parents in the ordinary duties and trials of life, but, in multitudes of instances, have followed them with their presence and their consolations into banishment and to prison.

At the accession of the late Emperor Alexander of Russia, many prisoners, who had been confined for political and other reasons in the preceding reign, were set at liberty.—"I saw," says Kotzebue, who was in Russia at this interesting period, "an old colonel of the Cossacks and his son brought from the fortress to Count de Pahlen's apartments. The story of this generous youth is exremely interesting. His father had been dragged, for I know not what offence, from Tscherkask to Petersburg, and there closely imprisoned. Soon afterward his son arrived, a handsome and brave young man, who had obtained, in the reign of Catharine II., the cross of St. George and that of Wolodimer. For a long time he exerted himself to procure his father's enlargement by solicitations and petitions; but, perceiving no hopes of success, he requested, as a particular favour, to be allowed to share his captivity and misfortunes. This was in part granted to him; he was committed a prisoner to the fortress, but was not permitted to see his father; nor was the unfortunate old man ever informed that his son was so near him. On a sudden the prison bolts were drawn; the doors were opened; his son rushed into his arms; and he not only learned that he was at liberty, but, at the same time, was informed of the noble sacrifice which filial piety had offered. He alone can decide which information gave him most delight."*

It is true, there have been instances of parents who have done more than this; who have not only been ready to suffer banishment or imprisoment, but have willingly and joyfully offered their lives for the welfare of their children. In the time of the French Revolution, General Loizerolles, availing himself of a stratagem in order to

* Kotzebue's Exile, p. 254.

effect the object, died upon the scaffold in the place of his son. It might not be easy to bring instances, although some such have probably existed, of children dying for their parents. But history furnishes some affecting cases, where the child has poured back into the parental bosom the fountain of life which had been received.—"The mother of a woman," says the writer referred to, § 168, "in humble life, being condemned at Rome, the jailer, rather than execute the sentence, wished from humanity to let her perish of famine. Meantime no one but her daughter was admitted to the prison, and that after she was strictly searched. But the curiosity of the man being aroused by the unusual duration of her survivance, he watched their interview, and discovered the daughter affectionately nourishing the author of her days with her own milk. The people among whom this incident occurred were not insensible of its virtue, and a temple dedicated to Piety was afterward erected on the spot. So was an aged father, under similar circumstances, preserved by similar means: he, too, was thus nourished by his daughter."

§ 362. Of the nature of the fraternal affection.

There is one other affection connected with the family or domestic relation, which bears the marks, although, perhaps, somewhat less distinctly than in the cases already mentioned, of a natural or implanted origin. We refer, as will be readily understood, to the Fraternal Affection, or the love of brothers and sisters. The love which we bear to our brothers and sisters, although, in the basis or essentiality of its nature, it is the same with any other love, has something peculiar about it, a trait not easily expressed in words, which, in our internal experience or consciousness of it, distinguishes it from every other affection.

We are aware that some will endeavour to explain the origin of this affection by saying, that it is owing to the circumstance of brothers and sisters being brought up together beneath the same roof, and thus participating in an early and long companionship. Nor are we disposed to deny, that this circumstance probably has some weight in imparting to it an increased degree of intensity. But there is a single fact, which furnishes an answer to the doctrine, that denies a distinct nature to the Fraternal Affection, and regards it as a mere modification of love in general, occasioned by the circumstance of early and long-continued intercourse. It is this. When other persons, not members of the same family, are brought up beneath the same roof, although we love them very much, yet we never have that *peculiar* feeling (distinct from every other and known only by experience) which flows out to a brother or sister. There is something in having the same father and mother, in looking upward to the same source of origin, in being nourished at the same fountain in infancy, in feeling the same life-blood course through our veins, which constitutes, under the creative hand of nature, a sacred tie unlike any other.

There are other views of the subject, besides that which has just been noticed, which contribute to show the connaturalness and permanency of this affection. A number of the remarks which have been made in support of the implanted or connatural origin of the Parental and Filial affections, will apply here. But we leave the subject to the decision of such reflections, as will be likely to suggest themselves to the mind of the reader himself

§ 363. On the utility of the domestic affections.

In the institution of the affections which have now passed under a rapid and imperfect review, and which, taken together, may be spoken of under the general denomination of the Domestic affections, we have evidence of that benevolence and wisdom which are seen so frequently in the arrangements of our mental nature. These affections are not only sources of happiness to individuals and families, diffusing an undefinable but powerful charm over the intercourse of life; they also indirectly exert a great influence in the support of society generally

It was, indeed, a strange notion of some of the ancients, of Plato in particular, that the domestic affections are at variance with the love of country; and that, in order to extinguish these affections, children should be taken from their parents at their birth, and transferred to the state to be educated at the public expense. But the domestic affections are too deeply planted, particularly that of parents, to be generally destroyed by any process of this kind; and if it were otherwise, the result would be as injurious to the public as to individual happiness. It is unquestionable, that one of the great supports of society is the family relation. Who is most watchful and diligent in his business? Who is the most constant friend of public order, and is most prompt in rallying to the standard of the law? Who, as a general thing, is the best friend, the best neighbour, and the best citizen? Not he who is set loose from family relationships, and wanders abroad without a home; but he, however poor and unknown to fame, who has a father and mother, wife and children, brothers and sisters; who sees his own sorrows and happiness multiplied in the sorrows and happiness of those around him; and who is strong in the advocacy and support of the common and public good; not only because it involves his own personal interest, but the interest and happiness of all those who are linked arm in arm with himself by the beauty and sacredness of domestic ties.

§ 364. Of the moral character of the domestic affections, and of the benevolent affections generally.

One of the most interesting inquiries in connexion with the domestic affections, and the benevolent affections generally, and one, too, on which there has been a great diversity of opinion, is, whether these affections possess a moral character, and what that character is. The more common opinion seems to have been, that all affections which are truly benevolent are necessarily, and from the mere fact of their being benevolent, morally good or virtuous. Nor is it perhaps surprising, that this opinion should be so often entertained. Certainly, as compared with the other active principles, coming under the general head of the Natural or Pathematic sensibilities, they hold the highest rank; and we frequently apply epithets to them which indicate our belief of their comparative pre-eminence. We speak of them, not only as innocent and useful, but as interesting, amiable, and lovely; and from time to time apply other epithets, which equally show the favourable place which they occupy in our regard. All this we allow; but still they are not necessarily, and in consequence of their own nature simply morally good.

The correct view on this subject we apprehend to be this; (the same that has been taken of other principles, that are analogous in their nature and operation.) So far as the benevolent affections are constitutional or instinctive in their action, they are indifferent as to their moral character, being neither morally good nor evil. So far as they have a voluntary action, they will be either the one or the other, according to the circumstances of the case. When, for instance, the mother hears the sudden and unexpected scream of her child in another room, and impetuously rushes to its relief, we allow the action to be *naturally* good, and exceedingly interesting and lovely; but we do not feel at liberty to predicate virtue of it, and to pronounce it *morally* good, because it is obviously constitutional or instinctive. If the act, done under such circumstances, be necessarily virtuous, then it clearly follows that virtue may be predicated of sheep, cows, and other brute animals, who exhibit, under like circumstances, the same instinctive attachment to their offspring. So far, therefore, as the benevolent affections are instinctive in their operation, they are to be regarded, however interesting and amiable they may appear, as neither morally good nor evil.

§ 365. Of the moral character of the voluntary exercises of the benevolent affections.

But so far as the benevolent affections are voluntary; in other words, so far as they exist in view of motives voluntarily and deliberately brought before the mind, they may be, according to the nature of the voluntary effort, either virtuous or vicious. Take, as an illustration, another instance of the operations of the maternal affection. The basis of this affection is unquestionably pure instinct. But it has, in addition to this, a voluntary operation; and this accessory operation, it is to be presumed, is in the majority of cases virtuous. Nevertheless, whenever this amiable and ennobling affection becomes inordinately strong, when under its influence the mother leaves the child to vicious courses, against the remonstrances of the sentiment of duty, its exercise evidently becomes vicious.—On the other hand, if the mother, perhaps in consequence of the improper conduct of the child, or a perplexing inability to meet its numerous wants, or for some other reason, finds its affection falling below the standard which is requisite in order to fulfil the intentions of nature, and in this state of things restores and invigorates its exercise by a careful and serious consideration of all the responsibilities involved in the maternal relation, it is equally clear that its exercise at once assumes the opposite character, not merely of amiableness, but of virtue

§ 366. Of the connexion between benevolence and rectitude.

We may add to what has now been remarked, that the highest and most ennobling form of benevolence exists in connexion with strict justice. Perfect justice is, by the constitution of things, indissolubly conjoined with the general and the highest good. All forms and degrees of benevolence, which are at variance, whether more or less, with perfect rectitude, although they are aiming at good or happiness, are nevertheless seeking something less than the greatest possible happiness. Even benevolence, therefore, is, and ought to be, subjected to some regulating power. Whenever we distinctly perceive that its present indulgence in any given case will tend, whatever may be its immediate bearing, to ultimate unhappiness and misery, we are sacredly bound by the higher considerations of duty to repress it. And there is as much virtue in repressing its action at such times as there would be at other times in stimulating it.

One of the most benevolent men of whom history gives us any account was Bartholomew Las Casas, bishop of Chiapa. In 1502 he accompanied Ovando to Hispaniola, who had been commissioned and sent out as the Spanish governor to that island. He there witnessed, with all the pain of a naturally benevolent heart, the cruel treatment which was experienced by the native inhabitants; the deprivation of their personal rights, the seizure of their lands, their severe toil, and inexorable punishment. He was deeply affected; and from that time devoted the whole of his subsequent life, a period of more than sixty years, to exertions in their behalf. Under the impulse of a most unquestionable benevolence, this good man recommended to Cardinal Ximenes, who was at that time at the head of Spanish affairs, the introduction of Negro slaves into the West India Islands, as one of the best methods of relief to the native inhabitants.

We introduce this statement for the purpose of illustrating our subject. The measures of Las Casas, which tended to introduce enslaved Africans into the Spanish islands, were the results, beyond all question, of a holy and exalted benevolence. But if he could have foreseen the treatment of the Negroes, still more dreadful than that to which the native inhabitants were subjected; if he could have beheld in anticipation the desolations which have spread over Africa in consequence of the Slave Trade, it would have been his duty, whatever good might have immediately resulted to the Indians, in whose behalf he was so deeply interested, to have checked and controlled his benevolent feelings, and to have endured the present rather than have been accessory to the future evil. The indulgence of his benevolence to the native inhabitants, under such circumstances and in such a form, (however amiable and interesting benevolence, in *itself considered*, undoubtedly is in all cases whatever,) would have been a violation of duty, and consequently a sin.—So false and pernicious is that system which ascribes to benevolence in its own nature, and independently of its relations to the law of rectitude, the character of virtue

§ 367. Of humanity, or the love of the human race.

Another of the implanted affections is HUMANITY, or the love of the human race.—On this subject there are only three suppositions to be made, viz., that man is by nature indifferent to the welfare of his fellow-man, or that he naturally regards him with feelings of hostility, or that he has a degree of interest in his welfare and loves him That man is by nature entirely indifferent to the welfare of his fellow-beings, is a proposition which will not be likely to meet with many supporters; still less the proposition, although some have been found to advocate it, that he is by nature and instinctively the enemy of man But, in endeavouring to support the third proposition, tha he has naturally a degree of interest in, and a desire foi the welfare of the members of the human race generally, expressed by the terms HUMANITY OF PHILANTHROPY, we wish it to be understood that we do not, as a general thing, claim for the exercise of this affection any marked intensity. It is too evident that it possesses but little strength compared with what it should; and that it falls far short of the Scriptural requisition, which exacts the same love for our neighbour as for ourselves. The fact undoubtedly is, that the principle is impeded in its action and diminished in its results by the inordinate exercise of the principle of SELF-LOVE, which is constantly recalling our attention within the restricted circle of our personal interests. But the affection of HUMANITY, although thus restricted in its action, and depressed far below the standard which its great Author justly claims for it, has nevertheless an existence.

This is shown, in the first place, from the great interest which is always taken, and by all classes of persons, in anything which relates to human nature, to man considered as a human being, irrespective, in a great degree, of his country and of the period of his existence. There are numerous other subjects of inquiry; and we undoubtedly feel a considerable degree of interest in whatever reaches us from different quarters of the earth in respect to their structure, climate, and resources. But it is chiefly when man is mentioned that the heart grows warm. We listen to the story of his situation and fortunes, even for the first time, as of one in whom flows the same fountain of life. When we touch a string here, we find a vibration in every human heart. The mere aspect of man, the mere sound of the human voice, unaided by a multitude of associations which often enhance their effect, awakens emotions of regard and interest. And seldom can we find a person so immersed in his own selfishness as boldly and openly to avow, that the pursuit of his personal interests, with whatever good reasons it may in itself seem to be justified, is a valid and honourable excuse for annulling the claims of humanity, and sundering the tie of universal brotherhood.

§ 368. Further proofs in support of the doctrine of an innate humanity, or love for the human race.

In the second place, the testimony of individuals who have been so situated as to put the natural sentiments of mankind in this respect to a fair trial, is favourable to the doctrine of the natural existence of humane or philanthropic feelings. We refer here, in particular, to the statements of travellers, who, either by design or by accident, have been placed, for a considerable time, among Savage tribes; without meaning, however, to exclude those who, in civilized lands, have been favourably situated for ascertaining the tendencies of the human heart. Kotzebue, for instance, who was suddenly seized and sent an exile into Siberia, where he remained some time, was thrown into the company of various classes of persons under such circumstances that he could hardly fail to form a correct judgment in the matter under consideration. The Narrative of his Exile, which is exceedingly interesting, discovers the human mind, considered as naturally disposed to the misery or happiness of the human race, under a decidedly favourable aspect. In the recollection of the good and the evil he had experienced, and in view of the numerous facts recorded in his book, he exclaims: "How few hard-hearted and insensible beings are to be met with in my Narrative! My misfortunes have confirmed me in the opinion, that man may put confidence in his fellow-man."

Almost all the travellers into the interior of Africa, Vaillant, Park, Sparman, Clapperton, Denham, the Landers, and others, although they travelled among tribes in the highest degree ignorant and degraded, constantly speak of the kindness they experienced.—On a certain occasion, Park, for reasons connected with the circumstance of his being an entire stranger in the country, was obliged to remain all day without food. About sunset, as he was turning his horse loose to graze, and had before him the prospect of spending the night in solitude and hunger, a woman happened to pass near him as she was returning from her employment in the fields. Astonished at seeing a white man, she stopped to gaze upon him; and, noticing his looks of dejection and sorrow, kindly inquired from what cause they proceeded. When Park had explained his destitute situation, the woman immediately took up his saddle and bridle, and desired him to follow her to her home. There, after having lighted a lamp, she presented him with some broiled fish, spread a mat for him to lie upon, and gave him permission to remain in her humble dwelling till the morning. Park informs us, that, during the chief part of the night, the woman and her female companions were occupied with spinning; and that they beguiled their labour with a variety of songs; one of which had reference to his own situation. The air was sweet and plaintive, and the words were literally as follows. "The winds roared, and the rains fell. The poor white man, faint and weary, came and sat under our tree. He has no mother to bring him milk, no wife to grind him corn. Let us pity the white man; no mother has he to bring him milk, no wife to grind him corn."

§ 369. Proofs of a humane or philanthropic principle from the existence of benevolent institutions.

It will be noticed, we do not assert that the principle of love to our fellow-men, considered simply as members of the human race, is as strong in the human mind as it should be. All we propose to assert and maintain is, that it actually has an existence there to some extent. And, among other proofs, we might, in the third place, properly refer to those numerous benevolent institutions, such as hospitals, infirmaries, asylums, houses of refuge charity schools, and charitable societies of every description, which exist in all parts of the world. It is true that institutions of this kind flourish most, and it is a circumstance exceedingly honourable to the tendency of the Christian religion, in Christian countries. But the fact undoubtedly is, that, on suitable inquiry, we may find evidences in a diminished degree, of benevolent efforts, and traces of benevolent institutions, such as have been now referred to, in lands not thus highly favoured. In the recently-published life of the Missionary Swartz, (ch xi,) we find the following incidental remark, which throws light upon the state of things in India. Speaking of the territory of Tanjore, the writer says, "Its capital bordering on the Delta of the Coleroon and the Cavary, is wealthy and splendid, adorned with a pagoda, which eclipses in magnificence all other structures in the South of India; and exceeding, in the number of its sacred buildings and *charitable institutions*, all the neighbouring provinces."

Among other facts kindred with those which have now been alluded to, it is well known, that when any portion of the human race have been subjected by fire, war, famine, the pestilence, or some convulsion of nature, to great affliction, an interest is felt, and efforts are made in their behalf in other countries. As an illustration of what we mean, it will suffice to remark, that when, some years since, the Greek nation, and, still more recently, the inhabitants of the Cape de Verd Islands, were in a state of extreme want, although they were a remote people, and scarcely known among us, a number of vessels, in both cases, were sent from this country to their assistance, loaded with provisions at the expense of private individuals. Many facts of this kind might be mentioned, which are obviously inconsistent with the idea that man is indifferent to the welfare of his fellow-man, much more that men are naturally hostile to each other.

§ 370. Other remarks in proof of the same doctrine.

In the fourth place, the principle of HUMANITY is requisite, in order to render human nature at all consistent with itself.—We have, for instance, implanted within us the desire of Esteem, which is universal in its operation. But why should we be so constituted as naturally to desire the esteem of those whom, at the same time, we naturally hate or are indifferent to? There is no question that Sociality, or the desire of society, is connatural to the human mind; but is it presumable that men are so created as earnestly to covet the society of others, when, at the same time, those whose company they seek are, by the constitution of nature, the objects of entire indifference or of decided aversion? We have within us, as we shall have occasion to notice hereafter, the distinct principle of Pity or Sympathy, which prompts us both to prevent suffering and to relieve it when it exists; a principle which no one supposes is designed by nature to be limited in its operation to the immediate circle of our relatives and friends, but which has men *as* such for its object, and the wide world for the field of its exercise. But on what grounds of wisdom or consistency is it possible that nature should prompt men to relieve or prevent the sufferings of others, whom she also imperatively requires us to regard with sentiments of hostility, or, at least, with unfeeling coldness? Furthermore, our Conscience requires us to treat our fellow-men, in all ordinary cases, with kindness, and we experience an internal condemnation when we do not do it; which would at least not be the case if we were the subjects of a natural hostility to them. —It is on such grounds we assert that human nature, in order to be consistent with itself, requires a principle of good-will or love to man, considered simply as possessing a kindred origin and nature.

§ 371. Of patriotism or love of country.

One of the most important modifications of that more general and extensive form of good-will or benevolence which extends to all mankind, is PATRIOTISM, or love of country. It seems to be the intention of nature, when we consider the diversities of customs and languages that exist, and particularly that, in many cases, countries are distinctly separated from each other, by large rivers, lakes, gulfs, mountains, and seas, that mankind, instead of being under one government, shall exist in separate and distinct communities or nations, each having its own institutions and civil polity. And such, at any rate, is the fact. We are not only members of mankind and citizens of the world, (a relation which ought to be more distinctly and fully recognised than it ever has been,) but are members, and, as such, have appropriate duties to fulfil, of our own particular community. And it is thus that a foundation is laid for that particular state of mind which we denominate Patriotism.

This affection we regard as secondary rather than original. It is that love which we exercise, and ought to exercise, towards the members of our species considered as such, heightened by the consideration that those towards whom it is put forth are sprung from the same race, inhabit the same territory, are under the same constitutions of government, speak the same language, and have the same interests. So that the love of our race, as it is modified in the form of love of our country, while it is more restricted, becomes proportionally more intense. And, in point of fact, it is unquestionably one of the predominant and ruling principles which regulate the conduct of men.

Nevertheless, we are not to suppose that there is necessarily any conflict between these two principles. For, in doing good to our country we are doing good to mankind, and to that particular portion of mankind which Providence, by placing them more immediately within the scope of our observation and effort, seems to have assigned as the especial field of our beneficence. At the same time it cannot be denied, that patriotism, in its irregular and unrestrained exercise, does sometimes, and but too frequently, interfere with Philanthropy, or the love of man. The passion of patriotism, as a general thing, has become disproportionate in degree, as compared with the love of the human race. The interests of our country, by being continually brooded over, are exaggerated to our perception; while those of mankind are too much lost sight of. There is too much ground for the feeling lamentation of Cowper:

> "Lands intersected by a narrow frith
> Abhor each other. Mountains interposed
> Make enemies of nations, who had else,
> Like kindred drops, been mingled into one."

§ 372. Of the affection of friendship.

Another interesting modification of that feeling of good-will or love, which, as men, we naturally bear to our fellow-men, is denominated Friendship. It is a passion so distinctly marked, that it well deserves a separate notice, although there are no good grounds for regarding it, considered as a distinct affection, as connatural. The love which we bear to our species is so diffused, that it cannot be said, as a general thing, to possess a high degree of strength. As it withdraws from the vast circumference of the human race, and contracts its exercise within the narrow circle of our country, it acquires increased energy. Retreating within the still more restricted limits which imbody those with whom we are most accustomed to associate, it assumes a new modification, being not only characterized by greater strength, but a source of greater pleasure. And this, in distinction from Humanity or Philanthropy, which extends to all mankind, as well as in distinction from Patriotism, which merely spreads itself over the extent of our country, we call FRIENDSHIP.

This affection, like the other benevolent affections which have been mentioned, includes in itself an emotion of pleasure, combined with the desire of good to its object. It exists, or may be supposed to exist, in respect to those persons who are not only so situated as to be the subjects of our intimacy, but possess such qualities as to be deserving of our esteem. It is, perhaps, a common remark, in connexion with this particular view of the subject, that a similarity of character is requisite as the basis of this affection. This, to some extent, is true; but the remark is not to be received without some limitation. It is certainly the case, that friendship is consistent with diversities of intellect. Persons who differ much in the quickness and amplitude of intellectual action, may nevertheless entertain for each other a sincere friendship. But it must be admitted, it does not readily appear how such friendship can exist in the case of persons who differ essentially in moral character. The fact that one of the parties is virtuous, the other vicious; that one of them attaches his highest veneration and esteem to that rectitude which the other regards as of no value, can hardly fail to interpose between them, as far as the reciprocation of friendship is concerned, an insuperable barrier

§ 373. Of the affection of pity or sympathy.

It is not unfrequently the case that we find around us objects of suffering; those who, from want, or disease, or some other cause, are justly entitled to the aid of their fellow-men. In order to meet this state of things, Providence has kindly implanted within us the principle of Pity, which prompts us, by an instinctive and powerful impulse, to render the aid which is so frequently needed. This benevolent affection differs from others, in being based upon a painful instead of a pleasant emotion. The occasion of the exercise of the affection of Pity or Sympathy is some case of suffering. On contemplating the scene of suffering, it is the result, in all ordinary cases, that we experience a painful emotion, which is followed by a desire to relieve the suffering object.

This principle is practically a very important one. It is a sentiment of Bishop Butler, expressed in connexion with this very subject, that the misery of men is much more directly, and to a much greater extent, under the power of others than their happiness. The sources of happiness, both mental and bodily, are to a great extent in ourselves; and although they are susceptible of increase through the instrumentality of the kind offices of others, yet not ordinarily in a very great degree. But it is in the power of any individual, who is thus evilly disposed, to plunge others, not one or two merely, but even whole neighbourhoods, into misery. The principle of Pity, which is called forth not only in the actual but also in the anticipated prospect of suffering, aids, in connexion with other causes, in keeping under proper restraint any tendency to a wrong exercise of this important power. It not only exercises the important office of preventing suffering, by operating, as it were, in anticipation, but it visits, watches over, and relieves it when it has actually occurred. And in this last point of view particularly, as well as in the other, it commends itself to our notice and admiration as a practical principle eminently suited to the condition and wants of man.

§ 374. Of the moral character of pity.

It is an opinion sometimes expressed, that an affection so amiable, and generally so useful as that of Pity, cannot be otherwise than virtuous It is not wonderful, when we take into view the interesting character of the affection, that such an opinion should be entertained ; but we cannot regard it as strictly correct. It is well understood, so much so as not to be considered a matter of doubt, that this affection operates in the first instance instinctively And it is easy to see the intention of nature in instituting this form of its action. In a multitude of cases where we can relieve the sufferings of our fellow-men, our assistance would come too late if we acted on the hesitating and cautious suggestions of reason. An instinctive action, therefore, is necessary. And, so far as the action of the principle is of this kind, it must be obvious that it is neither virtuous nor vicious.

But there is another view of this subject. The principle of sympathy may be checked in its exercise when it is too intense, or increased when deficient, under the influences of a deliberate and voluntary effort. And, under these circumstances, its action may have a voluntary character, being right or wrong according to the circumstances of the case. It is right when it is subordinated to the requisitions of an enlightened conscience; but otherwise it is wrong. And it may be wrong by excess as well as by defect. If, for instance, we happened to see a person severely but justly punished under the authority of law, we might exercise pity in his behalf. But if, under the mere impulse of pity, we should be led to attempt his rescue, in violation of the rights and interests of society, such an exercise of it would be wrong. Again, we can hardly fail to pity the wretchedness of the emaciated beggar who asks for our assistance; but if we are well persuaded that the bestowment of alms will only tend to encourage those vicious habits which have led to this wretchedness, it may become a duty both to check our sympathy and to withhold our aid.

At the same time we do not deny, that we may very justly draw inferences in favour of the virtuousness of that man's character in whom this interesting passion is predominant. And we say this, because, although sympathy does not necessarily imply virtuousness, yet, in point of fact, it is seldom the case that they are at variance with each other They generally run in the same track, acting harmoniously together.

§ 375. Of the affection of gratitude.

Another distinct modification of that general state of the mind which is denominated love, is the implanted or connatural affection of GRATITUDE. Although this, like the other benevolent affections, includes an emotion of pleasure or delight, combined with a desire of good or a benevolent feeling towards the object of it, it nevertheless has its characteristics, which clearly distinguish it from them. We never give the name of gratitude, for instance, to this combination of pleasant and benevolent feeling, except it arise in reference to some benefit or benefits conferred. Furthermore, GRATITUDE involves, as the basis or occasion of its origin, not only the mere fact of a good conferred, but of a *designed* or *intentional* benefit. If the benefit which we have received can be traced to some private or selfish motive on the part of the person from whom it comes, we may be pleased, as we probably shall be, with the good that has accrued to us; but shall cease, from the moment of the discovery of his motive, to entertain any gratitude to the author of it. Gratitude, therefore, can never be excited within us, except in view of what is in fact, or is supposed to be, true, unadulterated benevolence.

Different individuals manifest considerable diversity in the exercise of grateful emotions. There are some persons who exhibit, in the reception of the favours conferred upon them, but slight visible marks of grateful regard; others are incapable of such a passive reception of benefits, and are strongly affected with their bestowal. This difference is probably owing, in part, to original diversities of constitution; and is partly to be ascribed to different views of the characters and duties of men, or to other adventitious circumstances.

CHAPTER VII.

THE BENEVOLENT AFFECTIONS

LOVE TO THE SUPREME BEING.

§ 376. Man created originally with the principle of love to God.

In order to preserve the other principles of human nature in the position which the great Author of that nature has assigned to them, and to render their action just in itself and harmonious in its relations, we have reason to believe that there was originally in the human constitution a principle of love to the Supreme Being. This affection, it may well be supposed, was entirely analogous, both in its nature and its operations, to the other Benevolent Affections, possessing, like them, a twofold action, INSTINCTIVE and VOLUNTARY. It differed, however, greatly in the degree or intensity of its action; being rendered to its appropriate object, as might be expected from the unspeakably high and holy nature of that object, with all the energy of which the mind was capable. That man must have been created originally with such a principle of love, overruling and regulating all the subordinate principles, we think must be evident, in the first place, from the considerations furnished by Analogy.

In all the departments of the mind, so far as it has hitherto passed under our examination, we have seen evidences of contrivance and wisdom; everything has its place, adaptations, and uses; and nothing, so far as we can judge, is done imperfectly. If it were necessary in this inquiry to put out of view the Intellect, so wonderful in its adaptation and its resources, we should hardly fail to find, in the distinct departments of the Sensibilities, ample illustrations and proofs of this remark. The Instincts, which naturally arrest our attention first, have obviously their appropriate place and office; and although they rank lowest in the enumeration of our active principles, are yet indispensable. If man were constituted physically as he is at present, and yet without the Appetites, the next higher class of the principles involving desire, there would obviously be a want of adaptation between his mental and physical arrangements. The Propensities also, as we advance still upward, have each their sphere of action, their specific nature and uses; and are adapted with wonderful skill to the necessities of man, and to the relations he sustains. The same remark, and perhaps in a still higher sense, will apply to the Affections.—As a father, a man has a natural affection for his children, that he may thus be supported in the discharge of the arduous duties he owes to them; as a child, he has naturally an affection for his parents; and as man simply, he is evidently constituted with a degree of love for his fellow-man.

When we consider the relations which men sustain, still more important than those which are the basis of the principles which have been mentioned, are we not justified in saying, on the ground of Analogy, that there must have been originally in the human constitution a principle of love to the Supreme Being? If there was not originally in the mental constitution such a principle as love to God, was not the structure of the mind in that respect obviously at variance with what the Analogy of its nature in other respects requires? If, from the urgent necessities of our situation, there must be strong ties of love, binding together parents, and children, and brothers; if these ties must reach and bind with some degree of strictness all the members of the human family, on what principle can the doctrine be sustained, that man was originally created without an implanted love to that Being, who is infinitely more and better to him than an earthly brother or father?

§ 377. That man was originally created with a principle of love to God, further shown from the Scriptures.

In the second place, we have great reason to believe, from the testimony of the Scriptures, that man was, in the first instance, created with the distinct and operative principle of love to his Creator. At the creation, it is worthy of notice, that everything which came from the hands of the great Architect was pronounced to be GOOD. But if man, raised from nothingness into existence, furnished with high powers of thought and action, and supported by the daily gifts of the divine bounty, was created without a principle of love to his Maker, (analogous to the other implanted affections, only that it existed in an exceedingly higher degree, corresponding to the greatness of the object,) we cannot deny that we are utterly unable to perceive in such a result the basis of so marked a commendation, as far as the parents of the human race were concerned. It would seem, on the contrary, that such a work, framed with such a disregard of the most important relations, could not be pronounced good, even in the estimate of human reason, much less in that of a reason infinitely comprehensive and divine

But, furthermore, man is expressly said to have been created in the image of his Maker. That is to say, in the great outlines of his mental constitution, he was, in the first instance, a copy, (on a very limited scale, it is true,) but still a copy, in fact, of the Divine Mind. But we must suppose that God, both in his administration of justice and benevolence, is regulated by a wise and full consideration of the relations of things. He always loves from the very perfection of his nature, what is worthy to be loved; and if he created man in his own image, (that is to say, with affections and moral sentiments corresponding to the nature and relations of things,) He must have created him with a disposition to love himself. We are not at liberty to suppose that he could by possibility create a being who should either hate or be indifferent towards another being, whom he knew not only to be infinitely wise and good, but to sustain the relation of a Creator, preserver, and benefactor. A being thus created, so utterly wanting in those affections which are required by the immutable relations of things, could hardly be said, with any degree of truth, to be created in the image of God. We infer, therefore, from the statement of man's being created in the Divine image, that he was created with a principle of love to his Maker And the same reason leads us to believe, that the principle was paramount to every other; corresponding, as far as the limited powers of man would permit, to the infinitely exalted nature of its object. And, in addition to this, the analogy of the other implanted principles points to the conclusion, that, like them, it possesses a twofold action, instinctive and voluntary.

§ 378. Further proof that man was thus created.

Again, many of those passages of Scripture which are addressed to man in his present fallen state, appear to contemplate the restoration of this great principle. When the Saviour, on a certain occasion, was asked, in respect to the commandments, which of them was to be regarded as having the first or leading place, his answer was: "Thou shalt love the Lord thy God with all thy heart, and with all thy soul, and with all thy mind. This is the first and great commandment." Matt. xxii., 37, 38 This language implies, to say the least, the possibility of the existence of this principle; and particularly, that in a sinless or perfect state of the human race, it is indispensable.—Finally, that renovation of our nature, which is so frequently spoken of in the New Testament under the name of a New Creation or New Birth, and which is represented as being brought about by divine assistance, unquestionably, in the meaning of the writers of the Scriptures, involves the restoration of this essential element of the mental constitution. To be what he is required to be, man must be what he was before the Fall; and in order to be in this situation, the great requisite is, what has just been mentioned, to love God with all the heart.—We feel authorized, therefore, in asserting, that originally supreme love to God was an essential element of human nature; and that, at the present moment, it is, or ought to be in every human bosom, a distinct and operative principle. Its presence, as we shall be led to see in the succeeding section, makes man what he was designed to be; its absence furnishes an easy and philosophical explanation of those evils which, in the present state of things, so frequently press themselves on our notice.

§ 379. Relation of the principle of supreme love to God to the other principles of the pathematic sensibilities.

In giving an account, in their succession and place, of

the principles of action which go to constitute the department of the Pathematic sensibilities, we feel at liberty, from what has been remarked, to place at their head, both as most important in its results and as highest in rank, the principle of supreme love to God. If it be said, as undoubtedly it may be said with too much truth, that this principle of human action, considered as a distinct and permanent principle, is obliterated, it is nevertheless true that it is susceptible, with divine aid, of a restoration. If it be asserted that men are not naturally governed by it, it still remains certain, if the precepts of Scripture may be understood with their obvious import, that they *ought* to be governed by it.

Mental philosophy, as well as Divine Revelation, clearly indicates, that there has been at some period a great mental convulsion; that the glory of the human mind, although not absolutely extinct, is greatly obscured; and that man, in respect to his intellectual and moral condition, is truly and aptly described as a fallen being. And in this deplorable state of moral obliquity and mutilation he will continue to remain, if the views which have been proposed are correct, until the principle of supreme love to God is reinstated. The wisdom which we claim for the structure of human nature cannot be asserted with confidence to exist, except on the supposition that this great pillar of its support originally belonged to it, and may yet, by possibility, belong to it.

Now supposing this principle to exist in the human mind, either by being originally implanted as in Adam, or by being restored under the name of a Regeneration or New Creation, we naturally proceed to inquire what relation it holds to the other principles in this department of the mind, and what results are likely to attend upon it. In point of mere rank, (that is to say, in the position which it occupies and ought to occupy in our estimation,) we cannot hesitate to say that it stands first; not only before the Appetites and Propensities, but before all the other Affections, the class with which it is itself properly arranged; taking the precedence by an incalculable remove, not only of the love of country and the love of friends, but of the love of parents and children. "He that loveth father or mother more than me, is not worthy of me; and he that loveth son or daughter more than me, is not worthy of me." Matt. x., 37. The beneficial results connected with the exercise of this principle are such as might be expected from the pre-eminent rank it sustains. When it is in its full exercise, rendered to its appropriate object, in the language of Scripture, with all the heart, and mind, and soul, it may be regarded as a matter of course, that all the subordinate principles will be kept in their place. The appetites, the propensities, and the domestic affections still exist; but such is the ascendency of love to the Supreme Being, that every inordinate tendency is rebuked, and they all revolve in the circle which God in the beginning assigned to them.

§ 380. The absence of this principle attended with an excessive and sinful action of other principles.

Now take for a moment the opposite view, and let us see if we may not account for what has sometimes been called the Depravity of human nature, without the necessity of supposing the implantation of principles which, in themselves necessarily, and under all circumstances, are evil. If the principle of Supreme love to God be removed from the place which both Scripture and reason agree in assigning to it in the original constitution of the mind, one of the most important checks on the undue exercise of the subordinate principles is of course taken away. The love which is drawn from the great source of all good will naturally centre in ourselves, and the principles which have relation to our present enjoyment and interest will become predominant. Hence we see the disorders which all impartial inquirers, even heathen philosophers, acknowledge to exist in the human race; and which it is the aim of enlightened reason and philosophy, and particularly of religion in its instructions and its special influences, to rectify. The Appetites, which before had their appropriate place and offices, have now broken over their allotted limits, and are, on every hand, leading their victims into the various forms of excess and debauchery. The Propensities, many of which connect us closely with our fellow-beings, and in their proper exercise impart no small degree of strength and enjoyment to human character, have become inordinately intense in their action. Conscience, it is true, continues to repeat its remonstrances; and the Will, under the suggestions of Conscience, makes more or less of resistance; but as they are not sustained by the love of the Supreme Being, which could not fail, if it existed, to operate in their favour, the contest becomes unequal, and the efforts which they make are found to be unavailing. In this state of things, men who, under other circumstances, would have leaned, and loved to lean, on the great arm of the Almighty for support, now find their chief enjoyment in the pursuit of wealth and power, and in the unrestricted intercourse and the uncertain enjoyments of the world.—It is in such a condition of things as this that we find the true source of the follies and crimes which afflict the human race. The dethronement of God in the heart necessarily involves the predominance of principles which, however innocent and useful in their just exercise, become in their excess evil, and "only evil continually."

§ 381. Further illustrations of the results of the absence of this principle.

The topic of the last section is one of no small importance. The section, it will be noticed, consists chiefly of a statement of facts, without any attempt at explanations. As some persons may not at first readily perceive how it happens that the suspension or obliteration of the principle of love to God is necessarily or naturally attended with the evil results there ascribed to it, we will delay upon the subject a little longer. It is sometimes the case, that a mere additional illustration, placing the subject in a new light, will have the effect upon the mind of the inquirer of an argument or proof. If the suspension or obliteration of any other principle will be followed by results analogous to those which have been described as accessory to the extinction of love to God, we shall clearly have, in this circumstance, an evidence that the results in the last case have been correctly indicated. And, on the other hand, if the extinction or utter inaction of subordinate principles be not attended with irregularity and perversion in other parts of the mind, it will furnish a strong presumption that the extinction or utter inaction of the higher principles will, in its collateral results, be equally harmless. By the aid of these statements we may easily bring the subject, in a considerable degree, to the test of common observation. And what is the fact?

We will make the supposition, that, in the case of some individual, the domestic affections have for some reason become permanently extinct, either in their nature or in their action. Such instances, though not by any means frequently, may yet sometimes be found. The person in whom this obliteration or utter inaction of the domestic affections takes place, has no attachment for his children or any of his family such as he used to have. It is a matter of common observation and remark, that a person in such a situation will be much more likely than another to fall under the dominion of the lower appetites; to addict himself, for instance, to licentious practices, or to become a drunkard. While the domestic affections existed, while he looked with deep interest on his parents, his children, and his wife, he was furnished with powerful auxiliary motives to restrain his appetites. He saw distinctly, if he indulged them, they would not only interfere with his duties to his family, but would plunge them into deep disgrace and sorrow. So great influence had this view of his situation upon his mind, that he was enabled to sustain himself in opposition to the approaches of the evil habits which threatened him. But as soon as the domestic affections became extinct, as soon as the love of kindred was blasted in his bosom, he fell before them.

Again, if we suppose, in addition to the extinction of the domestic affections, the further obliteration of love to his country and of love to the human race, (and still more if we add the extinction of the principles of pity and gratitude,) the probability of his falling under the dominion of the bodily appetites, and of degrading himself to the condition of a brute, will be obviously increased by this state of things. With the removal of these leading principles of human action, there is, of course, a removal of an important class of motives which had a favourable tendency. And if it were possible for him to stand against the solicitations of the appetites before, he will be likely to fall now. The Will, whose office it is, under the direction of the Conscience, to regulate and restrain the appetites, received important assistance from the sources which have been alluded to; but with the removal of that assistance its power is proportionally diminished, and all hope is gone. The cravings of nature must have food of some kind; and if it fails to be furnished with the ennobling aliment which is generated in the love of our families, our country, and mankind, it will inevitably fatten itself on the mire of a debasing sensuality.—This is the common sense view of the subject; one which will be likely to commend itself to the sober judgment and acceptance of all.

It is clear that these illustrations will apply in their full strength to the principle of love to God. Just so long as this principle is predominant, it is impossible, as has been before stated, for the inferior principles to become excessive and morally evil in their action. We feel, under the influence of this exalting affection, that we cannot so much dishonour our Maker; we cannot estimate so lightly those claims of gratitude which He has upon us; we cannot so basely contemn our infinite obligations to his wisdom and benevolence, as to indulge for a moment any exercise of the passions which he has forbidden. They stand rebuked and withering in the presence of the object that has the dominion in our hearts. But only obliterate the principle of Love to God; and at once a thousand motives, which enabled us to keep them in their proper place, are lost in the extinction of the principle on which they rested; and other principles, infinitely below it, at once gain the ascendency.

CHAPTER VIII.

HABITS OF THE SENSIBILITIES.

§ 382. Meaning of the term habit.

We propose to bring the subject of this department of the Sensibilities to a conclusion by some slight references to the results of the law of Habit, considered in connexion with this portion of our nature. As we have already had occasion to make some remarks upon the general nature of Habit, and have seen in repeated instances its bearing upon mental action, it will not be necessary to spend much time upon that subject here. The term Habit, in its application to the various mental powers, expresses the simple fact, *that the mental action acquires facility and strength by repetition or practice.*

§ 383. Of habits in connexion with the appetites.

In considering the results of Habit, in connexion with that portion of the Natural or Pathematic Sensibilities which involves desire, viz., the Instincts, Appetites, Propensities, and Affections, we shall adhere to the arrangement which has hitherto been followed, with the exception of the Instincts, to which the law of Habit does not apply.—We proceed to remark, therefore, that there may be appetitive habits; in other words, that the Appetites, the class of sensitive principles next in order to the Instincts, acquire strength from repeated indulgence. The appetites in their first or original operation act instinctively; but it is incidental to their nature, as it is to all the modifications of Desire, that their gratification is attended with more or less of pleasure. In connexion with this experience of pleasure, we frequently stimulate them to action a second time, under circumstances when there would be but little, and perhaps no occasion, for a purely instinctive exercise. But the desire, as it is thus, by a voluntary effort, or, at least, by a voluntary permission, indulged again and again, rapidly becomes more and more intense till at last it is found to acquire a complete ascendency That such is the process appears to be proved by what unfortunately we have so frequent occasion to notice in those who are in the practice of taking intoxicating drinks. If they had indulged their appetite only a few times, they would undoubtedly have retained their mastery over it. But as this indulgence has been repeated often, and continued for a considerable length of time, the appetite growing stronger with each repetition, has gradually acquired the predominance, till it has brought the whole man, as it were, into captivity.—(See § 49.)

§ 390. *Of habits in connexion with the propensities.*

The Propensities, as well as the Appetites, are subject to the influence of this law; in other words, there may be propensive as well as appetitive habits. The principle of Sociality, for instance, has an instinctive action; but there is no question that we have the power, as it is undoubtedly our duty, to subject it to suitable regulation. But if, instead of doing this, we indulge it continually for the mere sake of the pleasure we experience, without regard to the other claims existing upon us, we shall find it rapidly acquiring undue strength, and every day will render it more difficult to regulate it properly. And, in point of fact, it is sometimes the case, that we find persons who, in consequence of an unrestricted indulgence of a principle otherwise naturally good, have brought themselves into such a situation, that retirement, which every reasonable man ought sometimes to desire, is always exceedingly irksome to them.

Perhaps not one of the Propensities can be named which may not be greatly strengthened in the same way. It is well known in what countless instances the desire of Possession, growing stronger by continued repetition, becomes an ascendant and controlling principle. We are not to suppose that the intense love which the miser has for his possessions, existed in him naturally and originally. We do, indeed, admit that the seed or element of it, the basis on which it rests, existed in him naturally, as it exists in all men. But how does it happen that it shows itself in this exaggerated and intense form? This is the work of the man himself, and for which the man himself is accountable, rather than the original tendencies of his nature. From morning till night, from day to day, and from year to year, the Possessory principle has been voluntarily kept in intense exercise. And the natural and necessary result has been, that it has become the ruling sentiment of the heart.

So of the desire of Power. In itself considered, power may properly be regarded as one of the various forms of natural good. And accordingly we are at liberty to take the ground, as was formerly seen in the remarks on that subject, that the desire of power, if duly subordinated, is not reprehensible. But in a multitude of instances, this desire is far from showing itself in the aspect of a subordinate principle. And the reason is, that it has acquired inordinate strength by repetition; a habit of mind has been formed, which has resulted in its becoming predominant. The individual, in whom it exists in this intense form, is not satisfied with anything short of the prostration of every other person at his own feet. It would hardly be going too far to say, that he looks upon the Supreme Being, when he contemplates his greatness and elevation, in the light of a rival and an enemy.

§ 385. Of habits in connexion with the affections.

Remarks similar to what have been made in respect to the lower active or motive principles, will apply, in like manner, to the higher class of the Affections. We sometimes see, for instance, decided indications of the result of Habit in the progress of the Malevolent Affections. A man entertains a degree of dislike to his neighbour; it appears perhaps at first in the form of a mere unpleasant suspicion; these suspicious and unpleasant feelings are frequently indulged; we see them gradually growing deeper and deeper, assuming under the influence of Habit a more fixed and determinate form, and ultimately appearing in the shape of malignant and permanent hatred.

The law of Habit applies, in the same manner, to the Benevolent affections. The parental affection is strong and decided in the very beginning of its existence. But the dependent situation of the beloved object on which it fastens, keeps it almost constantly in exercise. And thus, unless there are some improprieties in the conduct of the child, which check and diminish the results naturally following under such circumstances, it rapidly acquires immense strength. And hence it may be explained in part, that when a son or daughter, in the maturity of youth or on the verge of womanhood, is taken away by death, the grief of the parent, always great at such times, is more intense and excessive than when death takes place in infancy. The death of the child at the later period of life not only blasts a greater number of hopes, but as love, by a long-repeated, cumulative process, has been added and incorporated with love, it carries away, if one may be allowed the expression, a greater portion of the heart.

We may unquestionably apply these views to all those affections which are properly characterized as Benevolent, to Friendship, Patriotism, Gratitude, and Sympathy. He who is so situated that he is required to think much on the interests and good of his country, and whose love of country is in this way kept constantly in exercise, will be found, other things being equal, to exhibit in the day of trial a more intense ardour of patriotism than others. He who, by his untiring attentions to the poor, the sick, and the prisoner, has kept his sympathetic affections in action for a long series of years, will find the principle of sympathy more thoroughly consubstantial in his nature and more intensely operative, than if it had lain dormant. And we may add, that this doctrine, in all its extent, is applicable to the highest of all the Benevolent affections, that of love to God. This ennobling principle, this pre-eminent trait, which allies us not only to just men made perfect, but to angels, is an improvable one. Under the influence of Habit, we find it, even in the present life, going on from one degree of brightness and strength to another. The more we think of God, the more frequently we connect him with all our ordinary transactions, the more will the broad orb of his glory expand itself to our conceptions, and call forth the homage and love of the heart

§ 386. Of the origin of secondary active principles.

It is here, in connexion with the views of this Chapter, that we find an explanation of the origin of what are called SECONDARY principles of action. Some individuals, for instance, are seen to possess a decided passion for dress, furniture, and equipage. We are not to suppose that this passion is one which is originally implanted in the human mind, although it may be so permanent and so decided in its action as to have something of that appearance The probability is, setting aside whatever may be truly interesting or beautiful in the objects, that they are chiefly sought after, not so much for what they are in themselves, as for some form of good, particularly some esteem and honour, to which they are supposed to be introductory and auxiliary But the desire, existing in the first instance in reference to some supposed beneficial end, has been so long exercised, that we at last, in virtue of what may properly be called a Habit, so closely associate the means and the end, that it is exceedingly difficult to separate them. So that, after a time, we apparently have a real love or affection for the means itself, (the dress, furniture, equipage, or whatever it is,) independently, in a great degree, of the ultimate object, in connexion with which it first excited an interest in us.

There are some men, to illustrate the subject still further, who appear to have a strong love for money; we do not mean property in the more general sense of the term, but MONEY, the gold and the silver coin in itself considered, the mere naked issue of the mint. This is one of the various forms which the too common vice of Avarice sometimes assumes. But we cannot suppose that the love of money, in this sense of the terms, is a passion connatural to the human mind, and that men are born with it. It is loved, in the first instance, simply as a means, subordinate to some supposed beneficial end. The person has looked upon it for years as the means of enjoyment, influence, and honour; in this way he has formed a Habit of associating the means and the end; and they have become so closely connected in his thoughts, that, in ordinary cases, he finds himself unable to separate them.

Again, we are not to suppose that men are born with

a natural desire for the society of mice and spiders, such as we have reason to think they naturally entertain for that of their fellow-men. But in the entire exclusion of all human beings, we find the principle of sociality, deprived of its legitimate and customary sources of gratification, fastening itself upon these humble companions A man, as in the case of Baron Trenck and Count Lauzun, may form an acquaintance with these animals, which, aided by the principle of Habit, will, after a time, exhibit a distinctness and intensity, which are commonly characteristic only of the original passions.—In this way there may unquestionably be formed a series of SECONDARY appetites, propensities, and affections, almost without number. And we have here opened to us a new and interesting view of human nature, capable of being so applied as to explain many things in the history and conduct of men, which, however, we are not at liberty in this connexion to explore more minutely.

THE SENSIBILITIES.

PART SECOND.

THE MORAL SENSIBILITIES OR CONSCIENCE.

MORAL OR CONSCIENTIOUS STATES OF THE MIND.

MORAL SENTIMENTS.

CHAPTER I.

EMOTIONS OF MORAL APPROVAL AND DISAPPROVAL.

§ 387. Reference to the general division.

In entering upon the examination of the interesting and important department of the mental nature, which now presents itself to our notice, it is proper to revert a moment to that general division of the mind which we have endeavoured throughout to adhere to as the basis of our inquiries. The general classification, it will be recollected, was into the Intellect, the Sensibilities, and the Will. In passing from the purely intellectual region to that of the Sensibilities, we first find ourselves in the subordinate department of the Emotions. And, leaving the emotions, we may advance onward, and come in contact with the still more interior and remote department of the Will, either by passing through the region of the Desires on the one hand, or through the space occupied, if we may be allowed to use such expressions in connexion with the mind, by the feelings of Moral Obligation on the other. In accordance with this plan, we made it our first object to examine some of the leading emotions which come under the head of the Natural or Pathematic Sensibilities. And then, taking the direction of the Desires, endeavoured, in a variety of remarks on the Instincts, Appetites, Propensities, and Affections, to explain what may properly be included under that head.

Having completed, in such manner as we are able, that part of the subject, we propose to return again to the region of the Emotions, a part of which are included under the general head of the Moral Sensibilities, and to approach the Will in the opposite direction. In carrying this plan into effect, and in giving a philosophical account of the Moral in distinction from the Natural or Pathematic Sensibilities, we shall not delay to consider the general question, whether man has a moral nature or not. We take it for granted that he has. The well-known passage of the Apostle, not to mention other considerations, seems to be decisive on this point. "*For when the Gentiles, which have not the law, do by nature the things contained in the law, these, having not the law, are a law unto themselves; which show the work of the law written in their hearts, their Conscience also bearing witness, and their thoughts the mean while accusing, or else excusing one another.*"

§ 388. Classification of the moral sensibilities.

The Moral nature is less complicated than the Pathematic, although the general division of the Moral Sensibilities corresponds precisely to the general division of the Natural or Pathematic Sensibilities. As the Natural Sensibilities resolved themselves, in the first instance, into the subordinate classification of the Emotions and Desires, so the Moral Sensibilities, in a manner precisely corresponding, resolve themselves into the subordinate classification of moral Emotions and feelings of Moral Obligation. But both divisions of the Natural Sensibilities, it will be recollected, viz., the Emotive and the Desirous, were found to be susceptible of numerous minor divisions. It is not so in the moral department. The class of moral emotions, and the obligatory feeling or feelings of moral obligation, which are based upon them, will be found, exclusive of any subordinate divisions, to comprehend the whole subject.

It might be supposed, therefore, that this subject would be despatched in a few words. And so it would, if the discussion could properly be limited to the mere examination of these feelings. But the moral sentiments, both the emotive and the obligatory, sustain such important relations, and involve so many important consequences, that it seems to be proper, not only to examine them in their own nature, but also to consider them, to some extent, in their multiplied connexions.

§ 389. Nature of the moral emotions of approval and disapproval.

In accordance with what has been said in the foregoing section, we repeat that there are but two classes of mental states which belong, in strictness of speech, to the

Moral sensibilities, considered as being by nature an essential portion of the human mind; although it is very true that there are a number of things in the mind, such as the abstract conceptions of right and wrong, and the feelings of remorse, which have, both theoretically and practically, an important connexion with morals. The Moral Nature, properly so called, putting out of view the incidental relations it sustains, exists and developes itself, FIRST, in the moral Emotions, viz., of approval and disapproval; and, SECOND, in the feelings of moral Obligation.

While there are many kinds of the Natural or Pathematic emotions, such as the emotions of beauty, of sublimity, of the ludicrous, of cheerfulness, of surprise, of reverence, of shame, and the like, there is but one kind or class of Moral emotions. And these are known, considered as distinct states of mind, by the names by which they have just been described, viz., as feelings of APPROVAL and DISAPPROVAL. Of these states of mind we now proceed to give some account.—And our first remark is, that they are original feelings; which implies that, in the appropriate circumstances of their existence, they are called forth by the original or constitutional tendencies of the mind, and also that they are elementary or simple. Of course they are not susceptible of definition, since defining, except that sort of apparent defining which consists in the mere use of synonymous terms, is predicable only of what is complex. Hence, in their distinctive or appropriate nature, in that which constitutes them what they are, considered as separate from anything and everything else, they cannot be known by description, but by consciousness only. Nevertheless, we are not at liberty to suppose that their nature is either absolutely unknown, or, as a general thing, even misunderstood; inasmuch as the consciousness of such feelings is universal, and as no form of knowledge, it is generally admitted, is more distinct to our apprehension than that which has consciousness for its basis. Whoever, therefore, has had placed before him any case of right and wrong of such a nature that he could have, and did in fact have, a clear apprehension of it, in itself and in its relations, must, we suppose, have a knowledge (and if he has not, it is impossible he ever should have) of emotions of approval and disapproval.

§ 390. Of the place or position, mentally considered, of the emotions of approval or disapproval.

Moral emotions, or emotions of moral approval and disapproval, occupy a place, considered in reference to other departments of the mind, immediately successive to intellections or acts of the intellect.—In this respect they agree with the natural or pathematic emotions, which occupy the same position. It is, for instance, impossible for us to feel the beauty of an object, which is an act of the Natural sensibilities, without first having a perception or knowledge of the object itself. In like manner, it is impossible for us to approve or disapprove a thing, in the moral sense of the terms, without first having some perception, some knowledge of the thing approved or disapproved.

And as the natural emotions are immediately followed by Desires; so the moral emotions, viz., of approval and disapproval, (for these are all the states of mind that are properly comprehended under that phrase,) are followed, in like manner, by Obligatory feelings, or feelings of moral obligation. The position, therefore, of moral emotions, and they are found nowhere else, is between perceptions or intellective acts on the one hand, and Obligatory sentiments on the other. And as there can be no moral emotions without antecedent perceptions, so there can be no feelings of moral obligation without antecedent emotions of approval and disapproval. Accordingly, if we are said, in any given case, to be under obligation, either to do a thing or to abstain from doing it, we may always find a reason for our thus being under obligation in the antecedent action of the mind, viz., in our approval or disapproval, as the case may be, of the thing to which the obligation relates.

§ 391. Changes in the moral emotions take place in accordance with changes in the antecedent perceptions.

If the emotions of approval and disapproval, which are the basis of the subsequent feelings of moral obligation, are naturally founded upon antecedent perceptions, we may expect, and such is the fact, that they will change in their character in accordance with changes in those perceptions. If, for instance, a statement of facts is made to us, clearly establishing in our view a case of great crime, our emotions of disapproval are prompt and decided. But if it should happen that afterward some new facts are mingled in the statement, throwing a degree of doubt and perplexity upon what was believed to have taken place, the feelings of disapproval would at once become perplexed and undecided, in a degree precisely corresponding to the perplexity and indecision that, under the new circumstances, pervade the intellectual perception in the case. If still subsequently the introduction of other new facts should show that what was supposed to be a crime was directly the reverse, our moral emotions would undergo a new change, and, instead of condemning the transaction either more or less decidedly, would approve.

Nor is this changeableness in the character and the degree of the moral emotions to be regarded as implying any defect in the moral nature. On the contrary, it is unquestionably one of the most decisive indications of its value. If the moral nature were so constituted as not only to pronounce a thing right or wrong under certain given circumstances, but necessarily to adhere to that decision under essential changes in the circumstances, it certainly could not be regarded as a safe rule for men's guidance. A man kills another by means of the infliction of a heavy blow, and, as we suppose, with evil intention or malice prepense, and the action is at once disapproved and condemned by conscience. But it subsequently appears that the blow, which had the appearance at first of being intentional, was entirely a matter of accident; and the conscience or moral nature immediately conforms its decision to the new aspect of the transaction, and annuls the disapproving and condemnatory sentence which it had before pronounced. If it were otherwise, if it did not promptly and fully conform itself, by changes in its own action, to antecedent changes in the percipient or cognitive action, it would confound vice and virtue, guilt and innocence; and, as a rule of moral conduct, would not only be without value, but absolutely and exceedingly injurious.

§ 392. Of objects of moral approval and disapproval.

We are not to suppose that the sphere of that moral adjudication, which is involved in the existence of emotions of moral approval and disapproval, extends to all objects indiscriminately. It is a proper inquiry, therefore, and in some respects an important inquiry, what are the appropriate objects of approving and disapproving emotions.—In answer to this question, we remark in the first place that such objects are voluntary agents. The feelings in question, in their announcements of the right and the wrong of any case that comes before them, have nothing to do with things without life. And more than this, they require, as the objects of their exercise, something more than mere vegetable and animal life, viz., intellective, sensitive, and volitive life. In other words, they require, in the appropriate objects of their adjudication those attributes of perceiving, feeling, and willing, which are necessarily implied in voluntary agency.

(II.) In the second place, the legitimate objects of approval and disapproval are not only voluntary agents, but MORAL agents. No being is the object of moral emotions, (that is to say, no being can by possibility be approved or disapproved in the moral sense of the terms,) except such as have a conscience or moral nature. It is impossible that any others should have a knowledge of right and wrong; and, of course, impossible that they should conform themselves to the rule of right. Hence no one regards brute animals as the proper objects of these emotions.

(III.) Again, moral agents (this expression, of course, implies that they are also voluntary agents) are morally accountable; in other words, are the proper objects of moral approval and disapproval, in respect to those things only which are truly in their power. This remark, which limits the sphere of moral approval and disapproval not only to moral agents, but to what is actually in the *power* of moral agents, is practically an important one. So far as we can regulate our outward actions, we are accountable; that is to say, we are the proper objects of the emotions of moral approval and disapproval. So far as we can regulate the action of the intellect, the sensibilities, and the will, we are accountable also. So far as the action, whether physical or mental, is either involuntary or instinctive, it is not an appropriate object of the notice and adjudication of conscience; for all such action, although it belongs to, and is not separable from, the agent, is nevertheless not under his control.—Accordingly, when the moral agent, in the exercise of all his various powers, does what he ought to do, he stands approved. When, in the exercise of the same powers, he fails to do what he ought to do, he stands condemned. The extent of his capability is the basis of his duty; and the law of conscience is the measure of its fulfilment. And this simple statement intimates both the rule by which he is judged, and the vast amount of his responsibility.

CHAPTER II.

RELATION OF REASONING TO THE MORAL NATURE.

§ 393. Of the doctrine which confounds reasoning and conscience.

We are now prepared, in view of what has been said in the last Chapter, particularly in connexion with the subject of the grounds or principles on which changes take place in moral emotions, to proceed to another subject not more interesting than it is practically important. —The opinion has sometimes been advanced, that those moral decisions or judgments, which, as moral beings, we are capable of forming, are the direct results of REASONING. The advocates of this doctrine, rejecting the idea of a distinct moral principle or conscience, appear to regard the reasoning power as entirely adequate to the causation of all those results in the mind which have a moral aspect. In a word, they may be regarded either as denying entirely the existence of conscience, or, what is philosophically, if not practically, the same thing, as identifying it with mere ratiocination.

It is not surprising, on the whole, that this mistake,

which is certainly a very serious and prejudicial one, should have been committed, when we consider how close the relation is which reason sustains to conscience. It will be noticed that we speak without any hesitation of the doctrine referred to as a mistaken one. We do not suppose it to be necessary, after what has already been said, to attempt to show that reasoning and conscience are not identical, and that the moral nature has a distinct and substantive existence. Nevertheless, we freely admit the intimate and important relation which they sustain to each other. A relation so important, in a practical as well as in a philosophical point of view, that we shall delay here for the purpose of entering into some explanations of it.

§ 394. Of the close connexion between conscience and reasoning.

Reasoning, it will be recollected, is purely an intellectual process; consisting of successive propositions arranged together, and a succession of relative suggestions or perceptions, but, in itself considered, involving nothing which is properly called an emotion or desire. This single circumstance separates the reasoning power entirely from the moral nature; which, in its appropriate action, never originates, like the reasoning power, perceptions or new intellectual views, but merely moral emotions and feelings of moral obligation. Probably every one can say with confidence that he is conscious of a difference in the moral emotions of approval and disapproval, and the mere intellectual perceptions of agreement and disagreement, which are characteristic of reasoning. In the view of consciousness, there can be no doubt that they are regarded as entirely diverse in their nature, and as utterly incapable of being interchanged or identified with each other. The moral feeling is one thing; and the intellectual perception or suggestion, involved both in the process and the result of reasoning, is another.

Although the reasoning power and the conscience or moral being are thus distinct from each other in their nature, they are closely connected in their relations, as has been intimated already, inasmuch as the intellect, particularly the ratiocinative or deductive part of it, is the foundation or basis of moral action. We must first know a thing; it must first be an object of perception before we can take any moral cognizance of it. And this is not all. The moral cognizance, as we have already had occasion to explain, will conform itself with great precision to the intellectual cognizance. That is to say, it will take new ground in its decisions, in conformity with new facts perceived Consequently, we cannot rely perfectly on a moral decision which is founded upon a premature or imperfect knowledge. The more carefully and judiciously we reason upon a subject, the more thoroughly we understand it in itself and its relations, the more confidently may we receive the estimate which the voice of conscience makes of its moral character.

§ 395. Illustration of the preceding section.

The views of the preceding section may be easily illustrated. When, for instance, one man is alleged to have stolen the property of another, we find the conscience, as a general thing, ready to discharge the duty which the Author of our nature has assigned to it; but it is sometimes the case, that its decisions are arrested and postponed, in order to give time for the inquiries and conclusions of the reasoning power. Such inquiries inform us, perhaps, that the theft was long and coolly premeditated; and was committed, not only without any special temptation to it, but with a full knowledge of the aggravation of the crime. In view of this state of things, conscience immediately passes its decision. Perhaps our inquiries inform us, that the theft was committed at a time of extreme want and consequent great temptation; and, furthermore, was committed upon a species of property, in respect to which the right of individual possession is regarded by common consent as less strict and exclusive than in other cases. The conscience here, as in the former instance, condemns the criminal, but probably with a mitigated sentence. On further inquiry we learn, that although the property was taken, and that, too, much to the damage of the owner, it was taken wholly by mistake; it was a thing entirely accidental. In this case conscience, adapting itself to the newly-discovered circumstances, pronounces the supposed thief altogether guiltless.

The conscience, therefore, however distinct the two may be in themselves, is aided and supported by the various powers of perception and comparison, particularly by the reason. The reasoning power, however high the rank which we justly ascribe to it, sustains, in this case at least, a subordinate position; and is to be regarded as the servitor and handmaid of the moral power. And, moreover, the latter will vary in exact accordance, if there are no collateral disturbing influences, with the new facts and the new relations, which are from time to time presented by the former.—It is in consequence of this close connexion, and the important assistance rendered to conscience by reason, that they have sometimes been confounded together. But it is very essential to right views of the mind that this erroneous notion should be corrected, and that the precise relation, existing between these two distinct parts of our mental nature, should be fully understood.

§ 396. Of the training or education of the conscience.

We infer, from what has been said in this chapter, that there is such a thing, philosophically considered, as a training or education of the conscience. We propose to remark more fully on the subject of moral education in another place; but we may properly refer to it a moment here, in connexion with the views which have now been taken. No man is at liberty to say, in regard to any given case, that I am willing to refer this case to conscience, and to abide by the decisions of conscience, without first taking the pains to lay the case fully and fairly before the power that is to sit in judgment upon it We might as well expect the judge in a court of civil justice to give an upright decision without facts, without evidence, and without law, as to expect a correct decision from the spiritual judge, that exercises authority in the judgment-seat of the Sensibilities, without a full and fair presentment of the facts by the Intellect. And when we say it is necessary to make a full statement of the facts, we may add further, that they are to be stated not only in themselves, but also in their relations and bearings upon each other.—This is one form of moral training or moral education. In other words, in order to have a right conscience in respect to the vast multitude of things, which are the proper subjects of moral adjudication, it is necessary to extend the field of our knowledge; to know much, to think much, to compare much.

§ 397. Of guilt, when a person acts conscientiously.

The question has sometimes been started, Whether a person is in any case to be considered as guilty, and to be punished for actions done *conscientiously;* for instance, when certain ignorant Savages are supposed to act conscientiously in leaving their aged and infirm parents to perish. In view of what has been said in this Chapter, we seem to be prepared to answer this question in the affirmative.

We have seen that the moral nature, in consequence of its intimate connexion with the powers of perception and reasoning, is in some measure under our own control. On the one hand, it may be enlightened and guided; on the other, darkened and led astray, and in some cases be made to approve of actions of the most unworthy and sinful kind. Men, therefore, are to have a right conscience; this great and exalting principle is to receive, and ought to receive, the very first attention; and they are accountable whenever it is neglected. Otherwise we furnish a very easy and convenient excuse for all the cruelties of the Inquisition, for all the persecutions of the Protestants by the Catholics, for all the persecutions of the Protestants by each other, for all the acts of unkindness and tyranny which have ever been exercised upon individuals and communities.

And the position, that men are accountable and guilty for having a wrong conscience in proportion to their means of knowledge and their ability of rectifying the conscience, holds good in respect to the most ignorant and degraded Savage tribes, as well as in respect to civilized nations. It is true, no individual ought to assume the province of judging in all cases what that degree of guilt is; for no one is competent to it. All that is meant to be asserted is, that when persons feel an emotion of approval in doing wrong, (that is, in doing what is condemned by the general moral sentiments of mankind, and by the will and law of God,) and yet have within their reach neglected sources of knowledge, which, on being laid open to the mind, would have caused different feelings, they are criminal for such neglect of the information before them, and consequently cannot, under such circumstances, be rendered otherwise than criminal by any internal approbation.

CHAPTER III.

FEELINGS OF MORAL OBLIGATION.

§ 398. Feelings of moral obligation distinct from feelings of moral approval and disapproval.

It has been remarked in a former chapter, that the Moral Sensibilities, or Conscience, will be found, on an examination of its elements, to resolve itself into two classes of feelings, viz., Moral Emotions, and Obligatory feelings or feelings of Moral Obligation. Having given some account of Moral Emotions, viz., the feelings of moral approval and disapproval, which are all the states of mind that properly come under that head, we are now prepared to proceed to the consideration of the second class, viz., Obligatory feelings.

It is proper to remark here, that this class of mental states, considered as a separate and distinct class, has received but little notice in philosophical systems; having generally been confounded, under the familiar designations of conscience and the moral sense, with the moral emotions which have already been considered. On this account, therefore, and also for the reason that they have an important connexion with the actual operations and with the philosophy of the Will, it will be necessary to examine them with some degree of care.

§ 399. Proof of the existence of obligatory feelings from consciousness.

Our first inquiry relates to the actual and distinct existence of the states of mind which now come under consideration. The existence of feelings of this description is evinced, in the first place, by our own CONSCIOUSNESS. We might safely appeal to the internal conviction and the recollections of any man whatever, and ask whether there have not been periods in the course of his life in which he has experienced a new and authoritative state of mind; a peculiar, but undefinable species of mental enforcement, which required him to perform some particular act, and to avoid doing some other act, even when his interests and his desires seemed to be averse to the requisitions thus made upon him? And if so, we have here an instance of moral obligation, a feeling or sentiment of duty, the precise thing which is meant when we say we *ought* to do or *ought not* to do.

Take a common and simple illustration. A person, in passing along the streets, saw an old man sitting by the wayside who bore about him the most convincing marks of want, wretchedness, and sincerity in his applications for relief; he gave him bread, clothing, and money, conscious that it was done, not in view of any personal interest or gratification, or of any selfish object whatever, but under the impulse and guidance of a peculiar enforcement within, such as we commonly have when we speak of doing our duty; and if so, he then and there had a distinct knowledge of the moral sentiment or feeling under consideration. And this knowledge was from Consciousness.

§ 400. Further proof from the conduct of men.

The existence of feelings of obligation is further shown by the general conduct of men.—It cannot be denied that other motives, distinct from convictions of duty, often operate upon them. Their desires, hopes, fears, sympathies, their present and future interests, all have an effect. But it would certainly argue an evil opinion of human nature altogether unwarranted, to maintain that they are never governed by motives of a more exalted kind. In a multitude of cases they are found to perform what is incumbent upon them in opposition to their fears, in opposition to their sympathies, and their apparent interests. Different persons will undoubtedly estimate the amount of interested and selfish motives as greater or less, according as a greater or less portion of the good or evil of human nature has come within their own cognizance; but it is impossible, after a cautious and candid review of the principles of human action, to exclude entirely the elements of uprightness and honour. If there is any truth in history, there have always been found, even in the most corrupt periods of society, upright and honourable men. And if we are at liberty to infer men's character from their actions, as assuredly we are, we may assert with confidence that there are such at the present time. But a man of true uprightness and honour is one who acts from the sentiment of duty, the feeling of moral obligation, in distinction from motives of an inferior kind.

§ 401. Further proof from language and literature.

The existence of obligatory feelings is further proved, not only by each one's consciousness, and by the conduct of men generally, but by language and literature. In most languages, and probably in all, there are terms expressive of obligation or a sentiment of duty. No account could be given of the progress of society, and of the situation and conduct of individuals, without making use of such terms. If the words rectitude, crime, uprightness, virtue, merit, vice, demerit, right, wrong, ought, obligation, duty, and others of like import, were struck out from the English tongue, (and the same might be said of other languages,) it would at once be found unequal to the expression of the phenomena which are constantly occurring in the affairs of men. Now, as these terms occur, it is rational to suppose that they intimate something, that they have a meaning, that they express a reality. But it does not appear how this can be said of them, unless we admit the actual existence of obligatory feelings.

Turning our attention from single words and phrases, if we enter into an examination of the literature of a language, we shall come to the same result.—A great portion of every nation's literature is employed in giving expression and emphasis to moral principles and sentiments. They find a conspicuous place in the most valuable speculations, not of professed moralists merely, but of historians, poets, orators, and legislators. But their frequent introduction would seem to be altogether misplaced, unsuitable, and unmeaning, if there were no real and permanent distinction between virtue and vice, between the sacred requisitions of duty and those of mere personal interest.

§ 402. Further proof from the necessity of these feelings.

And in connexion with the observations which have been brought forward, we may further ask, What would men be, or what would society be, without the basis of moral obligation? There must be somewhere a foundation of duty. It does not appear how the bond which unites neighbourhoods and states can be maintained, with any requisite degree of permanency and strength, without something of this kind. Annihilate this part of our constitution, and would not civil society be dissolved? Would not violence, and wrath, and utter confusion immediately succeed? The natural desire of society, the sympathies, and the selfish interests of our nature might do something by way of diminishing these evil results, but could not wholly prevent them. With the dislocation of the great controlling principles which regulate the action of the moral world, there would soon be an utter confusion in the movements of society, and all the unspeakable evils attendant on such a state of things.

§ 403. Feelings of obligation simple and not susceptible of definition.

In view of what has been said, we assert with confidence that feelings of moral obligation, or obligatory feelings, in distinction from the antecedent acts of the Moral Sensibility, which consist in mere approval and disapproval, actually have an existence. In looking into their nature, in distinction from the mere fact of their existence, although we do not flatter ourselves with being able, by a mere verbal statement, to give a satisfactory notion of them, we would direct the attention to some characteristic marks. And the first observation to be made is, that these states of mind are simple. We cannot resolve them into parts, as we can any complex state of mind. And, as a necessary consequence of this, they are not susceptible of definition. Still we cannot admit that this simplicity, and the consequent inability to define them, renders men ignorant of their nature. It is true that the man who has never experienced the sentiment of obligation in his own bosom, can have no better means of knowing it from the descriptions of others than the blind man can have for understanding the nature of the colours of the rainbow. But such a case is hardly a supposable one; among all the tribes of men, and amid all the varieties of human degradation, it will probably not be found to exist; and we may, therefore, say with confidence, that every man knows what the feeling of obligation is, not less than he knows what the feeling of joy, of sorrow, and of approval is. In other words, men have as ready and clear an idea of it as of any other simple notion or feeling.

§ 404. They are susceptible of different degrees.

In obtaining this knowledge, however, which evidently cannot be secured to us by any mere process of defining, we must consult our consciousness. We are required to turn the mind inward on itself, and to scrutinize the process of interior operation on the various occasions of endurance, trial, and action, which so often intersect the paths of life. The same consciousness which gives us a knowledge of the existence of the feeling and of its general nature, assures us, furthermore, that it exists in various degrees. This fact may be illustrated by remarks formerly made in reference to another state of mind. The word *belief* is the name of a simple mental state; but no one doubts that belief exists in different degrees, which we express by a number of terms, such as presumption probability, high probability, and certainty. In like manner, the feeling of obligation may evidently exist in various degrees, and we often express this variety of degrees by different terms and phrases, such as moral inducement, slight or strong inducement, imperfect obligation, perfect obligation, &c.

§ 405. Of their authoritative and enforcing nature.

It may be remarked further in respect to obligatory

feelings, that they always imply action, something to be done. And again, they never exist except in those cases where not only action, but *effective* action, is possible, or is supposed to be so. We never feel under moral obligation to do anything which we are convinced, at the same time, is beyond our power. It is within these limits the feeling arises; and, while we cannot define it, we are able to intimate, though somewhat imperfectly, another characteristic. What we mean will be understood by a reference to the words enforcement, constraint, or compulsion. Every one is conscious that there is something in the nature of feelings of moral obligation approaching to the character of enforcement or compulsion; yet not by any means in the material sense of those terms. There is no enforcement analogous to that which may be applied to the body, and which may be made irresistible.

The apostle Paul says, "The love of Christ *constraineth* us." What is the meaning of this? Merely that the mercy of Christ, exhibited in the salvation of men, excited such a sentiment of obligation, that they found in themselves a great unwillingness to resist its suggestions, and were determined to go forth proclaiming that mercy, and urging all men to accept it. And it is in reference to this state of things we so frequently assert that we are bound, that we are obliged, or even that we are compelled to pursue a particular course in preference to another course; expressions which, in their original import, intimate the existence of a feeling which is fitted by its very nature strongly to control our volition. But, although these expressions point to this trait of the feeling, they do it but imperfectly and indistinctly, and consciousness alone can give a full understanding of it.

§ 406. Feelings of obligation differ from those of mere approval and disapproval.

It is possible that the question may be started why we do not class these feelings with Emotions, particularly those of a moral kind. And recognising the propriety of avoiding an increase of classes where it is not obviously called for, we shall endeavour to say something, in addition to what has already been intimated, in answer to this question.—We have not classed the mental states under examination with Emotions, in the first place, because they do not appear to be of that transitory nature which seems to be characteristic of all emotions. Ordinarily they do not dart into the soul with the same rapidity, shining up, and then disappearing, like the sudden lightning in the clouds; but, taking their position more slowly and gradually, they remain, like the sun, bright and permanent. In the course of an hour a person may experience hundreds, and even thousands, of emotions of joy or grief, of beauty or sublimity, and various other kinds. They come and go, return and depart again, in constant succession and with very frequent changes; but it probably will not be pretended that the feelings of duty, which are destined to govern man's conduct, and which constitute his most important principles of action, are of such a rapid, variant, and evanescent nature. A man feels the sentiment of duty now, and it is reasonable to anticipate, unless the facts presented to his mind shall essentially alter, that he will feel the same to-morrow, next week, next month, and next year. He may as well think of altering and alienating the nature of the soul itself, as of eradicating these feelings when they have once taken root, so long as the objects to which they relate remain the same in the mind's view.

§ 407. Feelings of obligation have particular reference to the future.

A second reason for not classing feelings of obligation with emotions, particularly moral ones, is the fact that obligatory sentiments have special reference to the future. Moral emotions are of a peculiar kind; they have a character of their own, which is ascertained by consciousness; but they merely pronounce upon the character of objects and actions that are either past or present; upon the right or wrong of what has actually taken place in time past, or is taking place at the present moment; with the single exception of hypothetical cases, which are brought before the mind for a moral judgment to be passed upon them. But even in these cases, as far as the action of the moral sense is concerned, the objects of contemplation are in effect present. The conscience passes its judgment upon the objects in themselves considered; and that is all. It goes no further.

But it clearly seems to be different with the feelings under consideration. The states of mind involving obligation and duty have reference to the future; to something which is either to be performed, or the performance of which is to be avoided. They bind us to what is to come. They can have no possible existence, except in connexion with what is to be done, either in the inward feeling or the outward effort. The past is merged in eternity, and no longer furnishes a place for action. Obligation and duty cannot reach it, and it is given over to retribution.

§ 408. Feelings of obligation subsequent in time to the moral emotions of approval and disapproval.

Another and third important circumstance to be taken into view in making out the distinction under our notice, is, that the sentiments or feelings of obligation are always subsequent in point of time to moral emotions, and can not possibly exist until preceded by them. The statement is susceptible of illustration in this way. Some complicated state of things, involving moral considerations, is presented before us; we inquire and examine into it; emotions of approval or disapproval then arise. And this is all that takes place, if we ourselves have, in no way whatever, any direct and active concern, either present or future. But if it be otherwise, the moral emotions are immediately succeeded by a distinct and imperative feeling; the sentiment of obligation, which binds us, as if it were the voice of God speaking in the soul, to act or not to act, to do or not to do, to favour or to oppose.

How common a thing it is for a person to say that he feels no moral obligation to do a thing, because he does not approve it; or, on the contrary, that, approving any proposed course, he feels under obligation to pursue it; language which undoubtedly means something, and which implies a distinction between the mere moral emotion and the feeling of obligation; and which tends to prove the prevalence of the common belief, that obligation is subsequent to, and dependent on, approval or disapproval.

On looking at the subject in these points of view, we cannot come to the conclusion to rank feelings of obligation with moral emotions, or with any other emotions, but are induced to assign them a distinct place. But it is not surprising, on the whole, that moral emotions are often confounded with them, when we consider the invariable connexion between the two just spoken of, and when also we consider the imperfection of language, which not unfrequently applies the same terms to both classes of mental states.

§ 409. Feelings of obligation differ from desires.

For the reasons which have now been stated, feelings of obligation are not classed with Emotions. We are next asked, perhaps, why they are not classed under the general head of Desires. And, in answering this question, we say in the FIRST place, that consciousness clearly points out a difference. It is believed that few matters come within the reach and cognizance of consciousness which can be more readily decided upon than the difference between our desires and our feelings of obligation We admit that, in the particular of their fixedness or permanency, and also of their relation to the future, the latter closely approach to the characteristics of the former; and yet a little internal examination will detect a distinction between them which is marked and lasting.

(2.) We may not only consult our own consciousness in this matter, but may derive information from a notice of the outward conduct of men. In speaking of men's conduct, we not unfrequently make a distinction; and we attribute it sometimes to the mere influence of their desires or wishes, and at other times to the predominance of a sense of duty, which is only another name for a sentiment or impulse within, which is morally obligatory. But there would evidently be no propriety in this distinction, if desire and feelings of duty were the same thing; and it would certainly be premature and unjust to charge men with universally making such a distinction when there are no grounds for it.

§ 410. Further considerations on this subject.

If there is not a fixed, permanent, and radical distinc

tion between desires and feelings of obligation, then there is an utter failure of any basis of morality, either in fact or in theory. It will readily be conceded that morality implies a will, a power of choice and determination. But the mere moral emotions, viz., of approval and disapproval, do not of themselves reach the Will. They operate on the Will through the feelings of obligation; that is to say, they are always succeeded by the latter feelings before men are led to action. All other emotions operate through the Desires. So that the will, in making up its determinations, takes immediate cognizance of only two classes of mental states, viz., Desires and Feelings of obligation. But brute animals, as a general statement, have all the desires that men have; we mean all those modifications of feeling which have been classed under that general head, viz., instincts, appetites, propensities, the various forms of affection, as resentment, love, the parental affection, &c. But still, being evidently destitute of all feelings of obligation, we never speak or think of them as possessing a moral character. We never applaud them for doing their duty, nor punish them for neglecting its performance. Our treatment of them proceeds on altogether different principles. And it would be the same with men if they were wholly destitute of feelings of moral obligation, and had no motives of action but the various forms of desire. They could never, in that case, be considered morally accountable. They would be without reward when they went right, and without rebuke when they went wrong.

CHAPTER IV.

UNIFORMITY OF ACTION IN THE MORAL SENSIBILITIES.

§ 417. Of uniformity in the decisions of the moral nature and the principle on which it is regulated.

The two classes of feelings which have been considered, viz., moral emotions, by means of which we approve and disapprove of actions, and the subsequent feelings of moral obligation, embrace all the states of mind which are properly and strictly included under the head of the Moral Sensibilities; although there are a number of collateral or incidental inquiries, some of which are worthy of notice. One of the most interesting of these inquiries relates to the Uniformity of moral decisions.—In entering upon the subject of the Uniformity of the decisions of our Moral Nature, we remark, in the first place, that there are two kinds of uniformity, viz., uniformity in fact or principle, and uniformity in manifestation or appearance. Uniformity in principle, which is the most important view of the subject, necessarily implies a rule or law by means of which the uniformity, which is alleged to exist, may be measured and known. And the rule or law upon which the uniformity of the moral nature is unquestionably based, is, that its decisions (excepting those extremely perverted acts which may justly be supposed to imply a state of moral alienation or insanity, and which do not properly come into consideration here) *will in all cases conform to the facts perceived;* in other words, will conform to the facts and their relations, as they exist in the view of the intellect.

Estimated by this law, we can hardly entertain a doubt that the decisions of conscience may justly be regarded as being, at the bottom, uniform throughout the world. It is not true, as some seem to suppose, that nature has established one code of morals for civilized and another for Savage nations; one law of rectitude on the banks of the Thames, and another on the banks of the Ganges; but in all parts of the world, in every nation and in every clime, on the borders of every river and on the declivities of every mountain, she utters the same voice, announces the same distinctions, and proclaims the unchangeableness of her requisitions.

§ 412. The nature of conscience, considered as a uniform principle of action, requires that it should vary in its decisions with circumstances.

It is well known, that one of the greatest and the only formidable objection which has been brought against the doctrine of a connatural Moral Sensibility or Conscience, is a want of uniformity in its decisions; in other words, that it approves at one time and in one place what it condemns at another time and place. The remarks which have been made enable us to meet this objection fairly and satisfactorily. We admit that there is a want of that kind of uniformity which, by way of distinction, we have denominated uniformity in manifestation or appearance; but it is not true (with the exception of those extreme perversions which come under the denomination of moral insanity or alienation) that there is a want of uniformity in fact or principle. It is the latter kind of uniformity only which we are desirous to witness as an attribute of the conscience. A uniformity of decision, based upon any other view, would be disastrous to its own authority. In meeting the objection, therefore, which has been referred to, all we have to do is to show that the moral sense or conscience conforms to its own law; in other words, is uniform in its action, relatively to the facts that are placed before it.

And our first remark here is, that the nature of conscience itself involves, that it must vary in its decisions in accordance with a variation or change of circumstances. And the important law of its own uniformity not only permits this, but requires it. As its uniformity exists in relation to the facts perceived, and involves the uniformity or sameness of those facts, it follows that a change in the facts and their relations will be attended by a change in the moral cognizance. The decisions of conscience, therefore, although erected upon a basis of uniformity, and although, in fact, uniform in reference to the principle which has been laid down, are nevertheless in their manifestations sometimes exceedingly diverse; like the multiplied forms of the kaleidoscope, which, although they always exist in accordance with fixed optical principles, are susceptible of almost every possible variety —Going on the supposition, therefore, that the general uniformity of the decisions of conscience is understood and acknowledged, we proceed now to give some account of its variations. And, in doing this, shall endeavour to show that they all take place in entire consistency with the permanent principles of its own nature; in other words, that the uniformity is real, and that the deviations are merely apparent

§ 413. Diversities in moral decisions dependent on differences in the amount of knowledge.

Diversities in the decisions of conscience will depend, in the first place, on differences in the amount of knowledge, whether such differences in knowledge be owing to differences of intellective power or to any other cause In other words, the conscience may be led astray, so far as to decide otherwise than it would under other circumstances, either by a want of facts, or by a false perception and estimate of facts. This simple statement, if properly applied, can hardly fail to explain numerous mistaken moral judgments, which have been adduced in opposition to the doctrine of a conscience.

We may illustrate this view of the subject by a case of this kind. Two men are required to give an opinion on some question which involves moral duty. The question we will suppose to be, whether it would be right, in a supposed case, to attempt a revolution in the civil government. Of these two individuals one will pronounce it to be right, the other will pronounce it to be wrong.—It is admitted that we have here a manifested or apparent deviation in the moral action. At the same time, it is unquestionably the fact, that it is not owing to a difference of structure in their moral nature, but rather to a difference in their perceptive and comparing powers.

The one who pronounces the attempt to be right, in consequence of his greater reach of thought, is able to foresee, after the first convulsive struggles, the subsidence of the angry passions into a state of permanent quiet, and the reorganization of the convulsed frame of society into greater strength and beauty. With these views he thinks it right to attempt to introduce a change into the government of the country. The other, whose intellectual vision is more limited, unable to extend the perceptive eye into the future, sees only the evils of the present moment; the discord and clamour, the breaking up of old habits and associations, the agony, and the blood. With these views he thinks it would be wrong to attempt the change in question. The moral nature, in each instance, pronounces according to the light which is placed before it; and in each case does what it would naturally be expected to do

The want of uniformity in this case, so far from being an evidence, as some seem to suppose, that there are no good grounds for the doctrine of a moral sense, is rather an evidence of the contrary. Although there is not an external or apparent uniformity, there is a uniformity in principle; that is to say, the conscience in each case decides according to the facts before it, which is the only proper ground of decision.

§ 414. Of diversities in moral judgment in connexion with differences in civil and political institutions.

We may reasonable expect, in the second place, to find diversities and occasional oppositions of moral judgment, in connexion with differences in civil and political institutions.—This statement might be illustrated by numerous instances from history. The objectors to a moral nature maintain, that theft or the unlawfully taking of the property of another is a crime; and that conscience, if it exists as a part of the mental constitution, will not fail to condemn it universally. And, in connexion with this, they bring forward the fact, that in some countries theft, instead of being condemned as it should be, prevails very much, and is scarcely regarded as a crime.

Under this head we may properly notice, in particular, the statement made by travellers, that some Savage tribes are very much given to theft. Captain Cook informs us, that when he visited the Sandwich Islands in 1778, the inhabitants exhibited a thievish disposition, taking everything which came within their reach. In explanation of this statement, it is to be remarked, first, that the idea of theft involves the idea of property; and that the right of property is more or less strict and absolute in different countries and under different political systems. In consequence of the richness of their soil and the favourable nature of their climate, there is no question that the right of property was held by the Sandwich Islanders to be less strict and exclusive than it is found to be in less productive countries. The familiar distinction of MEUM and TUUM, of our own and another's, was not so clearly drawn and so strenuously adhered to as it generally is in civilized nations; and the probability is, that nearly all the various forms of property were held in common. As the right of property was in their estimation less strict, the violation of it was less criminal; and they did not look upon the offender with that decided disapprobation which in other places would attach to him in taking the same articles. They probably regarded him with nearly the same feelings with which we regard a man who, in passing through an orchard that belongs to us, takes a few apples, or who occasionally draws water from our well. He takes our property, it is true; but as the right of property in those cases is held by common consent to be a loose or mitigated one, we do not call it theft nor regard it as criminal.

And further, in looking at Captain Cook's account a little more minutely, we see evidence in the narration itself of the correctness of this view. "At first," he says, "on entering the ship, they endeavoured to steal everything they came near, *or rather to take it openly, as what we either should not resent or not hinder.*" In another place he says, in explanation of their conduct, "they thought they had a *right* to everything they could lay their hands on." We learn also, that, after they were made to understand the English notions of property, and the penalty attached to a violation of it, they soon laid aside such conduct.—It is obvious, if they had attached the same ideas to taking property which we attach to stealing, they would not have taken it *openly*, as much so as if they supposed they either had a right to it, or that the owners would not resent or hinder their taking it.

§ 415. Of diversities and obliquities of moral judgment in connexion with speculative opinions.

We may reasonably expect, in the third place, that there will be diversities of moral judgment, based upon diversities in important speculative opinions in morals, politics, and religion, and, in truth, upon almost any subject.—Some years since the speculative opinion seems to have been prevalent through nearly the whole of the civilized world, that the Negroes were an inferior race, located in the graduation of rank somewhere between the brute animals and man. This was the speculative belief. And what has been the consequence? The fires of desolation have been kindled upon the coast of Africa; villages and towns have been destroyed; a continual war has been kept up among the native tribes; and probably forty millions of persons have been torn away from their native country, and consigned to perpetual slavery.

While this erroneous speculative opinion held possession, to a considerable extent, of the minds of men, the authority of conscience was paralyzed; her voice, if it was heard at all, was feeble, and scarcely excited notice. And why should it be otherwise? If the Negroes are truly an inferior race to white men, darkened in intellect and imbruted in the affections, incapable of taking care of themselves, and still more of any intellectual and social advancement, what harm is there in bringing them into vassalage, and making them grind, like the brute animals to which they are so nearly related, in the prison-house of the more favoured species? The difficulty is not so much with the conscience as with the erroneous opinion.

We learn from the Memoirs of the Rev. John Newton, of England, a man as much distinguished for his piety as for his intelligence and eloquence, that he was for some years personally engaged in the Slave Trade; and that, too, after he had professed, and to all appearance with great sincerity, to be guided by the principles of the Christian religion. Such were the prevalent notions in regard to the blacks, that the traffic does not appear to have occurred to him as being morally wrong. He expressly says: "During the time I was engaged in the Slave Trade, I never had the least scruple of its lawfulness." He pursued it without any of those compunctious visitings, which could not fail to have troubled him if he had regarded them, as surely they ought to be regarded, as children of the same common parent, and as participators, in the view of unprejudiced justice, in the same common inheritance of natural rights.

§ 416. Further illustrations of the influence of wrong speculative opinions.

The speculative opinion has formerly existed very extensively, and does still to some degree, that the civil authority has a right, in relation to its own subjects, to exact conformity in the matters of religion. And the result has been, that thousands and hundreds of thousands, at various times and in different countries, have been subjected to imprisonment, the torture, exile, and death. And those who have been the leading agents in these horrible transactions, from the persecutors of the Primitive Christians down to the Lauds and Bonners of later times, have perpetrated them, in their own estimation, with washed hands and a pure heart. They have gone from the Oratory to the dungeon of the Inquisition; they have, with unquestionable sincerity, looked up to Heaven for a blessing, as they have applied to their mangled victims the screw and the wheel of torture; they have arisen from the knee of supplication to kindle with a pious haste the fires of Smithfield, and to wield the exterminating sword of the St. Bartholomew. They have done all this merely in consequence of entertaining a wrong speculative opinion *conscientiously*.

§ 417. Influence of early associations on moral judgments

Our moral judgments, in the fourth place, are sometimes perplexed and led in a direction different from what they would otherwise be, by means of early associations. —The principle of association does not operate upon the moral capacity directly; it operates indirectly with considerable influence. When a particular action is to be judged of, it calls up in the minds of different individuals different and distinct series of accessory circumstances. It has the effect to place the thing, intellectually considered, in a different position. This difference in the tendencies of the associating principle can hardly fail to have considerable effect in modifying the sentiment of approbation or disapprobation resulting from the consideration of any particular action.

Accordingly, when vices are committed by near friends, by a brother or a parent, although they fill us with the deepest grief, (perhaps much greater than we should feel in the case of those who did not sustain so near a relation,) it is frequently the case that they do not excite within us such abhorrence of the actual guilt as we should be likely to feel in other cases. Our prepossessions in favour of the persons who have committed the crime, suggest a thousand circumstances which seem to us to alleviate its aggravation. We frame for them a multitude of plausible excuses, which we should not have thought of doing had it not been for the endearments and intercourse of our previous connexion.

Savage life also gives us an illustration of the views now expressed. Owing to the peculiar situation of those in that state, and the consequent early associations, a factitious and exaggerated importance is attached to mere courage; and gentleness, equanimity, and benevolence are, as virtues, proportionally depressed. In this way their moral judgments are not unfrequently perplexed and rendered erroneous.

§ 418. Of diversities in the moral judgment in connexion with an excited state of the passions.

Furthermore, there may be diversities of moral judgment; in other words, the moral nature may occasionally be perplexed and led astray in its action, under the influence of a state of excited passion.—The action of all the parts of the mind is a *conditional* one; that is to say, it takes place only under certain assignable circumstances It is, for instance, one condition of moral action, as we have repeatedly had occasion to notice, that there must be an antecedent perception of the thing, whatever it is, upon which the moral judgment is to be passed. This condition of moral action is violated in the case under consideration, as well as in others. In a time of great excitement of passion, the moral emotion which would have existed under other circumstances has failed to arise, because the soul is intensely and wholly taken up with another species of feeling. The perceptive and comparing part of the mind is not in a situation to take a right view of the subject, whatever it is. But after the present passion has subsided, so as to give the person an opportunity to inquire and reflect, the power of moral judgment returns And at once the individual, who has been the subject of such violence of feeling, looks with horror on the deeds which he has committed.

In this, and in all the cases which have been mentioned, the conscience will probably be found to be in harmony with itself. Its defective judgments are not owing to any defect in its own nature; but to the circumstance, owing to ignorance, to early training, prejudice, wrong associations, and inordinate passion, and perhaps some other causes similar in their results, that an imperfect or distorted view of the facts has been presented before it

---

CHAPTER V.

MORAL EDUCATION.

§ 419. Suggestions on the importance of moral education.

We do not feel at liberty to leave the subject of the Moral Sensibilities without offering a few remarks, chiefly of a practical nature, on the subject of moral education in general. It is perhaps unnecessary to occupy time in attempting to show the importance of such education, since no one can be ignorant of the deplorable consequences which follow from an utter neglect of it. But, notwithstanding the general concession of its importance, it has ever held a subordinate rank, compared with that purely intellectual education which deals wholly with the mere acquisition of knowledge.

While no one presumes to assert that moral education is unimportant, it must be acknowledged that it has been exceedingly neglected, in consequence of the greater value which has generally been attached to that training of the mind which has exclusive relation to its intellectual part. Children and youth have been taught with great zeal in everything where the head is concerned; in grammar, geography, arithmetic, geometry, astronomy, and the like; and in almost nothing which concerns the heart No pains have been spared in favour of the intellect, while the sensitive part of our nature, the moral emotions, the lower modifications of desire, and the affections, have been left to take care of themselves.

Supposing this to be nearly the true state of things, every reflecting mind must contemplate it with regret, and will look forward with great interest to the time, when moral education shall at least be put on a footing with intellectual, if it do not take the precedence of it Certain it is, that a firm and ample foundation is laid for this species of mental training, if the doctrines which have been advanced in the course of this Work are correct; FIRST, that we have *intellectually* the power of forming the abstract conceptions of right and wrong, of merit and demerit, which necessarily involves that there is an immutable standard of rectitude; and, SECOND, that, in the department of the Sensibilities, we have, in correspondence with the fact of such an immutable standard, the implanted principle of the Moral Sensibility or Conscience, which, in the Emotive form of its action, indicates our conformity to the standard of rectitude or divergency from it, and in its Obligatory action authoritatively requires conformity. We assert that we have here basis enough for a consistent and durable moral education; especially when we take into view the close connexion existing between the conscience and the intellect, particularly the reasoning power.

§ 420. The mind early occupied either with good or bad principles.

It may perhaps be suggested here, admitting the general fact of the great importance of moral education, that it would be better to leave the subject of morals until persons are old enough to decide on all subjects of this nature for themselves. This suggestion would be entitled to more weight, if it were possible, in the mean while, for the mind to remain a moral blank. But this does not appear to be the case. As the mind is continually operative, it is almost a matter of course that it receives, and, as it were, incorporates into itself, moral principles either right or wrong. We are surrounded with such a variety of active influences, that he who is not imbued with good cannot reasonably expect to be uncontaminated with evil. In order, therefore, to prevent the contaminations of vice, it is necessary to preoccupy the mind by the careful introduction and the faithful cultivation of the elements of virtue. Let the young mind, therefore, the minds of children and youth, be made the subjects of assiduous moral culture.

§ 421. Of the time when mora instruction ought to commence

We cannot but conclude, therefore, that a course of moral training ought to be commenced at an early period. It is a truth sufficiently established, that we begin to learn as soon as we begin to exist. The infant no sooner comes into the world, than the mind expands itself foı the reception of knowledge, as naturally as the floweı opens its rejoicing leaves to the rising sun. The earnestness which it discovers as it turns its eye towards the light or any bright object, its expression of surprise on hearing sudden and loud sounds, its strong propensity to imitate the actions and words of its attendants, all show most clearly that the work of intellectual developement is begun.

While no one doubts this early developement of the intellect, it has not been so generally admitted to be true of the pathematic and moral part of our nature. But there is no sufficient ground, as we have already had occasion to intimate, for a distinction in this respect; the developement of the head and the heart, of the intellect and the sentient nature, begins essentially at one and the same time. It is true that the perceptive or intellectual action is necessarily antecedent in the order of nature; but the sensitive action, both natural and moral, follows closely and perseveringly in its train. And this also may be added, viz., that the developement of the moral nature in its leading outlines appears to be sooner completed. Facts and the relations of facts, which are the subjects of the intellectual activity, are infinite. But the great principles of morals, however multiplied they may be in their applications, are in themselves few and simple. How few persons, at the age of fourteen or sixteen years, have completed their attainments in knowledge, and have fully unfolded and strengthened all their intellectual powers! And yet how many at the same age have established such a decided moral character, either for good or evil, as almost to preclude a hope of a correction of its deformi ties in the one case, or the enhancement of its beauties in the other!

§ 422. Of the discouragements attending a process of moral instruction

And here we would remark upon one discouragement which frequently attends the efforts of those who are so situated as to render it especially their duty to impart instruction to the young. We refer to the fact that it is sometimes, and but too frequently, the case, that they see but little immediate good results from their labours. They can see distinctly the advancement of their pupils in that knowledge which is appropriate to the intellect, but are less able to measure their progress in what pertains to the moral culture. Indeed, they too often believe that their instruction is seed sown upon stony ground, which is not only unproductive at present, but is absolutely and for-ever lost.

This is a great mistake. The truth is, that nothing is lost. The moral and religious instruction which is communicated to the youthful memory, is deposited in the keeping of a power which may sometimes slumber, but can never die. It may long be unproductive; it may remain for years without giving signs of vivification and of an operative influence; and yet it may be only waiting for some more favourable and important moment, when it shall come forth suddenly and prominently to view. No one, therefore, ought to be discouraged in the discharge of this duty. In nothing is the Scriptural declaration more likely to be fulfilled in its richest import. "Cast thy bread upon the waters, and thou shalt find it after many days."

Multitudes of illustrations might be introduced to confirm the views of this section. How natural is the following incident! And how agreeable, therefore, to sound philosophy!—"When I was a little child," said a religious man, "my mother used to bid me kneel beside her, and place her hand upon my head while she prayed. Ere I was old enough to know her worth, she died, and I was left much to my own guidance. Like others, I was inclined to evil passions, but often felt myself checked, and, as it were, drawn back by the soft hand upon my head

When I was a young man I travelled in foreign lands, and was exposed to many temptations; but when I would have yielded, *that same hand was upon my head*, and I was saved. I seemed to feel its pressure as in the days of my happy infancy, and sometimes there came with it a voice in my heart, a voice that must be obeyed; Oh, do not this wickedness, my son, nor sin against thy God."

§ 423. Of the importance, in a moral point of view, of adopting correct speculative opinions.

But, while we assert that there is ample basis in the mental constitution for a moral education, that this education ought to be commenced at an early period, and that such a course of training has its due share of encouragements, we acknowledge that it is not an easy thing in a few words to point out the characteristics, and to indicate the outlines of a system of moral culture. Accordingly, we shall not attempt it any further than to add a few general suggestions. We proceed, therefore, to remark, that suitable pains ought to be taken to introduce into the young mind correct speculative opinions.

It was seen in a former Chapter that the conscience acts in view of the facts which are before it. It will follow, therefore, if we adopt wrong opinions, whatever they may be, they will have an effect upon the conscience. If these opinions be important, be fundamental, they will be likely to lead us in a course which, under other circumstances, we should regard as wrong in the very highest degree. The belief that men by nature possess equal rights, is in itself nothing more than a speculative opinion; but this opinion, simple and harmless as it may seem in its enunciation, is at this moment shaking thrones, unbinding the chains of millions, and remodelling the vast fabric of society. The opinion that the rights of conscience are inalienable, and that no one can regulate by violent means the religion of another, is breaking the wheel of torture, and quenching the fire of persecution, and quickening into life the smothered worship of the world. The speculative opinion that Jesus Christ, the Son of God, appeared in the form of man, and by his death made an atonement for sin, is a truth, simple and ineffective as it may at first sight appear, which has already changed the face of domestic and civil society, and, like a little leaven which leaveneth the whole lump, is secretly regenerating the whole mass of human nature.

We infer, therefore, that it is highly important to consider well what truths we adopt. The doctrine that it is no matter what we believe, if we are only sincere in it, is derogatory to the claims of human reason, and full of danger. What persecutor, what tyrant, what robber, what assassin may not put in his claim for a sort of sincerity, and, in many cases, justly too? It is a sincerity, a conscientiousness based on all the wisdom which human intelligence, in its best efforts, can gather up, and nothing short of this, which stands approved in the sight of human reason and of a just Divinity.

§ 424. Of the knowledge of the Supreme Being, and of the study of religious truth generally.

And, in connexion with what has been said in the preceding section, we proceed to remark further, that all morality must necessarily be defective, in a greater or less degree, which proceeds on the principle of excluding RELIGION. It is true that a man who is not religious, (in other words, who has not a sincere regard for the character and institutions of the Supreme Being,) may do some things which, in themselves considered, are right and are morally commendable; but he does not do *all* that is right, he comes short in the most essential part. And his failure there renders it difficult, perhaps we may say impossible, to speak of him, with any degree of propriety and truth, as a right, that is to say, as a just or holy person.

We assert, therefore, that moral education must include, as a leading element, some instruction in regard to the existence and character of God, and those religious duties which are involved in the fact of his existence and character. Our conscience, the office of which is to adjust our duties to our ability and the relations we sustain, imperatively requires this. In the eye of an enlightened intellectual perception, God stands forth distinct from, and pre-eminent above all others, as an object infinitely exalted; and a want of love to his character and of adhe sion to his law is, in the view of conscience, a crime so grossly flagrant in itself as not to be atoned for by any other virtue. And not only this; a proper regard for the character of the Supreme Being has such a multiplicity of bearings and relations, in consequence of the diffusion of his presence, and the multiplicity of his acts and requirements, that the crime involved in the want of it seems to spread itself over the infinite number of transactions which, taken together, constitute the sum of life. So that the doctrine of the existence of God, received into the intellect, and attended, as it should be, with perfect love in the heart, is, beyond all question, the great foundation and support of a truly consistent moral life.

THE SENSIBILITIES, OR SENSITIVE NATURE.

SENSITIVE STATES OF THE MIND OR SENTIMENTS.

PART THIRD.

IMPERFECT OR DISORDERED SENSITIVE ACTION.

CHAPTER I.

DISORDERED AND ALIENATED ACTION OF THE APPETITES AND PROPENSITIES.

§ 425. Introductory remarks on disordered sensitive action.

WITH what has now been said on the subject of our moral nature, we bring the interesting and important department of the Sensibilities, in its two leading forms of the Natural or Pathematic Sensibilities, and of the Moral Sensibilities, to a conclusion. In saying this, however, we have reference to its regular and ordinary action, or that action which takes place in accordance with the ordinary and permanent principles of the Sensitive nature. But it remains to be added further, that there are instances here, as well as in the Intellect, of marked and disastrous deviations from the salutary restraint which these principles impose. In other words, there is not unfrequently an action of the Sensibilities which is so far out of the ordinary or natural line of the precedents of the heart and the morals, that it may be properly described, sometimes as an imperfect or disordered, and sometimes as an alienated action.—It is to the examination of this subject, a knowledge of which is obviously necessary to a comprehensive and complete view of the Sensibilities, that we now propose to proceed.

§ 426. Of what is meant by a disordered and alienated state of the sensibilities.

It may be proper to remark here, that an imperfect or disordered action of the Sensibilities may express merely an irregularity of action, something out of the common and ordinary course of action; or, as the form of expression is obviously a somewhat general and indefinite one, it may indicate something more. When, for instance, this irregular and disordered state passes a certain limit, goes beyond a certain boundary which is more easily conceived than described, it becomes Insanity or Alienation. That is to say, the merely irregular action becomes an insane or alienated action, when it becomes so great, so pervading, and so deeply rooted in the mind, that the individual has no power of restoration in himself. So that it would seem to follow, in view of this remark, that there may be a disordered state of the mind which is insanity; and, under other circumstances, a disordered state of the mind which is not insanity, or, rather, which is less than insanity. But in either case this condition of mind is not to be regarded, nor is it, in point of fact, a sound mental state. Although we may not be able to say specifically, in a given case, that the disorder has reached the point of insanity, yet it is certain that the mind in this disordered state, whether the disorder be greater or less, is presented to our view in a new and important aspect.

Unquestionably, a wide and interesting field of remark is opened here. Nevertheless, what we have to say will necessarily be brief, indicating rather the general trains of thought which naturally present themselves, than following them out into minuteness of detail. And in executing this plan, imperfect as it can hardly fail to be, we shall conform, so far as may be practicable, to those classifications of our Sensitive nature which have hitherto helped to aid our inquiries.

§ 427. Of the disordered and alienated action of the appetites

Accordingly we remark, in the first place, that there may be a disordered and alienated action of the Appetites.—It is well known that the appetites grow stronger and stronger by repeated indulgence. While the process of increased appetitive tendency is going on, there still remains, in the majority of cases, enough of remonstrance in the conscience, and of restrictive and aggressive energy in the Will, to ward off that state of thraldom which is rapidly approaching. But in some melancholy cases it is otherwise; the line of demarcation, which separates the possibility and the impossibility of a restoration, is passed; and from that time onward there is nothing but interminable sinking. Such cases as these may undoubtedly be regarded as coming within the limits of some of the multiplied forms of mental alienation.

The most frequent instances of mental alienation, as

ginating in a disordered and excessive energy of the appetites, are to be found in that numerous class of persons who habitually indulge in the use of intoxicating drugs, particularly ardent spirits. When the person who indulges in the use of intoxicating liquors has so increased the energy of this pernicious appetite as really to bring himself within the limits of mental alienation, there is no hope of a return by means of any effort which he himself is capable of making. He may have a clear perception of the misery of his situation; the desire of esteem may still arouse within him the recollection of what he once was and of what he still ought to be; the conscience may still speak out in remonstrance, though probably with a diminished voice; the will may continue to put forth some ineffectual struggles; but it is found to be all in vain. If left to himself, and not put under that constraint which is proper to persons in actual insanity, it may be regarded as a matter of moral certainty that he will plunge deeper and deeper in the degrading vice of which he is the subject, so long as the remaining powers of life shall support him in the process.

The individuals who are in this situation seem themselves to have a consciousness of this. They see clearly that in their own strength there is no hope. In repeated instances such persons have gone to keepers of penitentiaries and other prisons, and earnestly entreated for admission, on the ground that nothing short of strict seclusion within their massy walls would secure them against the ruinous indulgence of their appetite.—"The use of strong drink," says Dr. Rush, (Diseases of the Mind, ch. x.,) "is at first the effect of free agency. From habit it takes place from necessity. That this is the case, I infer from persons who are inordinately devoted to the use of ardent spirits being irreclaimable, by all the considerations which domestic obligations, friendship, reputation, property, and sometimes even by those which religion and the love of life can suggest to them. An instance of insensibility to the last, in an habitual drunkard, occurred some years ago in Philadelphia. When strongly urged, by one of his friends, to leave off drinking, he said, 'Were a keg of rum in one corner of a room, and were a cannon constantly discharging balls between me and it, I could not refrain from passing before that cannon in order to get at the rum.' "

§ 428. Disordered action of the principle of self-preservation.

As we advance upward from the Appetites to the region of the Propensities, such as the principle of self-preservation, the desire of knowledge, the desire of society, and the like, we shall find the latter, as well as the former, probably without an exception, subject, in certain individuals, to a greater or less degree of what may be termed a diseased or disordered action. We begin with the propensive principle of Self-preservation, or what may be designated in other terms as the natural desire of a continuance of existence. This principle, like the others of the same class, although not generally in so marked a degree, will sometimes manifest itself under such circumstances and in such a manner as obviously to show that its action is not a natural, regular, or healthy action. Persons under the influence of the disordered action of the principle which is connected with the preservation of life, multiply, as they would be naturally supposed to do, images of danger and terror which have no existence, nor likeness of existence, except in their own disordered minds. They not only see perils which are invisible to others, but are led to take a multitude of precautions which, in the estimation of those around them, are altogether unnecessary, and even ridiculous.

Pinel, under the head of Melancholy, mentions a case which may be considered as illustrating this subject. "A distinguished military officer," he says, "after fifty years of active service in the cavalry, was attacked with disease. It commenced by his experiencing vivid emotions from the slightest causes; if, for example, he heard any disease spoken of, he immediately believed himself to be attacked by it; if any one was mentioned as deranged in intellect, he imagined himself insane, and retired into his chamber full of melancholy thoughts and inquietude. Everything became for him a subject of fear and alarm. If he entered into a house, he was afraid that the floor would fall and precipitate him amid its ruins. He could not pass a bridge without terror, unless impelled by the sentiment of honour for the purpose of fighting"*

§ 429. Disordered and alienated action of the possessory principle.

There are instances, occurring with a considerable degree of frequency, of a disordered or alienated action of the desire of possession, or the Possessory principle. Some of these are voluntary; that is to say, are brought about by a course of action, of which the responsibility rests upon the individual. Others appear to be congenital or natural.—Among the class of confirmed misers, we shall be likely, from time to time, to find instances of the first class. There are individuals among this class of persons who have so increased the energy of the Possessory principle (Acquisitiveness, as it is sometimes conveniently termed) by a long voluntary course of repetition, that its action is no longer under the control of the Will, but has obviously passed over into the region of mental alienation. Such probably must have been the case with a certain individual mentioned by Valerius Maximus, who took advantage of a famine to sell a mouse for two hundred pence, and then famished himself with the money in his pocket. —It is difficult to tell, however, although a person may unquestionably become insane in his avarice, whether this is actually the case in any given instance, or whether, notwithstanding its intensity, it falls in some degree short of alienation.

§ 430. Instances of the second kind or form of disordered action of the possessory principle.

There are other instances of the disordered action of the principle of Acquisitiveness, which appear to be congenital or constitutional. In the case of the persons to whom we now have reference, the disposition to get possession of whatever can be regarded as property, whether of greater or less value, shows itself, not only in great strength, but at a very early period of life. There are a considerable number of cases of this kind to be found in the writings of Gall and Spurzheim; and there are some notices of similar cases in a few other writers. Dr. Rush,

* Pinel, as quoted in Combe's Phrenology, Boston ed. p. 241

for instance, in his Medical Inquiries, mentions a woman who was entirely exemplary in her conduct except in one particular. "She could not refrain from *stealing*. What made this vice the more remarkable was, that she was in easy circumstances, and not addicted to extravagance in anything. Such was the propensity to this vice that, when she could lay her hands on nothing more valuable, she would often, at the table of a friend, fill her pockets secretly with bread. She both confessed and lamented her crime."

Some of the facts which are given by Dr. Gall are as follows.—"Victor Amadeus I., King of Sardinia, was in the constant habit of stealing trifles. Saurin, pastor at Geneva, though possessing the strongest principles of reason and religion, frequently yielded to the propensity to steal. Another individual was from early youth a victim to this inclination. He entered the military service on purpose that he might be restrained by the severity of the discipline; but, having continued his practices, he was on the point of being condemned to be hanged. Ever seeking to combat his ruling passion, he studied theology and became a Capuchin. But his propensity followed him even to the cloister. Here, however, as he found only trifles to tempt him, he indulged himself in his strange fancy with less scruple. He seized scissors, candlesticks, snuffers, cups, goblets, and conveyed them to his cell. An agent of the government at Vienna had the singular mania for stealing nothing but kitchen utensils. He hired two rooms as a place of deposite; he did not sell, and made no use of them. The wife of the famous physician Gaubius had such a propensity to pilfer, that, when she made a purchase, she always sought to take something."*

§ 431. Disordered action of imitativeness, or the principle of imitation.

The proof that there is in man a principle of IMITATION, which impels him to do as others do, is so abundant as probably to leave no reasonable doubt upon the candid mind. This principle, as compared with its ordinary operation and character, is found in some individuals to ex

* Gall's Works, vol. iv., Am. ed., p. 132

hibit an irregular or diseased action. M. Pinel, as he is quoted by Dr. Gall, speaks of an idiot woman "who had an *irresistible* propensity to imitate all that she saw done in her presence. She repeats, *instinctively*, all she hears, and imitates the gestures and actions of others with the greatest fidelity; and without troubling herself with any regard to propriety."*—Under the form of Sympathetic Imitation, the disordered action of this principle becomes very important; so much so, that we shall leave the subject here for the purpose of considering it more at length than we could otherwise do, in a separate chapter.

§ 432. Disordered action of the principle of sociality.

The principle of Sociality, obviously one of the implanted propensities of our nature, may exist with such a degree of intensity as justly to entitle its action to be called a disordered, and, in some cases, even an alienated action. In connexion with this remark, it may be proper to revert a moment to the precise idea which we attach to the term alienation, considered as expressive of a state or condition of the mind. There may be an imperfection of mental action, there may be a disorder of mental action, which is nevertheless not an alienation of mental action. The term alienation properly applies to those forms of mental action which are so much disordered as to set at defiance any efforts of the Will to control them; in a word, they are involuntary. So that, in accordance with this statement, there may be either a disordered state of the principle of sociality or of any other principle, (that is to say, one which is irregular, but still is susceptible of correction under the efforts of the will;) or there may be, when this disorder is found to exist beyond certain limits, an alienated, an insane state. But, although this distinction should be fully understood, it is not necessary, in the remarks which, for the most part, we have occasion to make, that we should always keep it distinctly in view.

But to return to our subject. An irregular action of the social principle, whether it be truly alienated or exist

* Gall's Works, vol. i., p. 320.

in some lighter form of disorder, may show itself in two aspects, which are entirely diverse from each other, viz., either in a morbid aversion to society, or in a desire of society inordinately intense.—Persons to whom the first statement will apply are generally, and for the most part justly, designated as Misanthropes. Under the influence of some sudden revulsion of the mind, of some great disappointment, of some ill-treatment on the part of near relatives and supposed friends, or of some other powerful cause, the natural tie of brotherhood, which binds man to his fellow-man, is snapped asunder, and the unhappy individual flees to the solitude of the rock and the desert never more to return.

§ 433. Further remarks on the disordered action of the social propensity.

There is another class of cases, which in their character appear to be directly the reverse of those which have just been mentioned. Individuals, when they are cut off from society, particularly the society of their friends, are sometimes the subjects of a misery inexpressibly intense. The innocent but unfortunate Foscari, who was banished from Venice in 1450, died, apparently in consequence of the mere mental anguish which he suffered. Cases are also enumerated of death resulting from solitary confinement in prison.* There is an exceedingly painful disease, founded in a great degree upon the disordered action of the social principle, which is termed by physicians Nostalgia, but which is more commonly known under the familiar designation of HOME-SICKNESS. This disease, which is sometimes fatal, is said to have frequently prevailed among the Swiss when absent from their native country. The beautiful sky which shone over them in their absence from their native land, the works of art, the allurements of the highest forms of civilization, could not erase from their hearts the image of their rugged mountains and their stormy heavens. They had society enough around them, it is true; but it was not the society which their hearts sought for, or in which, in existing circumstances, they could participate. They bowed their heads under the influence of a hidden and irrepressible

* See the large ed. of this Work, vol. ii., § 144, 148.

sorrow; and in many cases not merely pined away, but died in the deep anguish of their separation.

In the year 1733, a Russian army, under the command of General Praxin, advanced to the banks of the Rhine At this remote distance from their native country, this severe mental disease began to prevail among the Russians, so much so that five or six soldiers every day became unfit for duty; a state of things which threatened to affect the existence of the army. The progress of this home-sickness was terminated by a severe order from the commander, (designed probably, and which had the effect to produce a strong counteracting state of mind,) that every one affected with the sickness should be buried alive *

§ 434. Of the disordered action of the desire of esteem.

There may be a disordered action of the desire of Esteem. This principle is not only an original one, but, as a general thing, it possesses, as compared with some of the other Propensities, a greater and more available amount of strength. It is a regard for the opinions of others, (a sense of character, as we sometimes term it,) which, in the absence or the too great weakness of higher principles, serves to restrict the conduct of multitudes within the bounds of decency and order. This principle is good and important in its place and under due regulation; but it is exceedingly apt to become irregular, unrestrained, and inordinate in its exercise. This view throws light upon the character of many individuals. It is here, probably, that we may discover the leading defect in the character of Alcibiades, a name of distinguished celebrity in the history of Athens. His ruling passion seems to have been not so much the love of POWER as the love of APPLAUSE. In other words, his great desire was, as has been well remarked of him, "to make a noise, and to furnish matter of conversation to the Athenians."

Pope, in the First of his Moral Essays, illustrates this subject, in his usual powerful manner, in what he says of the Duke of Wharton; the key to whose character he finds in the excessive desire of human applause.

* Dr. Rush on the Diseases of the Mind, 2d. ed., p. 113.

"Search then the ruling passion. There alone
The wild are constant, and the cunning known;
This clew once found, unravels all the rest,
The prospect clears, and Wharton stands confess'd.
Wharton, the scorn and wonder of our days,
Whose ruling passion was the LUST OF PRAISE.
Born with whate'er could win it from the wise,
Women and fools must like him, or he dies."

The inordinate exercise of this propensity, as is correctly intimated by Mr. Stewart, tends to *disorganize* the mind. The man who is under the influence of such an excessive appetite for the world's smiles and flatteries, has no fixed rule of conduct; but the action of his mind, his opinions, desires, hopes, and outward conduct, are constantly fluctuating with the changing tide of popular sentiment. It is nearly impossible that the pillars of the mind should remain firm, and without more or less of undermining and dislocation, under the operations of such a system of uncertainty and vicissitude.—Nor is this all. When persons who are under the influence of this excessive desire are disappointed in the possession of that approbation and applause which is its natural food, they are apt to become melancholy, misanthropic, and unhappy in a very high degree. In fact, numerous cases of actual Insanity, if we look carefully at the statements of writers on the subject of Mental Alienation, may probably be traced to this source.

§ 435. Disordered action of the desire of power.

Men become disordered in mind, and sometimes actually insane, not only by the inordinate indulgence of the desire of esteem and the desire of possession, but also, perhaps with no less frequency, under the influence of the exaggerated and intense desire of POWER. They are looking onward and upward, with an excited heart and constrained eye, to some form of authority, honour, and dominion, till this desire, strengthened by constant repetition, becomes the predominant feeling. Instances where the disorder of the mind arises in this way and exists to this extent are innumerable. But it is not always that it stops here. If the desire is suddenly and greatly disappointed, as it is very likely to be, the reaction upon the whole mind may be such as to cause disorder in all its functions, and leave it a wide mass of ruins.

The history of those who are confined in Insane Hospitals furnishes a strong presumption that such results are not unfrequent. Although the mind is deranged, the predominant feeling which led to the derangement seems still to remain. One individual challenges for himself the honours of a Chancellor, another of a King; one is a member of Parliament, another is the Lord Mayor of London; one, under the name of the Duke of Wellington or Bonaparte, claims to be the commander of mighty armies; another announces himself with the tone and attitude of a Prophet of the Most High. Pinel informs us that there were at one time no less than three maniacs in one of the French Insane Hospitals, each of whom assumed to be Louis XIV. On one occasion, these individuals were found disputing with each other, with a great degree of energy, their respective rights to the throne The dispute was terminated by the sagacity of the superintendent, who, approaching one of them, gave him, with a serious look, to understand that he ought not to dispute on the subject with the others, since they were obviously mad. "Is it not well known," said the superintendent, "that you alone ought to be acknowledged as Louis XIV.?" The insane person, flattered with this homage, cast upon his companions a look of the most marked disdain, and immediately retired

---

CHAPTER II.

SYMPATHETIC IMITATION.

§ 436. Of sympathetic imitation, and what is involved in it.

WE endeavoured, in its proper place, to illustrate the natural origin and the prevalence of the propensity to IMITATION. In connexion with the general truth of the existence of such a propensity, it is proper to observe here that there is a subordinate and peculiar form of imitation, which is deserving of a separate notice, and particularly so on account of its practical results. We speak now of what has been appropriately termed Sympathetic Imitation.

It is implied, in all cases of Sympathetic Imitation, that there is more than one person concerned in them; and it exists, in general, in the highest degree, when the number of persons is considerable. Some one or more of these individuals is strongly agitated by some internal emotion, desire, or passion; and this inward agitation is expressed by the countenance, gestures, or other external signs. There is also a communication of such agitation of the mind to others; they experience similar emotions, desires, and passions. And these new exercises of soul are expressed on the part of the sympathetic person by similar outward signs. In a single word, when we are under the influence of this form of imitation, we both act and feel as others. And this happens, not only in consequence of what we witness in them, and apparently for no other reason, but it happens *naturally;* that is to say, in virtue of an implanted or natural principle. The view which we are inclined to take of this principle is, that, although we may properly speak of it, on account of its close resemblance, as a modification of the more ordinary form of Imitativeness, yet, on the whole, it is so far distinct and specific in its character as to entitle it to be regarded as a separate part of our sensitive nature. As such it might have been treated of in another place; but in its ordinary action it is generally well understood; and we have delayed the consideration of it till the present time, because it is our principal object to give some account of its disordered or alienated action.

§ 437. Familiar instances of sympathetic imitation.

Abundance of instances (many of them frequent and familiar) show the existence of SYMPATHETIC IMITATION; in other words, that there is in human feelings, and in the signs of those feelings, a power of contagious communication, by which they often spread themselves rapidly from one to another.

"In general it may be remarked," says Mr. Stewart.

"that whenever we see in the countenance of another individual any sudden change of features, more especially such a change as is expressive of any particular passion or emotion, our own countenance has a tendency to assimilate itself to his. Every man is sensible of this when he looks at a person under the influence of laughter or in a deep melancholy. Something, too, of the same kind takes place in that spasm of the muscles of the jaw which we experience in yawning; an action which is well known to be frequently excited by the contagious power of example."*

To these statements, illustrative of sympathetic imitation, may be added the fact, that if there are a number of children together, and one of them suddenly gives way to tears and sobs, it is generally the case that all the rest are more or less affected in the same manner. Another case, illustrative of the same natural principle, is that of a mob when they gaze at a dancer on the slack rope They seem not only to be filled with the same anxiety, which we may suppose to exist in the rope-dancer himself; but they naturally writhe, and twist, and balance their own bodies as they see him do. It has also been frequently remarked, that when we see a stroke aimed and just ready to fall upon the leg or arm of another person, we naturally shrink, and slightly draw back our own leg or arm, with a sort of prophetic or anticipative imitation of the person on whom the blow is about to be inflicted.

§ 438. Instances of sympathetic imitation at the poor-house of Haerlem.

Multitudes of well-attested facts show the sympathetic connexion between mind and mind, and sympathy between the mind and the nervous and muscular system. Few are more interesting or decisive than what is stated to have occurred at Haerlem under the inspection of Boerhave.—"In the house of charity at Haerlem," says the account, "a girl, under an impression of terror, fell into a convulsive disease, which returned in regular paroxysms. One of the by-standers, intent upon assisting her, was seized with a similar fit, which also recurred at

* Stewart's Elements, vol. iii., chap. ii.

intervals; and on the day following, another was attacked; then a third, and a fourth; in short, almost the whole of the children, both girls and boys, were afflicted with these convulsions. No sooner was one seized, than the sight brought on the paroxysms in almost all the rest at the same time. Under these distressing circumstances, the physicians exhibited all the powerful anti-epileptic medicines with which their art furnishes them, but in vain. They then applied to Boerhave, who, compassionating the wretched condition of the poor children, repaired to Haerlem; and while he was inquiring into the matter, one of them was seized with a fit, and immediately he saw several others attacked with a species of epileptic convulsion. It presently occurred to this sagacious physician, that, as the best medicines had been skilfully administered, and as the propagation of the disease from one to another appeared to depend on the imagination, [the sympathy of imagination,] by preventing this impression upon the mind, the disease might be cured; and his suggestion was successfully adopted. Having previously apprized the magistrates of his views, he ordered, in the presence of all the children, that several portable furnaces should be placed in different parts of the chamber, containing burning coals; and that iron, bent to a certain form, should be placed in the furnaces; and then he gave these further commands; that all medicines would be totally useless, and the only remedy with which he was acquainted was, that the first who should be seized with a fit, whether boy or girl, must be burned in the arm to the very bone by a red-hot iron. He spoke this with uncommon dignity and gravity; and the children, terrified at the thoughts of this cruel remedy, when they perceived any tendency to the recurrence of the paroxysm, immediately exerted all their strength of mind, and called up the horrible idea of the burning; and were thus enabled, by the stronger mental impression, to resist the influence of the morbid propensity."

§ 439. Other instances of this species of imitation.

It would not be difficult to multiply cases similar to those which have been mentioned. A few years since, there was a man in Chelmsford, Massachusetts, who had a family of six children, one of whom became affected with the CHOREA, or St. Vitus's dance. The others, in the indulgence of that thoughtless gayety which is natural to children, amused themselves with imitating his odd gestures, until, after a time, they were irresistibly affected in the same way. At this state of things, which seems to be susceptible of an explanation in no other way than on the principles of sympathetic imitation, the family, as may naturally be supposed, were in great affliction. The father, a man of some sagacity as well as singularity of humour, brought into the house a block and axe, and solemnly threatened to take off the head of the first child who should hereafter exhibit any involuntary bodily movement, except the child originally diseased. By this measure, which proceeded on the same view of the human mind as the experiment of Boerhave just mentioned, a new train of feeling was excited, and the spell was broken.*

It may be added, that not only those in the same family and in the same building have been seized, but the contagion has sometimes spread from one to another, (by the mere imitation of sympathy as we suppose,) over whole towns, and even large districts of country. This was the case in a part of the island of Anglesey in 1796; and still later in this country, in some parts of Tennessee.†

CHAPTER III.

DISORDERED ACTION OF THE AFFECTIONS.

§ 440. Of the states of mind denominated presentiments.

WE proceed now to remark, that there may be a disordered action of the Affections or Passions, as well as of the lower principles of the Sensitive nature; and this remark is designed to apply to both classes of the Affections, the benevolent and those of an opposite kind. We do not pro

* Powers's Essay on the Influence of the Imagination, p. 32.

† See Edinburgh Med. and Surg. Journal, vol. iii., p. 446

pose, however, in this Chapter, to confine ourselves very strictly to the Affections, properly so called; but shall introduce some collateral or connected subjects, which may be regarded as too interesting to be omitted, and at the same time as too unimportant to require a distinct place They may be expected, moreover, to throw indirectly some light upon the leading topic of the chapter. We begin with the subject of PRESENTIMENTS.

Many individuals have had at certain times strong and distinct impressions in relation to something future; so much so that not the least doubt has remained in their own minds of its being something out of the common course of nature. It is related, for instance, of the nonconformist writer, Isaac Ambrose, whose religious works formerly had some celebrity, that he had such a striking internal intimation of his approaching death, that he went round to all his friends to bid them farewell. When the day arrived, which his presentiments indicated as the day of his dissolution, he shut himself up in his room and died. Mozart, the great musical composer, had a strong presentiment that the celebrated Requiem which bears his name would be his last Work. Nothing could remove this impression from his mind. He expressly said, "It is certain I am writing this requiem for myself; it will serve for my funeral service." The foreboding was realized. It is stated of Pendergrast, an officer in the Duke of Marlborough's army, that he had a strong foreboding that he would be killed on a certain day. He mentioned his conviction to others, and even made a written memorandum in relation to it. And the event was such as he had foretold it would be.* Henry the Fourth of France, for some weeks previous to his being assassinated by Ravaillac, had a distinct presentiment, which he mentioned to Sully and other men of his time, that some great calamity was about to befall him.

Some cases of Presentiments can undoubtedly be explained on natural principles. Some accidental circumstance, a mere word, the vagaries of a dream, any trifling event, which happens in the popular belief of the time and country to be regarded as a sinister omen, may have

* Boswell's Life of Johnson, vol. ii., p. 48.

been enough in some cases to have laid the foundation for them; and the subsequent fulfilment may have been purely accidental. Nor is it necessary, so far as we are able to perceive, to suppose that in any cases whatever there is any supernatural or miraculous interposition. But, if this is not the case, it is difficult to account for the deep conviction which sometimes fastens upon the mind, a conviction upon which arguments and persuasions are found to make no impression, except upon the ground that the action of the Sensibilities is in some degree disordered. But of the specific nature of that disorder, the trait or circumstance which distinguishes it from other forms of disordered mental action, it is difficult to give any account.

§ 441. Of sudden and strong impulses of the mind.

There is another disordered condition of the mind, different from that which has just been mentioned, and yet in some respects closely allied to it. Some persons, whose soundness of mind on all ordinary occasions is beyond question, find in themselves at certain times a sudden and strange propensity to do things, which, if done, would clearly prove them, to some extent at least, deranged. As an illustration, a person of a perfectly sane mind, according to the common estimate of insanity, once acknowledged, that, whenever he passed a particular bridge, he felt a slight inclination to throw himself over, accompanied with some dread that his inclination might hurry him away. Such slight alienated impulses are probably more frequent than is commonly supposed. And they exist in every variety of degree; sometimes scarcely attracting notice, at others bearing the broad and fatal stamp of dangerous insanity.

Dr. Gall mentions the case of a woman in Germany, who, having on a certain occasion witnessed a building on fire, was ever afterward, at intervals, subject to strong impulses prompting her to fire buildings. Under the influence of these impulses she set fire to twelve buildings in the borough where she lived. Having been arrested on the thirteenth attempt, she was tried, condemned, and executed "She could give no other reason, nor show any other motive, for firing so many houses, than this impulse which drove her to it. Notwithstanding the fear, the terror, and the repentance she felt in every instance after committing the crime, she went and did it afresh."* Would not sound philosophy, to say nothing of the requisitions of religion, have assigned such a person to an insane hospital rather than to the block of the executioner?

The same writer, who has collected numerous valuable facts in relation to the operations of the human mind mentions the case of a German soldier, who was subject every month to a violent convulsive attack. "He was sensible," he proceeds to remark, "of their approach; and as he felt, by degrees, a violent propensity to kill, in proportion as the paroxysm was on the point of commencing, he was earnest in his entreaties to be loaded with chains. At the end of some days the paroxysm and the fatal propensity diminished, and he himself fixed the period at which they might without danger set him at liberty. At Haina, we saw a man who, at certain periods, felt an irresistible desire to injure others. He knew this unhappy propensity, and had himself kept in chains till he perceived that it was safe to liberate him. An individual of melancholy temperament was present at the execution of a criminal. The sight caused him such violent emotion, that he at once felt himself seized with an irresistible desire to kill, while, at the same time, he entertained the utmost horror at the commission of the crime. He depicted his deplorable state, weeping bitterly, and in extreme perplexity. He beat his head, wrung his hands, remonstrated with himself, begged his friends to save themselves, and thanked them for the resistance they made to him."†

§ 442. Insanity of the affections or passions.

From the instances which have been given, it will be seen that sudden and strong impulses, indicating a disordered state of the mind, may exist in reference to very different things, and also in very various degrees. The cases last mentioned were of such an aggravated nature,

* Gall's Works, vol. iv., Am. ed., p. 105

† Ib., vol. i., p. 329.

that they may properly be regarded as instances (and perhaps the same view will apply to some other cases of a less marked character) of actual alienation or insanity. And, as such, they may be correctly described as instances of the insanity of the Affections or Passions.

The insanity of the passions is a state of mind somewhat peculiar, even as compared with other forms of insanity. The powers of perception, in cases of insanity of the passions, are often in full and just exercise. The mind may possess, in a very considerable degree, its usual ability in comparing ideas and in deducing conclusions. The seat of the difficulty is not to be sought for in what are usually designated as the intellectual powers, in distinction from the sensitive nature, but in the passions alone. The victim of this mental disease does not stop to reason, reflect, and compare; but is borne forward to his purpose with a blind and often an irresistible impulse

Pinel mentions a mechanic in the asylum Bicetre, who was subject to this form of insanity. It was, as is frequently the case, intermittent. He knew when the paroxysms of passion were coming on, and even gave warnings to those who were exposed to its effects to make their escape. His powers of correctly judging remained unshaken, not only at other times, but even in the commission of the most violent and outrageous acts. He saw clearly their impropriety, but was unable to restrain himself; and, after the cessation of the paroxysms, was often filled with the deepest grief.

§ 443. *Of the mental disease termed hypochondriasis.*

The seat of the well-known mental disease termed Hypochondriasis, is to be sought for in a disordered state of the Sensibilities. It is, in fact, nothing more nor less than a state of deep depression, gloom, or melancholy. This is the fact; and we never apply the term hypochondriasis to a state of the mind where such gloom or melancholy does not exist; but it is nevertheless true, that the occasion or basis of the fact may sometimes be found in a disordered condition of some other part of the mind One or two concise statements will illustrate what we mean.

One of the slighter forms of hypochondriasis can perhaps be traced to inordinate workings of the Imagination. The mind of the sufferer is fixed upon some unpromising and gloomy subject; probably one which has particular relation either to his present or future prospects. He gives it an undue place in his thoughts, dwelling upon it continually. His imagination hovers over it, throwing a deeper shade on what is already dark. Thus the mind becomes disordered; it is broken off from its ordinary and rightful mode of action; and is no longer what it was, nor what nature designed it should be.

There is another, and still more striking form of hypochondriasis, which is connected in its origin with an alienation of the power of belief. As in all other cases of hypochondriasis, the subject of it suffers much mental distress. He is beset with the most gloomy and distressing apprehensions, occasioned, not by exaggerated and erroneous notions in general, but by some fixed and inevitable false belief.—One imagines that he has no soul; another, that his body is gradually but rapidly perishing; and a third, that he is converted into some other animal, or that he has been transformed into a plant. We are told in the Memoirs of Count Maurepas, that this last idea once took possession of the mind of one of the princes of Bourbon. So deeply was he infected with this notion, that he often went into his garden and insisted on being watered in common with the plants around him. Some have imagined themselves to be transformed into glass, and others have fallen into the still stranger folly of imagining themselves dead.—What has been said confirms our remark, that, although hypochondriasis is, in itself considered, seated in the sensibilities, yet its origin may sometimes be found in a disordered state of some other part of the mind.

It is also sometimes the case, that this disease originates in a violation of some form of sensitive action. It is not only, as its appropriate position, seated in the sensibilities, but it sometimes has its origin there. It is related of a certain Englishman, a man of generous and excellent character, that his life was once attempted by his brother with a pistol. He succeeded, however, in wresting the pistol from his brother's hand, and, on examination, found it to be double charged with bullets. This transaction, as might be expected in the case of a person of just and generous sentiments, filled him with such horror, and with such disgust for the character of man, that he secluded himself ever after from human society. He never allowed the visits even of his own children. It is certainly easy to see, that, under such circumstances, the sensibilities may receive such a shock as to leave the subject of it in a state of permanent dissatisfaction and gloom. In other words, he may in this way and for such reasons become a confirmed hypochondriac.

§ 444. Of intermissions of hypochondriasis, and of its remedies.

The mental disease of hypochondriasis is always understood to imply the existence of a feeling of gloom and depression; but this depressed feeling does not exist in all cases in the same degree. In all instances it is source of no small unhappiness; but in some the wretchedness is extreme. The greatest bodily pains are light in the comparison. It is worthy of remark, however, that the mental distress of hypochondriasis is, in some persons, characterized by occasional intermissions. An accidental remark, some sudden combination of ideas, a pleasant day, and various other causes, are found to dissipate the gloom of the mind. At such times there is not unfrequently a high flow of the spirits, corresponding to the previous extreme depression.—As this disease, even when mitigated by occasional intermissions, is prodigal in evil results, it becomes proper to allude to certain remedies which have sometimes been resorted to.

(1.) The first step towards remedying the evil is to infuse health and vigour into the bodily action, especially that of the nervous system. The nerves, it will be recollected, are the great medium of sensation, inasmuch as they constitute, under different modifications, the external senses. Now the senses are prominent sources of belief and knowledge. Consequently, when the nervous system (including, of course, the senses) is in a disordered state, it is not surprising that persons should have wrong sensations and external perceptions, and, therefore, a wrong belief. If a man's nerves are in such a state that he feels precisely as he supposes a man made of glass would feel, it is no great wonder, when we consider the constitution of the mind, that he should actually believe himself to be composed of that substance. But one of the forms of the disease in question is essentially founded on an erroneous but fixed belief of this kind. Hence, in restoring the bodily system to a right action, we shall correct the wrong belief if it be founded in the senses; and, in removing this, we may anticipate the removal of that deep-seated gloom which is characteristic of hypochondriasis.—(2.) As all the old associations of the hypochondriac have been more or less visited and tinctured by his peculiar malady, efforts should be made to break them up and remove them from the mind by changes in the objects with which he is most conversant, by introducing him into new society, or by travelling. By these means his thoughts are likely to be diverted, not only from the particular subject which has chiefly interested him, but a new impulse is given to the whole mind, which promises to interrupt and banish that fatal fixedness and inertness which had previously encumbered and prostrated it.—(3.) Whenever the malady appears to be founded on considerations of a moral nature, the hypochondriasis may sometimes be removed, or at least alleviated, by the suggestions of counteracting moral motives. If, for instance, the despondency of mind has arisen from some supposed injury, it is desirable to suggest all well-founded considerations which may tend to lessen the sufferer's estimate of the amount of the injury received. When the injury is very great and apparent, suggestions on the nature and duty of forgiveness may not be without effect.—But, whatever course may be taken, it is desirable that the attention of the sufferer should be directed as little as possible to his disease, by any direct remarks upon it. It was a remark of Dr. Johnson, whose sad experience enabled him to judge, that conversation upon melancholy feeds it. Accordingly, he advised Boswell, who, as well as himself, was subject to melancholy of mind, "never to speak of it to his friends nor in company."

§ 445. Disordered action of the passion of fear.

The passion of FEAR, inasmuch as there are various objects around us which are or may be dangerous, is obviously implanted in us for wise purposes. But it not unfrequently exhibits an irregular or disordered action. This disordered state of the affection may discover itself, when considered either in reference to the occasion on which it exists, or in reference to the degree in which it exists. In some cases, for instance, it is connected with objects which, in the view of reason and common sense ought not to excite it. Some persons are afraid to be alone in the dark; it is exceedingly distressing to them. Others are afraid (so much so, perhaps, as to be thrown into convulsions by their presence) of a mouse, or a squirrel, or an insect.

Again, fear may exist with such an intensity as essentially to affect the mind, and even cause insanity. Probably the power of this passion is not well understood. Certain it is, that terrible results have often followed from the attempts of persons, particularly of children, to excite it in others, even in sport. Many instances are on record of individuals who have been permanently and most seriously injured, either in mind or body, or both, by a sudden fright.

Sometimes, especially when connected with permanent causes, it gradually expands and strengthens itself, till it is changed into DESPAIR. The distinctive trait of Despair, in distinction from all other modifications of fear, is, that it excludes entirely the feeling of hope, which exists in connexion with fear in other cases. Despair may exist, therefore, in a greater or less degree, and with a greater or less amount of mental anguish, in accordance with the nature of the thing, whatever it is, which occasions it. When great present or future interests are at stake, and the mind, in relation to those interests, is in a state of despair, the wretchedness which is experienced is neces sarily extreme.

§ 446. Perversions of the benevolent affections.

There are some singular perversions of the benevolent affections which are worthy of notice here It is not unfrequently the case, that persons in a state of mental alienation are entirely indifferent to, and sometimes they even hate, those whom at other times they love most sincerely and deeply. It is, perhaps, difficult to explain this, although it is practically important to know the fact.—Dr. Rush, in speaking of a singular apathy or torpor of the passions, which is sometimes found to exist, says: "I was once consulted by a citizen of Philadelphia, who was remarkable for his strong affection for his wife and children when his mind was in a sound state, who was occasionally afflicted with this apathy, and, when under its influence, lost his affection for them all so entirely, that he said he could see them butchered before his eyes without feeling any distress, or even inclination to rise from his chair to protect them."—(2.) There are other cases, where there seems to be not merely an extinction of the benevolent affection, but its positive conversion into hatred. The same philosophic physician mentions the case of a young lady who was confined as a lunatic in the Pennsylvania Hospital in the year 1802. One of the characteristics of her insanity was hatred for her father. She was gradually restored; and, for several weeks before she was discharged from the Hospital, discovered all the marks of a sound mind, excepting the continuance of this unnatural feeling of hatred. On a certain day she acknowledged with pleasure a return of her filial attachment and affection, and soon after was discharged as cured.*—(3.) There are other cases where insanity is the indirect result of the mere intensity of the benevolent affections. In cases of this kind the affections are so strong, so intense, that they are unable to withstand the shock of sudden and great opposition and disappointments.—"A peasant woman," says Dr. Gall, "became insane three times; the first at the death of her brother, the second at the death of her father, and the third at that of her mother. After she had recovered the third time she came to consult me. As she was very religious, she complained to me of her unfortunate disposition to be afflicted, at the loss of persons who were dear to her, more than religion permits; an evident proof that she had yielded to

* Rush on the Diseases of the Mind, p. 255, 345

grief, although she had combated it by motives which were within her reach." Pinel also mentions the case of a young man who became a violent maniac a short time after losing a father and mother whom he tenderly loved It is true that in these cases the proximate cause of the insanity is sorrow or grief; but the remote cause, and that without which the unfortunate result would not have existed, is an unrestrained and excessive position of the benevolent affections.—It may be proper to add here, that sudden and strong feelings of joy have, in repeated instances, caused a permanent mental disorganization, and even death itself.—"The son of the famous Leibnitz died from this cause, upon his opening an old chest and unexpectedly finding in it a large quantity of gold. Joy, from the successful issue of political schemes or wishes, has often produced the same effect. Pope Leo X. died of joy, in consequence of hearing of a great calamity that had befallen the French nation. Several persons died from the same cause, Mr. Hume tells us, upon witnessing the restoration of Charles II. to the British throne; and it is well known the doorkeeper of Congress died of an apoplexy, from joy, upon hearing the news of the capture of Lord Cornwallis and his army during the American revolutionary war."*

CHAPTER IV.

DISORDERED ACTION OF THE MORAL SENSIBILITIES.

§ 447. Nature of voluntary moral derangement.

THE moral, as well as the natural or pathematic Sensibilities, the Conscience as well as the Heart, may be the subject of a greater or less degree of disorder and alienation. There are probably two leading forms, at least, of moral derangement, viz., VOLUNTARY, and NATURAL OR CONGENITAL.—In regard to voluntary moral derangement, we remark, as an interesting and practically important fact,

* Rush on the Diseases of the Mind, p. 339.

that man may virtually destroy his conscience. There is sound philosophy in the well-known passage of Juvenal, "NEMO REPENTE FUIT TURPISSIMUS." The truth implied in this passage is unquestionably applicable to all persons, with the exception of those few cases where the moral derangement is natural or congenital. A man is not in the first instance *turpissimus*, or a villain, because his conscience makes resistance, and will not let him be so But if the energies of the will are exercised in opposition to the conscience; if, on a systematic plan and by a permanent effort, the remonstrances of conscience are unheeded and its action repressed, its energies will be found to diminish, and its very existence will be put at hazard. There is no doubt that in this way the conscience may be so far seared as to be virtually annihilated. Multitudes have prepared themselves for the greatest wickedness, and have become, in fact, morally insane, by their own voluntary doing. There is a passage in Beaumont, in his "King and no King," which strikingly indicates the progress of the mind in such cases.

> "There is a method in man's wickedness;
> It grows up by degrees. I am not come
> So high as killing of myself; there are
> A hundred thousand sins 'twixt it and me,
> Which I must do. *I shall come to't at last.*"

We say in such cases the conscience is virtually annihilated. And by this remark we mean that it is inert, inefficient, dormant, paralyzed. We do not mean that it is dead. The conscience never dies. Its apparent death is impregnated with the elements of a real and terrible resurrection. It seems to gather vivification and strength in the period of its inactivity; and, at the appointed time of its reappearance, inflicts a stern and fearful retribution, not only for the crimes which are committed against others, but for the iniquity which has been perpetrated against itself.

§ 448. Of accountability in connexion with this form of disordered conscience.

If the moral sensibility, under the system of repression which has been mentioned, refuses to act, the question arises, whether, at such a time, a person is morally accountable for his conduct. As his conscience does not condemn him in what he does, is the transaction, whatever its nature, a criminal one? There can be but one answer to this question. If the individual is not condemned by his conscience, it is the result of his own evil course. We may illustrate the subject by a case which is unhappily too frequent. A man who commits a crime in a state of drunkenness, may plead that he was not, at the time, aware of the guilt of his conduct. And this may be true. But he was guilty for placing himself in a situation where he knew he would be likely to injure others, or in some other way commit unlawful acts. His crime, instead of being diminished, is in fact increased. It is twofold. He is guilty of drunkenness, and he is guilty of everything evil, which he knew, or might have known, would result from his drunkenness.

In like manner, a man is not at liberty to plead that he was not, in the commission of his crimes, condemned by conscience, if it be the fact that he has, by a previous process, voluntarily perverted or hardened the conscience. On the contrary, it would be fair to say, as in the case of drunkenness, that he has increased his guilt; for he has added to the guilt of the thing done, the antecedent and still greater crime of aiming a blow at the mind, of striking at the very life of the soul. Practically he is not self-condemned, for the mere reason that he has paralyzed the principle by which the sentence of self-condemnation is pronounced. But in the eye of immutable justice there is not only no diminution of his guilt, but it is inexpressibly enhanced by the attempts to *murder*, if we may so express it, the principle which, more than anything else, constitutes the dignity and glory of man's nature (See § 403.)

§ 449. Of natural or congenital moral derangement.

The other form of moral derangement is NATURAL or CONGENITAL. We do not know that we are authorized to say that men are by nature, in any case whatever, absolutely destitute of a conscience; nor, on the other hand, have we positive grounds for asserting that this is not the case. There is no more inconsistency or impossibility in a man's coming into the world destitute of a conscience than there is in his being born without the powers of memory, comparison, and reasoning, which we find to be the case in some idiots. But certain it is, that there are some men who appear to have naturally a very enfeebled conscience; a conscience which but very imperfectly fulfils its office; and who, in this respect at least, appear to be constituted very differently from the great body of their fellow-men. They exhibit an imbecility, or, if the expression may be allowed, an *idiocy* of conscience, which unquestionably diminishes, in a very considerable degree, their moral accountability. A number of those writers who have examined the subject of Insanity have taken this view, and have given instances in support of it.

"In the course of my life," says Dr. Rush, "I have been consulted in three cases of the total perversion of the moral faculties. One of them was in a young man; the second in a young woman, both of Virginia; and the third was in the daughter of a citizen of Philadelphia. The last was addicted to every kind of mischief. Her wickedness had no intervals while she was awake, except when she was kept busy in some steady and difficult employment." He refers also to instances in other writers.

Dr. Haslam, in his Observations on Madness, has given two decided cases of moral derangement. One of these was a lad about ten years of age. Some of the traits which he exhibited were as follows. He early showed an impatience and irritability of temper, and became so mischievous and uncontrollable that it was necessary to appoint a person to watch over him. He gave answers only to such questions as pleased him, and acted in opposition to every direction. "On the first interview I had with him," says Dr. Haslam, "he contrived, after two or three minutes' acquaintance, to break a window and tear the frill of my shirt. He was an unrelenting foe to all china, glass, and crockery-ware. Whenever they came within his reach, he shivered them instantly. In walking the street, the keeper was compelled to take the wall, as he uniformly broke the windows if he could get near them; and this operation he performed so dexterously and with such safety to himself, that he never cut his fingers. To tear lace and destroy the finer textures of female ornament seemed to gratify him exceedingly, and he seldom walked out without finding an occasion of indulging this propensity. He never became attached to any inferior animal, a benevolence so common to the generality of children. To these creatures his conduct was that of the brute; he oppressed the feeble, and avoided the society of those more powerful than himself. Considerable practice had taught him that he was the cat's master; and, whenever this luckless animal approached him he plucked out its whiskers with wonderful rapidity; to use his own language, '*I must have her beard off.*' After this operation he commonly threw the creature on the fire or through the window. If a little dog came near him, he kicked it; if a large one, he would not notice it. When he was spoken to, he usually said, 'I do not choose to answer.' When he perceived any one who appeared to observe him attentively, he always said, 'Now I will look unpleasant.' The usual games of children afforded him no amusement; whenever boys were at play he never joined them; indeed, the most singular part of his character was, that he appeared incapable of forming a friendship with any one; he felt no consideration for sex, and would as readily kick or bite a girl as a boy. Of any kindness shown him he was equally insensible; he would receive an orange as a present, and afterward throw it in the face of the donor."

This unfortunate lad seems sometimes to have been sensible of his melancholy condition. When, on a certain occasion, he was conducted through an insane hospital, and a mischievous maniac was pointed out to him who was more strictly confined than the rest, he said to his attendant, "This would be the right place for me." He often expressed a wish to die; and gave as a reason, "That God had not made him like other children."

§ 450. Of moral accountability in cases of natural or congenital moral derangement.

The question recurs here, also, whether persons who are the subjects of a natural or congenital moral derangement are morally accountable, and in what degree. If there is naturally an entire extinction of the moral sense, as in some cases of Idiocy there is an entire extinction of the reasoning power, which, although it may not frequently happen, is at least a supposable case, there is no moral accountability. A person in that situation can have no idea of what right and wrong are; nor can he be conscious of doing either right or wrong in any given case; and, consequently, being without either merit or demerit in the moral sense of the terms, he is not the proper subject of reward and punishment. He is to be treated on the principles that are applicable to idiots and insane persons generally.

In other cases where the mental disorder is not so great, but there are some lingering rays of moral light, some feeble capability of moral vision, the person is to be judged, if it is possible to ascertain what it is, according to what is given him. If he has but one moral talent, it is not to be presumed that the same amount of moral responsibility rests upon him as upon another who possesses ten. The doctrine which requires men, considered as subjects of reward and punishment, to be treated alike, without regard to those original diversities of structure which may exist in all the departments of the mind, not only tends to confound right and wrong, but is abhorrent to the dictates of benevolence. Many individuals, through a misunderstanding of this important subject, have suffered under the hands of the executioner, who, on the principles of religion and strict justice, should have been encircled only in the arms of compassion, long-suffering, and charity

MENTAL PHILOSOPHY.

DIVISION THIRD.

THE WILL.

VOLITIONS, OR VOLITIONAL STATES OF MIND.

CHAPTER I.

GENERAL NATURE OF THE WILL.

§ 451. The will the third and last department of the mind.

MAN has the INTELLECT, by which he perceives; the SENSIBILITIES, by which he feels; and also the WILL, by which he acts. This is the third and last great department of the mind. We proceed now to complete this abridged and concise view of the mind, by giving a brief account of the WILL.

§ 452. On the nature of the will.

And here let us interpose a word of caution. It is not to be inferred, when we speak of one part of the mind in distinction from another, and of passing from one part or power to another, that the mind is a congeries of distinct existences, or that it is, in any literal and material sense of the terms, susceptible of division. Varieties of action do not necessarily imply a want of unity in the principle from which they originate. The mental principle, therefore, is indivisible. In itself it is truly and essentially a unity, though multiplied, in a manner calculated to excite the greatest astonishment, in its modes of application. It is merely one of these modes of its application, or, rather, one of these modes of its exercise, which is indicated by the term Will. Accordingly, the term Will is not meant to express anything separate from the mind; but merely embodies and expresses the fact of the mind's operating in a particular way.

And hence the Will may properly enough be defined the MENTAL POWER OR SUSCEPTIBILITY BY WHICH WE PUT FORTH VOLITIONS.—And, in accordance with this definition, if we wish to understand more fully what the nature of the power is, we must look at its results, and examine the nature of those states of mind which it gives rise to.—"It is necessary," says Mr. Stewart very justly, "to form a distinct notion of what is meant by the word *volition*, in order to understand the import of the word *will;* for this last word properly expresses that *power* of the mind, of which volition is the *act*, and it is only by attending to what we experience while we are conscious of the act, that we can understand anything concerning the nature of the power."*

§ 453. Of the nature of the acts of the will or volitions.

Of volitions, which are the results of the existence and exercise of the volitional power, we are unable to give any definition in words, which will of itself make them clearly understood. They are simple states of the mind, and that circumstance alone precludes the possibility of a definition, in any strict and proper sense of the term. It is true, we may call them determinations or decisions of the mind, or resolutions of the mind, or acts of choice, and the like, but this is only the substitution of other terms, which themselves need explanation; and, of course, it throws no light upon the subject of inquiry. And hence we are thrown back upon our consciousness, as we are in all cases where the nature of the simple states of mind is the matter of investigation. And whenever we have made this appeal to the internal experience, and have received its testimony, we are then placed in the possession of all that knowledge which the nature of the case seems to admit of. And we must suppose that every one has, in some degree, done this. It is not presumable, at least it is not at all probable, that men who are constantly in action, pursuing one course and avoiding another, adopting one plan and rejecting another, accepting and refusing, befriending and opposing, all which things, and many others, imply volitional action, are still ignorant of what an act of the Will is.

§ 454. Volition never exists without some object.

Although we are obliged to depend chiefly upon

* Philosophy of the Moral and Active Powers, Appendix i., § 1.

consciousness for a knowledge of the nature of volitions, it is still true that we can make some statements in respect to them which may aid us in forming our opinions. Among other things, it is an obvious remark, *that every act of the will must have an object.* A very slight reflection on the subject will evince this. It is the same here as in respect to the act of thought, of memory, and of association, all of which imply some object, in reference to which the mental act is called forth.

"Every act of the will," says Dr. Reid, "must have an object. He that wills must will something; and that which he wills is called the object of his volition. As a man cannot think without thinking of something, nor remember without remembering something, so neither can he will without willing something. Every act of will, therefore, must have an object; and the person who wills must have some conception, more or less distinct, of what he wills."*

§ 455. It exists only in reference to what we believe to be in our power.

Another circumstance may be pointed out in illustration of volitions, viz., *that they never exist in respect to those things which we believe to be wholly beyond our reach.* As no man believes that it is in his power to fly in the air like a bird, so we never find a person putting forth a volition to do so. As no man believes that he can originate what never had a being before; in other words, that he can create a new existence out of nothing, so we never find a man determining, resolving, or willing to that effect. Indeed, we are obviously so constituted, that, whenever we believe an object to be wholly and absolutely beyond our power, volition does not and cannot exist in respect to it. The farmer, for instance, in a time of severe drought, desires rain, but he does not will it. He is conscious of a desire, but he is not conscious of a volition. The very nature of the mind interposes in such a case, and effectually obstructs the origina-

* Reid's Essays on the Active Powers, Essay ii., ch. i.

tion of the volitional act. And this is so promptly and decisively done, and done too in all cases without exception, that we find it very difficult even to *conceive* of anything which we are certain is wholly beyond our power, as being an object of the will's action. There may be a desire in such cases, but there is no volition.

And the usage of language will be found to throw light on this distinction, making the term DESIRE applicable both to what is within our reach and what is not; and the term VOLITION applicable only to the former. In some cases we speak of willing or determining to do a thing, while in others we invariably limit ourselves to the mere expression of a wish or desire. Accordingly, it would comport with and be required by the usage of language, if our thoughts and conversation were directed to those matters, to say, that we determine or *will* to walk, but *desire* to fly; that we *will* to build a house, but *desire* to create a world.

§ 456. Volition relates to our own action and to whatever else may be dependent upon us.

Although the statements thus far made tend to throw some light upon the nature of the Will's acts, something further remains to be remarked. It does not seem definite enough merely to assert, that volitions relate solely to those things which are in our power, or are believed to be so. We may inquire further what is meant by being in our power, and how far the import of the phrase may justly extend itself.—And hence it is necessary to add, that volitions relate, in the first place, to our own action, either some bodily movement or some act of the mind. In saying this, however, we do not mean to say that volition is necessarily limited to the *present* action. We may will to perform something of the simplest kind, which will exact, in its execution, merely the present moment, or something of a more complicated nature, which will require no inconsiderable time. Any series of actions, intellectual or bodily, capable of being performed by us, which the understanding can embrace as one, and by means of any relations existing among them can consolidate into one, the will can resolve upon as one. So that the action, dependent upon volition, may be the mere movement of the foot or finger; or, it may be the continuous labours of a day, a week, or a year, or some long and perilous expedition by land or sea. It is just as proper to say that a man wills to take a voyage to England, as to say that he wills to put one foot before the other in stepping from his door to the street.

Volition may exist, in the second place, in respect to anything and everything which is truly dependent upon us, however circuitous and remote that dependence may be. It is proper to say that a merchant has determined or willed to fit a vessel or a number of vessels for sea, and to send them to different parts of the world, although his own direct and personal agency in the thing is hardly known. The effect of his volition, extending far beyond his own direct and personal capabilities, controls the acts of a multitude of individuals who are dependent on him. Previous to the commencement of his celebrated expedition into Russia, the Emperor Napoleon undoubtedly brought all the objects relative to the intended expedition distinctly before his understanding; the number and the kind of troops, the arms and ammunition with which they were to be furnished, the means of subsistence in the various countries through which they were to pass, and the expenses incident to the arming and support of a body so numerous. The action of the intellect enabled him to assimilate and combine this vast complexity of objects into one. Although numberless in its parts and details, it assumed, as it passed before the rapid glances of his understanding, an identity and oneness, which, for all the purposes of volition and action, constituted it one thing. And, accordingly, it is altogether proper to say, that Napoleon purposed, determined, or *willed* the expedition into Russia, although the agencies requisite to carry it into effect were not lodged directly in himself, but in millions of subordinate instruments, that were more or less remotely dependent upon him. Certain it is, if he had not put forth his volition, the subordinate instrumentalities, however numerous and powerful in themselves, would never have united in and secured the result in question.

§ 457. Volitions involve a prospective element.

Another mark or characteristic of volitions, by which they are distinguished from some, though not from all states of the mind, is, that they have exclusive relation to the future, to something which is to be done.—A volition is "futuritive" in its very nature; it involves in itself, and as a part of its own essentiality, a prospective element; it has no capacity of turning its eye backward, but always looks forward.

An intellective or perceptive act rests in itself. As soon as it assumes the form of a cognition or knowledge, it accomplishes, so far as its own nature is concerned, the mission for which it was sent. It takes its position, and there it stands; furnishing an occasion, it is true, for other feelings to exist and to operate, but in itself remaining not only complete, but satisfied and quiescent.

But it is not so with a volition, which, from its very nature, cannot rest satisfied with the mere fact of its own existence. If we may be allowed the expressions, it continually reaches forth its hand to grasp objects which have not as yet a being. In other words, it always has in view something which is to take place hereafter; something which is to be done, the completion of which is, therefore, necessarily future. This trait is an element of its nature, or, rather, is naturally and necessarily involved in its nature, and may be regarded as one of the characteristics which help to distinguish it from the perceptive and emotive states of the mind at least, if not from others.

§ 458. Volitions may exist with various degrees of strength.

There is one additional characteristic of volitions

worthy of some notice, viz., that the volition does not always exist with the same degree of force. Undoubtedly every one must have been conscious, that the exercise of the voluntary power is more prompt and energetic at some times than others. We are aware that it is liable to be objected to this statement, that if we will to do a thing, there can be nothing less than the volition; and that it is necessarily the same under all circumstances. And it is undoubtedly true, that we never will to do an act with anything less than a volition; and that, if there be any act of the will at all, it is one truly and fully so. That is to say, the act is in all cases the same, as far as its intrinsic nature is concerned. And yet we may confidently urge, there is no inconsistency in saying that it may exist with different degrees of force.

The existence of a mental state, which is always the same in its nature, in different degrees, is not peculiar to volition. The same trait is characteristic of the mental act in all cases where we yield our assent or belief. The state of mind which we denominate BELIEF is undoubtedly always the same in its nature, but admitting of various degrees. We determine these differences of strength in the feeling by means of that same internal consciousness which assures us of the existence of the mere feeling itself. In other words, we are conscious of, or feel our belief to be sometimes weaker and at other times stronger, which we express by various terms, such as presumption, probability, high probability, and certainty. And by appealing in the same way to our consciousness of what takes place within, we shall probably come to the conclusion that we put forth the act of volition with much greater strength at some times than others; that at some times it is so feeble as hardly to be distinguished from a mere desire or wish, and is scarcely recognised as a volition, while at other times it is exceedingly marked and energetic.

CHAPTER II.

ON THE LAWS OF THE WILL.

§ 459. On the universality of law.

THE will is free; but it is also true, that it acts *in connection with law.* In entering specifically upon the question, whether the will is susceptible of determinate principles or laws of action, we may reason in support of that view, in the first place, from the general likeness or analogy of nature. If the universe is everywhere legibly inscribed and written over with the great truth, that all things are subject to law, are we not furnished with a strong presumption that we shall not discover an exception in any part of man's mental nature? As to the alleged fact on which we base this presumption, there can be no doubt of it.—Let us look, in the first place, at material things. The parts of the earth are kept in their relative position by the operation of some fixed law; the various immense bodies, composing the system to which the earth belongs, are made to revolve in obedience to some unalterable principle; there is not even a plant, or a stone, or a falling leaf, or a grain of sand, which can claim an exemption from regulation and control. And what is true in these few instances, is true in all. No certain and undoubted exception can be found.

And this great truth holds good also of things which have life and intelligence. Objects of a spiritual or mental nature (if not in precisely the same sense in which the assertion is applicable to matter, yet in some true and important meaning of the expressions) have their appropriate and determinate principles of being and action. There may, indeed, be some things which are as yet unexplainable by man; there may be some objects of knowledge, to the full understanding of whose nature limited human reason cannot as yet reach; but still the vast majority of objects, coming within the ordinary range of our inspection, obviously tend to found and to foster the general conviction, that there are laws wherever there are existences, whatever the kind or nature of the existence.— There is, therefore, undoubted truth in the remark of Montesquieu, with which he introduces his great work on the Spirit of Laws, where he says, after some suggestions on the meaning of the term, "all beings have their laws, the Deity his laws, the material world its laws, the intelligences superior to man their laws, the beasts their laws, man his laws."

§ 460. Remarks of Hooker on the universality of law.

"Of law," says the learned Hooker in a passage often quoted, "no less can be said than that her seat is the bosom of God, her voice the harmony of the world; all things in heaven and earth do her homage, the very least as feeling her care, the greatest as not exempted from her power; both angels and men, and creatures of what condition soever, though each in different spheres and manner, yet all with uniform consent admiring her as the mother of their peace and joy."*

It is a sublime truth, that law, the great bond of the universe, finds its origin and support in the bosom of the Deity, and is, in its basis or elements, co-substantial with his nature; and going forth from that primitive and prolific centre in every possible direction, like rays from the sun, embraces, harmonizes, and controls every form and modification of being, whether intelligent or unintelligent. And how full of grandeur and of consolation is the thought! If we could suppose that even a single unintelligent atom had broken loose from the countless extensions and applications of the great Principle of Unity, which is only another name for that law which binds one existence to another, and both to a third, and all to the great central and superintendent Power, it would not fail to fill us with misgivings and anguish. The doctrine of the universality of law, which is the same as the universality of power under the guidance of fixed

* Hooker's Ecclesiastical Polity, book i.

principles, recommends itself to the heart as well as the understanding, and dispenses happiness while it controls conviction. Is any one prepared to say that he is not rendered happy in the recollection that God is around us and in us? Is it not a source of consolation, that his paternal eye rests for ever upon our path; that he knoweth our lying down and rising up, our going out and coming in? And that, while he superintends the minutest actions and events pertaining to ourselves, He extends abroad, amid the numberless varieties of existence, the watchfulness of his pervading control,

"And fills, and bounds, connects and equals all?"

§ 461. A presumption thus furnished in favor of the subjection of the will to law.

It is not necessary to pursue this subject, when contemplated under this general form, at much length. What has been said will answer our present purpose. If the doctrine of the universality of law be tenable, what shall we say of the Will? Does not the position, that the Will is not subject to laws, imply an anomaly in the universe? Whatever is not under some sort of control, but is entirely irregular, contingent, and exempt from all conditions, is necessarily irresponsible to the supervision of any thing, even God himself. We have, then, an exceedingly strong presumption, when we look at the subject in the most general light, in favour of the proposition that the Will has its laws.

CHAPTER III.

LAWS OF THE WILL IMPLIED IN THE PRESCIENCE OR FORESIGHT OF THE DEITY.

§ 462. The notion which men naturally form of the Deity implies foreknowledge.

In further proof of the general proposition that the Will has its LAWS, we now enter very briefly upon some distinct trains of thought. In the present chapter we propose to bring forward in its support the Prescience of the Deity.

And we naturally remark, in the first place, that the idea which all men agree in forming of the Deity implies foreknowledge. We do not have reference in this remark to the light which Revelation throws upon this subject, but refer merely to the notion of the Deity which men form of themselves. In all countries and among all classes of men; in the cheerless hut of the Esquimaux; in the rude dwellings of the uncivilized tribes inhabiting the islands of the Pacific; in the tent of the vagrant Arab, as well as among those who are refined by the arts and enlightened by science, we find the notion of a God. The conception may indeed be a feeble and imperfect one, compared with that developed in the Scriptures; but, feeble as it is, it always includes the idea of Prescience or Foresight in a much higher degree than is possessed by men. The very heathen would scoff at the idea of a God whose knowledge is limited to the present moment.

§ 463. The prescience of God directly taught in the Scriptures.

The divine prescience or foresight is distinctly made known in a multitude of passages of Scripture. The Supreme Being himself, in the language ascribed to Him by the prophet Isaiah, asserts, "I am God, and there is none like me, *declaring the end from the* *beginning*, and from ancient times the things that are not yet done." "Known unto God," says the apostle James, "are all his works, *from the beginning of the world*."*

Nor does the doctrine of God's foreknowledge rest upon general statements alone; but we have instances, again and again, of predictions, uttered long before the events came to pass, which were strictly fulfilled. The deluge was predicted one hundred and twenty years before it came on the face of the earth. It was foretold that the children of Israel should be in bondage four hundred years. The cruel conduct of the Syrian Hazael, and the deliverance wrought out by the hand of the Persian Cyrus, are matters of precise and specific prediction. The destruction of Babylon and of Nineveh, with many of the circumstances attending their overthrow, was predicted also. The coming and the preaching of Jesus Christ, and particularly his humiliation, trials, and death, were foretold by the mouths of holy men many years, and even ages, before the events themselves took place. The destruction of Jerusalem (not to mention other instances equally decisive in their bearing on this subject) was depicted long before it happened, and with a wonderful particularity and vividness.—In view of these facts, and others like them, we have only to make the remark that predictions so numerous and specific, and so exactly fulfilled, could not have been uttered without the possession of foreknowledge or prescience on the part of their author.

§ 464. The foreknowledge of events implies the foreknowledge of volitions.

And it is further to be noticed, in regard to many, if not all the events which have taken place in accordance with such predictions as those referred to in the last section, that they were dependent on the volitions of men. The voluntary actions of men necessarily imply the antecedent exercise of volitions; and,

* Isaiah xlvi., 9, 10; Acts xv., 18.

such being the fixed relation between volitions and actions, it is difficult to suppose that any being whatever should foresee the actions of men without a foresight, at the same time, of their volitions. As an illustration, it was foretold to Abraham that his descendants should go into Egypt, and should take up their residence there; but such a prediction evidently implies a knowledge of all the circumstances under which this event should take place, including, in particular, every motive and every volition connected with it. Such a prediction implies a knowledge, not only of the volitions and acts of the immediate agents in the events foretold, but of those persons also who were concerned in them incidentally and collaterally. In the present case, it implies a knowledge of the jealousies of Joseph's brethren, and of their perverse and wicked conduct in selling him to the Ishmaelites; it implies a knowledge of the wants, interests, and motives of the Ishmaelites themselves, not to mention the situation and motives of other individuals and bodies of men, which were undoubtedly among the preparatory steps and means to the wonderful events which followed.

Every one knows that events of the greatest magnitude are dependent upon circumstances apparently the most trivial. It is a remark of Dr. Dwight, that the "motions of a fly are capable of terminating the most important human life, or of changing all the future designs of a man, and altering the character, circumstances, and destiny of his descendants throughout time and eternity."* Now, if these things are so, it cannot for a moment be conceded that God foreknows and predicts events without a knowledge of all those circumstances, even the most trivial, upon which those events may, by any possibility, be dependent. In particular, and above all, He must be minutely and fully acquainted with the volitive acts or volitions of the immediate agents in them. In foreseeing events in which men are concerned, He must, of course, foresee what men will do; but it is incon-

* Dwight's Theology, Sermon vi.

ceivable that he should know this without knowing what volitions they will put forth.

§ 465. Application of these views to the will.

But if it satisfactorily appears that God foreknows all things, particularly the volitions of men, then it clearly follows that the volitional power or Will has its laws. The opposite of an action which is in harmony with law is perfect *contingency;* and the very idea of contingency or of contingent action implies that it is something which cannot possibly be foreknown. Whatever is foreknown must be foreknown to exist at a particular time or place, or under some particular circumstances; but that action or event, which it is ascertained and certain will exist at a particular time or place, or under any particular and definite circumstances, cannot, with any propriety of language, be deemed a perfectly contingent one. Since, therefore, nothing which is foreknown is contingent, and since the volitions of men are obviously the subjects of foreknowledge, it follows that there must be some definite laws or principles by which the action of the voluntary power is, to some extent, regulated.

§ 466. The views of this chapter in harmony with the doctrine of the influences of the Holy Spirit.

As in some respects closely connected with the views of this chapter, we may here, with propriety, refer to the Scripture doctrine that God, through the influences of the Holy Spirit, has the power, and, when in his providence He sees fit, exerts the power, of enlightening, sanctifying, and guiding the minds of men. The reader of the Bible will naturally be reminded here of the Saviour's interesting expressions on this subject, which are found in the concluding chapters of the Gospel of John: "I will pray the Father, and he shall give you another Comforter, that he may abide with you for ever." "And the Comforter, which is the Holy Ghost, whom the Father will send in my name, He shall teach you all things, and bring all things to your remembrance, whatsoever I have said unto you." John xiv., 16, 26.—"So they, being sent forth by the Holy Ghost, departed unto Seleucia."—"Then Saul, who is also called Paul, filled with the Holy Ghost, set his eyes upon him, and said, Oh full of all subtlety," &c.—"And were forbidden of the Holy Ghost to preach the word in Asia." Acts xiii., 4, 9; xvi., 6.—"Which things also we speak, not in the words which man's wisdom teacheth, but which the Holy Ghost teacheth." 1 Cor. ii., 13.—"Holy men of God spake as they were moved by the Holy Ghost." 2 Pet. i., 21.

All these passages, and others like them, necessarily imply that the human mind, whatever may be true of its freedom and responsibility, is, nevertheless, susceptible of being held in subordination to the all-pervading and transcendent control of the Supreme Intelligence.

CHAPTER IV.

LAWS OF THE WILL IMPLIED IN THE PRESCIENCE OR FORESIGHT OF MEN.

§ 467. Man as well as Deity susceptible of foresight.

It may, perhaps, be objected by some that the argument drawn from the prescience of the Deity is less satisfactory than it would otherwise be, in consequence of the unspeakable elevation and incomprehensibleness of the Divine Mind. That the divine mind is, in some respects, incomprehensible by man, is true; but it does not follow that an argument, founded upon what we know and can understand of the divine nature, is therefore incomprehensible or even obscure. But whatever weight, whether more or less, may be conceded to this objection, we come to another view of the subject, analogous indeed to that of the last chapter, but drawn from a different source, and level to every one's comprehension. Man himself, restricted and dimmed as his conceptions undoubtedly are, has a prescience of the future, a foresight of what is to come to pass, as well as the adorable Being who made him. Not in an equal degree indeed, but still in some degree. And this fact also goes to confirm the position which we are now examining in regard to the Will.

§ 468. Prescience or foresight of men in respect to their own situation and conduct.

In the first place, man can foretell (we do not say with perfect certainty, nor is that at all essential to our argument) his own situation, actions, and success at some future time.

Take a very simple illustration. A man proposes to go to Boston or New-York, or to some place of common resort, no matter where it is, for the purpose of transacting business there. The execution of a design of this nature, although it is difficult to mention one more common and simple, implies the putting forth of hundreds and thousands of volitions. And it is undoubtedly the fact, that the object in view cannot be effected without this great number of volitions. And yet we perceive that this person goes forward with confidence, and that he makes his calculations without fear, and with a feeling of certainty that he will be able to execute them. He evidently proceeds upon the supposition (although he may not be fully conscious of it at the time, and may never have made it a matter of distinct reflection) that the operations of the Will exist in reference to some fixed principles; and particularly in connexion with motives in their various kinds and degrees. And looking at his proposed undertaking with care, and understanding well the claims, both of interest and duty, which are involved in it, he determines or wills in reference to the general plan before him, whatever it may be, without even doubting that all the future acts of the voluntary power will be accordant with its requisite details; and that, in due season, it will be brought to a fulfilment in all its parts. But we may assert with confidence, that this could never be done if volitions were entirely contingent; in other words, if they were without laws. For if this last were the case, he would be just as likely to go to Providence as Boston, to Albany as New-York, or to any other place whatever, as to that where he first determined to go; and would be just as likely to do the direct opposite as that particular business which he designed to accomplish at his first setting out.—And the views, applicable in this particular case, will apply to the multiplied occurrences and duties of every week and day. And they furnish of themselves, and independently of every other argument which may be brought up, but little short of a demonstration of what we are attempting to establish.

§ 469. Foresight of men in respect to the conduct of others.

In the second place, men are able to foretell, with a considerable degree of certainty, the situation, actions, and success of others at some future time. This is so notorious as not unfrequently to have elicited the remark, that there is a certain regular order in the conduct of men, in some degree analogous to the regular course of things, which we never fail to observe in the physical world. Men may everywhere be found who would no more hesitate to predict the precise conduct of their neighbours in certain assignable circumstances, than they would to predict that trees of a certain kind would grow in a given situation.

Some instances will illustrate what we mean.—A poor man goes to a rich man in the same neighbourhood, who is a confirmed and inexorable miser, for the purpose of borrowing a sum of money, but without being willing to give the customary interest of twenty per cent., and unable at the same time to furnish adequate security for the principal. Everybody knows that the miser will refuse his money at once. They expect and predict it with hardly less confidence than they predict, that a stone thrown into the air will immediately fall to the earth's surface. "A prisoner," says Mr. Hume, "who has neither money nor interest, discovers the impossibility of escape, as well when he considers the obstinacy of his guards as the walls and bars with which he is surrounded; and in all his attempts for his freedom, chooses rather to work upon the stone and iron of the one, than upon the inflexible nature of the other." This remark of Mr. Hume is an important one, and, without question, is essentially correct. Undoubtedly it is sometimes the case, that prisoners endeavour to effect their escape by working upon the passions and will of their guards; but in a vast majority of cases they consider their chance of escape much better by means of attempts made upon the stone and iron that enclose them. They understand so well the connexion between motive and volition, between interest and duty on the one hand and the resolves of the will on the other, that, with the knowledge they possess of the characters and situation of those who are appointed to act as their guards, they consider their escape by means of any collusion with them, or any assistance from that source, as an utter impossibility.

§ 470. Other familiar instances of this foresight.

But we will now proceed to give some instances which are less remote from common observation. The reader may perhaps recollect some remarks of Dr. Paley, relative to our constant dependence on our fellow-men. "Every hour of our lives we trust and depend upon others; and it is impossible to stir a step, or, what is worse, to sit still a moment, without such trust and dependence. I am now writing at my ease, not doubting (or, rather, never distrusting, and, therefore, never thinking about it) but that the butcher will send in the joint of meat which I ordered; that his servant will bring it; that my cook will dress it; that my footman will serve it up; and that I shall find it on the table at one o'clock."*—And this is a state of things which is constantly occurring, not only in the matter of the daily food necessary for the support of our lives, but in a thousand other instances. The merchant depends upon his clerks; the manu-

* Moral Philosophy, book iii., chap. v.

facturer upon his numerous operatives of all classes and conditions; the farmer, who works upon a large scale, depends upon the hands of others as much as he does upon the labour of his own hands; the commander of a vessel constantly reckons upon the efficient co-operation of his sailors; the leader of armies relies upon the movements of vast bodies of men made with the utmost precision in the most trying circumstances. And it is the same in all situations, and among all classes of men, as any one, who will in the least trouble himself to exercise his recollection, will be abundantly satisfied. But if all these persons operated by mere accident, and without regard to any fixed principles; if it were a matter of entire contingency whether they should perform their engagements or not, it is easy to see that all the sources of enjoyment and even of existence would be destroyed, and the foundations of society speedily broken up.

§ 471. Argument from the regularity of voluntary contributions.

In connexion with the topic now before us, viz., that we are able to foretell, with a considerable degree of certainty, the situation and actions of others at some future time, we request the attention of the reader to a class of facts which are somewhat peculiar. It cannot have escaped the notice of any one as in some degree a characteristic of modern times, that there are a multitude of benevolent associations, whose receipts depend wholly upon *voluntary* contributions. But, notwithstanding the fact of their income being wholly voluntary, which, if experience had not shown to the contrary, would be exceedingly discouraging, they proceed in their affairs with nearly or quite the same confidence as if they had a fixed capital to operate with. They send out missionaries, establish schools, translate the Scriptures, explore unknown and barbarous countries, plant colonies, erect churches, and engage in other important and expensive undertakings, without a cent of money except what comes from voluntary gifts. They make their calculations beforehand as to what they can accomplish in a given time; and not unfrequently incur heavy expenses in anticipation of their receipts. Their true capital is a knowledge of the operations of the human mind under certain assignable circumstances. These circumstances they are in a good degree acquainted with; and hence are enabled to anticipate the amount of their receipts for a given time with almost as much accuracy as the merchant or farmer, who has an actual capital already in his possession to operate with. Does not this circumstance go, with others, to show that the Will has its laws?

§ 472. Of sagacity in the estimate of individual character.

We now proceed to introduce to the consideration of the reader another view of the subject of this chapter, which is exceedingly interesting in itself, besides furnishing an argument deserving of some attention. It is not uncommon to find men who exhibit a sort of quickness or sagacity in the estimate of individual character, which is sometimes described by the phrase, *a knowledge of the world, or of human nature.* This knowledge is undoubtedly possessed by all persons to some extent; but not unfrequently individuals are found who possess it in a remarkably high degree. In some men it may be said not only to assume the appearance, but even to approximate the nature of a *prophetic* anticipation or foresight; and when this is the case, it is an acquisition, as no one can be ignorant, of great power and value. The late Mr. Dumont, of Geneva, in his Recollections of Mirabeau, has noticed this ability in one of its more striking forms.—Speaking of the political life of that celebrated man, especially in its connexion with his knowledge of men and his political foresight, he goes on to say, "It was by the same instinctive penetration that Mirabeau so easily detected the feelings of the Assembly, and so often embarrassed his opponents by revealing their secret motives, and laying open that which they were most anxious to conceal. There seemed to exist no political enigma which he could not solve. He came at once to the most intimate secrets, and his sagacity alone was of more use to him than a multitude of spies in the enemy's camp. I used sometimes to attribute the severity of his judgments to hatred or jealousy, but it has been justified by succeeding events, and there was not a man of any consequence in the Assembly, the sum of whose conduct did not correspond with the opinion which Mirabeau had formed of him.

"Independently of this natural gift, this intellect of penetration, his life had been so agitated, he had been so tossed upon the sea of human existence, as he used to say, that he had acquired vast experience of the world and of men. He detected, in a moment, every shade of character; and, to express the result of his observations, he had invented a language scarcely intelligible to any but himself; had terms to indicate fractions of talents, qualities, virtues, or vices—halves and quarters—and, at a glance, he could perceive every real or apparent contradiction. No form of vanity, disguised ambition, or tortuous proceedings could escape his penetration; but he could also perceive good qualities, and no man had a higher esteem for energetic and virtuous characters."*

It cannot be necessary to add anything to show how this instance, and others like it, (for the political history of every age brings to light some men of this stamp,) connects itself with and illustrates our subject.

§ 473. Foresight of the conduct of masses of men and nations.

It is not too much to say that we are able, not only to predict with a considerable degree of certainty the conduct of individuals in any given circumstances, but we may do the same of whole classes of men, and even nations. Hence the remark which Lord Bacon has somewhere made, and which is strikingly characterized by its poetical as well as its philosophical spirit. "The shepherds of the people," he says, "should understand the *prognostics of state tempests;* hollow blasts of wind seemingly at a distance, and secret swellings of the sea, often precede a storm."

* Dumont's Recollections of Mirabeau, chap. xiv.

But we may carry this view into some particulars which are deserving of notice. The results, for instance, of a popular election, if certain data are ascertained, are often considered as settled, even before the day of voting has arrived; although the conclusions thus formed are based in part upon opinions relative to whole classes of men, who differ from each other in their callings, interests, and prejudices.

Again, the speculations in the public or national stocks are very frequently prompted by the opinions, which those who are engaged in such speculations are able to form of the course which states and nations will take in some future time.

One of the most striking facts, involving the foresight or prescience of the conduct of large masses of men, is the financial estimate which is annually made by governments. It is well known that the amount of property invested in commerce, with the annual returns of revenue to the government, is every year estimated in advance, and with very considerable accuracy, by the treasury departments of all civilized nations.

Reasoning from what has taken place in times past, we may predict, with a good degree of accuracy, what number of letters will be written and circulated through a nation at any future time. The number of letters is indicated by the amount of postage; and this is a matter which the governments of nations have thought it important to them to ascertain. If a person will take the pains to examine the total receipts of the Postoffice Department of the United States, in the successive years from 1790 to 1830, he will notice, with but few exceptions, and those easily explained, a gradual and very regular increase in the amount; the increase being such as would naturally be expected from the augmentation of the wealth and population of the country.

It would seem, in looking at the statistical tables for this purpose, that in the year 1815 there was an increase decidedly greater than would be naturally expected in ordinary circumstances. But this was probably owing (and equally satisfactory reasons will be found for other equally marked variations) to the recent return of peace with Great Britain, which at once gave a new and expanded impulse to the business transactions of the country.

We presume it will be found also on inquiry, that the number of letters not taken from the subordinate offices, and returned from time to time to the General Postoffice, or DEAD LETTERS so called, is nearly the same from year to year, or varying so as to correspond to the variation in the number of letters received. It is stated by Laplace, that the number of dead letters remaining at and returned from other offices to the Postoffice at Paris is, in ordinary times, nearly the same from one year to another. The same thing has been stated of the Dead Letter Office, as it is called, in London.—All these things conclusively evince that the actions of men, whether considered individually or in masses, are not left to chance or mere accident.

NOTE.—For a more detailed and satisfactory examination of this part of our subject, including not only a specific statement of a number of volitional laws, but also an explanation of the relational harmony and consistency of Law and Freedom, we are compelled by our narrow limits to refer to the volume on the Department of the Will, of which these statements are an abridgment.

CHAPTER V.

ON THE FREEDOM OF THE WILL.

§ 474. Of the freedom of the will, and of the relation of its freedom to its subjection to law.

WE proceed now to another view of this important subject. If it be true that the will, in its action, harmonizes with law, in such a sense at least that its action cannot be regarded as wholly accidental, it is also true that the WILL IS FREE.

Law and Liberty necessarily go together. If it could be shown that the will acts, irrespective of any determinate methods and principles of action; in other words, if laws were not in any sense predicable of the will, (such for instance as the great law of motives,) then it would of course follow, that it is the subject of mere contingency and accident, which entirely and fully comes up to the utmost idea of fatality. And it would be found to be a fatalism of the worst kind, an unintelligent fatalism.—But having shown that the Will has its laws, we secure in that single fact the possibility of liberty, which we could not have without it. We are, accordingly, in a situation in which the liberty of the Will, that important and noble attribute of a morally accountable nature, is not necessarily excluded, which would certainly be the case if the will were driven about hither and thither, without any possible foresight of what is liable to take place, and without any regularity of action.

§ 475. Circumstances or occasions under which freedom of the will exists.

Although, in entering into the subject of the freedom of the Will, we do not profess, in this abridged view of it, to go into verbal explanations and definitions, something may nevertheless be said in relation to the occasions or circumstances under which it exists. If there is perfect harmony in other parts of the mind, there will be perfect freedom in the Will; if every appetite, and propensity, and passion is precisely what it should be, the voluntary power cannot possibly experience any pressure which will interrupt or diminish that degree of liberty which is essential to, or compatible with its nature.

This topic may perhaps be susceptible of illustration by a reference to the Supreme Being. If freedom can, with propriety and justice, be predicated of any being whatever, it is certainly predicable of the Supreme Being; and predicable not only in general terms, *but of the Will in particular.* We hazard nothing in saying, that liberty of the Will is possessed by Him in the highest possible degree. And we cannot conceive how it should be otherwise, when we consider that the elements, both moral and intellectual, by which it is surrounded, are in harmony with each other.—And if we turn our attention to any other high and holy beings, such as are nearest in glory to the Supreme Author of all things, it is the same. All the various elements, which go to constitute them intelligent and moral beings, are restricted to their proper place, and operate in their due proportion. Their perceptions, so far as they go, are in perfect accordance with the truth of things. Their emotions are such as God, who takes supreme delight in perfect rectitude, can entirely approve. Every desire which they exercise is in its right place; their love to God is just such as it should be; their love to other holy beings corresponds precisely to the nature of the object towards which it is directed; their aversion to sin and sinful beings is just such, and fully and entirely such, as is appropriate and right; and it is precisely the same in respect to every other emotion and desire. And the consequence is, there is no disturbing force in the neighbourhood of the Will; there is no possible motive to sway it from the line of perfect rectitude; and hence it is true, that their Will, although it always operates in the direction of the highest rectitude and good, is always at liberty; and this liberty exists, too, in the highest possible degree. And hence we assert, in respect to all minds, whether they are higher or lower in the scale of being, that perfect harmony is the appropriate element of perfect freedom; and that every diminution of harmony will be attended with a corresponding diminution of liberty. And this is as true of the separate parts or powers of the mind as of the whole; and is as true of the Will as of any other part.

§ 476. Evidence of the freedom of the will from consciousness.

Having made the foregoing remarks in explanation of the nature of the freedom of the Will, and of the occasions on which it exists, we are now prepared to proceed to a consideration of the proofs in support of the position that there is such a freedom. And we accordingly remark, that the doctrine of the freedom of the will is sustained, in the first place, by CONSCIOUSNESS.—When we assert that men have a knowledge of the Freedom of the will by Consciousness, we mean merely to declare, that such knowledge is the result of an inward conviction, an internal experience. In other words, every man knows himself, in the exercise of volition, to be free. It is a knowledge which we possess, not by deduction, but by a species of intuitive conviction; not by inference, but by an original perception.

We will only add, that the argument from Consciousness is as decisive, as it is plain and simple. Some writers, indeed, have been disposed to rely upon this argument alone. They consider it (and perhaps it may be admitted with entire justice and correctness) as conclusive against any considerations which may be adduced adverse to it. "Our own free will," says Mr. Stewart, "we know by consciousness; and we can have no evidence of any truth so irresistible as this."

§ 477. Objection to the argument from consciousness.

It ought to be noticed, however, that from time to time, a few individuals have been found who have asserted the opposite, viz., a consciousness of internal compulsion or slavery. Surprising as such a declaration is, we are bound in candour to receive it as truly indicating the internal experience of those who make it, although it may be in opposition to the testimony of thousands and even hundreds of thousands to one. But these exceptions do not at all overthrow our argument. If there truly be such exceptions, they can undoubtedly be explained in entire consistency with the general truth, that the Freedom of the will is ascertained and proved by the consciousness of mankind. Is it not true, is it not accordant with common experience and with the Scriptures even, that any man and every man may enslave himself? And, when that is the case, what could we expect but that consciousness, the true index of what takes place within, should bear its testimony to a state of thraldom?

If, then, these persons are not conscious of Freedom of the will, may we not safely say, it is not the work of their Creator, but their own?

Certain it is, if we permit any one of the appetites, propensities, or passions continually to extend and strengthen itself by being continually repeated, it will eventually gain the ascendency over and subdue all the rest of the mind. If, for instance, a man indulges, year after year, the consuming propensity of AMBITION, it ultimately so disorders the proper action of the mental powers, and acquires such immense strength, that he feels himself driven by a sort of compulsion; he undoubtedly recognises in himself, as he asserts to be the case, the impulse of a species of destiny, which, however, is of his own creation. By his own criminal improvidence, and not by any inward and irresistible fatality, he has lost control of the helm, and is driven forward amid billows and tempests to his destruction.

Such cases undoubtedly exist, but they cannot with propriety be regarded in any other light than that of exceptions to the general rule, and which are susceptible of an explanation in consistency with the general experience of mankind. That experience (the inward testimony or consciousness which the great mass of mankind has) most decidedly testifies to the liberty of the will.

CHAPTER VI.

FREEDOM OF THE WILL IMPLIED IN MAN'S MORAL NATURE.

§ 478. Of the elements of man's moral nature.

WE may further argue the matter of the freedom of the will from man's moral nature. That man has a moral nature we cannot suppose to be a matter of doubt. Without such a nature he could not be the subject of a moral government; and although he might possess all knowledge, he would necessarily be without virtue and vice; and neither praise nor blame, neither rewards nor punishment, could ever attach to his conduct.

There is nothing inconceivable or inconsistent in the supposition of a being so constituted as to be possessed of intellect, propensities, passions, and will, and yet to be incapable, by his very constitution, of framing those notions and of exercising those feelings which are implied in a moral nature. But such is not the constitution of man. While he is endowed with intellect, and appetites, and propensities, and passions, and will, God has seen fit to elevate and ennoble him, by constituting him a moral and religious being. The elements of his moral nature (in accordance with that striking wisdom ever manifested in God's works, which accomplishes great results by simple means) are few in number, and are to be found chiefly in his ability to frame the abstract notions of right and wrong, in the feelings of moral approval and disapproval, in those states of the mind which are known as feelings of remorse, and in feelings of moral obligation.—All these states of mind, which, taken together, constitute man a moral being, and without which he could not sustain or possess that character, are based upon and imply the fact, as will more fully appear in the separate examination of them, of the freedom of the will.

§ 479. Evidence of freedom of the will from feelings of approval and disapproval.

In stating the argument which may be deduced on this subject from our moral nature, we proceed to remark, in the first place, that the freedom of the will is implied in, and is shown by, the moral feelings of approval and disapproval. We are so constituted, that, whenever we behold a person performing a virtuous action, demeaning himself with entire kindness, good faith, and justice, we at once feel a sentiment of approval. On the other hand, if we see a person pursuing a different course, one which is obviously characterized by falsehood, ingratitude, and injustice, we at once feel an emotion of disapproval. But if it should be suddenly disclosed to us that the agent, whom we thus, according to the circumstances of the case, either approve or condemn, was not in the possession of freedom of will, it is undeniable, that all such approval or disapproval would at once cease. We should no more think of approving an action, however beneficial it might be, which was known to be performed without freedom of will, than of pronouncing a man worthy of moral approbation for a purely natural gift, such as symmetry of form, a musical voice, or striking outlines of the countenance. More properly, we should think nothing about it. To approve under such circumstances would, by the very constitution of our nature, be an impossibility. The existence of liberty, therefore, is, in this respect, and so far as these feelings are concerned, fundamental to our moral nature.

§ 480. Proof of freedom from feelings of remorse.

There is another class of mental states, constituting a part of man's moral nature, to which similar remarks will apply; we refer to feelings of remorse. These feelings are entirely distinct from those of approval and disapproval. We are capable of approving or disapproving when our attention is directed solely to the conduct of others; but we never feel *remorse* for what others do, and it is impossible that we should. Feelings of remorse have relation to ourselves alone. We experience them when our own conduct, and not that of others, is the subject of moral disapproval. They are painful feelings, but the suffering is of a peculiar kind, altogether different from mere sadness or grief; and hence they may be regarded as having a character of their own, and as separate in their nature from all other states of the mind. The existence of these states of mind implies, on the part of the person who is the subject of them, a conviction of the freedom of the will.

It can hardly be thought necessary to adduce facts and arguments in support of what has been said. If a person feels an internal condemnation or remorse for what he has done, it certainly must be on the ground that he was at liberty to will and to do otherwise. It cannot be doubted that this position is fully and universally admitted.—There may be fears and sorrows, undoubtedly; there may be regrets and sufferings, in cases which are not dependent on any determinations of our own; but there cannot possibly be REMORSE, which implies a sense of guilt as well as the experience of sorrow, without a conviction, deep as the basis of the mind itself, that, in doing the criminal action, we willed and acted freely, and not by compulsion. If, therefore, feelings of remorse exist, as they not unfrequently do, they furnish a strong proof in support of the liberty of the will.

§ 481. Without the possession of liberty of will man could never have framed the abstract notions of right and wrong.

Among other things having a relation to man's situation and character as a moral being, it is to be noticed that he is so constituted as to be able to form the abstract notions of right and wrong, or of virtue and vice, which are only other and synonymous expressions for right and wrong. These conceptions (which are thoughts, and not emotions; the creations of the Intellect, and not the exercises of the Sensibilities or heart) are truly great and ennobling; and it may perhaps be said of them, more than of any other part of our moral nature, that they are the basis of moral reasoning, and the foundation of moral anticipation and hope. They disclose to the mind, like light coming from heaven and shining vividly into its depths, the great fact that there is a real, permanent, and immutable distinction between good and evil. Strike out and annihilate these primary conceptions, and you at the same moment obscure and destroy the glory of man's mental nature, and blot out, at least as far as all human perception is concerned, the brightest feature in the character of all other mental existences.

But these leading ideas, so fundamental to everything of a moral and religious nature, could never have been formed without a conviction of the liberty of the will. The occasions undoubtedly, on which they are suggested and exist in the mind, are instances of voluntary conduct, either our own or that of others, where we either approve or disapprove. Without such occasions offered to our notice, and without such attendant emotions of moral approval or disapproval, it may be asserted without any hesitation, that men would never have formed any conceptions in the abstract of right and wrong, of rectitude and the opposite; and, consequently, could never have beheld, as they now clearly do, as if inscribed by the radiant finger of God, a great line of demarcation, remaining always and immutably the same, between good and evil, between holiness and sin. But, as has already been stated, it is always implied in the feelings of approval and disapproval, that the person, whose conduct is either approved or disapproved, possessed liberty of the will. Without a firm conviction that such was the case, the emotions could never have existed; and, consequently, there could never have occurred, in the history of the human mind, that state of things which is the basis of the origin of the abstract notions of right and wrong, of rectitude and want of rectitude, of virtue and vice, which are only different expressions for the same thing. We have, therefore, in this view of the subject, a new proof that the liberty of the will is positively and necessarily involved in the fact of our possessing a moral nature.

§ 482. Proof from feelings of moral obligation.

There is a distinct class of mental states, entitled, in every point of view, to an important place in man's moral constitution, which may be termed Obligatory feelings, or feelings of moral obligation. Of these states of mind we do not profess to give a definition. As they are elementary and simple, they are necessarily undefinable. But we cannot doubt that every one must have more or less frequently experienced them, and that every one knows what their nature is. And this class of feelings also furnishes an argument on the subject before us.—We deem the assertion within the bounds of truth and of the common opinion of mankind, when we say that no man ever does or ever can experience in himself the feeling of moral obligation to do a thing, so long as he feels himself to be actually destitute of liberty to do it. And this is equally true, whether the destitution of liberty relates to the outward and bodily action or to the action of the will. Does a man feel himself morally accountable for the performance of an action to which he is driven by some bodily compulsion? Or does he feel himself accountable for a failure to perform an action, from the performance of which he is kept by actual bodily restraint? And if the mind is constrained and driven by a compression and violence, corresponding, as far as the different nature of the two things will permit, to such compulsion of the body, can there be any more conviction of accountability, or of any form of moral obligation in the one case than in the other? But if the existence of feelings of obligation be undeniable, and if the existence of such feelings be incompatible with the absence of freedom, and if both these truths are based on the consciousness and confirmed by the universal acknowledgments of mankind, then it follows, of course, that men do in fact feel and recognise, and that they fully and assuredly know their freedom.

§ 483. Evidence from men's views of crimes and punishments.

Again, the freedom of the will is clearly implied in the views which we find to be generally adopted by men in respect to crimes and punishments. This view of our subject is closely connected with that which has just been given; and essentially the same illustrations as were introduced in the last section will apply here.

If a man is laid under bodily constraint, and, in that situation, is the agent or rather instrument in the performance of an action involving great loss and suffering to others, such action is never considered a crime and deserving of punishment, in whatever light it might be regarded under other circumstances. This is undeniable. And we always take the same view when the mind is actually laid under constraint as when the body is; with this difference merely, that constraint of the body is a matter easily ascertainable, while that of the mind can be learned only with a greater or less degree of probability. The power of the will is a gift or trust, as much so as the power of perception, and is a definite thing; in some persons it is greater, in others less; but in all cases it has its limits. Whenever, therefore, there is an utter disproportion between the strength of the motive and the power of the will, (so much so, perhaps, as to render it essentially the same as if the will were wholly destitute of power,) the will is universally understood to be, at such times, under a greater or less degree of constraint. And if, under such circumstances, a crime be charged upon a person, we graduate the degree of it, (looking upon it as higher in some cases and lower in others,) in precise conformity with the degree of constraint, so far as we can judge what it is.

"There are cases," says Dr. Reid, "in which a man's voluntary actions are thought to be very little, if at all, in his power, on account of the violence of the motive that impels him. The magnanimity of a hero or a martyr is not expected in every man and on all occasions.—If a man, trusted by the government with a secret which it is high treason to disclose, be prevailed upon by a bribe, we have no mercy for him, and hardly allow the greatest bribe to be any alleviation of his crime. But, on the other hand, if the secret be extorted by the rack or the dread of present death, we pity him more than we blame him, and would think it severe and unequitable to condemn him as a traitor."—And he afterward gives the reason of these different judgments, viz., that while the mere love of money leaves to a man the entire power over himself, the torment of the rack or the dread of present death are so violent motives, that men who have not uncommon strength of mind are not masters of themselves in such a situation, and, therefore, what they do is not imputed to them as a crime at all, or is thought less criminal than it would otherwise be.

§ 484. Prevalent opinions of mankind on this subject.

The argument under this general head, so far as it has now been gone into, has been stated in particulars; and it is probably more satisfactory, when stated in this way, than in any other. But something may be said on the subject of the freedom of the will, as connected with our moral nature, when it is considered, as it were, in the *mass*. The body of mankind undoubtedly look upon this subject, in its great outlines and as a whole, without attempting to penetrate and seize its elements. And, without unduly yielding to popular prejudices or abating from the dignity of philosophy, we may safely assert, that this is an inquiry on which an appeal may with propriety be made to the common experience, and the common convictions and expressions of the great body of men. And we no sooner make the appeal than we find that the testimony from that source is unanimous and unequivocal.

There are some truths which are so deeply based in the human constitution, that all men of all classes receive them and act upon them. They are planted deeply and immutably in the soul, and no reasoning, however plausible, can shake them. And, if we are not mistaken, the doctrine of the freedom of the will, as a condition of even the possibility of a moral nature, is one of these first truths. It seems to be regarded by all persons, without any exception, as a dictate of common sense and as a first principle of our nature, that men are morally accountable, and are the subjects of a moral responsibility in any respect whatever, only so far as they possess freedom, both of the outward action and of the will. They hold to this position as an elementary truth, and would no sooner think of letting it go, than of abandoning the conviction of their personal existence and identity. They do not profess to go into particulars, but they assert it in the mass, that man is a moral being only so far as he is free. And such a unanimous and decided testimony, bearing, as it obviously does, the seal and superscription of nature herself, is entitled to serious consideration.

In view of the various suggestions of this chapter, we are abundantly authorized in the assertion, that the liberty of the will is implied, and fully and clearly implied, in the fact of man's possessing a moral nature; and that, if he possesses such a nature, he possesses freedom.

§ 485. Both views are to be fully received.

In respect, then, to the two distinct doctrines of the will's freedom and its subjection to law, there remains nothing to be done but the cheerful, ready, and complete reception of both. The doctrine, that the will has its laws, is very important, considered in connexion with the relation which men sustain to the Supreme Being. This view places the will in subordination to that higher and more glorious Intelligence, from whom the laws, to which it is amenable, proceed. By adopting this doctrine, we are enabled to understand how his full and perfect superintendence can be maintained. He has himself assured us that he is intimately acquainted with the outward actions of men; that he knoweth their down-sitting and uprising; and it is a pleasing and consoling thought, that his care and exact scrutiny may be extended even to the mind itself. Who will not rejoice to be, in soul as well as in body, in the hands of God? Who will feel that there could be any better provision for his security than is thus furnished by the constancy and nearness of the Divine presence? Who will attach any value even to independence itself, when purchased at the measureless expense of an exemption from the superintendence of the Deity?

§ 486. The doctrine of the will's freedom equally important with that of its subjection to law.

On the other hand, the doctrine that the will is free, in any correct and intelligible sense of that term, is of equal practical importance, since it is obviously essential to man's moral character and accountableness. It is a great truth, which demands to be received with entire and unwavering confidence, that God has made man in his own image; and that, in doing this, he has seen fit to constitute him with the attributes of freedom and power, as well as with the other attributes which are requisite to a rational and morally accountable nature. In the sphere which is given him, (whether more or less limited in extent,) he has not only the ability, but is under the requisition of acting for himself. No plea of inability can ever be admitted as an excuse for negligence, still less for utter inaction. There are claims, therefore, binding upon every man, which he cannot resist. So that the truest and highest philosophy is to be found in that passage of Scripture, "Work out your own salvation with fear and trembling, for it is God which worketh in you both to will and to do, of his own good pleasure." It expresses the great truth, and, we may add, the great *mystery*, of the harmonious combination of power and dependence. And it is the same in other things as in religion, that, if we will act for ourselves under the impulse of right feelings, our Maker will take compassion upon us, and act in our behalf; that, if we will faithfully do our duty, God will be as faithful to help us. Not an hour is spent in effort of any kind, in conformity with the directions of an enlightened conscience, and, to use the expressions which Milton's genius has made so familiar,

"As ever in our great Taskmaster's eye,"

which is not attended with a divine blessing. The doctrine of a combination of freedom on the part of men, with complete superintendence on the part of God, brings God and men into harmony with each other; it fully makes men co-workers with God, and yet under the twofold condition, without which God can neither be a sovereign nor man a moral agent, of responsibility and dependence.

CHAPTER VII.

ON THE POWER OF THE WILL.

§ 487. Proof of power in the will from the analogy of the mind.

THE Will acts in harmony with law. But it is also true, as we have seen in the preceding chapter, that the Will is free. And we proceed further to say, that the Will possesses, not only freedom, but POWER. Power is not only predicable of the mind in a general way, but it is predicable of its parts, and particularly and emphatically so of our volitional nature. The analogy running through our mental constitution furnishes some grounds and authority for this remark. Men universally speak (and they undoubtedly believe they have good reason so to do) of the power of sensation, of the power of perception, of the power of memory, of imagination, of reasoning. The structure of all languages (for they appear to be all alike in this respect) proves what they think; and we may add, proves what they *know* on this subject. It is natural for the man who perceives to say that he has the power of perception; the man who remembers or reasons, asserts without hesitation, that he has the *power* of remembering or reasoning; and it is impossible to convince these men, either that these expressions are improperly applied, or that they are nugatory and convey no distinct meaning.—But if there is truly a foundation for such expressions, and if there is a propriety and truth in the use of them, is there not equal propriety in speaking of the POWER of the WILL? If every other mental action clearly and convincingly indicates to us the existence of an innate energy corresponding to such action, it cannot be supposed that the act of willing alone, which is a pre-eminent and leading exercise of the mind, exists independently of any actual basis of voluntary energy. The analogy, therefore, of the mental constitution, (for we are undoubtedly at liberty to reason from analogy in this case, as well as others,) distinctly leads to the result that power is appropriate to, and is an attribute of, the Will.

§ 488. Proof of power in the will from internal experience.

That power is predicable of the will, as well as of any other faculty of the mind, or of the mind as a whole, is evinced not only by the analogy running through the mental structure, but by other considerations. Among other views to be taken of the subject now before us, may we not, in this inquiry as well as in others, make an appeal to our own internal experience? In other words, have we not, beyond all doubt, a testimony within us, a direct and decisive internal evidence of power in the acts of the Will? Do we not feel and know it to be so?—Let us take a familiar instance as a test of these inquiries. When a person wills to go to a certain place, or wills to do a certain thing, does the volition appear to have been wrought within himself by an extraneous cause? Does it appear to have been created and placed there without any personal agency and effort? Or does it rather distinctly and satisfactorily indicate to him an energy of his own? Few persons, it is believed, will hesitate as to what answer to give.

Our consciousness, therefore, distinctly assures us, that, within the limits constituting its appropriate sphere, the action of the will truly originates in its own power. It wills, because it has the power to will. It acts, because it possesses that energy which is requisite to constitute the basis of action. In the language of one of the characters of the great English dramatist, when pressed for the reasons of a certain course of proceeding,

"The cause is in my *Will;* I *will* not come."

§ 489. **Proved from the ability which we have to direct our attention to particular subjects.**

In one particular at least, our internal experience seems to be clear and decisive, viz., that we are able to direct our attention to some subjects of inquiry in preference to others. It is admitted that we cannot call up a thought or a train of thought by a mere and direct act of volition; although we have an *indirect* power in this respect, which is not without its important results. But when various trains of thought are passing through the mind, we are enabled, as it is presumed every one must be conscious, to direct our attention and to fix it firmly upon one thought or one train of thought in preference to another. It is undoubtedly the tendency of association to remove the thought or the train of thought, whatever it is, from the mind; but the power of the Will, where it is decisively exerted, can counteract this tendency, and keep the mind in essentially the same position for a greater or less length of time. And it does not appear what explanation can possibly be given of the fact, that we thus frequently delay upon subjects, and revolve them in our contemplation, except on the ground of a real and effective energy of the Will.

§ 490. **Proof of power in the will from observation.**

Furthermore, the phenomena of human nature, as they come within our constant observation, cannot be explained, except on the supposition that the Will is not the subject of any extraneous operation or power, in such a sense as entirely to exclude power or agency of its own. Do we not often see instances of persons, in whom vigour of the Will is a characteristic and predominant trait; and whose character and conduct cannot be explained, except on the ground that they possess a voluntary energy of their own, and that, too, in a high degree? Men have often been placed in the most trying circumstances, called to endure the pains of imprisonment, and hunger and thirst, and torture and exile and death; and they have undergone it all with a most astonishing fortitude and calmness, without shedding a tear or uttering a lamentation. Here is something difficult to be explained, unless we take into consideration that innate power which we assert to be an attribute of the Will.

Whatever may be said of the fervid sincerity of his religion or the natural benevolence of his heart, are we able satisfactorily to explain the character and deeds of the illustrious Howard, except by taking this view? "The energy of his determination," says a judicious and valuable writer, "was so great, that if, instead of being habitual, it had been shown only for a short time on particular occasions, it would have appeared a vehement impetuosity; but, by being unintermitted, it had an equability of manner which scarcely appeared to exceed the tone of a calm constancy, it was so totally the reverse of anything like turbulence or agitation. It was the calmness of an intensity, kept uniform by the nature of the human mind forbidding it to be more, and by the character of the individual forbidding it to be less."*

The case of Howard, marked and extraordinary as it is, does not stand alone. Every age of the world and every class of society have their men of this stamp. Extraordinary endowments of the will are as necessary to support society, and to meet the exigencies of our situation, as extraordinary endowments of intellect. But, unfortunately, though they are given in the discretion and wisdom of the great Dispenser of all mental gifts, they are not always wisely and righteously employed. A multitude of instances, of a character both good and evil, will occur to every one; among others, Alexander, Cæsar, Regulus, Charles XII., Hannibal, Columbus, the Apostle Paul, Cromwell, William Tell, Chatham, Nelson, Ledyard, Mungo Park, Napoleon, John Knox, Luther, Whitefield, Wesley, and numerous others, whose names are permanently enrolled in the religious and political history of men. The language of Ledyard will show the intensity of determination existing in such men. "My distresses have been greater than I

* Foster's Essay on Decision of Character.

have ever owned, or ever *will* own to any man. I have known hunger and nakedness to the utmost extremity of human suffering; I have known what it is to have food given me as charity to a madman; and I have at times been obliged to shelter myself under the miseries of that character to avoid a heavier calamity. Such evils are terrible to bear, but they never have yet had *power to turn me from my purpose.*"

§ 491. Illustration of the subject from the command of temper.

The fact that men are not governed by a fatality impressed upon them from an exterior cause, but have an efficiency in themselves, may be further illustrated from the control which they are seen to exercise over their passions, in what is called *command of temper.* Few sayings are more celebrated than that of Socrates on a certain occasion to his servant, that he would beat him if he were not angry. Hume, who is entitled to the credit of being a careful observer of human nature, speaks expressly of the remarkable command of temper which was possessed by Henry IV. of England; and it is not uncommon to find this trait pointed out by historians and biographers as one worthy of particular notice. The biographer of our illustrious countryman, Mr. Jay, says, that "he sought not the glory which cometh from man, and the only power of which he was covetous was the *command of himself.*"* And this power, although he was obliged to contend with a natural irritability of temper, he exhibited in a very high degree.

§ 492. Further illustrations of this subject.

It would not be difficult to specify other distinguished men, both of our own and other countries, who knew how to conciliate the actings of a sensitive and enkindled heart with the coolest circumspection and the most perfect self-command. But this is not necessary, since the trait in question is one daily coming within our notice. It is not uncommon, in almost every village and neighbourhood, to observe

* Life of John Jay, vol. i., chap. xii.

persons of naturally quick feelings, and whose passions are obviously violent, and are prone to foam and toss about like the waves of the sea, who nevertheless have those passions under complete control, even in the most trying circumstances.

And is it not a duty to exercise this control over the passions? "He that ruleth his spirit," says Solomon, "is better than he that taketh a city." And again, "He that hath no rule over his own spirit, is like a city that is broken down and without walls." "Be ye angry," says the Apostle, "and sin not; let not the sun go down upon your wrath." Here, then, is a great practical fact in the philosophy of the mind, and upon which important and solemn duties are based, viz., that the passions are under our control. But where is the power that controls them? It is not enough to say that this power of regulation and control is deposited in the understanding. It is true that the understanding can suggest various and important reasons why this control should be exercised; but it cannot of itself render those reasons effective and available. The greatest light in the Understanding, and even if it were carried into the region of the Affections and the Conscience, could never bring this great result to pass without the co-operation of the effective energies of the Will.

§ 493. **Illustrated from the prosecution of some general plan.**

We find further illustration and proof of that energy which is appropriate to the Will, in instances where individuals adopt and pursue, for a length of time, some general plan. Not unfrequently they fix upon an object, which involves either their interest or their duty, and prosecute it with a perseverance and resolution which is truly astonishing. Nor is this state of things limited to those who have been elevated by rank, or have had the advantages of learning. It is often the case, that we see this fixedness of purpose, this unalterable resolution, among those who have been greatly depressed by poverty, and who are ignorant as well as poor.

"In the obscurity of retirement," says the author of Lacon, "amid the squalid poverty and revolting privations of a cottage, it has often been my lot to witness scenes of magnanimity and self-denial, as much beyond the belief as the practice of the great; a heroism borrowing no support, either from the gaze of the many or the admiration of the few, yet flourishing amid ruins and on the confines of the grave; a spectacle as stupendous in the moral world, as the Falls of Niagara in the natural." And can we explain this greatness of soul, this fixedness of purpose, this indomitable resolution, which is displayed in every condition of society, in humble as well as in elevated life, consistently with the supposition that the Will has no power?

But there are other facts of a higher character and a more general interest, as they involve the welfare, not only of individuals and families, but of whole classes of men. They are too numerous to be mentioned here; but they are recorded, and will long continue to be so, in the faithful register of grateful hearts. Are there not many individuals, who, like the benevolent Clarkson, have fixed upon some plan of good-will to men, embracing a great variety and degree of effort, and have pursued it amid every form of trial and opposition for years and tens of years? The individual just referred to proposed the simple object of the Abolition of the Slave Trade. To this one object he consecrated his life and all his powers. He permitted no opposition to divert him from his purpose. But amid great apathy of the public mind, and great opposition on the part of those who were personally interested in his defeat; amid the most arduous labours, attended with a thousand discouragements, and protracted for many years; in rebuke, and sickness, and sorrow, this one object was the star that guided him on, the light that sustained him, and which he followed without giving way to his trials or relaxing in the least from his efforts until it was secured.

§ 494. The subject illustrated from the course of the first settlers of New-England.

The course of the first settlers of New-England is an instance favourable for the illustration of the subject before us. Their simple object was to find a residence somewhere where they could live in the full and free exercise and enjoyment of their religion. And this was an object which, under the circumstances of the case, was not to be carried into effect without great firmness and perseverance. They left behind them, in their native country, a thousand objects which the world holds most dear. Despised and outcast, they came to these inhospitable shores in sorrow, and weakness, and poverty. They suffered from the want of provisions, from the prevalence of wasting sickness, from the storms and cold of winter, and from the watchful jealousy and hostility of the savage tribes. Though sincerely and ardently religious, it cannot be denied that they had their seasons of discouragement; and often feared and often doubted. But when all without was darkness, and when even the inward lights burned dimly, the high purpose which they had once deliberately and prayerfully formed remained unchanged. They held on by the anchor of a determined RESOLVE. So that it can be said with almost strict truth, that the Will sustained them when the Heart was broken.

§ 495. Illustrated by the fortitude exhibited by Savages.

We might go on multiplying illustrations of this subject almost without number; drawn, too, from every class of men, and from every condition of society, savage as well as civilized. We have often thought that the life of the savage warrior furnished an interesting philosophical problem. Let the reader go with us a moment to yonder dark and boundless forest. Behold beneath the light of the uncertain and shuddering moon, the fire kindled which is destined to consume the victim taken in war. View him fastened to the stake, his flesh slowly consumed, and, as it is burning, torn piecemeal from his blackened bones.

What inexpressible suffering! And yet this dark son of the forest, this poor ignorant child of nature, betrays no weakness of purpose, sheds no tear, utters no exclamation of impatience. His enemies can take from him his distant wigwam, his wife and children, his burning body, his expiring life; but the sudden death-song, rising loudly and triumphantly, is a proof that they have not taken, nor are they able to take from him, the firm resolve, the unconquerable Will.

Here are the facts which are presented before us; not all, indeed, which can be brought forward, and perhaps they are not those which are best adapted to our purpose. But, such as they are, they are undeniable. They are inscribed on every page of the history of the human race. And we may challenge philosophy or anything else satisfactorily to explain them, except on the ground of the innate energy, not merely of the mind as a whole, but of the volitional faculty in particular.

QUESTIONS

QUESTIONS

TO

UPHAM'S ABRIDGMENT OF MENTAL PHILOSOPHY

BY THE REV. L. L. SMITH,

OF NORFOLK, VA.

CHAPTER I.

Qu. Sect.

1. 1. Is the human mind a unit, or composed of many departments?
2. Its three leading divisions?
3. How are the states of mind, the results of these leading departments, expressed?
4. 2. What is the intellect?
5. In what two points of view may the intellectual part of man be considered?
6. Upon what does the existence of intellectual states of external origin depend?
7. How is this shown?
8. What are intellectual states of internal origin?
9. 3. What kind of knowledge is first acquired?
10. Does the mind of the new-born infant possess any knowledge?
11. How is it first brought into action?
12. How does it appear that there is a correspondence between the mind and outward material objects?
13. To what may the soul be compared?
14. Explain the points of resemblance.
15. 4. What two general principles are here laid down?
16. The first proof of the truth of these principles?
17. 5. The second proof of it?
18. What are the first ideas of the human race?
19. To what may the history and origin of all our notions be traced?
20. When do we begin to compare, and reason, and seek for causes and effects?
21. In what way is knowledge most easily imparted to children?
22. 6. The third proof of the truth of these principles?
23. Why is the vocabulary of savage tribes so limited?
24. To what does the growth of languages correspond?
25. What do we learn from the history of all languages?
26. Illustrate the fact that the words of all languages, expressive of the mind, had an external origin.
27. What conclusion may you derive from this fact?
28. 7. The fourth proof of the truth of these principles?
29. Illustrate these facts.
30. What facts are stated of the deaf and dumb man of the city of Chartres?
31. What inference would you deduce from them?
32. 8 Give an account of James Mitchell.

CHAPTER II.

Qu. Sect.

1. 9. Is sensation a simple or complex state of mind?
2. Why can it not be defined?
3. Is its simplicity its only characteristic?
4. By what peculiarity is it distinguished?
5. Why can we not speak of the sensations of joy and sorrow?
6. Mention several of the sensations.
7. 10. Where has it, by some, been supposed that sensation is located?
8. Where is it really located?
9. How, then, should we regard the organs of sense? and illustrate
10. 11. Are our sensations copies, pictures, or images of outward objects?
11. Do they possess any of the qualities of outward objects?
12. What do you mean by this?
13. 12. Is the affection of the mind coetaneous with, or subsequent to, the operation of external bodies on the mind?
14. The character and extent of this operation?
15. The extent of our knowledge on this subject?
16. What change takes place subsequently to the change in the organ of sense?
17. What do we know of the connection between mind and matter?
18. 13. How does perception differ from sensation?
19. How is the term sometimes used?
20. Define it.
21. 14. Is it a complex or a simple state of the mind?
22. Distinguish between it and sensation.
23. What would be the nature and extent of our knowledge, if we nac but sensation alone, without perception?
24. 15. What do we know of matter?
25. Under what two heads have the qualities of material bodies beei ranked?
26. How are the primary qualities known; and what are they?
27. Why called primary?
28. What do you mean by solidity?
29. Show that water is solid in this sense.
30. The Florentine experiment? and what did it prove?
31. 16. The secondary qualities of bodies, how divided?
32. What are included under the first class?
33. What is meant when we say a body has sound, color, etc.?
34. Mention some of the second class of secondary bodies.

CHAPTER III.

1. 17. Is the possession of organs of sense essential to the possession of that knowledge which we are accustomed to ascribe to them?
2. How is this shown?
3. How does it appear that they are essential to human knowledge?
4. 18. Can the senses be separated from the nervous system?
5. Can they perform their duty if the brain be injured?
6. Can they, if the nerves be tightly compressed?
7. What may be inferred from these facts?
8. What is the sensorial organ?
9. What is essential to the sensations of hearing, seeing, etc.?
10. 19. How is the sensation of smell produced?
11. 20. What is the olfactory nerve?
12. Is there any necessary connection between the smell and surrounding objects?
13. How does it happen that we are not merely sensible of the particular sensation, but refer it at once to the particular external object that produces it?

Qu. Sect
14. 21. Show that this mental reference is made with great rapidity.
15. Why is it so?
16. What three things are involved in the process of perception?
17. 22 What is the organ of taste?
18. Is it confined to the tongue?
19. Why do we speak of particular bodies as sweet, or sour, etc.?
20. What do we mean when we call them sweet or sour?

CHAPTER IV.

1. 23. How is sound produced?
2. What is the organ of hearing?
3. Why are the ears placed in the side of the head?
4. How are they formed, and why so formed?
5. What is the tympanum of the ear?
6. By what is the sound communicated to the mind?
7 24. Are the sensations of sound more or less numerous than the words in the English language?
8 How would you illustrate this fact?
9. How many simple sounds are there, according to Dr. Reid?
10. How are varieties and shades of difference of the same tone produced? and illustrate.
11. 25 How do we know the place whence sounds originate?
12. What renders our ignorance of their place, previous to experience, less surprising?
13. Illustrate this fact.
14. How do we learn to distinguish the place of things?
15. How is this shown?
16. If a man, born deaf, were suddenly restored to his hearing, where would he locate the sounds he might hear?
17. What alone would teach him their true source?

CHAPTER V.

1. 26. The principal organ of the sense of touch?
2. Why located principally in the hand?
3. In what respect does the sense of touch differ from those of hearing, tasting, smelling?
4. 27. What knowledge would we derive from the sense of smelling alone?
5. What additional ideas would we derive from these sensations?
6. What feelings would these ideas excite in the mind?
7. If we had no other sense, how should we regard these feelings?
8. How do we get the idea of externality or outwardness?
9. What would be our condition without the senses of touch and sight
10. How does the sense of touch give us the idea of outwardness?
11. 28 How do we arrive at the idea of extension?
12. Why can not the idea of extension be resolved into others?
13. The foundation of the idea of *form* in bodies?
14. Dr. Brown's definition of form?
15. Which is antecedent in the idea of nature, the idea of form or of extension?
16. 29. The two significations of the words heat and cold?
7. What are the qualities in bodies which give us the sensation of heat and cold?
18. Mention some of the various opinions respecting them.
19. Do they resemble the sensations they occasion?
20. 30. When is a body called hard or soft?
21. How do we arrive at the sensation of hardness?
22. Why is it difficult to make this sensation an object of reflection?
23. In what cases is it not at all difficult?

Qu. Sect.
24. Why is it important to attend to it?
25. 31. To what sense would you ascribe the feelings expressed by the terms uneasiness, weariness, sickness, and the like?
26. What remarks are made of hunger and thirst?
27. Why is it difficult to state what sense they should be ascribed to?
28. 32. What two things always exist when we speak of extension, or resistance, or heat, or color, etc.?
29. Do they resemble one another?
30. How, then, can one give us a knowledge of the other?
31. How would you illustrate this?
32. What is the relation between the sensation and the outward object?

CHAPTER VI.

1. 33. The most valuable of the five senses?
2. Show its superiority over the touch.
3. To what is the eye compared?
4. The medium on which it acts?
5 To what science does a description of the eye belong?
6. 34. What would be the effect if the rays of light that first strike the eye were to continue on, in the same direction, to the retina?
7. How is this prevented?
8. What is the retina?
9. The last step we are able to trace in the material part of the process in visual perception?
10. How is the image conveyed to the mind?
11. 35. What knowledge do we derive originally from the sense of sight?
12. Can we obtain the idea of color from any other sense?
13. What knowledge is generally, though erroneously, ascribed to the sense of sight?
14. 36. Is extension a direct object of sight?
15. How do we get the idea of extension?
16. Can we get it from any other or all of the four remaining senses?
17. Why do any suppose that this idea is due to the sense of sight?
18. 37. How do we get the idea of figure?
19. To what is it often attributed?
20. Do we really see prominences or cavities in solid bodies?
21. What do we see in them?
22. Why do we then suppose that we really see them?
23. How is the fact that we do not see them proved?
24. 38. What was the problem submitted to Mr. Locke; and his decision?
25. The first idea conveyed to the mind on seeing a globe?
26. How is it corrected?
27. How is the truth of this statement shown?
28. Why do we ever attribute to sight the knowledge that is acquired by touch only?
29. 39. How is a knowledge of magnitude first obtained?
30. The difference between tangible and visible magnitude?
31. What fact is stated in support of the doctrine that the knowledge of magnitude is not an original intimation of sight?
32. 40. What is said of the visible magnitude of objects seen in a mist?
33. How is this fact accounted for?
34. To what may it, in part, be attributed?
35. 41. Mention three reasons why the sun and moon seem larger in the horizon than in the meridian.
36. 42. What is meant by the term distance?
37. Is the perception of distance an acquired or an original perception?
38. How do all objects, in the first instance, appear to us?
39. Why do they not appear so now?
40. What facts are stated on this subject?

Qu. Sect.
41. 43. How do we learn to estimate distances?
42. How do landscape and historical painters take advantage of this fact?
43. 44. Why do we often misjudge in estimating the width of rivers, plains etc.?
44. Why also in estimating the height of steeples, the distance of the stars, etc.?
45. Why does the horizon seem further off than the zenith?
46. 45. The effect, in the apparent distance of objects, of a change in the purity of the air?

CHAPTER VII.

1. 46. Repeat the law of habit.
2. How is this known?
3. Can it be resolved into any more general or elementary principle?
4. What is indicated by the term habit?
5. Mention some of the things to which we apply the term.
6. 47. Is it confined to the mind?
7. Its effects on the bodily organs?
8. Mention several respects in which individuals are distinguished from one another by habit.
9. 48. What is said of habits of smell?
10. What facts are stated illustrative of this truth?
11. 49. The effects of habit on taste?
12. What practical view of this subject presents itself here? and illustrate.
13. State the three-fold operation in such cases.
14. The only remedy for one whose habits are so confirmed? and why?
15. 50. Show that the sense of hearing is capable of cultivation.
16. In whom is it very acute? and why?
17. What facts are stated of the blind?
18. 51. Mention some facts showing that the sense of touch is susceptible of cultivation.
19. The case of John Metcalf?
20. How are books for the blind prepared?
21. 52. Cases of James Mitchell and Julia Brace?
22. What has Diderot conjectured of those that are deprived of both sight and hearing?
23. 53. Show that the law of habit affects the sight.
24. What persons possess the sense of sight in greatest perfection?
25. How is this accounted for?
26. The case of the lady at Geneva, mentioned by Bishop Burnet?
27. What may we learn from such facts?
28. 54. What important remark is here made with reference to our sensations?
29. How is it explained?
30. 55. By what are habits often modified?
31. Illustrate.
32. Quote the remarks of Dr. Reid.
33. 56. Does the mind perceive the complete figure of the object at once?
34. Mr. Stewart's opinion?
35. How, then, does it happen that we appear to see the object at once?
36. 57 Mention some circumstances that tend to confirm Mr. Stewart's views on this subject.
37. 58. Mention the facts stated by Sir Everard Home.
38. (The history of Caspar Hauser?)

CHAPTER VIII.

Qr. Sect.
1. 59. What is meant by conceptions?
2. How do they differ from the ordinary sensations and perceptions?
3. Illustrate.
4. How do they differ from ideas of memory?
5. How are they regulated in their appearance and disappearance?
6. What is meant by the power of conception?
7. 60 What striking fact in regard to our conceptions is mentioned? and illustrate.
8. What facts are related of the celebrated traveler, Carsten Niebuhr?
9. Of what senses are the conceptions least vivid?
10. How do you explain the fact that our perceptions of sight are more easily and distinctly recalled than others?
11. 61. On what, besides association, does the power of forming conceptions depend? and illustrate.
12. What fact is stated of Beethoven?
13. 62. Illustrate the influence of habit on conceptions of sight.
14. 63. What is remarked of the subserviency of our conceptions to description?
15. In what does the perfection of description consist?
16. The best rule for making the selection of particulars?
17. Why is it easier to give a happy description from the conception of an object than from an actual perception of it?
18. What great element of poetic power is mentioned?
19. 64. State several facts to show that our conceptions are attended with a momentary belief.
20. Why only momentary?
21. In whom is this particularly observed?
22. What fact is stated of Dr. Priestly?
23. 65. In what cases is the belief in our mere conceptions the more evident and striking?
24. What is related of one of the characters sketched by Sir Walter Scott?
25. 66. How are the effects produced on the mind by exhibitions of fictitious distress explained?
26. What else does this fact explain?

CHAPTER IX.

1. 67. Into what two classes are our mental affections divided?
2. 68. The first characteristic of a simple idea?
3. 69. The second characteristic?
4. What is essential to a legitimate definition?
5. Why will not this process apply to our simple thoughts and feelings?
6. If an individual professes to be ignorant of the terms we use when we speak of simple ideas and feelings, how can we aid him in understanding them?
7. (Can you illustrate this remark?)
8. 70. The third characteristic of a simple mental state?
9. What does Mr. Locke mean by chimerical ideas? and why does he so style them?
10. Illustrate.
11. 71. Which were first in origin, our simple or our complex states of mind?
12. What simple notions are embraced in our complex notions of external material objects?
13. Of what are our complex ideas made up?

Qu. Sect.
14. Which are most numerous, the simple or the complex states of mind?
15. To what may the ability of originating complex thoughts and feelings be compared?
16. 72 What opinion has been advanced by some with respect to the priority of the simple mental states? and illustrate.
17. How is this appearance explained?
18. 73. Are our thoughts and feelings made up of others, or complex in the material sense of the expression?
19. What, then, constitutes their complexness?
20. How is this subject illustrated?
21. How is the language which expresses the composition and complexity of thought to be regarded?
22. 74 What do you understand by the term analysis?
23. What is the distinction between the analysis of material bodies and of complex thoughts?
24 When do we perform mental analysis?
25. Analyze the term government.
26. 75. To what is the doctrine of simplicity and complexness of mental states applicable?
27. Are the acts of the will simple or complex?
28. What are our simple ideas?
29. Are our ideas of external objects simple or complex? and illustrate.
30. 76. What are some of the elements presented in the term loadstone?
31. Also in the term gold?

CHAPTER X.

1. 77. What is abstraction?
2. What are abstract ideas?
3. Into what two classes may they be divided?
4. 78. What are particular abstractions? and illustrate.
5. The distinctive mark of particular abstract ideas?
6. Does the abstraction exist in the object itself, or only in the mind?
7. 79. Does the mind possess a separate faculty adapted solely to this particular purpose?
8. Is it nearer to the truth to speak of the process or the power of abstraction?
9. What must necessarily take place in every case of separating a particular abstract idea?
10. What is said of the principle of association in abstraction?
11. Illustrate.
12. What, then, is the process of the mind in abstraction?
13. 80. What are general abstract ideas?
14. How are they distinguished from the great body of our other complex notions?
15. How are general abstract ideas expressed?
16. 81. What fact shows that we find no practical difficulty in forming these classifications?
17. What is the process in classification?
18. Illustrate.
19. 82. Are our early classifications always correct?
20. Why are they sometimes incorrect, and how are they corrected?
21. 83. Give an illustration of our earliest classifications?
22. 84. Does the general idea embrace every particular which makes a part of the corresponding object?
23. Illustrate.
24. Why called *abstract* ideas?
25. Why called *general*?
26. 85. What is said of the ability which the mind possesses of forming such ideas?

Qu. Sect.
27. What power does this give us?
28. Why should we not be able even to number without this ability?
29. 86. State the process in forming general abstract truths.
30. 87. What is the difference between the speculations of philosophers and of common men?
31. Why are their general reasonings not so difficult in performance as is apt to be supposed?
32. What is said of the speculations of the great bulk of mankind?

CHAPTER XI.

1. 88. What is attention?
2. Is it a separate intellectual faculty?
3. Is the distinct and exclusive mental perception all of attention?
4. What is it that keeps the mind intense and fixed in its position?
5. 89. When is the attention said to be slight, and when intense?
6. How do we commonly judge of the degree of attention given to a subject?
7. What is it that induces us to bestow much time on any subject?
8. What remark is made of Julius Cæsar's and Bonaparte's power of attention?
9. 90. On what does memory depend, and how is this shown?
10. Mention five facts that confirm this statement.
11. Quote Shakspeare's remark on this subject.
12. 91. What important direction is here given, and the reason for it?
13. State the disadvantages of attempting to learn too many things at once.
14. The most important part of education?
15. How is this effected?
16. By what process is the mind weakened?
17. 92. Is it an easy matter to keep the attention fixed on one subject?
18. The cause of the difficulty?
19. By what is intense attention always accompanied?
20. What is the only thing that will confine the minds of men in scientific pursuits?
21. What does Mr. Locke say on this subject?
22. What anecdote is related of D'Alembert?

CHAPTER XII.

1. 93. What are dreams?
2. Why have they excited so much attention?
3. Can any one be found that has never dreamed?
4. 94. The first thing that arrests our attention in dreams?
5. How is it accounted for?
6. What facts are related of Condorcet and Franklin?
7. What of Coleridge?
8. The inference from these facts?
9. Why did President Edwards think it needful to notice his dreams?
10. 95. What other circumstance affects our dreams?
11. State the two facts related in evidence of this.
12. What other cause still of dreams is mentioned?
13. State the facts mentioned in evidence of this.
14. What else has considerable influence in producing dreams, and giving them a particular character?
15. 96. The first cause of the incoherency of dreams?
16. What keeps the train of our thoughts coherent and uniform while we are awake?
17. 97. The second cause of the incoherency of dreams?
18. Is the mind ever inactive?

Qu. Sect.
19. To what are our thoughts and feelings during sleep compared?
20. 98. How do objects and events appear to us in dreams?
21. The first cause of this apparent reality?
22. How is this explained?
23. When are our conceptions most distinct and vivid? and why?
24. 99 The second cause of the apparent reality of dreams?
25 Illustrate.
26 In what case does belief always attend our perceptions?
27. 100. How do we estimate time in dreaming? and illustrate.
28. Repeat the anecdote related by Dr. Abercrombie.
29. Relate that of Count Lavalette.
30. 101. How is this estimate of time explained by some?
31. The true explanation?
32. Repeat the remarks of Stewart.

PART II.

CHAPTER I.

1. 102. In what way have we seen the mind connected with the material world?
2. Is all our knowledge derived from the senses?
3. The natural progress of all true knowledge?
4. Locke's doctrine?
5. 103. The two sources of knowledge according to him?
6. Mention certain ideas which could not be derived from external things.
7. What might be styled the "internal sense?"
8. The name commonly given to it?
9. 104. In making the human soul a subject of inquiry, what distinction may be drawn?
10. What inquiry naturally arises here?
11. How is it answered?
12. Could we have had any knowledge without the senses?
13. 105. Is, then, the whole amount of our knowledge to be ascribed directly to an external source?
14. What is all that can be said with truth on this point?
15. What are ideas of reflection?
16. Are the sources of human thought, the internal and the external distinct or confounded?
17. 106. Mention some of the notions which are to be ascribed to the internal sense.
18. Can the mind remain for any length of time inactive?
19 What do you mean by thinking?
20. Is its origin internal or external?
21. The origin of doubting?
22. What is all we can say of it?
23 How is belief occasioned?
24. What do we denominate certainty?
25. 107. Mention other ideas of internal origin?
26 How is it determined that these are of internal origin?
27. Sum up what has been said in this chapter.

CHAPTER II.

Qu. Sect.

1. 108. How is the word suggestion used?
2. Who first proposed the use of this term?
3. What class of ideas does he attribute to it?
4. What are some of the ideas which Stewart attributes to it?
5. What, for example, does he say of duration?
6. 109. What is said of the idea of existence?
7. The origin of the notion of mind?
8. The origin of personal identity?
9. 110. Why does the author decline to explain the nature of unity?
10. How has it been defined?
11. How does the idea of it originate?
12. What is the process by which we form numbers?
13. 111. The nature of succession?
14. What simple fact forms the occasion on which the idea of succession is suggested to the mind?
15. Why can it not be defined?
16. Show that it can not be referred to any thing external.
17. 112. The distinction between it and the idea of duration?
18. Which exists first in the order of nature, succession or duration?
19. Why do we know nothing of duration when we are asleep?
20. 113. How is the priority of the *notion* of succession proved? two facts
21. 114. What is time?
22. How is it measured?
23. How does it differ from duration?
24. What is eternity?
25. 115. The origin of our idea of space?
26. How is it shown not to be external?
27. What other consideration shows the same thing?
28. What is your idea of space?
29. 116. When did we first get the idea of space?
30. What is it supposed may have been the original occasion of the rise of this idea?
31. What other supposition still more probable is mentioned?
32. 117. The origin of the idea of power?
33. Can there be any accountable existence without it? and why not?
34. 118. State the three-fold occasion of the origin of this idea?
35. 119. The origin of the ideas of right and wrong?
36. Show that this arrangement of them has an important connection with the theory of morals.
37. Can right ever become wrong, or wrong right?
38. 120. Which are first in the order of nature, right and wrong, or merit and demerit?
39. What is implied in merit and demerit?
40. Can the ideas of merit and demerit be defined?
41. 121. How is reason defined?
42. Why does the author prefer the term suggestion, as designative of the origin of the ideas we have been considering, to the word reason?
43. Mention other ideas which should be referred to suggestion.
44. 122 Is original suggestion the basis of ideas only?
45. The basis of the comparative intellect?
46. Mention several elementary propositions which are prerequisites to the exercise of the deductive faculty.

CHAPTER III.

Qu. Sect.

1. 123 The second source of our internal knowledge?
2. What is consciousness?
3. What three distinct notions does every instance of consciousness embrace?
4. Illustrate.
5. 124. Can we be conscious of thoughts or emotions that have agitated us in times past?
6. Can we be conscious of material or immaterial objects which are external to the mind? Illustrate.
7. Are we conscious of the existence of our own minds?
8. Of what, then, are we conscious?
9. 125. What is said of the belief attendant on the exercise of consciousness?
10. The reason of such belief?
11. What is said of one that seriously rejects the testimony of his own consciousness?
12. 126. Are the ideas, states of mind, etc., that come within the range of con sciousness, few or many?
13. Mention several of the various degrees of belief that are matters of consciousness.
14. Mention the names of other intellectual acts and operations that are expressive of the subjects of our consciousness.
15. What emotions does it include?
16. What complex emotions or passions does it include?
17. What moral and religious emotions also?
18 What consideration shows us that this enumeration might be carried to a much greater extent?

CHAPTER IV.

1. 127. What is remarked of the expression, "The mind brings its thoughts together," etc?
2. What is the meaning of it?
3. What is relative suggestion?
4 What ultimate fact in our mental nature is spoken of here?
5. 128. What is said of the relations of things and of thoughts? and illustrate.
6. Mention several terms that express the ideas of relatio .
7. 129. What are correlative terms?
8 The advantage derived from their use?
9. 130. Why is it difficult to classify our relations?
10. Repeat the seven classes enumerated.
11. What is said of the relation of identity and diversity?
12. Illustrate.
13. Show the utility of this relation.
14. 131. What is said of the relation of degree? and illustrate.
15 By what terms are such relations expressed?
16. Show how, from this relation alone, the importance of the power of relative suggestion is shown.
17. 132. In what respect are the relations of proportion peculiar?
18. In what are they particularly discoverable?
19. 133. Under what circumstances do we form the idea of the relations of place?
20. What is meant by position or place?
21. Illustrate.
22. Why can we form no idea of the position of the universe considered as a whole?
23. What is meant by the words high and low, near and distant?

Qu. Sect.

24. 134. How do time and place resemble each other?
25 Are our notions of time relative or absolute?
26 Under what aspect is all time contemplated?
27. What do we mean when we say of any event, it happened on such a day, say July 4th, 1776? and illustrate.
28. Under what head, then, may all dates be classed?
29. 135. What is meant by relations of possession?
30. How soon do we learn this relation? and illustrate.
31 Does it increase or diminish in strength?
32 What class of words have their origin here?
33. Show that the verb "to be" often expresses this relation.
34. Mention certain complex terms which involve this relation.
35. 136. What does the notion of cause and effect, as it first exists in the mind, include?
36 What constitutes the full notion of cause?
37. What of effect?
38 To what do we give the name of events?
39. 137. Mention several terms in which the relation of cause and effect is embodied, and illustrate.
40. 138. What connection has relative suggestion with reasoning in general?
41. What relations are embraced in demonstrative reasoning?
42. What in moral reasoning?

CHAPTER V.

1. 139. Why do we take up the subject of association and memory before that of the reasoning powers?
2. 140. What is mental association?
3. Give an illustration of it.
4. Another, from Chateaubriand.
5. 141. Do we know why it is that our thoughts and feelings succeed one another in a regular train?
6. What is the extent of our knowledge on this subject?
7. What is meant by the laws of association?
8. Repeat the most important of them.
9. 142. What do we mean by saying that new trains of ideas and new emotions are occasioned by resemblance?
10. How is this fact explained?
11. Illustrate it.
12. Quote the remark of Lander.
13. Is the association which is founded on resemblance limited to objects of sight?
14. Repeat the poetry on this subject.
15. 143. Show in what way resemblance operates as an associating principle.
16. Give several illustrations of this.
17. Repeat the comparison of Akenside.
18. Why do we often speak of nature as animated, etc.?
19. 144. What is the law of contrast?
20. Give the outlines of Count Lemaistre's story of the leper.
21. The foundation of antithesis?
22. 145. The law of contiguity? and illustrate.
23. When we speak of the crucifixion of our Savior, what thoughts are suggested to our minds?
24 What when the American Revolution is named?
25 Which of the primary laws of association is the most extensive in its influence?
26. What forms the basis of the calendar of the mass o men?
27. Illustrate.
28 146 The law of cause and effect?

Q. Sect.

29. Show that this is one of the primary principles of our mental associations.
30. Illustrate the law.
31. Mention the incident related by Locke.
32. Repeat the remark of Shakspeare.

CHAPTER VI.

1. 147 Repeat the four secondary laws of mental association.
2. Show that they are not of minor importance.
3. To what are the primary and secondary laws compared?
4. 148. Repeat the first law of lapse of time.
5. Illustrate this law.
6. What apparent exception to this law is mentioned?
7. What two remarks are made on this point?
8. 149. Repeat the law of repetition, and illustrate.
9. What is said of the operation of this law in particular arts and professions?
10. 150. Repeat the law of coexistent emotion.
11. Why are bright objects more readily recalled than faint ones?
12. Why are those events in our history that were attended with great joy or sorrow longest remembered?
13. 151. In what respect are there original differences in the mental constitution of men?
14. In what channel do the associations of the great mass of mankind run? and why?
15. What original differences are often seen in men? Illustrate.
16. Repeat the substance of what is said of Newton.
17. 152. What two classes of persons are spoken of here as originally different?
18. How does Milton illustrate the difference?
19. What other thing is mentioned as modifying our trains of thought?
20. Recapitulate the primary and secondary laws of association.

CHAPTER VII.

1. 153. Why is the subject of memory taken up after that of association?
2. To what is memory essential?
3. What is memory?
4. Is it a simple or complex action of the intellectual principle?
5. What does it imply?
6. What is meant by this?
7. Illustrate the distinction between our conceptions and memory.
8. 154. In what cases is our belief controlled by our remembrances?
9. How do we know when to rely on our memory?
10. What would be our condition without such a reliance?
11. 155. What is remarked of the ability to remember?
12. Relate several instances of great memory.
13. 156. What is circumstantial memory?
14. Explain it at large.
15. What kind of memory prevails among uneducated people?
16. 157. How is this illustrated by Shakspeare?
17. 158. What is philosophic memory?
18. By what is it sustained?
19. What is remarked of Montaigne?
20. 159. Under what two forms does every department of science present itself to our notice?
21. Which form does the circumstantial memory rapidly embrace?
22. Quote Mr. Stewart's remarks on this topic.
23. 160. What is intentional recollection?

Qu. Sect.
24. Are our trains of associated thought voluntary?
25. Can we will to remember any particular event?
26. In what does our chief power in quickening and strengthening the memory consist?
27. 161. How do we set about to recall any circumstances which we wish to remember? Two ways.
28. 162. Give the illustration furnished by Dr. Beattie.
29. How else are these views illustrated?
30. 163. What are the two prominent marks of a good memory?
31. To what is tenacity of memory compared?
32. Do men of philosophic minds usually possess a ready memory?
33. 164 The first direction for improving the memory?
34. The remark of Stewart on this point?
35 The advantage of always endeavoring to understand what we study?
36. The second direction, etc.?
37. Illustrate the benefit of such classification.
38. The third direction?
39. How illustrated?
40. Two advantages of studying geography with maps, etc.?
41. Give another illustration of this rule in the reading of history.
42. 165. The fourth direction?
43. Mention an instance of the utter violation of this rule.
44. The fifth rule?
45. 166. What other help to memory is here noticed?
46. What remark is made of Dr. Johnson on this point?
47. Show how it is that a strict regard to truth is a help to memory.

CHAPTER VIII.

1. 167. What opinion of Lord Bacon is here noticed?
2. Why is it of importance to examine it?
3. What question suggests itself here?
4. How is it answered?
5. What does our experience teach us on this point?
6. Repeat the poetic quotation.
7. 168. On what does the ability of the mind to restore its past experiences depend?
8. What admitted facts render this probable?
9. What important views do these facts confirm?
10. What is the proximate cause of the great acceleration of the intellectual acts in cases of drowning?
11. 169. What fact is stated of the influence of disease on the mind?
12. 170. State the facts related of the American traveler.
13. 171. State those related of the young German woman.
14. What inferences did Coleridge draw from this instance?
15. 172. What is implied in the term education?
16. What is said of the effect of a single remark?
17. What effect should such a consideration have on us?
18. Why is it so important to introduce truth and right principles into the mind of a child?
19. 173. What other practical remark is suggested by these considerations?
20. What objection has been raised to the Scriptural doctrine of a final judgment?
21. What gives it all its plausibility?
22. Can the power of reminiscence ever die?
23. Repeat the poetry on this subject.

CHAPTER IX.

Qu. Sect.

1\. 174 To what are we indebted for our knowledge of the operations of the faculty of reasoning?

2\. Is reasoning identical with, or involved in, consciousness?

3\. What is it that gives us a knowledge of our own existence?

4\. What of the operations of our minds?

5\. What enables us to reason?

6\. For what knowledge are we indebted to reason?

7\. What is the office of reason?

8\. 175 How is reasoning defined?

9\. What are propositions?

10\. May a proposition exist in the mind without being expressed in words?

11\. What are the parts of a proposition?

12\. Define each, and illustrate.

13\. How have propositions been divided?

14\. Define each, and illustrate.

15\. To what are propositions compared?

16\. 176 How many propositions are essential to every process of reasoning?

17\. Is the arrangement of propositions arbitrary?

18\. Are they brought into existence by an act of volitiŏn?

19\. By what are they suggested?

20\. 177 Give an illustration of the preceding statement.

21\. Illustrate the manner in which this consecution of propositions takes place.

22\. What is all the direct voluntary power possessed in such cases?

23\. 178. State the grounds of the selection of propositions.

24\. How does the mind discover the agreement or disagreement of the propositions presented to it?

25\. In what does the difference in the various kinds of reasoning consist?

26\. 179. On what does reasoning necessarily proceed?

27\. Show that this must be so.

28\. Are the propositions assumed always expressed?

29\. What are primary truths?

30\. 180. What things are assumed in reasoning?

31\. 181. Do all persons possess the faculty of reasoning to the same extent?

32\. On what does the difference depend? Three things.

33\. Why is knowledge necessary?

34\. Why is premeditation essential to one who would reason well on any subject?

35\. 182. What is said of the power of habit in reasoning? and illustrate.

36\. 183. The great instrument of reasoning?

37\. What is said of persons who are suddenly called upon to state their arguments in public debate?

38\. What is said of Oliver Cromwell?

39 184. Give another illustration.

40 To what is this perplexity often owing?

41\. What are these mental habits referred to?

CHAPTER X.

1\. 185. In what respects does demonstrative reasoning differ from every other species of reasoning?

2\. What are the subjects of it?

3\. What are abstract ideas?

4\. What topics come under this head?

5\. What are the subjects of moral reasoning? and illustrate.

6\. 186 What is essential to every process of reasoning?

Qu. Sect.

7. What are the preliminary truths in demonstrative reasoning?
8. Mention certain general facts in natural philosophy which may be considered as first principles.
9. What are axioms? and illustrate.
10. Can we complete a demonstration by their assistance alone?
11. 187. Why is it necessary, in demonstrations, to consider but one side of a question? and illustrate.
12. How does this differ from moral reasoning? and illustrate.
13. 188. Do demonstrations admit of different degrees of belief?
14. Show why they can not.
15. What is the case in moral reasoning, and why?
16. 189. What is the proper use of diagrams in demonstrations?
17. In what respect does demonstrative reasoning resemble every other kind of reasoning?
18. How does it appear that diagrams are not essentially necessary in demonstrations?
19. What remark does Cudworth make on this subject?
20. What is a definition?

CHAPTER XI.

1. 190. The subjects of moral reasoning?
2. Show its importance.
3. Does skill in demonstrative reasoning make one a good reasoner in moral subjects also?
4. The effect of demonstrative reasoning on the mind?
5. 191. Point out the resemblance and dissimilarity between this and moral reasoning.
6. Which kind is attended with knowledge?
7. Are the conclusions from moral reasoning necessarily doubtful?
8. Illustrate.
9. What is moral certainty?
10. 192. What do we mean by analogy?
11. What is analogical reasoning?
12. Illustrate.
13. The proper use of such reasoning?
14. 193. What is inductive reasoning?
15. Illustrate.
16. What is said of the belief which attends such reasoning?
17. The results of such reasoning?
18. 194. What is remarked of accumulated arguments in demonstrations?
19. What in moral reasoning? and the grounds of this opinion?
20. Illustrate.

CHAPTER XII.

1. 195. What is logic? and its object?
2. 196. The first direction in relation to reasoning?
3. What is the opposite of a desire of the truth?
4. What are the great enemies of truth?
5. Why is this rule of importance particularly in public debate?
6. 197. The second rule?
7. In what ways is this rule often disregarded?
8. The practice of special pleaders?
9. At what should dialecticians aim?
10. 198. The third rule?
11. What kind of evidence have we when the inquiry is one of a purely abstract nature?
12. What in the examination of material bodies?
13. In which is the conclusion most relied on?

Qu.	Sect.	
14.		In what cases do we rely on testimony?
15.		To what extent do we rely on this?
16.		In what cases have we the evidence of induction?
17.		In what the evidence of analogy?
18.	199.	What is a sophism?
19		What is said of them?
20.		Mention four species of sophism.
21.		Explain the ignoratio elenchi, and illustrate.
22.		Explain and illustrate the petitio principii.
23.		What is arguing in a circle?
24.		Explain the non causa pro causa, and illustrate.
25.		Explain the fallacia accidentis.
26.	200.	What further direction is given?
27.		What remark is made of the meaning of words in every language?
28.	201.	What other sophism is common?
29.		In what does this fallacy consist?
30.		What is said of Alexander and Charles XII.?
31.		What of Cæsar and Catiline?
32.	202.	What remark is here made of adherence to our opinions?
33.		Why should we not always give up an opinion when objections are raised which we can not answer?
34	203.	What is said of contending for victory instead of truth?
35.		How is it often done?
36.		What remark has been made of persons that addict themselves to this practice?
37.		The cause of such a result?
38.		What is said of Chillingworth?

CHAPTER XIII.

1.	204.	Under what general head does imagination come?
2.		With what are we apt to associate the exercises of the imagination?
3.		What is said of one that possesses a creative and well-sustained imagination?
4.	205.	What further remark is made of the imagination?
5.		What does D'Alembert say of it?
6.		What does he say of Archimedes?
7.		In what three respects do the deductive and imaginative powers resemble each other?
8.		In what do they differ?
9.		What are the objects of each?
10.		Contrast the two.
11.	206.	What is imagination?
12.		What are the materials from which new creations are made?
13.		To what have they been compared?
14.		How is the difference between the imagination of the mass of mankind, and of poets, painters, and orators, illustrated?
15.		Why do we speak of imagination as a complex operation of the mind?
16.	207.	State in full the process of the mind in the creations of the imagination.
17.	208.	What name do we give to this complex state, or series of states of the mind?
18.		Why is it important to have a single term expressive of it?
19.		Is imagination an original and independent faculty?
20.		What is it, then?
21.	209.	The illustration of Dr. Reid?
22.	210.	What question naturally suggests itself here?
23.		How is it answered?
24		Is any voluntary power exercised over our conceptions?

Qu. Sect.
25. 211. How was Milton enabled to form his happy conception of the Garden of Eden?
26 Has his conception ever been realized on earth?
27. 212 What erroneous opinion on this subject has widely prevailed?
28. Give an illustration.
29. What practical application does this view admit of?
30. What is said of Scott and Bunyan?
31. 213. How is this subject illustrated in the case of Byron?
32. Quote the remark of Sir Joshua Reynolds.
33. 214. What have some supposed respecting the utility of the imagination?
34. Why is this a reflection on the Creator?
35 In whom has the power of the imagination shown itself most conspicuously?
36. What is said of them?
37. In what instances has the imagination contributed to national glory and national happiness?
38. Mention other benefits of it.
39. What has Addison said of it?
40. 215. In what important point of view may it be considered?
41. What remark is made on this?
42. Why are many able reasoners so dull and uninteresting?
43. How may reasoning be made interesting?

CHAPTER XIV.

1. 216. Are the operations of the mind always uniform?
2. What occasions these deviations from fixed laws
3. On what does the action of the will depend?
4. On what the sensibilities?
5. The two-fold action of the intellect?
6. Which is first in the order of time?
7. Which in the order of nature?
8. What is essential to the action of the external intellect?
9. The inference from this fact?
10. 217. What subject does this fact elucidate?
11. What are conceptions?
12. What are excited conceptions?
13. What are apparitions?
14. What kind claim our especial attention, and why?
15. 218. What two things are to be noticed in explanation of them
16. What fact is stated of children?
17. Quote the remark of Cowper.
18. That of Beattie.
19. Illustrate the fact that excited conceptions are called into existence by anxiety of mind, etc.
20. Illustrate the fact in the case of Mrs. Howe.
21. 219. What is said of excited conceptions of sound? and illustrate.
22. What incidents in the life of Johnson and Napoleon does this explain?
23. 220. What is the first cause of permanently vivid conceptions or apparitions?
24. Why is this conjectural?
25. What fact is it necessary to keep in mind in order to understand the applicability of this cause
26. How is this illustrated?
27. How does this case explain the cause of apparitions?
28. How is this explanation confirmed?
29. 221. The second cause of apparitions?
30. State the case of Nicolai.

Qu. Sect
31. 222 How was he relieved?
32. 227 The third cause of apparitions?
33. State the case recorded in the Philosophical Journal.
34. 224 The fourth cause of apparitions?
35. What general remark is made in confirmation of this cause?
36. What proportion of the blood is sent immediately from the heart into the brain?
37. In what way does nitrous oxide affect the brain?
38. What opinion do these facts seem to confirm?
39. By what fact is it controverted?
40. 225. State the fact related in illustration of the fourth cause of apparitions.
41. 226. The fifth cause of apparitions?
42. What is said of hysteria?

CHAPTER XV.

1. 227. Meaning of the term insanity?
2. What do we usually understand by it?
3. What is partial, and what is total insanity?
4. 228. What is remarked of disordered sensations?
5. State a case of a disordered sensation of touch.
6. The case of Mendelsohn?
7. 229. The distinction between sensation and perception?
8. When are our perceptions likely to be disordered?
9. State facts on this subject.
10. 230. What conviction is essential to a sound mind?
11. What fact is related of the Rev. S. Browne?
12. 231. What produces insanity of consciousness?
13. State the case of the watchmaker.
14. 232. Is original suggestion or relative more frequently disordered?
15. Why is the latter so frequently so?
16. 233. What is light-headedness?
17. The characteristics of the light-headed?
18. 234. State the case of Lavater.
19. 235. What is said of disordered memory?
20. The three kinds of it?
21. Illustrations of the second kind?
22. Illustrations of the third?
23. 236. When is the inability to reason total?
24. Is this usually the case?
25. The most common form of alienated reason? and illustrate.
26. 237. Describe the case of Don Quixote.
27. 238. How do men of sensibility sometimes become mentally disordered?
28. The case of Rousseau?
29. 239. Three kinds of insanity, or alienation of the power of belief?
30. What is remarked of the first kind when the inability to believe is great?
31. What of the second?

DIVISION II.

INTRODUCTION.

Qu. Sect.
1. 240. How has the mind been divided?
2. Are these divisions strongly marked?
3. In what do they differ?
4. How is it ascertained that they differ in their nature?
5. Which comes first in order?
6. 241. What is essential to the action of the sensibilities?
7. How is this shown?
8. If our intellectual powers were dormant, what would be the effect on the sensibilities?
9. To what is the activity of the sensibilities proportioned?
10. 242. How are the sensibilities divided?
11. By whom was the term pathematic introduced?
12. To what state of mind is it applicable?
13. 243. What different views do the natural and moral sensibilities appear to take of the objects in respect to which they are called into exercise?
14. What would be the effect of obliterating from man's constitution his conscience?
15. In this case, by what would his movements be dictated?
16. What would be the center around which his motives of action would revolve?
17. What teaches him to act with reference to the glory of God?
18. 244. Which division of the sensibilities occupy the higher rank?
19. Which are higher in our estimation, the instincts or the appetites?
20. The appetites or the affections?
21. What other remark is made of our moral sensibilities?
22. 245. Do brutes possess moral sensibilities?
23. What do they possess in common with man?
24. What, then, is the ground of distinction between men and brutes?
25. 246. How are the natural sensibilities divided?
26. Which come first in the order of time and nature, the emotions or the desires?
27. How is this fact otherwise stated?
28. Show that this fact is necessarily so.
29. 247 How are the moral sensibilities divided?
30. To what do the obligatory feelings correspond?

PART I.—CLASS I.

CHAPTER I.

1. 248 Why can not a verbal explanation be given of the emotions?
2. Why can not any thing simple be defined?
3. How do we learn the nature of the emotions?
4. 249. The place of the emotions considered with reference to other mental acts?

Qu. Sect.
5. What is said of the desires?
6. What do we mean when we speak of any thing as pleasant to us?
7. What is essential to a feeling of moral obligation?
8. On what are our desires founded?
9. On what our emotions?
10. 250. By what are our desires followed?
11. By what our obligatory feelings?
12. How is it shown that our emotions are founded on our intellections?
13. Illustrate.
14. 251. By what are emotions characterized?
15. To what are they compared?
16. How do they differ from the desires and feelings of moral obligation?
17. What are some of the varieties of our emotions?
18. Why is it essential to understand the distinctions that exist in the sensibilities?

CHAPTER II.

1. 252. The two characteristics of the emotion of beauty?
2. 253. What objects do we call beautiful?
3. What do we mean, then, when we say an object has beauty?
4. 254. How are beautiful objects distinguished from other objects?
5. Why does the mind experience a pleasant emotion in view of certain objects?
6. 255. How may the term beauty be regarded? and why?
7. What are some of the occasions of the emotions of beauty?
8. What is remarked of the human countenance?
9. What does a mathematician regard as beautiful? a logician?
10. What, then, is the province of beauty?
11. 256. Are all objects equally fitted to cause the emotion of beauty?
12. What important inquiry does this suggest?
13. 257. What must be taken for granted in answering this question?
14. How do we know that we have a susceptibility to beauty?
15. Have the emotions of beauty fixed causes or antecedents?
16. Can the antecedents exist and not be followed by these emotions?
17. What is meant by the æsthetic power of objects?
18. 258. What figure is universally regarded as beautiful?
19. What was Hogarth's line of beauty?
20. In what natural objects do we find this line?
21. 259. What two kinds of beauty are mentioned here?
22. What is intrinsic beauty?
23. Mention some objects that possess it.
24. 260. What other forms have beauty?
25. Quote the remark of Mr. Alison.
26. 261. What is said of the square?
27. What other forms of beauty are mentioned, and what is said of them?
28. What does Mr. Alison say of the tripod?
29. What explanatory remark is made in connection with the foregoing statements, and how is it illustrated?
30. 262. What is said of the beauty of colors?
31. By what considerations is this opinion supported?
32. What is remarked of infants?
33. What of savages?
34. What of the uneducated?
35. Who are most pleased with gaudy colors?
36. 263. What additional proof is given of the fact that colors are of themselves fitted to cause emotions of beauty?
37. What facts are mentioned of the early life of James Mitchell?

Qu. Sect.

38. 264. When are sounds termed beautiful?
39. What sounds are disagreeable?
40. What are entirely indifferent?
41. Quote Mr. Alison's remarks.
42. 265. How are musical sounds characterized?
43. Are they intrinsically beautiful, or so from association only?
44. The first consideration that goes to prove this?
45. What is said of brutes in this connection?
46. The second consideration to prove that there is an intrinsic beauty in musical sounds?
47. The third consideration, etc.?
48. What fact is related of a Jesuit missionary?
49. 266. The fourth consideration?
50. What is said of Caspar Hauser in this connection?
51. 267. On what does the permanency of musical power depend?
52. What does this prove?
53. 268. What other element of beauty is mentioned?
54. What motions are pleasing?
55 What remarks are made of ascending columns of smoke?
56. 269. What kinds of motion are agreeable?
57. Why is long-continued swift motion disagreeable?
58. Why very slow motion?
59. What kinds of motion are the most agreeable?

CHAPTER III.

1. 270. What two positions on the subject of beauty are laid down in this section?
2. The remark of Stewart on this subject?
3. Can association originate or create any thing?
4. To what is it compared?
5. 271. Is it possible for an object to become beautiful by association merely?
6. Illustrate.
7. 272. What gives the country half its charms?
8. What invests with beauty the Rock of Plymouth?
9. Repeat the poetry of Rogers.
10. 273. Mention several instances of national associations.
11. Mention several in colors.
12. What is often the effect on the countenance of a single crime?
13. 274. With what are the sources of associated beauty coincident?
14. 275. Give a summary of what has been said on this subject. 1st, 2d, 3d 4th, 5th.

CHAPTER IV.

1. 276. What is remarked of emotions of sublimity?
2. Illustrate the progression from the gentle to the sublime.
3. In what respect do emotions of sublimity differ from those of beauty?
4. 277. Why are they undefinable?
5. How do we, then, obtain a knowledge of them?
6. How do we measure the sublimity of an object?
7. 278. What is the first source of sublimity mentioned?
8. Quote the remarks of Stewart and of Washington Irving.
9. 279. Mention another source of sublimity.
10. Illustrate.
11. 280. Mention a third source.
12. Quote Burke's remark.
13. 281 A fourth source? and illustrate.

Qu. Sect.
14. Give the Scripture quotation.
15. 282. A fifth source? and illustrate.
16. The remark of Coleridge?
17. 283. A sixth source? and illustrate.
18. 284. A seventh source? and illustrate.
19. Is the emotion in these instances to be ascribed to one cause only?
20. 285. How does it appear that these are objects originally sublime?
21. 286. How is this proved?
22. How illustrated in the case of Sir William Jones?
23. 287. To what is a share of the emotion to be attributed?
24. How is this shown?

CHAPTER V.

1. 288. What is said of the emotions of the ludicrous?
2. What modifies the pleasure we experience from them?
3. 289. The origin of the feeling?
4. Does the discovery of new relations in every case give rise to it?
5. Mention several instances in which it does not.
6. What else is necessary to the production of these emotions?
7. 290. With what are they closely allied?
8. In what does wit consist?
9. 291. The first method which wit employs in exciting emotions of the ludicrous?
10. What are such descriptions termed?
11. Is it morally right to attempt to burlesque what is truly great?
12. Repeat the examples from Hudibras.
13. 292. The second method which wit employs to excite emotions of the ludicrous?
14. What is it termed?
15. How does it differ from the former kind?
16. Repeat the example.
17. What are included in this division of wit?
18. Repeat an example of this kind?
19. 293. What subject closely borders on wit?
20. Illustrate what you mean by humor and the humorous.
21. Are such feelings useless?
22. The reasons for such an opinion?
23. 294. Is ridicule the proper weapon to use against vice?
24. In what cases is it allowable?
25. What writers have treated of this subject in full?

CHAPTER VI.

1. 295. What is cheerfulness?
2. What are joy and delight?
3. What is gladness?
4. 296. The opposite of these emotions?
5. The distinction between melancholy and sorrow?
6. The distinction between grief and sorrow?
7. How do grief and sorrow show themselves?
8. 297. What is surprise?
9. What is astonishment?
10. What is wonder?
11. The utility of this emotion?
12. Show in what manner it is useful.
13. 298. What is dissatisfaction?
14. How does it differ from displeasure?
15. How from disgust?
16. 299. What is diffidence?

Qu. Sect
17. How does it differ from modesty?
18. Its utility?
19. What is shame?
20. How characterized?
21 By what is it occasioned?
22. 300. The foundation of the respect we pay to the mass of mankind?
23 What is reverence?
24. What is adoration?
25. Recapitulate the emotions that have been touched upon.

PART I.—CLASS II.

CHAPTER I.

1. 301 Of what two kinds of sensibilities does the author treat?
2. How are the natural sensibilities divided?
3. What is said of desire?
4. What is essential to every appetite, propensity, and affection?
5. 302 Why can we not define the desires?
6. How, then, do we obtain a knowledge of them?
7. 303 Why is it important to obtain a definite idea of the place of desires?
8. Do desires follow intellections immediately or not?
9. How is this shown?
10. The proximate and causative occasion of desires?
11. What fact is mentioned in illustration of what has been said?
12. What fixed law of the mind is stated?
13. 304. Which are the more permanent emotions or desires?
14. To what are our emotions compared?
15. What illustration is given of the strength and permanency of desires?
16. 305. What additional characteristic of desires is mentioned?
17. From what do they differ in this respect?
18. In what do our emotions terminate?
19. In what our desires?
20. Give a reason for their fixedness, and illustrate.
21. 306. Are our desires pleasant or painful?
22. What other characteristic circumstance distinguishes them from other mental states?
23. With what does the enjoyment vary?
24. 307. Are all our desires equally strong?
25. On what does their strength depend?
26 On what does the strength of our emotions depend?
27. 308. What other characteristic attribute of our desires is mentioned?
28. What does Hobbes term desire?
29. Does it always terminate in action?
30. What is necessary to this?
31. Does the tendency exist if action does not follow desire?
32. Does this tendency exist in other departments of the mind?
33 What would man be with intellect alone?
34 What with emotive sensibilities alone?
35. How illustrated?
36. In what exists the tendency to excite movement?
37. The office of the will?
38. 309. How are the desires modified?
39. How classified?

Qu. Sect.
40. 310. What two-fold action have all these principles, instincts excepted?
41. Why are instincts excepted?
42. Why is it important to notice this two-fold action?

CHAPTER II.

1. 311. What are instincts?
2. What is implied in the term instinctive?
3. Are the instinctive tendencies of men or of brutes the most frequent and effective?
4. Why should they be?
5. The proof that the instinct of the lower animals is strikingly adapted to the exigences of their situation?
6. 312. Mention a striking fact illustrative of the nature of the instinctive principle.
7. Mention a remarkable fact in relation to bees.
8. Can you prove that this is instinct?
9. 313. The first instance of instinct in man?
10. The second?
11. The third? and illustrate.
12. 314. The fourth? and illustrate.
13. The fifth? and illustrate.
14. 315. The design of our instincts?
15. What power predominates in man, and what in brutes?

CHAPTER III.

1. 316. The prominent appetites?
2. How do they differ from instincts?
3. Their three characteristics?
4. 317. The use of the appetites?
5. Illustrate.
6. What is said of the lower animals in this respect?
7. Why can not our appetites be called selfish?
8. Are they ever strong enough to enslave us?
9. What is remarked of one so enslaved?
10. 318. Give an instance of an acquired appetite.
11. Explain the origin of such appetites.
12. The only way to avoid the forming of such habits?
13. 319. Explain the instinctive and the voluntary operation of the appetites.
14. The basis of the morality of the appetites?
15. In what do virtue and vice consist, considered in relation to the appetites?

CHAPTER IV.

1. 320. In what respect do the propensities differ from the instincts?
2. And from the appetites?
3. Enumerate the propensities.
4. On what are they all founded?
5. 321. How is it shown that the desire of self-preservation is one of our propensities?
6. What is sometimes stronger than this?
7. Can it ever be extinguished?
8. 322. Its two-fold operation? and illustrate.
9. 323. Show that curiosity is one of our propensities.
10. What class of works depends almost wholly on curiosity for readers?
11. 324. What is said of the deaf and dumb with reference to this propensity?

Qu. Sect.
12. How was this shown in James Mitchel?
13. Repeat the poetry on this subject.
14. 325. Illustrate its two-fold operation.
15. How may it be stimulated or restrained?
16. When is it virtuous, and when vicious?
17. Illustrate with reference to the astronomer.
18. 326. Show that the propensity to imitation is natural.
19. How do children acquire the use of oral language?
20. In what various ways do they manifest this propensity
21. 327. Is this principle one of utility?
22. Show how.
23. What practical inference may we deduce from this?
24. 328. Show that the desire of esteem is natural to man.
25. Show that it is not confined to children.
26. Show that it is not founded on personal and interested considerations.
27. Show that it operates strongly with reference to the future.
28 329. Show that it is favorable to human happiness, and illustrate.
29. Sylla's remark of Julius Cæsar?
30. By what is this desire checked?
31. 330. Show that children very early form a notion of the relation of possession.
32. 331. On what does the morality of this desire depend?
33. When is it morally right, and when wrong?
34. What is remarked on the duty of this desire?
35. By what Scripture is it enforced?
36. 332. What is said of its ordinary action?
37. Why is it usually inordinately strong?
38. What is covetousness?
39. What is avarice?
40. 333. What is power?
41. How is this shown?
42. How is it shown that the desire of power is natural to the mind? and illustrate.
43. 334. In what cases is its exercise virtuous, and in what vicious?
44. What is ambition?
45. 335. To what actions does the desire of happiness lead us?
46. 336. What is this desire called?
47. How is it distinguished from selfishness?
48. 337. Repeat Wardlaw's remark on self-love.
49. How do the Scriptures appeal to self-love?
50. 338. Of what propensity has our desire for society been sometimes regarded as a modification?
51. Show that it is not so.
52. How may this principle be perverted?
53. 339. The first evidence of the existence of this principle?
54. The second evidence of its existence?
55. 340. How is the strength of it shown?
56. Give two other illustrations of it.
57. 341. What strange notion of Hobbes is noticed?
58. On what is civil society founded?
59 Repeat the quotation from Cowper.

CHAPTER V.

1. 342. How are the affections distinguished from the other forms of our propensive nature?
2. The relative ranks of our sensibilities?
3. 343. How do the affections differ from the appetites and propensities?
4. What does the term affection denote?

Qu. Sect.

5 How are the affections divided?
6. How are these two classes distinguished?
7. What term is used as synonymous wth affection?
8. 344. What is anger?
9. What modifications of it are mentioned?
10. 345. By what is anger occasioned?
11. Show that it is instinctive, and illustrate.
12. 346. The design of the Creator in implanting this principle in man?
13. Is instinctive resentment morally wrong?
14. The basis of morality?
15. 347. How may we impart to instinctive resentment the character of accountability?
16. The proper occasion of resentment?
17 What is injury?
18. The final cause of instinctive resentment?
19 The final cause of voluntary resentment?
20. How does it dispense its retribution?
21. When is resentment right, and when wrong?
22. 348. One of the chief causes of excessive resentment?
23. The three checks to it?
24. What is remarked of the pain it occasions?
25. What of its outward signs?
26. 349. The first consideration calculated to check it?
27. The second?
28. The third?
29. The fourth?
30. In what is the Christian code distinguished from every other?
31. 350. How does peevishness differ from anger?
32. To what are both compared?
33. 351. What is envy, and what is remarked of it?
34. How is it accounted for?
35. 352. What is jealousy?
36. How is it characterized?
37. To what is its strength proportioned?
38. In whom is it most frequently found?
39. What is remarked of it?
40. 353. What is revenge?
41. How does it differ from resentment?
42. Is it ever right?
43. 354. How is fear occasioned?
44. Why ranked among the malevolent affections?
45. To what is its strength proportioned?
46. What is said of it when extreme?
47. The danger of frightening others?
48. What is despair?

CHAPTER VI.

1. 355. The basis of the malevolent affections?
2. The basis of the benevolent ones?
3. What is implied in the affection love?
4. What are some of its modifications?
5. What are some of the different kinds of it?
6. 356. The two-fold action by which it is characterised?
7. Is parental affection voluntary or implanted?
8. The first consideration in support of this view?
9. The second?
10. The third?
11. The fourth?
2. 357. The fifth?

Qu.	Sect.	
13.	358.	Mention a fact illustrative of this.
14.	359.	How does filial affection differ from parental?
15.		Show the wisdom of the Creator in this.
16.	360.	The first proof that filial affection is implanted?
17.		Illustrate this remark.
18.		The second proof of this fact?
19		The penalty which nature has attached to a want of filial affection?
20.		What other considerations might be adduced in evidence of the same fact?
21	361.	An illustration of filial affection.
22		An illustration of parental love.
23	362	How has fraternal affection been accounted for?
24		What one fact shows that this explanation is an insufficient one?
25	363	Show the wisdom of the Creator as manifested in the domestic affections.
26.		What strange notion of Plato is mentioned?
27.		Show that the reverse is the fact.
28.	364.	Do these affections possess a moral character?
29.		The common opinion, and the reasons for it?
30.		Show the error of it, and illustrate.
31.	365	When are these affections vicious, and when virtuous?
32.	366.	What is essential to the highest and most ennobling form of benevolence?
33.		In what cases is it wrong to indulge a benevolent feeling toward an individual?
34.		Give an account of Bishop Bartholomew las Casas.
35		How did his benevolence defeat its own intention?
36.	367.	Is man by nature indifferent to the welfare of others?
37		Is he naturally an enemy to his brother man?
38.		What is philanthropy?
39.		What principle checks its exercise?
40.		How is it shown to be natural?
41.		Illustrate.
42.	368.	A second argument in favor of this truth?
43.		How illustrated?
44.		Narrative of Mungo Park?
45.	369.	A third proof of this fact?
46.		Are such institutions confined to Christian countries?
47.		Mention other facts illustrative of this truth.
48.	370.	A fourth proof of this fact?
49.		Illustrate.
50.	371.	What is patriotism?
51.		The manifest intention of nature on this subject?
52.		Is patriotism a secondary or an original affection.
53.		Show that there is no contrariety between patriotism and philanthropy.
54.		Repeat the remark of Cowper.
55.	372	Of what is friendship a modification?
56		How does it resemble the other benevolent affections?
57.		Is similarity of character requisite as the basis of friendship?
58.		What is essential?
59	373.	How does pity differ from the other benevolent affections?
60		Sentiment of Bishop Butler on this subject?
61		The office of pity?
62	374.	Is this affection instinctive or voluntary?
63		The great advantage of its being so?
64.		When is its exercise right, and vice versa? and illustrate.
65.		Why do we judge favorably of the pitiful?
66.	375.	How is gratitude distinguished from the other benevolent affections?
67.		What is essential to it?

CHAPTER VII.

Qu. Sect.
1. 376. What principle does the author suppose was originally implanted in man?
2. The first argument in favor of this?
3. 377. The second argument, drawn from the Scriptures?
4. What is meant by man's being created in the image of God? and the argument from this?
5. 378. The third argument from texts of Scripture?
6. The fourth argument from the new birth?
7. 379. What fact is taught us by both philosophy and revelation?
8. What facts prove that man is a fallen being?
9. What principle should stand first in rank of those by which man is governed?
10. How would this regulate all the others?
11. 380. How is human depravity accounted for?
12. 381. How is this illustrated?
13. Show how the obliteration of the principle of love to God would lead to the enslaving of man to his appetites and passions

CHAPTER VIII.

1. 382. What simple fact does the term habit express?
2. 383. What are appetitive habits?
3. How are such habits acquired?
4. 384. What are propensive habits? and illustrate.
5. 385. To what other affections does it apply? and illustrate.
6. 386. What are secondary principles of action?
7. Their origin? and illustrate.

PART II.

CHAPTER I.

1. 387. How has the mind been divided?
2. The place of the emotions?
3. Through what departments must we pass to arrive at the will from the emotions?
4. Prove from Scripture the existence of conscience.
5. 388. Into what do the natural sensibilities resolve themselves?
6. Into what the moral?
7. Why might it be supposed this subject would be dispatched in a few words?
8. Why is it not?
9. 389. How does the moral nature develop itself?
10. How many kinds of moral emotions are there?
11. By what names are they known?
12. What is implied in calling them original feelings?
13. Why are they not susceptible of definition?
14. How are they known to exist?
15. 390. What position do moral emotions occupy with respect to acts of the intellect?
16. What other emotions occupy the same place?
17. By what are the moral emotions immediately followed?
18. What is implied in our being under obligations to do, or not to do any particular act?

Qu. Sect.

19. 391. In what cases are the moral emotions liable to change?
20. The necessity of this?
21. 392. The appropriate objects of moral approval, etc.?
22. What are not such objects?
23. With what is duty commensurate?

CHAPTER II.

1. 393. With what have some confounded conscience?
2. Why is this a natural mistake?
3. 394. What is reasoning?
4. The distinction between the reasoning power and the moral nature?
5. The basis of moral action?
6. 395. Illustrate this truth.
7. 396. Is conscience susceptible of being educated?
8. Mention one form of moral education.
9. 397. Can a person who has acted conscientiously be considered guilty in so acting?
10. In what does such guilt consist?
11. The consequences of denying this doctrine?
12. Repeat the doctrine on this subject.

CHAPTER III.

1. 398. Into what two classes of feeling does conscience resolve itself?
2. 399. How do we ascertain the existence of feelings of moral obligation?
3. Illustrate.
4. 400. In what other way, also, do we ascertain their existence?
5. Illustrate.
6. 401. In what other way still is it shown?
7. Mention some of the terms that prove their existence.
8. 402. What would be the state of society without this part of our constitution?
9. 403. The first characteristic mark of these feelings?
10. 404. The second mark, etc.? and illustrate.
11. 405. The third mark, etc.?
12. What is meant by the terms enforcement, constraint, compulsion, as applied to this feeling?
13. The apostle's meaning in the passage, "The love of Christ constraineth me?"
14. 406. The first reason assigned for not classing feelings of obligation with emotions?
15. Illustrate.
16. 407. The second reason?
17. What is said, in this connection, of moral emotions?
18. 408. A third reason? and illustrate.
19. What language shows the prevalence of the common belief on this subject?
20. 409 The first reason why feelings of moral obligation are not classed with desires?
21. The second reason, etc.?
22. 411 The third reason?
23. How do the mere moral emotions operate on the will?
24. Why have brute animals no moral character?
25. Why are they not accountable?

CHAPTER IV.

Qu.	Sect.	
1	411	What two kinds of uniformity are there in the decisions of our moral nature?
2.		The law on which uniformity in principle is founded?
3.		Are the dictates of unperverted conscience the same every where?
4.	412.	What objections have been urged against the doctrine of a connatural conscience?
5.		What must be shown in order to meet this objection?
6.		The first remark on this subject?
7		To what is conscience compared? and point out the resemblance.
8	413.	The first reason assigned for the diversities of the decisions of conscience?
9.		Illustrate this truth.
10.	414.	The second reason? and illustrate.
11.		How is the thievishness of the Sandwich Islanders accounted for?
12.		Show that this is the true explanation.
13.	415.	The third reason? and illustrate.
14.		What is said of the Rev. John Newton?
15.	416.	How is persecution for religious opinions accounted for?
16.	417.	The fourth reason, etc.? and illustrate.
17.	418.	The last reason for these diversities? and illustrate.

CHAPTER V.

1.	419.	What is said of the importance of moral education?
2.		Why has it been so much neglected?
3.	420.	What suggestion has been made on this subject?
4.		Why is it entitled to no weight?
5.		What is necessary in order to prevent the contamination of vice?
6.	421.	What facts show the early development of the intellect?
7.		How early does the moral nature begin to develop?
8.		At what age is the moral character sometimes formed?
9.	422.	What discouragement often attends our efforts to improve the moral character of the young?
10.		Why should we not be discouraged?
11.		What incident is mentioned illustrative of this subject?
12.	423.	Why should we take pains to introduce into the mind correct speculative opinions?
13.		Illustrate the great importance of such opinions.
14		What is said of the doctrine that "Sincerity is every thing?"
15	424.	What is essential to sound moral education?
16		The office of conscience?
17		How does conscience regard a want of love to the divine character?
18		The foundation of a moral life?

PART III.

CHAPTER I.

1	425.	The subject of this chapter?
2.	426.	What is insanity?
3.		May the mind be disordered without being insane?
4.	427.	The consequence of disordered appetites?
5.		Mention instances of such.

Qu. Sect.
6. Give an illustration of the power of appetite.
7. 428. How does the principle of self preservation show itself to be disordered? and illustrate.
8. 429. How the possessory principle? and illustrate.
9. 430. Examples of constitutional thieves?
10. 431. Examples of constitutional mimics?
11. 432. What is implied in the term alienation?
12. What two kinds of alienation are mentioned?
13. In what two ways may an irregular action of the social principle show itself?
14. 433. What is said of Foscari?
15. What is nostalgia?
16. What is said of the Swiss? and of the Russian army in A.D. 1733?
17. How remedied?
18. 434. The effect of the desire of esteem on the character?
19. The effect when disordered?
20. The ruling passion of Alcibiades?
21. The effect of the inordinate exercise of this propensity?
22. 435. The effect of the disordered action of the desire of power?
23. Mention the case recorded by Pinel.

CHAPTER II.

1. 436. What is sympathetic imitation?
2. 437. The remark of Stewart?
3. What facts illustrate its truth?
4. 438. Relate the occurrences at Haerlem.
5. 439. Relate those at Chelmsford, Mass.

CHAPTER III.

1. 440. What do you mean by presentiments?
2. The case of Isaac Ambrose?
3. The case of Mozart?
4. The case of Pendergrast?
5. The case of Henry IV. of France?
6. How may some cases be explained?
7. Can all such be?
8. 441. What other disordered condition of mind is mentioned? and illustrate.
9. The cases mentioned by Dr. Gale?
10. Mention other cases.
11. 442. What is said of the insanity of the passions?
12. 443. What is hypochondriasis?
13. To what may it sometimes be traced?
14. Mention several cases of it.
15. That of the Englishman?
16. 444. How is this disease characterized?
17. The first step toward remedying it?
18. The second step?
19. The third step?
20. Remark of Dr. Johnson?
21. 445. How does the disordered action of the passion of fear show itself?
22. The distinctive trait of despair?
23. 446. What strange fact is here mentioned?
24. Fact mentioned by Dr. Rush?
25. Second fact?
26. Fact mentioned by Dr. Gall?
27. Instances of death from joy?

CHAPTER IV.

Qu. Sect.
1. 447. The two leading forms of moral derangement?
2. Remark of Juvenal? and explain it.
3. Repeat the poetry on this subject.
4. Can conscience die?
5. 448. May an individual sin in obeying conscience?
6. In what would such a sin consist? illustrate.
7. 449. Can a man be born without a conscience?
8. Case mentioned by Dr. Haslam?
9. 450. Are such persons accountable?
10. Are men, as subjects of moral government, to be treated alike?

DIVISION III.

CHAPTER I.

1. 451. How has the mind been divided?
2. What is the Intellect?
3. What the Sensibilities?
4. What the Will?
5. 452. What caution is here given?
6. How may the Will be defined?
7. What remark of Mr. Stewart is quoted?
8. 453. Why can we not define the word *Volitions?*
9. How, then, can we ascertain what they are?
10. Why have we a right to assume that no one is ignorant of what is meant by an act of the Will?
11. 454. The first thing pointed out in illustration of Volitions?
12. Repeat Dr. Reid's remark.
13. 455. The second circumstance mentioned?
14. Illustrate this remark.
15. What usage of language throws light on the distinction here mentioned?
16. 456. What further inquiry still is made?
17. To what do our volitions relate, in the first place?
18. Illustrate this remark.
19. To what, in the second place?
20. Illustrate this remark.
21. 457. The third mark or characteristic of Volitions?
22. How are they distinguished from intellective or perceptive acts?
23. 458. The fourth characteristic of Volitions?
24. What objection is liable to be made to this statement?
25. How is this objection shown to be untenable?

CHAPTER II.

1. 459. Is the Will *free*, or in bondage?
2. Does it act in connection with law, or without law?
3. The first argument from analogy that it acts in connection with law?
4. Show that the *fact* on which this presumption is founded is undoubted.
5. Is this truth confined to inanimate things?
6. Quote the remark of Montesquieu.

Qu. Sect.
7. 460. Quote the remark of Hooker.
8. How is this a most consolatory thought?
9. (What did our blessed Redeemer say on this point? See Matt., x., 29-31.)
10. 461. The inference from this truth in relation to the Will?

CHAPTER III.

1. 462. The second argument offered in proof of the position that the Will has its laws?
2. Is the divine foreknowledge universally admitted?
3. 463. Prove it from the Scriptures.
4. 464. On what are the actions of men dependent?
5. The inference from this?
6. Illustrate.
7. The remark of Dr. Dwight, and the author's observations thereon?
8. 465. The inference from these facts?
9. What is the opposite of an action which is in harmony with law?
10. What is implied in the idea of contingent action?
11. Can any thing which is foreknown as certain be contingent?
12. What necessary conclusion then follows?
13. 466. What Scripture doctrine is closely connected with this view?
14. Repeat some of the passages here quoted.
15. What do they imply?

CHAPTER IV.

1. 467. What objection to this argument is mentioned?
2. How is it answered?
3. What other view of the subject is presented?
4. 468. What are some of the things man can foretell, with reference to himself?
5. Give an illustration.
6. What fact does this teach us with reference to our volitions? How is this shown?
7. 469. What can man foretell with reference to others?
8. What remark has this fact elicited?
9. Give an illustration.
10. Quote the remark of Hume.
11. Repeat the remarks of Paley with reference to this subject.
12. What other instances are mentioned?
13. The argument derived from these facts?
14. 471. What other facts of a somewhat peculiar nature are here mentioned?
15. What do they show?
16. 472. What other view of this subject is presented?
17. What is said of Mirabeau?
18. 473. What other fact still is mentioned?
19. Repeat Bacon's remark.
20. Mention several other facts.

CHAPTER V.

1. 474. The subject of this chapter?
2. Under what circumstances might it be said that the Will was subject to mere accident?
3. What then would be the result?
4. 475. What would follow from perfect harmony in other parts of the mind?
5. What illustration is here given?
6. What is remarked of the holy angels?

Qu. Sect.
7. The inference from these facts?
8. 476. The first argument in proof of the freedom of the Will?
9. Explain what is meant by this.
10. What is said of this argument?
11. The remark of Mr. Stewart?
12. 477. Are all persons conscious of freedom?
13. What is said of the apparent exceptions?
14. Can any man enslave himself?
15. Illustrate.
16. What is remarked of such cases?

CHAPTER VI.

1. 478. The second argument in proof of the freedom of the Will?
2. How is it shown that man has a moral nature?
3. In what are the elements of his moral nature to be found?
4. What fact is implied in man's possessing such a nature?
5. 479. State the argument from the moral feelings of approval and disapproval.
6. 480. The argument from the feelings of remorse?
7. 481. The argument from the abstract notions of right and wrong?
8. What remark is made of these conceptions of right and wrong?
9. 482. What is said of our feelings of moral obligation?
10. Why can they not be defined?
11. How do they prove that the Will is free?
12. 483. The argument from men's views of crimes and punishments?
13. The remark of Dr. Reid?
14. 484. The prevalent opinion of mankind on this subject?
15. The argument derived from this opinion?
16. 485. What two distinct doctrines have now been stated on this subject?
17. What is said of the first, the Will's subjection to law?
18. 486. What of the second, the Will's freedom?
19. Can any plea of inability ever be admitted as an excuse for negligence or sin?

CHAPTER VII.

1. 487. The subject of this chapter?
2. Of what is power predicable?
3. Illustrate what you mean by this.
4. 488. The first proof of the fact that power is predicable of the Will?
5. Illustrate.
6. What then are we taught by consciousness?
7. 489. The second argument in proof of this fact?
8. What control have we over our trains of thought?
9. What explanation can be given of this fact?
10. 490. The third proof of power in the Will?
11. Illustrate.
12. What remark is made of Howard?
13. What does Ledyard say of himself?
14. 491. In what other way is this subject illustrated?
15. What saying of Socrates is quoted?
16. 492. Solomon's declaration on self-control?
17. The argument deduced from this power?
18. 493. What other proof of power of Will is given?
19. What remark is made by the author of Lacon?
20. On what supposition only can we explain this fixedness of purpose?
21. 494. What illustration is given in this section?
22. 495. What illustration is furnished by the conduct of savages?
23. How alone can such facts be explained?

www.ingramcontent.com/pod-product-compliance
Lightning Source LLC
LaVergne TN
LVHW021231110826
845150LV00002B/301

* 9 7 8 1 4 2 5 5 6 2 8 7 8 *